WOMEN AND HOUSEHOLDS IN INDONESIA

NORDIC INSTITUTE OF ASIAN STUDIES
NIAS Studies in Asian Topics

15. Renegotiating Local Values
    Merete Lie and Ragnhild Lund
16. Leadership on Java
    Hans Antlöv and Sven Cederroth (eds)
17. Vietnam in a Changing World
    Irene Nørlund, Carolyn Gates and Vu Cao Dam (eds)
18. Asian Perceptions of Nature
    Ole Bruun and Arne Kalland (eds)
19. Imperial Policy and Southeast Asian Nationalism
    Hans Antlöv and Stein Tønnesson (eds)
20. The Village Concept in the Transformation of Rural Southeast Asia
    Mason C. Hoadley and Christer Gunnarsson (eds)
21. Identity in Asian Literature
    Lisbeth Littrup (ed.)
22. Mongolia in Transition
    Ole Bruun and Ole Odgaard (eds)
23. Asian Forms of the Nation
    Stein Tønnesson and Hans Antlöv (eds)
24. The Eternal Storyteller
    Vibeke Børdahl (ed.)
25. Japanese Influences and Presences in Asia
    Marie Söderberg and Ian Reader (eds)
26. Muslim Diversity
    Leif Manger (ed.)
27. Women and Households in Indonesia
    Juliette Koning, Marleen Nolten, Janet Rodenburg and Ratna Saptari (eds)
28. The House in Southeast Asia
    Signe Howell and Stephen Sparkes (eds)
29. Rethinking Development in East Asia
    Pietro P. Masina (ed.)

WOMEN AND HOUSEHOLDS IN INDONESIA
CULTURAL NOTIONS AND SOCIAL PRACTICES

Edited by
Juliette Koning, Marleen Nolten, Janet Rodenburg
and Ratna Saptari

LONDON AND NEW YORK

Nordic Institute of Asian Studies
Studies in Asian Topics Series, No. 27

First published in 2000
by Curzon Press

Published 2013 by Routledge
2 Park Square, Milton Park, Abingdon, Oxfordshire OX14 4RN
711 Third Avenue, New York, NY, 10017, USA

First issued in paperback 2016

Routledge is an imprint of the Taylor & Francis Group, an informa business

Typesetting by the Nordic Institute of Asian Studies

© Nordic Institute of Asian Studies 2000

While copyright in the volume as a whole is vested in the Nordic Institute of Asian Studies, copyright in the individual papers belongs to their authors. No paper may be reproduced in whole or in part without the express permission of the author, publisher or editors.

British Library Catalogue in Publication Data

Women and households in Indonesia : cultural notions and social practices. - (NIAS studies in Asian topics ; 27)
1.Women - Indonesia - Social conditions 2.Households - Indonesia
I.Koning, Juliette
305.4'2'09598

ISBN 13: 978-1-138-98721-0 (pbk)
ISBN 13: 978-0-7007-1156-7 (hbk)

CONTENTS

Contributors viii
Preface xii

SECTION I: INTRODUCTION 1

1. Food for Thought: Reflections on the Conference and the Set-up of this Book 3
   Marleen Nolten
2. Women, Family and Household: Tensions in Culture and Practice 10
   Ratna Saptari

SECTION II: DOMINANT NOTIONS OF FAMILY AND THE HOUSEHOLD 26

3. Colonial Ambivalencies: European Attitudes towards the Javanese Household (1900–1942) 28
   Elsbeth Locher-Scholten
4. Representations of Women's Roles in Household and Society in Indonesian Women's Writing of the 1930s 45
   Barbara Hatley and Susan Blackburn
5. Reconstructing Boundaries and Beyond 68
   Sylvia Tiwon
6. Beyond Women and the Household in Java: Re-examining the Boundaries 85
   Diane Wolf

SECTION III: CHALLENGING THE HOUSEHOLD CONCEPT 101

7. Houses, People and Residence: The Fluidity of Ambonese Living Arrangements 102
   Keebet and Franz von Benda-Beckmann
8. Bitter Honey: Female Agency and the Polygynous Household, North Bali 142
   Megan Jennaway
9. The Salty Mouth of a Senior Woman: Gender and the House in Minangkabau 163
   Joke van Reenen

SECTION IV: MOBILITY, DOMESTIC ARRANGEMENTS AND FAMILY LIFE 180

10. Different Times, Different Orientations:
    Family Life in a Javanese Village 181
    Juliette Koning
11. Negotiating Gender, Kinship and Livelihood Practices
    in an Indonesian Transmigration Area 208
    Becky Elmhirst
12. Staying Behind:
    Conflict and Compromise in Toba Batak Migration 235
    Janet Rodenburg

SECTION V: BEYOND THE DICHOTOMIES 262

13. Women's Networks in Cloth Production and Exchange in Flores 264
    Willemijn de Jong
14. Networks of Reproduction among
    Cigarette Factory Women in East Java 281
    Ratna Saptari
15. Hidden Managers at Home:
    Elite Javanese Women Running New Order Family Firms 299
    G.G. Weix

Bibliography 315
Glossary 345
Overview of the papers presented at the WIVS conference 350
Index 352

TABLES

4.1	Seven publications by Indonesian women's organizations of the 1930s	48
7.1	Composition of Ambonese and Butonese houses	111
8.1	Comparison between male and female marriage destinies in *desa adat* Punyanwangi	148
8.2	Number of men contracting plural marriages in *desa adat* Punyanwangi	157
8.3	Number and sex of children of first marriages of polygynous men	159
14.1	Household type by land ownership, Kayuwangi, 1988	286
14.2	Household position of cigarette workers (women and men) by household type, Kayuwangi, 1988	287

FIGURES

1.1	Map of Indonesia – research locations	2
7.1	Map of Hila, Ambon	109
7.2	Kinship diagram of the Patti family	114

CONTRIBUTORS

Franz von Benda-Beckmann is professor of law and rural development in Third World countries at the Agricultural University Wageningen (the Netherlands). His major fields of research are the relations between legal complexity and the management of natural resources, social (in)security of rural population groups, and legal anthropological theory and methodology. He has done fieldwork in Malawi, West Sumatra and the Moluccas. He is the author of *Rechtspluralismus in Malawi* (1970), *Property in Social Continuity* (1979) and numerous articles on legal pluralism, social security and property issues. Together with Keebet von Benda-Beckmann he co-edited a number of books, among them *Between Kinship and the State: Law and Social Security in Developing Countries* (1988) and *Natural Resources, Environment and Legal Pluralism* (1997). At present he and Keebet von Benda-Beckmann are involved in a research project on the management of natural resources and social security in plural legal settings in Indonesia and Nepal.

Keebet von Benda-Beckmann is professor of anthropology of law at the Faculty of Law, Erasmus University Rotterdam. She obtained her PhD degree at Nijmegen University based on field research on dispute management in West Sumatra. She did field research on local forms of social security in Islamic Ambon, Eastern Indonesia and has published extensively on issues of legal pluralism and social security. She co-authored a book on the *Emancipation of Moluccan Women in the Netherlands* (1992) and co-edited a variety of books on socio-legal issues, among them *Water Rights, Conflict and Policy in Nepal* (1997).

Susan Blackburn has a PhD from Monash University, and now lectures there on Southeast Asian politics and gender in Asian politics. She is also director of the Development Studies Centre. Her past publications include *Jakarta: a History* (1997; under her former name, S. Abeyasekere). At present she is conducting research on Indonesian women in the twentieth century.

Becky Elmhirst is a lecturer in human geography at the University of Brighton. She obtained her PhD in Environment and Development from the University of London in 1997. Her publications include articles on gendered resource management in transmigration areas and inter-ethnic resource politics in trans-migration areas. She is working on a book entitled *Gender, Environment and Culture: a Political Ecology of Transmigration in Indonesia*. Her research focuses on intra-household relations, community resource politics and environmental change in Indonesia. She is currently working on a new project which investigates the household-level links between migrant factory work and rural land use in a Sumatran transmigration area.

Barbara Hatley teaches Indonesian studies and is director of the Centre of Southeast Asian Studies at Monash University. Her main research interests are in the fields of Indonesian performance, literature and gender studies. Her

CONTRIBUTORS

recent publications include articles on *Gender Concepts and Performances in Java* (in *Power and Difference: Gender in Island Southeast Asia* edited by J. Atkinson and S. Errington (1991) and *Gender, Nation and Indonesian Literature* (in *Imagining Indonesia: Cultural Politics and Political Culture* edited by J. Schiller and B. Martin-Schiller (1997).

Megan Jennaway studied social anthropology at the Australian National University and the University of Sydney before receiving her doctorate in medical anthropology from the University of Queensland's Tropical Health Program. She is currently revising her thesis, 'Sweet Breath and Bitter Honey: HIV/AIDS and the Embodiment of Desire Among North Balinese Women', for publication by the University of Chicago Press. She has had several articles published in anthropological anthologies and journals, as well as contributing book reviews to journals such as *RIMA* and *Anthropological Forum*. In between her academic work she also writes fiction and immerses herself in the mothering of three young children.

Willemijn de Jong was born in the Netherlands and received her PhD degree in 1985 at the University of Zurich with an ethnolinguistic dissertation about Greek labour migrants in Switzerland. Since 1980 she has worked as a lecturer at the Anthropology Department of the University of Zurich, and is currently an assistant professor. In 1996 she finished a postdoctoral thesis (habilitation) about work, marriage and gender in a weaving region on Flores in Indonesia.

Juliette Koning obtained her PhD (1997) in anthropology at the Centre for Asian Studies, University of Amsterdam. Her thesis, 'Generations of Change, a Javanese Village in the 1990s' discusses changing village, family and personal life in a context of rapid transition, as was characteristic for Java during the last two decades. At present she is research fellow at Wageningen Agricultural University within a research project studying 'Legal Pluralism, Natural Resource Management and Social (In)Security in Indonesia'. Earlier articles discuss family planning, 'development' programmes, and state–village relationships in Indonesia. More recently she has been studying the effects of the economic and political crisis in Indonesia on land, labour and social security mechanisms.

Elsbeth Locher-Scholten obtained her PhD in history at Leiden University in 1981 on the basis of a dissertation concerning colonial policies: *Ethiek in Fragmenten: Vijf Studies over Koloniaal Denken en Doen in de Indonesische Archipel 1877–1942*. This was also the subject matter of her second book, *Sumatraans Sultanaat en Koloniale Staat. De Relatie Djambi-Batavia (1939–1907) en het Nederlandse Imperialisme* (1994). She was the co-editor of two volumes on Indonesian women: *Indonesian Women in Focus: Past and Present Notions* (1987/1992) and *Women and Mediation in Indonesia* (1992). She is currently lecturer in history at Utrecht University and is working on a book on *Gender in Colonial Indonesia (1900–1942)*.

Marleen Nolten studied geography at the University of Utrecht. She has worked on gender-specific research and training projects in Malaysia and

Indonesia, through respectively the University of Utrecht and the University of Leiden. She is the co-editor of *Geography in Development: Feminist Perspectives on Development Geography* (1989) and has published on gender issues and a variety of other subjects in, for example, *Geografisch Tijdschrift* and *The Malaysian Journal of Tropical Geography*. Her latest publications include *Women in Pacific Asia* edited by T. van Naerssen and P. Druijven (1997). In 1996 she joined the Netherlands Organisation for International Development Cooperation and now divides her time between working at the Special Programmes Desk and raising two children.

Joke van Reenen studied anthropology at the Amsterdam Free University. From 1984 to 1990 she was a visiting staff member at Andalas University (Dep. of Sociology and Anthropology), Padang, West Sumatra. In 1996 she received her PhD at the University of Leiden, with her study *Central Pillars of the House: Sisters, Wives, and Mothers in a Rural Community in Minangkabau, West Sumatra* (CNWS Publications). She currently works as WID-specialist on an irrigation project in Lampung, Indonesia.

Janet Rodenburg is a social anthropologist and a graduate from the University of Amsterdam. In 1993 she obtained her PhD at the same university on the basis of her study on the relationship between outmigration and gender roles in North Sumatra. She is the author of *In the Shadow of Migration. Rural Women and Their Households in North Tapanuli, Indonesia* (1997, KITLV Press) and has written widely on gender and migration, e.g. in the United Nations report *Internal Migration of Women in Developing Countries* (New York, 1993). She worked as a lecturer at the University of Leiden and the University of Copenhagen and has been involved in various consultancy jobs. At present she is project co-ordinator at the International Rehabilitation Council for Torture Victims (Copenhagen), focusing on health and human rights in Asia.

Ratna Saptari obtained her PhD in anthropology from the University of Amsterdam. She is currently coordinator of the research programme 'Changing Labour Relations in Asia' at the International Institute of Social History, Amsterdam. She has published a number of articles on cigarette factory workers in Indonesia and on labour issues and NGOs in Indonesia, among them 'The Differentiation of a Rural Industrial Labour Force: Gender Segregation in East Java's *Kretek* Cigarette Industry' in P. Alexander, P. Boomgaard and B. White (eds), *In the Shadow of Agriculture* (1991). Together with Brigitte Holzner, she has also written a textbook in Indonesian entitled *Women, Work and Social Change: an Introduction to Women's Studies* (Grafiti Pers. Jakarta).

Sylvia Tiwon obtained her doctorate at the Fakultas Sastra of the University of Indonesia, before obtaining her PhD from the University of California at Berkeley. At present she is associate professor of Indonesian at the Department of South and Southeast Asian Studies at the same university and works on the theme of 'Women in the Production of Discourse'. She has published extensively on literature and on gender issues and is the author of the book *Breaking the*

Spell: Colonialism and Literary Renaissance in Indonesia, which is currently in press at the Semaian Series, Leiden University.

G.G. Weix is associate professor of anthropology and director of women's studies at the University of Montana. Her research is focused on political economy, gender and cultural studies in Indonesia, particularly North Java. She has published articles in *Indonesia, Visual Anthropology Review* and two international conference proceedings in Indonesia and Singapore. She is currently preparing a book for publication with Duke University Press.

Diane Wolf is associate professor of sociology at the University of California at Davis. Her publications include 'Daughters, Decisions and Dominations: an Empirical and Conceptual Critique of Household Strategies' in *Development and Change* (1990) and 'Female Autonomy, the Family and Industrialization in Java' in *Gender, Family and Economy: the Triple Overlap*, edited by R.L. Blumberg (1991). She is the author of *Factory Daughters, Gender, Household Dynamics, and Rural Industrialization in Java* (1992). She is currently conducting research on the identities and family issues among children of recent Filipino and Vietnamese immigrants to California. She is also beginning a project on Jewish identity, particularly the production of Holocaust memory and history.

PREFACE

The aim of this book is to examine critically the usefulness of the 'household' concept within the culturally diverse context of Indonesia and to explore in more detail the position of women within and beyond the existing domestic arrangements. This has been the focus of classical household and kinship studies for many decades, yet there is still much to learn about the way women deal with two major forces that shape and define their everyday reality. The first constitutes local traditions, encapsulated in familial and kin-based institutions; the second concerns the universalizing and authoritarian ideology of the Indonesian regime. Both provide prescriptions and prohibitions concerning family, marriage, womanhood (and manhood). The boundaries of households and other forms of domestic arrangements are to a certain extent defined by these.

Women are often caught between different and sometimes conflicting notions and practices in relation to family and household. How they themselves consciously or unconsciously challenge or accommodate to such forces is the main issue we deal with in this book. It is through women's agency that boundaries become blurred, either because women redefine certain prescriptions or because there is a wide gap between culture and practice as many women face the realities of struggling to make a living. Therefore, our attempt to 'reconstruct' the household is not confined to defining household boundaries, composition and on-the-ground inter- and intra-household relations but to the ways in which at various levels women's agency finds different formats and functions.

This book originates from a conference entitled 'Indonesian Women in the Household and Beyond' that was held in The Netherlands in 1995. At this conference, in total 29 participants from seven countries presented in-depth case studies and contributed pictures to an exhibition on various types of domestic arrangements of those present at the conference, and those whom we met during our research. These domestic arrangements ranged from one-woman households to nuclear households and to all kinds of extended families (some solely consisting of family members, some including friends or other acquaintances).

During the presentations and discussions the colourful exhibition continuously reminded us of the complexities of analysing women in relation to households. It also made us reflect on the link between the researcher and the researched, the resemblances between us but also the major differences in our lives, as well as the tensions that occur when comparing notes on ideals and reality. For the Indonesian researchers in particular, shifting forward and backward between the position of object and subject was an intensive – sometimes enriching, sometimes schizophrenic – experience.

PREFACE

The conference was a joint undertaking of the WIVS (Inter-disciplinary Forum on Indonesian Women's Studies) and the KITLV (Royal Institute of Linguistics and Anthropology). It was generously supported by the International Institute of Asian Studies, Neys van Hoogstraten Foundation and the Leids Universitair Fonds, as well as the Royal Institute of Linguistics and Anthropology. We appreciate the support of Jolanda den Hollander, who made many of the administrative arrangements for the conference.

In a way, this volume is also the product of a continuing dialogue among the members of the WIVS during our regular meetings in The Netherlands. We are obliged to Mies Grijns, Anke Niehof and Joke van Reenen for the lively arguments and the discussions that helped to clarify and enrich the ideas expressed in this book. Although we were not able to include all the papers in the present volume, we would like to express our gratitude to all the participants for the intellectual energy and excitement they brought to the sessions, an impression of which is included in the introduction. We trust that the essays, with their rich empirical material derived from Indonesian cases, will contribute to the ongoing theoretical discussion on women and households. As such the book will be of interest to anthropologists, sociologists and specialists in gender studies.

The Editors

SECTION I: INTRODUCTION

The two chapters in this first section are the introduction to this edited volume. The chapter by Marleen Nolten 'Food for Thought: Reflections on the Conference and the Set-up of this Book', reflects in detail on the issues that were 'food for thought' during the conference on 'Indonesian Women in the Household and Beyond' held in 1995. She gives a lively account of the discussions that evolved around topics such as conceptualizing the household, form and function, domestic arrangements, the gap between ideologies and realities, and more. Her account not only gives a good impression of the discussions that took place and that finally laid the basis for this book, but it also proves an insight into the papers that were not included. The second part of her chapter introduces the various sections and chapters of the present volume.

The chapter by Ratna Saptari 'Women, Family and Household: Tensions in Culture and Practice', maps out the general tensions emerging from the existence of dominant representations on womanhood, family and household and the realities of gender relations and women's agency as these are mediated through households. Her chapter provides a theoretical background to the sections in this book on 'Dominant Notions of Family and Household', 'Challenging the Household Concept', 'Domestic Arrangements and Mobility', and 'Beyond the Dichotomies'.

WOMEN AND HOUSEHOLDS IN INDONESIA

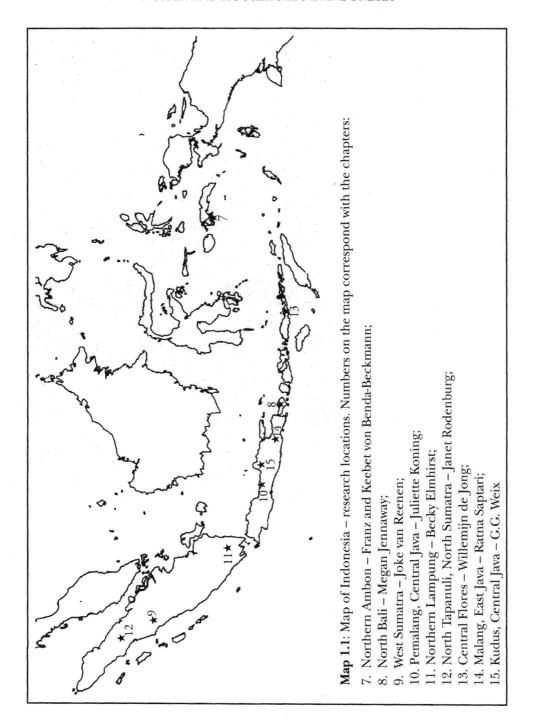

Map 1.1: Map of Indonesia – research locations. Numbers on the map correspond with the chapters:

7. Northern Ambon – Franz and Keebet von Benda-Beckmann;
8. North Bali – Megan Jennaway;
9. West Sumatra – Joke van Reenen;
10. Pemalang, Central Java – Juliette Koning;
11. Northern Lampung – Becky Elmhirst;
12. North Tapanuli, North Sumatra – Janet Rodenburg;
13. Central Flores – Willemijn de Jong;
14. Malang, East Java – Ratna Saptari;
15. Kudus, Central Java – G.G. Weix

1

Food for Thought
Reflections on the Conference and the Set-up of this Book

Marleen Nolten

INTRODUCTION

The call for papers by the Interdisciplinary Forum on Indonesian Women's Studies for its third international conference early in 1995 led to the submission of an overwhelming number. Many of these contained refreshing, exciting ideas on the apparent links between women and households (an overview of the papers presented is listed at the end of the book). As only a limited number of papers could be accommodated in the current book, we shall start off with a summary of the rich discussion that developed during the cold and windy conference week at the end of September 1995 and highlight some of the major conclusions that were drawn on the basis of the presented papers. Subsequently we shall focus on the set-up of the volume.

ON FORM, FUNCTIONS AND FLEXIBILITY OF DOMESTIC ARRANGEMENTS

From the outset it has been apparent that the enormous variety in domestic arrangements in Indonesia calls for a careful approach when defining 'households': that we need to be clear about underlying assumptions and that the boundaries that go with demarcating units should always be subject to interrogation. What we can see and quantify (a particular dwelling, a group of people sharing a roof and/or a common cooking pot, the size and composition of this group) may only reveal part of the social reality of individuals. There may be major dividing lines among kin, family and non-kin members (Van Bemmelen). Subjective perspectives ('I happen to live here, but my home is elsewhere') may throw an unexpected light upon relations that people nurture, and the value they attach to arrangements that do not necessarily include permanent co-residence (Elmhirst, Koning, Rodenburg).

We furthermore need to have a thorough understanding of the functions that 'households' or other arrangements fulfil. In many papers the universality of the harmonious production-consumption unit was questioned (Holzner) or functions in the field of distribution and retention were analysed (de Jong, Weix). Other functions include reproduction and the sharing of domestic responsibilities, the provision of care, affection and social security, the shaping of political bonds, the celebration of cultural festivities, spending free time together or the preservation of ancestral identity (Kariani Purwanti).

It was commonly acknowledged that it very much depends on the individual whether or not a specific 'household' will be able to meet all one's needs. Furthermore we need to take into account the way and pace in which 'households' change and develop, as children for example grow older and marry, and parents are not longer able to work and so become dependent on others. Individuals go through the various phases in their life-cycle. Can we say that the same applies to 'households'? This question is particularly relevant as Indonesian life expectancy has been steadily rising: it has doubled from 30 at the beginning of this century to 60 years at the turn of the millennium. Although on the whole we cannot (yet) speak of an 'ageing of the Indonesian population', this demographic phenomenon has enormous consequences for society as a whole, as well as a major impact on domestic arrangements.

THE FAR-FROM-HARMONIOUS NUCLEAR HOUSEHOLD

Living under the same roof with a group of people may facilitate the development of multi-stranded relationships. But it also forms a potential source of tension – personal conflicts appear to be major factors in breaking up households. We had lengthy discussions about the general appeal that nuclear households appear to have and the tendency for households to 'nuclearize' in terms of form (to comprise solely parents and children, living in a separate dwelling) and in function (the strengthening of interaction patterns within this limited group of people). One of the explanations given was that small living arrangements decrease the control of other (kin/family) members and bring apparent freedom to a couple and their children in terms of making one's own decisions and leading one's own life. It is also a way in which financial obligations can be limited to a small circle, which is an important incentive in areas where the cash economy is growing in importance. For some people inhabiting a one-family house is the equivalent to being modern or Western. Altogether the nuclear household is often seen as refuge from the harsh world outside.

Yet in various papers it was shown that life might actually become more complicated. Living up to the ideal of the harmonious nuclear household means that domestic tensions are being obscured. New networks have to be created in order to meet the nuclear household's needs. Young Komering couples in South Sumatra, for example, increasingly prefer not to co-habitate with other family members and to build their own houses. But as they continue to depend on the support of relatives in raising their offspring, often huts are built as close to the parents' homes as possible. Or they arrange for their children to live with relatives while attending school (Yusmadiana and Yusnaini).

It was also recognized that the household is permeable and that it may be 'intruded' upon by outsiders. Whereas in former times a sister would, for example, baby-sit on the basis of mutual reciprocity, now a baby-sitter has to be hired. Or the sister may ask to be paid for her services. Market relations also enter the home in the case of homeworking mothers in East Java, who pay their children when they help in the production or may even pay them to play outside (Holzner).

In the light of the complex world around us, it remains very tempting to extrapolate (state) ideas on ideal households to local-level situations or to take neat units such as nuclear households as a point of departure in research and planning. While convenient for planners, this approach does not fit reality (Wolf). An illustrative example comes from West Java, where in 1980 the government established a new smallholders' coconut estate. The ideal blue-print farmer families (in the policy documents referred to as 'the plasma') in reality turned out to be much smaller than was foreseen, despite the fact that they were sometimes extended with grandparents (which had not been expected). Moreover, the average age of the children was lower than anticipated, while the small household size could primarily be ascribed to divorce frequency, both of which had not been foreseen. Consequently the various calculations concerning labour input all had to be readjusted (Grijns).

THE INDIVIDUAL PERSPECTIVE AS A STARTING POINT

The immense variety in 'households' that were presented in the papers made us realize that arrangements may take on spatial forms, fulfil functions, and change at a pace that may well go beyond our imagination as well as beyond our personal frameworks of reference, being members of urban, Western, middle-class, etc. households ourselves. A brief inventory of the concepts includes: the *pekarangan* on Bali, a house compound that is occupied by two or more households (Nakatani); the *kajan* on Kalimantan, a space shared by several individuals which may comprise a nuclear household (Thambiah); residential units consisting of two-generation households in Flores, that are primarily units of production and distribution (de Jong); and the intriguing courts of Central Java (Djajadiningrat). It was commonly agreed that it is useful to analyse local, indigenous concepts and the indigenous meanings attached to them.

Some participants proposed to go a step further and to discard household concepts and their apparent boundaries altogether, since they believe that social realities can only be fully understood when taking the individual perspective as a starting point (F. and K. von Benda-Beckmann, Van Reenen). Following the same line of thought, Dharmaperwira and Nolten argued that women provide and receive security and care through a whole range of networks, of which the household may be only one.

Others disputed the existence of illusive boundaries by arguing that the dichotomies that have evaded Western feminist theories and for some time served as useful instruments in explaining women's worlds are not applicable to the Indonesian situation. Here demarcations between the household and the outside, between the private and the public, and the corresponding roles and identities and functions that go with the different spheres are much less clear-cut. In various studies it was shown how women skilfully balance their lives between the home and the outside and may shift the locus of negotiation into the home, into the factory and back to the home again (Saptari, Weix, Nakatani). It was also demonstrated how women's engagement in production enables them to deal strategically with uncertainties in the reproductive sphere (Niehof).

On Contradictions, Compromises and Congruencies in Women's Lives

From various case studies it appeared that there is an immense gap between daily realities and the ideologies which exist at the national level right down to the personal level, and which are translated into notions about ideal households and ideal roles and identities for men and women. Gender ideologies are, in a sense, difficult to grasp and often contradictory within themselves and between each other (Dawson). They reach the research communities via colonial policies, formal state ideologies, government plans and religious institutions (Locher-Scholten, Schouten). They are communicated to us through the educational system, through books, journals, magazines and performances (Blackburn and Hatley).

The very contradictions that characterize ideologies at the various levels and at times lead to untenable situations (as women are simply not able to live up to all the expectations), at the same time appear to give women room for manoeuvre and the possibility to shape their lives in their own way. Women select what seems useful, modify it and act on it (Schouten).

Indeed, women's agency was a central issue in many of the papers that were presented, demonstrating that women play an active role in shaping their own lives and that of others, within households, between households and in arrangements that go beyond households (Davis). This is not to say that women do not often find themselves in undesirable positions. They might find themselves coping with tensions in an effort to combine reproductive and productive activities through homeworking (Holzner); feel humiliated and insecure – and not able to prevent their husband from engaging in a polygamous marriage (Jennaway); find themselves to be poor and alone, detesting the day that they convinced their husband that it would bring fortune to the family if he would *mangaranto* [migrate] (Rodenburg); be physically and psychologically battered, and not able to defend their rights as they are taught to uphold the myth of the harmonious household (Sciortino and Smyth).

At another level too, various mechanisms are used to bridge the discrepancy between reality and ideals. As Elmhirst showed in her study among young girls in two villages in southern Sumatra, the unmarried daughters of migrant households were supposed to stay in the village as wage labourers (the ideal). Unmarried daughters of the local households on the other hand, were allowed to migrate and earn the family an income through factory work on Java. By allowing the girls to migrate and become 'invisible', an acceptable situation had been created, ideologically perhaps less pure but financially more rewarding.

Sometimes cultural notions and social practices do, however, converge. Jufri and Watson showed how slowly but surely formal state ideologies start influencing the daily practice of the independent and strong women in Minangkabau and Kerinci Sumatra. Being exposed to an external ideology that considers them subordinate to men, women indeed internalize this ideology which actually starts to influence the gender division of labour.

All in all, valuable insights were gained in the functions that various domestic arrangements fulfil (of for that matter fail to fulfil) for women and vice versa. What is more, the various papers provided us with an overview of the immense variety in domestic arrangements throughout Indonesia.

THE SET-UP OF THE BOOK

This book critically examines the usefulness of the household concept by focusing on the interaction between outside forces that shape domestic arrangements and women's place in them. It unravels the multiple perspectives that need to be combined in order fully to understand how women create a balance between what is ideally expected of them and the demands that the realities of daily life make on them. We should note that the studies precede 1997, the year that Indonesia faced the beginning of what would turn out to be a major economic and political crisis.

In the second part of this section Ratna Saptari introduces the major themes that run through all the chapters. It starts off with a general, theoretical overview which provides the reader with some basic insights into the interrelation between macro- and micro-level processes in the structuring of domestic units and kin-based networks, with special emphasis on the role of the state. It then focuses on efforts to separate domestic arrangements from other social units and networks, and the problems we may encounter when applying analytical dichotomies. Finally, the role of female agency within the larger structures is highlighted. These main themes are further elaborated in four thematic clusters.

The chapters in section two focus on the dominant notions of the family and the household in colonial and present-day Indonesia. It illustrates how the views of the (colonial) elite were transformed into major forces that have come to shape gender ideologies in the Peninsula. Hence, the focus is on the impact of state policies during the twentieth century and the extent to which journals and novels propagated and reinforced elite ideas. Moreover a critical analysis is made of the effects of various approaches in household studies. Despite the fact that (colonial) policies, state propaganda and the media definitely have had a great impact in shaping living arrangements physically, economically, socially as well as culturally, from the various chapters it becomes very clear that it is impossible to speak of 'the' Indonesian household or for that matter of 'the' role of women. Obviously, these strong external forces have not prevented the existence of intriguing deviations from the dominant cultural notions regarding form and function of living arrangements.

In the third section the household concept is further challenged by taking women's perspectives as a point of departure. The authors unequivocally contest the notion that the household is the most suitable unit when trying to analyse and understand women's realities, gender relations and the dynamics that underlie them. Instead it is argued that complex realities can only be fully understood when taking the individual residence perspective as a point of departure. Only then can we properly understand the magnitude of the various networks in which people are engaged, assess the needs and interests of those who are part of them, and understand the role of women in establishing and maintaining, and at times sabotaging and destroying, a variety of relationships.

In the fourth section the impact of migratory patterns on domestic arrangements and family life is examined by means of three micro-studies. Migration, be it spontaneous or planned, has always been characteristic of past and present Indonesia and the effect of spatial divisions on the form and function of domestic arrangements has been enormous. The authors in this section too, show that New Order family ideology and policy have little congruence with daily life in migration communities. The authors even go a step further than mainstream migration studies by closely examining the role of women, either as active migrants – be it voluntary or involuntary – or as those staying behind while providing basic support to the migrants.

In the fifth and final section several of the dichotomies that have become such a common frame of analysis in feminist literature are revisited. In feminist studies a sharp distinction is often made between private and public spheres, as well as a distinction between reproductive and productive work, and the roles, functions and responsibilities that go with it at the individual level. Yet the case studies presented show that, despite the fact that space is engendered, these demarcations between the home and workplace are often much more fluid than we are inclined to think. Moreover, roles and functions that women fulfil in various spaces are not only negotiable, but may also be interdependent and mutually beneficial.

Present-day Indonesia is undergoing major transformations. The reinforcement of ideas about ideal domestic arrangements and the stereotyping of women's role have been strong tools in the state's efforts to create coherence within the Peninsula and to shape national identity. Yet uniformity in forms and functions of domestic arrangements and of those who are part of it, is the exception rather than the rule. The current clamour for diversity, inclusion, democracy and self-destination also very much applies to the domestic realm of people's lives.

2

Women, Family and Household
Tensions in Culture and Practice

Ratna Saptari

INTRODUCTION

This chapter attempts to map out the general tensions emerging from the existence of dominant representations of womanhood, family and household and the realities of gender relations and women's agency as these are mediated through households.

For more than a century, debates on the nature of the family have occupied the attention of Western scholars and policy-makers alike, leaving a long trail of ideas which we have alternately embraced and abandoned. Universal assumptions concerning the nuclear family based on the conjugal unit can be traced back to both evolutionist and functionalist thinking in social science. In 1871 Lewis Henry Morgan had already attempted to show that the nuclear family was a universal characteristic of modern societies. He outlined the progression of domestic arrangements in his evolutionary scheme, from simple to more complex forms, from a condition of promiscuity to group marriage and polygamy, ultimately leading to monogamy (Cheater 1991: 19). On the other hand, in the 1920s, Malinowski argued that the conjugal relationship and by extension, the family, was universal since it fulfilled a universal human need, namely emotional relations and child-rearing (see Collier and Yanagisako 1981).

In the 1960s some anthropologists had already argued against the idea of the universal nuclear family as represented by the evolutionists and functionalists and pointed out the Western bias of both scholars and policy-makers. This line of argument gained momentum as feminist scholars, in particular, questioned the natural fit between women and the family. It was contended that the concept of the family as it was then seen, was actually a product of European history. It was exactly when, as a result of the Industrial Revolution, middle-class fears of social disintegration found their expression in the public sphere in the early half of the nineteenth century that the family became the 'moral unit' from which citizens and members of society were to be produced and maintained. Feminists also very strongly argued that the family was not necessarily the vehicle for social solidarity and support as often contended, but the medium through which women's subordination was reproduced (Hartmann 1979).

With the attempt to demystify the family came also the need to understand its actual workings. If the family was not the arena of nurture and solidarity that it was assumed to be, what then was it?[1] Since in order to understand its operation, researchers needed to identify its boundaries, debates then shifted to defining these boundaries. Feminists argued that although 'family' and 'household' were closely linked concepts, they were not necessarily identical (Rapp 1982; Yanagisako 1979; White 1980; Harris 1981; Wolf 1990; Kabeer 1994). The emphasis underlying this argument has not always been the same, however. For some, the family is primarily defined by biological and kin relations and is related to procreative and reproductive functions, whereas households are social units which consist of a set of individuals who usually share a common residence and conduct a set of activities coined by the term 'domestic'.[2] Although the inclusion or exclusion of members into households is often based on kinship and family ties, it is not exclusively so. Put more simply, family is associated with kinship and household with propinquity.

Another basis for separating the two concepts is made by Rapp when she states that 'households are the empirically measurable units within which people pool resources and perform certain tasks'; whereas family is a more normative term, namely those who should be living together or the 'more extended network of kin relations that people may activate selectively' (Rapp 1982: 169–70). This distinction between the normative and empirical usefully reminds us of the duality of structures in analysing the family and household, a point to which I shall return below.

Having pinpointed the criteria by which family and household are distinguished, there still exists much disagreement regarding the distinction based on kinship vs. propinquity. The fact that domestic arrangements have different forms and functions both in the past and present has been shown by many (see among others Goody 1972; White 1980). Domestic units can be regulated by different combinations of kinship systems and residential patterns i.e. matrilineal–uxorilocal/virilocal; patrilineal–virilocal/uxorilocal; bilateral and virilocal or uxorilocal patterns of lineage and residence. These features are not just a relic of some distant past, as evolutionists will have it, but are still strongly present in modern-day social relations.[3] Co-residentiality in particular becomes problematic to define when we take into account various domestic arrangements such as:

> residential groupings that move through a seasonal cycle of dispersal and concentration ... the movement of personnel between dwelling units, particularly in societies where there is great mobility between these units ... the huts or houses that share a common yard, which

may or may not be enclosed from other yards, and whether to include servants, apprentices, boarders, and lodgers as members of the household (Yanagisako 1979: 164).

Most chapters in this volume attest to this diversity in domestic arrangements.[4] However in the last decade we have also been faced with the increasing emphasis in social science on deconstructions of state representations and on the workings of state hegemony, particularly as they relate to women and the household.[5] With the growing strength of state regimes and their ability to manipulate media, educational systems, legislation, social institutions, and public policy, state-induced representations would in many ways influence the way people think, particularly with regard to women and the household. With the development of the state and centralized control, various administrative measures central to the functioning of the state needed an easily definable social unit upon which it could place its claims, and the nuclear family household has become the most convenient unit for this purpose. The enactment of taxes and dues imposed upon the citizens; the necessity for census-taking; the need to clarify property rights between that of the state and that of the individual; and the introduction of land reform, all enhanced the need clearly to demarcate the boundaries of the social units that are to form the focal point of these government measures. The household defined by relations of propinquity and kin became the simplest tool for state administration (Harris 1981; White 1980; Kabeer 1994; see also F. and K. von Benda-Beckmann and Wolf, this volume).

Wedged between these general phenomena our task is then to map the tensions of hegemonical notions of family and external interventions into family life, household structures and domestic arrangements on the one hand, and the persistence of cultural variations and local subversions, on the other. In other words, we become highly attentive to the tensions between structure and agency, culture and practice. Although this chapter is not meant to find conceptual solutions to these contradictions, it attempts to reflect on the findings revealed by the contributions in this book. The section below will first examine the debates regarding the nature of 'structures', which will be followed with a brief overview of the trends shown in Indonesian history. This then will lead to a discussion on the dilemmas concerning the concept of agency, and this will be the focus of the last section.

THE STRUCTURES THAT BIND?

It has long been argued by anthropologists that dichotomies and symbolic structuring is ever-present in shaping social relations and dictating the rituals of life. Although the majority of scholars recognize the existence of dichotomies, there is much disagreement concerning the nature of these dichotomies, how they have emerged and how they are maintained. The view that dichotomies are part of mental structures pervading human societies in their rituals and daily lives irrespective of time and spatial differences (as contended by structuralism), flourished in the 1970s only to rapidly fade away again.[6] Class-based feminists have attempted to link the emergence of dichotomies with the emergence of bourgeois ideology among the middle-classes in nineteenth-century Europe.[7] In the late 1980s Foucauldian theory recast the concept of power and domination, and introduced them into the analysis of dominant ideologies and the creation of dichotomies. In this framework, power is exercised from within society rather than from above, through surveillance and discourse rather than by physical punishment or explicit coercion. Through these mechanisms, definitions of what is 'normal' and 'abnormal' are forged and maintained. The lived system of meanings and values is therefore hegemonic, although as Raymond Williams reminds us, hegemony is never complete and is always vulnerable to subversion (Williams 1977). Much feminist theorizing has examined the content of discourse and has analysed representations of women and the family which constitutes it.

These basic premises are significant when we examine the chapter of Tiwon in the first section of this volume, juxtaposing it with that of Locher-Scholten. On the one hand Tiwon shows how 'regimes of truth' concerning women and womanhood (i.e. their exclusion from the public domain) are part and parcel of the nationalist construction, whether colonial or postcolonial. This is represented in print, public ceremonies, legislation and in public policies in the form of dichotomies of femininity and masculinity with their respective unequivocal associations. On the other hand, Locher-Scholten attempts to show the ambivalence in Dutch colonial attitude towards women where a clear distinction is made between high-status, priyayi women, and working-class women. Priyayi families constituted large extended households, relations within the family were dictated by *adat* [tradition], and the women were seen to be submissive to their husbands. Working-class women were considered to come from small families and their legal positions and property rights were considered better than those of European women (see Locher-Scholten this volume). Blackburn and Hatley (this volume), through their analysis of novels and magazines, also show the ambiguous messages and representations as women themselves attempt to find a voice in the public domain of the 1930s where, on the one hand, the nuclear family was an accepted fact but, on the other hand, relations within it were not necessarily harmonious.

The two positions sketched above may not be contradictory, since hegemonical representations portraying one single image of womanhood may operate at the same time as those acknowledging the heterogeneity of women and the ambivalencies of rulers as well as the ruled. However, it is worthwhile to indicate the tensions in the process of representation itself and also in interpreting such representations.[8] Added to this, Wolf brings another dimension into the picture as she focuses on the way in which households are represented by scholars. Indeed, the process of labelling and naming social phenomena is not the domain of the rulers alone but also those who claim to represent the subjects of study.

In attempting to understand the concurrence of these different representations, one could take into account what Alice Schlegel has termed the different 'levels of meaning'. Applying this term for the examination of gender ideology in Hopi society, she distinguishes two levels of meaning: the 'general meaning', namely 'what women and men are in an abstract sense'; and the 'specific meaning', i.e. 'the definition of gender according to a particular location in the social structure or within a particular field of action' (Schlegel 1990: 24). Thus it may be that the specific meaning of gender in any particular instance may depart from the general, and that specific meanings may appear to be antithetical to one another. The meaning ascribed to gender has more to do with social reality, whereas general meanings are abstracted from ritual, literature, myth, symbolic objects and other aspects of expressive culture. Although we may question this sharp distinction between the abstract and specific, we cannot deny the different levels of abstraction in representations of womanhood as portrayed by the discussion above. Nevertheless, how the two levels of meaning interact and redefine each other should be the subject for further investigation.

Apart from the tensions in the regimes of representations, any analysis of operation of state hegemony and its impact on women and the family must also take into account the discrepancies between state design, its implementation and its actual impact at local level (see von Benda-Beckmann 1991). Even if state policy is more or less consistent and non-contradictory, the implementation may be less so. Gordon among others, in looking at state practice in the West, has argued that 'state patriarchy' cannot explain the often contradictory, even self-defeating aspects of policy (Gordon 1990). Gordon shows that contradictions emerge from various sources: the fragmented and inconsistent goals of policy-makers and the struggles surrounding the enactment of certain policies. This approach also underlines the role of women's activism in challenging policies and national power structures as well as the heterogeneity of women's groups and the different interests that women's groups represent (Gordon 1990: 30). Thus, the actual impact of state policy on domestic units and on the gender division of labour is a highly complex process, the outcome of which can only be ascertained at the local level. Furthermore, although its political range is the broadest in scope, the state is not the only institution involved in the creation of gender ideology. The role of counter ideologies either represented by religion, by *adat* [customary law] or by communal practice have always made the translation of state ideology anything but a smooth process. The struggle surrounding the 1974 marriage law (see Tiwon this volume), and the contentions regarding land reform and land redistribution both in the 1960s and the present period, reflect such complexities.

Empirical research has also shown that although state structures are clearly visible in all aspects of life, they are not all-pervasive (Sullivan 1989; Blackwood 1995). As has been shown in community studies in the Indonesian New Order period, for instance, public ceremonies at local level are usually attended only by local village officials and their wives whereas those outside the official world observe and do not participate.[9] Because of the exclusion of ordinary people from these ceremonies, social and political behaviour splits into official and non-official spheres (see Sullivan 1994). It seems that as official policy regarding citizenship and sanctioned behaviour for the common people has become more rigid and inflexible, people have been forced to accommodate to the official line and yet at the same time they retain some of their freedom of movement. The idea of the nuclear family and the loyal housewife is particularly preserved in the official sphere. As Sullivan stresses in her study of an urban kampung community:

> No kampung woman is likely to perceive herself or any of her neighbours as either a dainty, cultured little helpmate or a potent citizen of the Republic. In the kampung universe she is a neighbour first, a mother second and a wife last (Sullivan 1989: 78).

The exclusion of women from public affairs may be seen as the medium through which they avoid state surveillance.

On the other hand, the state has also appropriated local cultural symbols from its various ethnic groups to boost the attractiveness of its development projects. In doing so the initial interpretation of such symbols may be appropriated by the state but, at the same time, may be the means by which the actual enactment of such programmes can be left to the discretion of local leaders. An example is shown by the concept of Bundo Kanduang, which is a general term applied to any senior woman. A senior woman in a matrilineal society such as Minangkabau has wide-ranging power over her sublineage both in terms of family relationships, management of family land, and in ceremonial affairs. However the New Order state has appropriated this term, through its ibu teladan [model mother] awards, and translated Bundo Kanduang in terms of women who are good homemakers and child-rearers. Despite this appropriation by the state, social relations as circumscribed by the interplay of tradition, Islam and the social economic exigencies have not moulded themselves to the dictates of the Indonesian state (Blackwood 1995: 130–40).

Such questions present the problematics of any analysis on dominant representations. Since such representations are created within specific political constellations and serve a specific purpose, they are inherently subject to challenges and reinterpretations as political bases shift and change. And yet different political groupings in different historical moments may share the same interest in retaining certain types of depictions, despite the different contexts in which such ideologies are created and maintained. Furthermore, within the multifarious context of Indonesian power and politics, we should consider what hegemonic representations mean for women at different levels of the social hierarchy; for women in urban and rural structures, in 'public' and 'private' domains, in upper, middle and lower classes, and in the 'centre' (Jakarta/Java) and 'periphery' (outside Jakarta/Java).

WOMANHOOD AND THE FAMILY IN INDONESIAN HISTORY

Feminist literature has paid some attention to the links between state formation, domestic units and women's position in them both in the history of Western and non-Western societies. In anthropology, Sacks (1979) linked the devaluation of women's position to the erosion of the power of kin-group autonomy. She argued that the state undermined women's status by eroding the economic and political integrity of kin groups; the process of state-making tended to favour women's roles as wives, to the detriment of their personal autonomy. Leacock made a more direct link between state formation, the creation of a market economy with changes in property holdings and the formation of the nuclear family (Silverblatt 1991: 146). All of these scholars saw that the domestication of women was a process directly and indirectly spurred by commercialization, individualization and state formation rather than a systematically planned scenario designed and implemented by state patriarchy or by patriarchal elements within the state.

Quite often the stringency or leniency in the control of sexuality and citizenship was founded on the degree of centralized or decentralized system of rule enacted by the ruling powers.[10] The (re)definition of women's place is also linked to crucial moments in history where the state, or ruling factions within the state, need to take certain measures to gain legitimacy, control and power. The legal framework of marriage and divorce, welfare provision, financial and legal responsibilities, fiscal obligations, rights to physical movement, constraints on the physical location of economic activities, rules concerning hours and remuneration of work, eligibility for the transfer of income, land reform, taxation programmes in the public sector, and collective bargaining agreements in the private sector, are all areas in which women's position and identity is defined by the state (Moore 1988: 128–85; Walby 1990: 150–72).

In the Indonesian case, it has often been remarked that in Southeast Asia, even from the pre-colonial times, women enjoyed a relatively high status compared to their counterparts in South and East Asia (Stoler 1977; Atkinson and Errington 1990; Reid 1988). Reid for example, argues that the influence of Islam, Christianity, Buddhism and Confucianism have not undermined their status. This is inferred from such indicators as bride-price, residence pattern after marriage, divorce, pattern of pre-marital sexual activity and easy divorce, and interracial unions. Women were also active in the public domain, as can be seen from their involvement in diplomatic missions and in trade, and from the fact that women rulers were not unknown.[11] Islam – which made women legally and economically dependent on their husbands – also restricted their rights to initiate divorce. However, this impact, according to Reid, was mostly felt by the wealthy urban mercantile elite and not by the ordinary working population (Reid 1988: 147–57).[12]

The arrival of the colonial powers initially did not bring major changes in the gendered representations as enacted by the state. It was only when systematic appropriation of surplus became part of colonial policy and village organization was redesigned to cater to the needs of the colonial regime, that direct interventions were made towards domestic units.[13] The redefinition of these structures can be provided by two examples: changes resulting from the enactment of the Cultivation System in Java (1930s) and those emerging from the corporate Plantation System in North Sumatra (late nineteenth century).

The cultivation system, which was introduced in the 1830s in Java by the Dutch, was based on the traditional mode of appropriation through the enactment of land taxes. In many parts of Java, two types of land tenure systems had existed since the colonial period, namely the system of inheritable individual possession and that of communal possession. The basis on which the nature of these shares changed was very closely linked to the needs of the colonial state in obtaining labour for its forced cultivation system. Therefore the target of these policies was primarily the male land-owning and land-cultivating members of the community,[14] since it was the men who were mainly allowed to hold land shares (although land based on individual heritable possession was accessible to women). Indeed, although women were quite conspicuous in indigenous agriculture, it is argued that they were almost absent in the production of cash crops for the European market (Boomgaard 1981; Locher-Scholten 1987).[15] In this case women's exclusion emerged from the adoption of traditional ways of recruiting labour already reported in pre-colonial times (see Burger 1975). This meant that with the separation of production systems, i.e. one geared towards subsistence and the other towards the European market, there has been a gradual dichotomization of spheres, the boundaries of which were quite flexible since colonial labour demands changed rapidly following the changes in policy. Although this dichotomization did not imply the domestication of women, it did mark the different relationship men and women had to the colonial bureaucracy and the more strictly defined household through which the colonial state recruited its labour.

The other example in the superimposition of colonial policy on existing social structures which resulted in the redefinition of household units can be provided by the corporate plantation system in North Sumatra. Ann Stoler has shown that in the plantations of the late nineteenth century, where Javanese-indentured workers constituted the labour, single male workers were at first recruited. Women coolies made up only 10–12% of the plantation workforce. These women were recruited not only as cheap labourers but also primarily as 'magnets' for the male workers to provide sexual services, deemed to be important by the corporate managers as there was a scarcity of women and also because of the systematic denial of stable social and domestic ties (Stoler 1986: 51). The units consisted of single men living in compounds within the plantation grounds. During the Depression when estates were running out of funds, attempts were made to create a resident labour pool. As a result 'pseudo colonies' were created which could only be inhabited by workers who had married (and been employed for at least five years) and they had the right to use the house and garden only on the basis of their continued employment in the company. Therefore nuclear households were created, which contrasted sharply with the Batak communities surrounding the plantation. A look at the social contours of present-day North Sumatra with its diverse domestic structures of patrilineal Batak and bilateral Javanese nuclear households can only be understood through the history of plantation politics. In the Javanese and North Sumatran examples the definition of household boundaries were colonial creations but these are embedded in different social contexts.

The representation of womanhood and its role in the family has not only been a franchise of the state. Contending notions have coloured the colonial setting as both anti-colonial and church-based discourses used gendered metaphors in staking their claim and attempting to achieve their goals. Gouda mentions how the use of parental and sexual metaphors were part of both colonial and nationalist discourse. However whereas the Dutch used these parental metaphors to legitimize colonial authority, nationalist espousal of them in different nuances was meant to subvert and mock the colonial rhetoric of legitimacy (Gouda 1998: 237–38).

The emergence of women's organizations in the early twentieth century paved the way for the articulation of women's own representations, even though these were never far from the prevailing dominant notions[16](see Wieringa 1995). Debates on the marriage law, and on access to employment as well as education, were however key issues brought up by these organizations. The national independence movement brought with it the involvement of women in the public sphere through these women's organizations. Sukarno repeatedly included women in his appeal for national unity; however, while he saw women as indispensable to the revolution, they were still distinguished from men in their contribution to the revolution. As Wieringa points out, women were to participate equally, but not on equal terms or under equal conditions (Wieringa 1995: 95). What distinguished this period from the New Order era is that in the presence of relative democracy, the emergence of women's organizations, whether as part of political parties or as independent ones, offered the possibility for women to articulate their political interests unshackled by the doctrines of the state (although still tied to their parties).

In the New Order, the domestication of women has been quite a strong feature within state ideology and programmes. The Suharto regime laid down the basic principles of gender relations as they manipulated family ideology towards one based on the nuclear form with a clear distinction between the male household head as the representative and provider of the family, and the female housewife and mother as the husband's supporter, the children's nurturer and the society's guardian of morals and culture. This has manifested itself in the ghettoization of women's activities in the so-called wife-organizations and the emphasis of women's roles as first and foremost that of safeguarding family well-being and general social welfare (see also Sen 1998; Sullivan 1994; Suryakusuma 1996; Tiwon 1996; Wieringa 1995). The Family Welfare Programme (PKK) enacted at all levels of the bureaucracy operates to install state notions of womanhood and the family. The family planning programme is closely associated with this official representation of womanhood as pictures depicting a father, mother and two children (i.e. the nuclear family) are distributed in more than 100,000 villages in all the Indonesian provinces.[17] Educational primary textbooks have shown the clear gender division of labour between mother and father with pictures depicting the mother in the house and father going out to work. In 1995 the minister launched the year of 'the dual role' which is an affirmation of this representation, as the economic reality of the majority of Indonesian women pushes them out of the home. The archetypal juxtaposition of, on the one hand, the ideal woman associated with marriage and the family and, on the other, the bad and dangerous women outside the family realm portrays the consequences for those who do not conform (see Wieringa 1995; Tiwon 1996). The representation of womanhood at the national level is associated with a clear middle-class and Java-centric bias, as official ceremonies and public affairs place women as attentive companions to their husbands with their Javanese traditional garb depicting elegance and confinement (see Tiwon this volume).

And yet these representations are also open to different interpretations. The fact that the New Order state has emphasized the dual role of women (as housewife and working woman) has been interpreted in different ways by feminist scholars. Some have seen this as a means to justify the secondary role women play in the labour market or in production relations (Wolf 1992). Others have tended to view this as the conflictual role that women in reality have with the state, where on the one hand women basically are seen as housewives but their role in paid work cannot be ignored. Sen, for instance, argues that the early New Order ideal of the domesticated woman had begun to change as she pointed out that 'the 1993 Garis Besar Haluan Negara [Broad Outlines of State Policy] removed any reference to child-rearing which had appeared in previous edition of the document' (Sen 1998: 43).

WOMEN'S AGENCY AND HOUSEHOLDS

As scholars gradually turned away from structural analyses, there has been an equally obsessive trend towards looking at the dynamism and creativity of 'agents' or 'actors' in finding ways to 'outwit the system' or to survive in the face of repressive conditions. As many papers in our conference have also stressed the importance of looking at women's agency, it is appropriate here to devote some space to this issue. The concept of 'agency' has been often used to describe different things. Giddens' concept of agency hinges on the idea of individuals who are capable of creatively responding to and changing the circumstances in which they find themselves (Giddens 1984). However, others have used it in a very wide sense, embracing the broad concepts of action and strategies. In using the term, we often avoid any attempt to analyse what it implies for the person's structural positioning, rather, the focus is more on what it means for an individual's subjective experience. In this sense there is no reference to the implication of such activities for the person's longer-term well-being and social position.

If we view agency in terms of how it affects an individual's position within existing power structures, we can conceptually distinguish different types. It may mean simply the capability to maximize one's ability to undertake the tasks and duties allocated to a person. Yanagisako has shown in her study of the Japanese-American families in the United States that it is the wife's relationships with other women (i.e. her agency) outside the household that have managed to maintain the continuity of the ideal typical nuclear family with men as the recognized heads of the economic and jural spheres (Yanagisako 1977: 219). Therefore women's agency in this case helps to reassert the unequal gender relations in the household. This is also true of Sharma's study in an urban Indian community, on the networks women make with their sisters-in-law which function as a support group for the enactment of their roles as wives. Agency may also mean the ability to stretch the boundaries defining one's social space. This has been shown in Diane Wolf's study on factory women in Java (1992) and various chapters in this volume.

Quite often the need for economic survival allows more freedom of movement for women. However, a woman's position cannot be judged solely by this measure. As we delve more deeply into the realm of practice, various possibilities emerge from this situation: a woman's income-earning capacity may improve her decision-making position and control at home, but it may not significantly change her subordinate position there; or her situation may depend on how much she earns, whether her husband has a stable income, and whether there are other individuals to whom she can delegate her domestic tasks. In the case of the Toba Batak women examined by Rodenburg (this volume), despite living in a patrilineal and patrilocal system, the women's social space and decision-making position is elevated because of the absence of their husbands who have migrated to Java. Megan Jennaway shows the ambiguous nature of polygynous households where the institution of co-wives 'is a threat underpinning the maintenance of monogamy and a safety net for those marginal women whose conjugal interests have been seriously compromised' (Jennaway this volume). The fact that certain kin networks are suspended and others are encouraged due to the agency of the women is shown by F. and K. von Benda-Beckmann and also van Reenen (this volume).

In our analysis on agency we do not intend to dismiss action that does not induce visible changes in power relations or 'structures'; the impact of action is too complex to be measured by simple indicators and it is also important to examine what certain actions mean for individuals in terms of their attempts to create space for themselves. Yet we argue for a more dynamic analysis, involving an examination of the interplay between action and social implications, whether in the short or long term.

Following these discussions we then come to the question of the types of domestic structures which either constrain or enable women's agency. Should we follow the general proposition put forward by scholars of European and North American societies, that with the nuclearization of the household came also the domestication of women? In the chapters that follow it will be shown how, first of all, the nuclearization of households has not been universal in practice. In fact apart from Saptari, and to a certain degree Koning, most of the case studies show the absence of nuclear households and the prevalence of co-residential arrangements based on extended kinship units, or social networks cutting across co-residential units. However, domestic forms do not in themselves say anything about the direction which women's agency is taking. Some show that the smaller the unit, the more limited the obligation to provide financial support for other members of the household. Others say that the larger and the looser the boundaries, the more space a woman has to initiate her own strategies for her interests. Most of the chapters in this book point to the importance of networks in supporting the needs of women or domestic units in the performance of domestic responsibilities or economic activities or obtaining access to economic resources (F. and K. von Benda-Beckmann, de Jong, van Reenen and Saptari).[18] Although not all these papers focus on the central role of women-centred networks, other studies have shown their importance in supporting or undermining certain forms of domestic arrangements and unequal gender relations. These networks are also considered to increase women's space for manoeuvre in the face of structural constraints.

Some examples may shed more light on the aspects brought up in the discussion. In looking at Japanese families in the United States, Yanagisako for instance has shown how, with increased individualization and the enhancement of the autonomous nuclear family ideal, women-centred networks are able to establish ties between nuclear households without threatening the economic and jural independence of nuclear families (Yanagisako 1979: 219). Lamphere (1974: 103) shows that the type of women's networks and women's strategies developed through the creation of such networks, are dependent on the type of domestic group and the larger social and economic structures that influence their social space. In China, women create two types of strategies: inside and outside the household. Inside the household, women build close ties within the uterine family to counteract their subordinate position. Outside the household, women form neighbourhood groups and create a space for themselves through gossip and opinion-forming strategies that may undermine their husband's position. In Africa, women may form two types of networks – those they create with other women as they conduct extra-domestic economic activities and those that they create with their male kin. Both types of strategies influence their position vis-à-vis their husbands. In modern industrial societies, where working-class men often work outside the home, mother–daughter ties are the focus of the networks (Lamphere 1974). In her study on rural India in the 1970s, Sharma also points out that women's networks are often complex and ambivalent. This is because in a patrilocal system, a woman's most important relations are with her sisters-in-law, who are at the same time her neighbours.

In building networks with them, a woman obtains assistance but this is for the purpose of fulfilling her obligation as wife (Sharma 1980: 193). In an urban *kampung* community in Indonesia, Sullivan shows that the networks that a woman builds with her neighbours may break the formal dichotomy of private–domestic and public–non-domestic domains that are deemed to characterize Western societies (Sullivan 1994: 150). What she terms as rewang [help] networks performed during slametans [communal rituals] bridge the distance between women and men as women are included and assume definite roles in a situation that is culturally seen as formal and public (Sullivan 1994: 116, 163).

In all these cases, the types of networks and what they mean for women as well as for intra-household relations and the maintenance of domestic boundaries are contingent on the rules of descent, residential patterns, marital relations and access to resources. Not all networks have the same meaning for women, and a specific network may have different meanings for different groups of women. However, it is clear that in intra- and inter-household relations, any analysis of the meaning of domestic arrangements for women's position should not underestimate the importance of women's networks. In focusing on women's networks it is useful to identify the various constitutive components, namely: the degree of role differentiation among members of the network; the female kin or non-kin typology forming the solidary core of the network; the cohesion of this core (and of the larger network); the types of activities conducted by the networks; and the kind of services that flow through the network.

While kin-based networks are important, we must also remember that domestic functions may also be served by non-kin-based networks. As Yanagisako reminds us, 'Why do we regard solitaries [individuals living alone] as constituting households, while we exclude institutions like orphanages, boarding schools, men's houses and army barracks?' (Yanagisako 1979: 164). One example we can mention for Indonesia is the case of factory dormitories, where single or married women who are separated from their natal or conjugal families live, and who therefore rely on one another to undertake domestic activities (see Singarimbun and Sairin 1995). These women rely on the exchange of services with their dormitory mates for shopping, cooking and emotional support. Many of the married women with children, however, leave their offspring in the homes of their parents or grandparents.

Conclusion

As we have moved away from a functionalistic mode of analysis, where social norms, role expectations and the practical application of such norms were to meet the reproductive needs of society, we are now more aware of the gap and discontinuities between culture and praxis, between different sets of normative rules, and between the different uses of norms in daily life. This chapter has attempted to highlight a number of issues that illustrate these contradictions. Representations of womanhood and family and definitions of household boundaries have taken different forms and meanings in different periods of Indonesian history. It cannot be denied that the presence of the state or a centralized form of power is necessary to the enactment of dominant notions of family and women, yet each period has reflected different constellations of power and different tensions in the creation and maintenance of such notions. At the symbolic level there is never one single base for cultural domination. Diverse representations have always existed, yet the consolidation of these different notions depends on the balance of power and on the level in which such tensions are negotiated.

It has been shown that not only in the implementation of such representations, differences in interpretation and the ability to ensure the proper translation of such notions continue to exist. Responses to such representations may vary, but one strong feature of Indonesian political life is that dual spheres based on what is official and unofficial have been created.

When we examine the nature of women's agency within such fixed yet at the same time fluid representations, we can see how their position within households is an expression of multifarious factors. The composition of domestic arrangements, whether large or small units, does not in itself define the extent to which women can improve their bargaining position. Women's networks, which are created either through or in spite of their membership in households, have also functioned ambiguously in promoting their agency. On the one hand, women's networks are a source of support and solidarity, yet on the other hand they quite often reproduce the unequal structures of which they are a part. It is only through our examination of the interplay between these different levels of analysis that we can understand how culture and practice intersect and form the environment in which women live.

Acknowledgements

I would like to thank the external reviewer and particularly Juliette Koning, Marleen Nolten and Janet Rodenburg for their helpful comments on earlier versions of this chapter. The latter three have also shown great patience and understanding in waiting for its final completion.

Notes

1   The assumption held by scholars and policy-makers that households are unified wholes where there is a unity of interests of the different household members has been much criticized (see Wolf 1990 and Wolf this volume). Such views are upheld for instance by neo-classical economics where economic decision-making is assumed to be made within the walls of the households with the central decision-maker being the male household head. Particularly for policy-making, such a perception is useful because of the practical solution it provides to the complex flow of resources and

benefits to and from households (see Dwyer and Bruce 1988: 3). Such views can also be associated with traditional Marxist thinking where the identification of the class position of individuals assumes the natural unity and homogeneity of households (Humphries 1977).

2 This refers, among others, to food production, consumption, sexual reproduction and child-rearing. See Yanagisako (1979: 164–65).

3 Different terms have been used to refer to domestic units such as 'domestic group', 'co-residential unit', 'hearthhold' and 'household'. Variations in the terms used reflect not only the diversity in functions and types of domestic units existing in different societies, but also in what we view as central to the existence of such units.

4 See particularly F. and K. von Benda-Beckmann, van Reenen, Elmhirst, Rodenburg, Koning, de Jong, and Saptari, this volume.

5 Donzelot stresses how mechanisms regulating society are closely connected with prevailing social images of the family and of the idea of 'normality' which have in turn been maintained by educational institutions and by the manipulation of various kinds of legislation and policies (Donzelot 1977; see also Barrett 1990).

6 Simone de Beauvoir (1952) and, later on, Ortner (1974) stressed the subordinate position of women through the perceived link between women and the domestic, women and nature. A dialectical pattern of binary opposition characterizes all societies, Western or non-Western, namely the opposition between the masculine and feminine. Since maleness is consistently associated with culture and femaleness with nature, males are placed in a dominating and women in a subordinate position as culture exploits nature (Beauvoir 1952; see also Jaggar 1983; Moore 1988; Sanday 1990). In Western society, the family, the home and the 'domestic' are conceptualized as a single unit which is defined in juxtaposition to the public sphere of work, business and politics.

7 See for instance Hall (1979); Barrett (1990); Alexander (1984).

8 One should also be reminded that the media through which such discourses are manifested are as important as the content of the discourse itself.

9 Because of the rigid structure imposed on village life, participation in official functions is limited to those who are members or spouses of the official structures, thereby excluding all of those outside them.

10 This is clearly shown, for instance, by Comaroff, who, in looking at the changing boundaries of the domestic and public domains among the Tshidi in Africa, found that 'When the world was highly centralized and hierarchical ... the active public sector placed great stress on the closure of the domestic unit – and sharpened the division between the spheres. Under conditions of decentralization, the public domain barely existed ... the managerial quality of the social field was reduced, and the mechanisms that integrated and stratified domestic units within the overarching polity were eclipsed' (Comaroff 1987: 68–72).

11 Reid mentions that six of the 32 rulers of the kingdom of Bone since it was established in the fourteenth century were women.

12 Many scholars have inserted a cautionary note to descriptions of women's high status as they do not take into account the dynamics of power within the local context (Ong and Peletz 1995: 7; Wolf, this volume). Reid's illustration of fifteenth-century kingdoms of Southeast Asia also suggests that apart from the fact that several indicators could provide evidence of women's high status, they were also objects of exchange (as wives, concubines and daughters) by local kings and treated as their possessions (Reid 1993).

13 This does not imply that villages were unchanging and static. The movement of people from one village to another even in the early colonial period, has been registered. This also implies that domestic units, whether households or extended families, had already enjoyed flexible boundaries since the eighteenth and nineteenth centuries.

14 The qualifications that had to be met by those who were allowed these shares were among other things: a) the obligation to provide labour services (in this case to work approximately 66 days a year for the cultivation of crops for the colonial state); b) the person had to be married; c) the person must possess a farmyard and a house – all this referred to male household heads (Kano 1977: 15)

15 Boomgaard also contends that it is because women have been pulled into indigenous agriculture that their labour time in the production of handicrafts dropped sharply.

16 The articulation of their voices did not start with these organizations but had been expressed by women from the higher elite circles such as Kartini, about whom much has been written (see among others Tiwon 1996). Seven women from this elite class were interviewed for the Dutch enquiry on 'The Declining Welfare of the Native Population of Java and Madura'. The issues that they brought up were not restricted to family matters: they encompassed education for women, marriage reforms, combatting prostitution, greater opportunities for women to appear in public, sex education, equal wages for equal work, improvements for the economic position of peasants and training for peasant women (Vreede de Stuers 1960: 174–75).

17 As Stivens has shown, this official representation differs somewhat from Malaysia, where although the state has domesticated kinship relations undermining its productive functions and emphasizing its reproductive tasks, it has not reduced kin-based units to that of nuclear families. According to her, the outcome has been a range of modified extended family forms which are often female-centred (Stivens 1985).

18 Marleen Nolten and Frieda Dharmaperwira, whose paper was not included, focused on the role of these networks in supporting the position of middle-class women despite huge physical distance.

SECTION II: DOMINANT NOTIONS OF FAMILY AND THE HOUSEHOLD

National policies and the ideologies that underlie them have been strong forces in shaping gender ideologies as well as cultivating ideas about the ideal Indonesian household and women's role in it. This holds true for the colonial situation as well as for the more recent process of nation-building. The four chapters in this section closely examine the views of the elite, the ways in which these were translated into colonial and temporary state policies, how these views were propagated through journals and novels, and how they influenced the manner in which households were approached.

Elsbeth Locher-Scholten in her chapter on 'Colonial Ambivalencies: European Attitudes towards the Javanese Household (1900–1942)', analyses how male colonial authorities perceived Javanese households through a bifocal lens. *Priyayi* households were seen as units of socialization whereas peasant households were seen as units of production. Women's roles in both types of households were valued differently and so were the colonial policies that were directed towards them. Whereas the concept of the housewife was popularized among Christian rural women and among women of the elite, the productive work of women from peasant households was recognized as an economic asset, and actually used for the betterment of the colonizers.

The next chapter complements this argument. Susan Blackburn and Barbara Hatley examine in their study on 'Representations of Women's Roles in Household and Society in Indonesian Women's Writing of the 1930s', the content of journals and novels in different periods of history and the impact these had on the role and identity of the elite. The authors conclude that despite restrictive norms on the household and women's roles, women themselves showed their inventiveness and explored alternative views and ways for giving vent to their expressions.

By focusing on the discourse of the current 'regime of truth', Sylvia Tiwon in her contribution entitled 'Reconstructing Boundaries and Beyond', looks at the contemporary process of women's exclusion within the project of nation-building. This process of exclusion depends on cultural traits derived from 'traditional' symbols of the feminine and has its origins in the discourse of the colonial state. Eventually this leads to a situation where not only women (irespective of class, race or religion) are excluded from the creation of the Indonesian state, but where indeed large segments of the Indonesian population are being marginalized as they do not conform to dominant state ideologies.

Diane Wolf provides an overview of the different approaches concerning household studies in Java. In her chapter entitled 'Beyond Women and the Household in Java: Re-examining the Boundaries', the author argues for flexibility in defining households, relations between household members, and relations between households and larger institutions. She takes into account not only the structural prescriptions of household or family membership but also the agency of household members, particularly women in their capacities as mothers, wives and daughters.

3

Colonial Ambivalencies
European Attitudes towards the Javanese Household (1900–1942)

Elsbeth Locher-Scholten

INTRODUCTION

Households are historical phenomena. As basic organizational units of human society they should not be essentialized. They change according to time and place and accommodate to social, economic and political circumstances. Households – in the so-called 'private sphere' – are influenced by public policies, which reflect and reinforce prevailing norms and values on to inter-household relations or on the 'proper place' of their constituting members.

Consequently, when studying the Indonesian household, colonial influences upon the Indonesian family, exerted through official policies as well as cultural discourses, have to be taken into account. How did Europeans from the upper class (the colonial government and private European institutions such as the Association of Housewives in the Dutch East Indies and the missions) view the Indonesian household? Did they want to mould it into a specific shape? Did they export their Western norms of the family or did they consider their colonized subjects to be too different to be bothered with these notions (Said 1984)? In short, what kind of influences on the Indonesian household from the colonial period can be pointed out?

This question is also relevant with regard to historical continuities. Present-day Indonesia is often compared to the colonial regime (Anderson 1990, Ricklefs 1991: 225). The Suharto government has formulated a state ideology concerning the household in which the cult of domesticity is a central theme and in which a traditional labour division between the sexes is propagated. Women should be at home, be responsible for the household and the education and socialization of the children, while men are considered the breadwinners and representatives of the household in the outside world. In the ideology of the PKK (*Pembinaan Kesejahteraan Keluarga*, Family Welfare Guidance), an organization for village development which is directed at women, the Indonesian government has created a harmonious family model along middle-class lines. By means of this organization households in the *desa* [village] are reached (de Regt 1993). To what extent did the Indonesian *Orde Baru* [New Order] draw upon the colonial example? Are the roots of the PKK to be found in the colonial period? Did colonialism favour 'the domestication' of Javanese women and has it thus linked Western ideology to present-day practice?

In order to find answers to these questions, I shall focus on the colonial perceptions of the Indonesian household of both (male) colonial authorities and Western private institutions (the Christian missions, the Association of Housewives in the Indies) and on some Indonesian reactions to those perceptions. My analysis is restricted to the period 1900–1942. This was the heyday of colonialism; so if colonial policies exerted any influence on Javanese households at all, it should have been in that period. Because Dutch colonialism in Indonesia was highly Java-centred, I shall concentrate on the Javanese household. Colonial influences were oldest and strongest in Java; it was here that the largest section of the European population was living (80% in 1930). However, European perceptions were not shaped by European perceptions of the Javanese family. Europeans came to the East with their own ideological luggage concerning the household. For a proper understanding of colonial views, we should therefore turn to prevailing views on the household in Europe first.

CONTEXTUAL IDEOLOGIES

The Western family ideology changed considerably in nineteenth-century Europe. Industrialization, urbanization and economic growth resulted in a more explicit labour division between the sexes, an 'emotionalization' of social life, and the growing isolation of the nuclear family. The cultural product of these changes was the middle-class cult of the family. Within this cult true womanhood meant functioning as a wife and mother, bound within the private sphere of the home. In the first half of the twentieth century the household activities were professionalized through education and training, which strengthened the household position of women even further. By means of a 'civilizing offensive', those values were propagated among the working classes as well.

Historical research has shown that the separation between the public and the private sphere has never been absolute. The secluded position functioned as a springboard for a more public role for women. Public institutions like the government gradually took responsibility for the defence of private family values. In spite of these developments, however, at the end of nineteenth century, women – certainly those of a better-to-do social position – were anchored firmly within the household.

It was this middle-class value system that Dutchmen brought to the Indies. Although nineteenth-century colonialists could be the 'black sheep' of the family or the misfits who had failed in Dutch society, twentieth-century Dutchmen coming to the Indies were of a different breed. They had generally followed higher education; they as well as their wives had assimilated middle-class values. Moreover, this value system was reinforced by the leisured-class character of colonial society that every European entered automatically when coming to the Indies. European households copied the Javanese elite household with regard to domestic servants. Especially in the cities, which were the major place of residence for the majority of European women, these servants provided women with plenty of leisure time and the privileges of elite behaviour (Locher-Scholten 1994: 19–40).

Colonial perceptions of the Javanese household were not only framed by Western notions of the household, they were also part and parcel of a broader colonial ideology, of prevailing values, attitudes and ideas about the Javanese in general. In the twentieth century this ideology never offered a uniform pattern of ideas. Yet, even if a sliding scale can be detected in opinions of conservative and progressive colonial groups concerning the possibilities and the pace of the development of the Javanese population, all groups shared a class-bound approach. All followed the Indonesian class division of *priyayi* [elite] and *tani* [peasants]. Europeans had always had a special connection to the ruling Javanese elite, on which they were dependent for the exercise of their rule.

Recognition of the indispensable power of this elite, together with a dislike of its inefficiency and 'unmanageableness', and rejection of its 'power abuse', had coloured colonial attitudes to varying degrees. In the twentieth century these attitudes had come together in evolutionary policies concerning the formation of a more efficient administrative and professional elite. Education and steadfast striving would enable the *priyayi* of higher and lower descent to climb the social ladder to a Western level of development.

In contradistinction, the Javanese masses should develop – or be developed – as an economic healthy population first. Economic and welfare policies were directed towards that goal; village education too was geared to that same end. While Westernization as an explicitly formulated policy was reserved for the Javanese elite, the masses were considered to live in a distinct world. They were perceived as the 'Other' and – being considered different in race, class and culture – Orientalized (Locher-Scholten 1992). As I shall argue, this more general, ideological class-bound pattern can also be traced in colonial attitudes towards the Javanese household. Bifocal spectacles, tinted with Western notions, thus shaped, sharpened or blurred colonial perceptions of this household.

SOURCES ON THE JAVANESE HOUSEHOLD

Colonial views on the Javanese household can only be analysed indirectly. Even in Holland, the family was rarely discussed as such, but only as part of measures concerning marriage, education and social policies (de Regt 1993: 219–239). The composition of the family, the desired number of children for instance, fell outside the realm of government control. Here, however, demographic material was available at least. In the Indies social policy was a weak and late offshoot of colonial rule, and demographic analysis an as yet rather unrefined instrument of research. European opinions on the Javanese household as an economic unit of production and consumption can be deduced from budget, labour and food research, which got off the ground in the interwar years (Boeke 1926, Huizenga 1958); from government debates about female labour and girls' education; from publications of non-governmental organizations like the missions; from fiction and non-fictional reports; and, to some extent, from the census of 1930, which analysed demographic aspects.

Concrete data on the Javanese household are hard to find. As a budget researcher wrote in 1926: 'The Native household is for non-Natives almost a closed book' (Boeke 1926: 232). Facts about the structure of the inter-household patterns, the number of household members, the family rules, the budget, the diet, the ideology, all those quantitative and qualitative data that would have given us more insight in internal household relations, would remain largely unknown during the colonial period. One had to wait until the early 1960s before writing on the internal dynamics of the Javanese household got off the ground (Geertz 1961).

The census makers of 1930 for instance, who organized the most extensive census of the pre-war period, had omitted to count the composition and size of the indigenous households. Figures concerning household members, children, servants, tenants or boarders were excluded, as well as those concerning types of families, such as nuclear or extended, childless, or one-person households. Neither did the census inquire after residence patterns (for instance whether individual or with more households under one roof). It only counted the heads of the household and the number of houses. The family or household head was defined as the person in the family 'who earns the most important share of the means of existence', i.e., the main wage-earner. Following Dutch census practice, the Dutch term *gezin,* which has the double meaning of nuclear family and household, was formulated in terms of the household: 'all who live together or are considered to live together, i.e. to share the house' (*Volkstelling van Nederlandsch-Indië 1930* 1934: 59). The census certainly betrayed a Western bias. By putting wage-earner and head of the household on the same footing, it excluded other important wage-earners in the household and made the more fluid Javanese patterns in this respect invisible (See also Locher-Scholten 1987: 84–88).

It is easy to criticize the census for the scarce and biased information it presented. However, we should bear in mind that this was the first time that household data had been collected on such a scale. It was announced as a first step to gain information on the complicated and locally differing family formations of the Indies archipelago: 'That unit of cohabitation [which] is demographically and sociologically of eminent importance in this country' (*Volkstelling 1930. III, Oost-Java,* 1934: 59; *Volkstelling 1930. VIII.* 1936: 2).[1] In view of the complicated household patterns, it was not yet considered feasible to start household statistics as had been done in the Netherlands. At this stage only a bare minimum of averages could be calculated, and that minimum was provided.

In 1930 Java and Madura had nearly 8 million male and more than 1.1 million female family heads. The census confirmed Western and Javanese expectations. Where marriage was a most common status of the Javanese, most family heads were married men. More than 10% of all households, however, were female-headed (12.5%). These were more common in rural areas than in cities or municipalities, more in East Java than in the princely states of Central Java. The census makers could not explain these regional differences. Statistics did not support their explanation, that female-headed household coincided with a male population surplus and male labour migration. Most of the female heads of family were widows or divorced women (80%); 18% were married. Imprecise generalizations were offered as far as the average family size and the number of persons living in one house were concerned: respectively 4.5 and 4.7. This implied that under one roof more than one household head could be found (*Volkstelling 1930 III. Oost Java*: 59–67, *Volkstelling 1930 VIII, Overzicht voor Nederlandsch-Indië*: 27).

It was hardly surprising then, in view of these meagre results, that the report found that definitive conclusions on household structure and organization were impossible: as yet, too little was known about the composition of the household. This assessment of lack of information was as modest as it was factual. Hence we had better consider European opinions on the Javanese household, since lack of factual knowledge did not prevent Europeans from making statements or formulating policies with regard to the topic.

Two Types of Households

In line with existing class differences in Java and following the Javanese *priyayi* class distinction, Dutch colonial authors usually discerned two forms of households in Java: those of princes, regents and other Indonesian civil servants (*priyayi*) on the one hand, and those of peasants, including other wage-earners like coolies or *warong*-holders [small shop holders] on the other. 'Royal houses, regents' families to a lesser extent, are large patriarchal families [*grootgezinnen*]; the others more small families [*klein-gezinnen*]' (*Onderzoek naar de mindere welvaart der Inlandsche bevolking op Java en Madoera. (MWO) IX b3. Verheffing van de Inlandsche vrouw*, Batavia: Papyrus, 1914a: 1). The plight of married women within the former group was deplored because the *adat* [tradition] required submissiveness to their husbands as well as the practice of polygamy. Peasant women had less to fear, since having more than one wife required some wealth (*Onderzoek naar de mindere welvaart der Inlandsche bevolking op Java en Madoera (MWO) XII* 1914 c). Intellectually these peasant women might be little developed; however, their legal position and property rights were considered better than those of women in Europe. In spite of this recognition, Resident H.E. Steinmetz, compiler of the extensive research report on the economy of Java, the Lesser

Welfare Report, noted in 1914 a gradual improvement in the legal rights of women 'due to Western influence and personal development'. Implicitly he referred to *priyayi* woman. His views are illustrative for the curious blend of colonial perceptions of Javanese women in the household, as appears from colonial reports. His respect for the autonomy and equality of (rural) women coincided with his pleas for a better standard of education for women and with his complaints about weak family life, which he considered one of the reasons for Javanese poverty (*Oorzaken der mindere welvaart* 1914: 6). Unmistakably, these pleas and complaints concerned *priyayi* women. His use of the generalizing term 'the Javanese woman' resulted in a confusion of classes.

In order to avoid a similar blurring of distinctions, I shall deal with perceptions and policies concerning peasant and *priyayi* households separately. There is another reason to do so. Colonial opinions attributed to both types of households two different functions. While the peasant household was judged according to its economic production, the *priyayi* household was criticized with regard to its social reproduction: its (weak) socializing impact on its youthful members. In both household functions, women allegedly held a key position.

Peasant Households

A Javanese peasant household might be a nuclear family plus one or more parents, poor relatives or boarders. Persons without a house or yard, who lived in the house or on the compound of a wealthier neighbour, who shared meals and/or earned an income by working for the owner of the house, could also belong to the household (Maijer 1894: 261). Of course, as a research report of 1941 stated, exceptions to this rule did exist, such as: families with unmarried adults who provided their own food; families with married and financially independent children, who lived with their parents and shared meals; the rare polygamous family heads who belonged to more than one household; bachelors living together (Huizenga 1958:38). Different household forms were also recognized incidentally in budget research projects of the 1920s and 1930s. But for research reasons, these projects usually took uniform and comparable households as their norm: for instance, households in which members (except for the household head and his wife) did not earn an income and whose expenses could be controlled by the household head (Boeke 1926: 235).[2] In other research projects, households were not defined at all (Ochse and Terra 1934).

As far as those budget researches provided figures on the size of households, they mentioned 2–15 persons. However, since this economic re-search was directed to specific subjects such as domestic budgets, division of labour and diet, it does not offer any clue regarding the position of women. In this research peasant households were unified entities in which female roles and functions as well as inter-household relationships were made invisible.

This was not what might have been expected, for colonial recognition of the economic function of the household and of women had a long tradition.

Already in the eighteenth century, the East India Company (VOC) had recognized Javanese households, including women, as economic production units. Following Javanese customs, the VOC had taken the Javanese *cacah*, a term translated as 'household', as the basic unit for tax collection.[3] In the nineteenth century, the financial autonomy of *tani* [peasant] women had been noticed. *Tani* women had been admired for taking responsibility for the family income, their work, their (supposed) equality to their husbands and their autonomy in the family (Raffles 1817: 109, Sollewijn Gelpke 1879–80). This did not imply family conflicts. On the contrary, Europeans offered idealized pictures of the happy and harmonious family of the *tani* and romanticized peasant life (*Onderzoek naar de mindere welvaart der Inlandsche bevolking op Java en Madoera (MWO). X a. De Volkswelvaart op Java en Madoera. Eindverhandeling van 't onderzoek naar de mindere welvaart der Inlandsche bevolking* 1914b: 34–35, Maijer 1894: 238–243).

The recognition of the importance of the female labour contribution to the household's well-being prevailed in official colonial discourse on the Javanese peasant household. This was reflected in policies concerning lower-class Javanese women. The colonial government did not show signs of disapproval of this household pattern, in which women worked outside the house. Three examples from the 1920s and 1930 illustrate this point: the debate on minimum wages; the regulation of women's night labour; and transmigration strategies.

The debate on minimum wages for labourers in Java is an illustration of implicit views on the Javanese households and (lack of) concrete policies. This debate started in 1919 when the government installed an advisory commission on the subject. At the end of the First World War rising prices and stagnant wages had created a situation of poor wages and malnourishment in Java. The succinct commission's report of 1920 was unanimous about the necessity to introduce minimum wages in industries. However, the commission was divided concerning the question of whether minimum wages should be calculated as individual or household wages. The progressive minority opted for family wages. The earnings of the wife should be considered only 'as a reserve' in case of emergency (an ill husband, support given to the older generations, unemployment, large number of children). In contradistinction, the majority wanted individual wages, since it considered this a subtle means to delay marriage among Javanese. Individual wages would prevent starting up a family at too young an age (*Verslag van de arbeidscommissie betreffende de wettelijke vaststelling van minimumloonen voor werknemers op Java en Madoera* 1920). In the end, no one won. The introduction of minimum wages was postponed because wages were raised in the early 1920s as a result of union strikes, and because problems of implementation and control were considered paramount. The government, moreover, expressed a need for more information. Active policies in this respect were thus restricted to ongoing budget research (Huizenga 1958).

The debate on female night labour offers a second example of European perceptions of the Javanese household. In 1925, a legal restriction to female night labour was a point of discussion in the Indies proto-parliament, the *Volks-*

raad. Progressives, advocating a stringent restriction or total ban on female night labour, defended the interests of the family: married women, exhausted from night work, would neglect their children. Conservative colonial spokesmen championed the interests of the European agricultural estates, which were to a large extent dependent on female labour: in sugar production 25% of the total workforce consisted of women, while in tea and coffee estates the figure was 45%. Their perception of indigenous society was largely inspired by self-interest. They considered female night labour in the Indies 'a perfectly natural institution' and pointed to the fact that Javanese peasant norms deviated from Western ones, and they should therefore not interfere. It resulted in a governmental compromise: a restriction in hours and an obligation for European estates to inform the government of exceptions to this rule. Female night labour would remain largely intact. In the 1920s, colonial progressives thus voiced the ideology of a 'women's proper place'; progressiveness implied 'domesticity'. The government, however, did not bolster this ideal with an active policy of wage and labour regulations (Locher-Scholten 1992).

That the colonial government had an interest in the labour power of Javanese peasant women was most clearly demonstrated in transmigration policies. After initial failures in the transmigration of Javanese peasants to South Sumatra, it was stipulated in the early 1930s that only families or households should be selected. The family unit not only guaranteed calm and order (*rust en orde*) in the new settlements, but productive working units as well. Young people, who could work hard, were preferred. Their departure from Java diminished future population growth there. However, families with many young children should be passed by, since working members of the family (women included) could not carry those burdens in the pioneering phase of the transmigration project. 'Do not transmigrate pregnant women; in the first year the colonist household cannot do without the labour force of the woman', one of the so-called Ten Commandments for the Transmigration stated (Heeren 1967: 16). The working power of Javanese women was thus implicitly recognized and used. No need to store those women away in the household.

These three examples illustrate that the relevance of the Western cult of domesticity for Javanese *tani* women was indeed a point of discussion among Europeans. However, this did not result in an extension of this cult to peasant or wage-earning women in Java. Policies to mould Javanese *tani* household according to Western models did not materialize. The colonial government needed the household as an economic unit to keep (agricultural) production going. The role of Javanese women as economic producers was confirmed by statistics: in 1930 one-third of the working population in Java was female, a high percentage compared to the one-quarter in the Netherlands in the same year. Nearly 40% of all working women were found in indigenous agriculture (Locher-Scholten 1992: 96).

Education did not change this labour pattern. Peasant girls were left untouched by Western household ideals. In 1928, the large majority of all schoolgirls in Java and Madura (nearly 70%) followed basic (three years) education in co-ed schools in their own language (Bemmelen 1982 Appendices: 19). A minority might find a place in a school of the Christian missions (see below). In the 1930s, education in home economics for *desa* girls was a popular subject in European and *priyayi* circles. Uplifting those women, for instance, was discussed in the 1930s in the Dutch language journal *Widoeri*[4] for former students of the Kartini and Van Deventer schools. Lessons in home economics were considered to be a means to that end. These debates, however, were far removed from the harsh reality of *desa* life, as the following quotes underline:

> If only she [the peasant woman] would stay at home and learn to care better for her children by meeting her housewifely obligations, then enough time would remain to earn an extra income by doing some light agricultural labour, or rather, to spin, to weave, to make batik.

Or :

> The peasant woman's fundamental ignorance prevents her from using her time efficiently; if she could comprehend her household tasks more clearly, she and her family would live more economically (Gouda 1995: 107).

In spite of those discussions, such education was not provided for in colonial Indonesia (Resink-Wilkens 1936). Policies to change female economic activities in the lower classes were not formulated.

The existing Javanese household structure served not only as a social cornerstone (like in Europe), but also as an economic asset. This does not imply that colonialism in general left the Javanese *tani* households untouched. They underwent the influence of a growing monetization, of demographic change and population growth, of smaller land holdings, of state regulations concerning access to land, of production for the export and the world economy. European perceptions of the *tani* household, however, did not stimulate direct changes of this unit. The colonial government lacked the political will and – notwithstanding its hierarchical organization – the proper means to influence the household. State organization via the *desa* administration to reach this lowest stratum of society has only been perfected in post-revolutionary Indonesia. Hence, to return to our earlier question, we cannot point out a direct line of continuity between colonial policies directed at rural households and the present-day PKK.

THE *PRIYAYI* HOUSEHOLD

While the economic function of peasant women was underlined, colonial attention *vis-à-vis* the other function of households, its socializing task, was reserved to the regents' class. Households of princes, and of higher and lower *priyayi*, were large and loosely knit communities. Besides the male head of the household, they might include his four official wives, his *selir* or co-wives, their children, his parents and siblings plus the servants (Maijer 1894: 25).[5] Royal families could count hundreds of people. Around 1900 a *priyayi* daughter complained that she had 53 mothers and 83 brothers and sisters, most of whom she did not know;[6] the Sultan of Jogya had 70 children in 1910 and more than 200 grandchildren, of which the exact number was not given (*MWO* 1914a: 25). It implied a loose organization of household tasks like cooking and cleaning, and shifting residence patterns, which made the functioning in economic terms, the internal division of labour, of income and consumption patterns as well as the emotional relationships rather obscure.

For political reasons, this type of household (here identical with family) was not the most popular in colonial opinion, since it produced the seeds for internal strife and division. Dutch Calvinism frowned upon polygamy also for moral reasons. Socially and emotionally *priyayi* households were not considered ideal. They apparently lacked the conditions to educate a new generation and to introduce them to the desired Western norms of activity, thrift and responsibility. The main colonial solutions to this social deficit, as far as women were concerned, were twofold. Reformers opted for Western education for girls on the one hand; on the other hand they defended a stable family life through a regulation of rules concerning child marriages, divorce and polygamy or the *selir* system. Both options coincided with the ideas of the *priyayi* daughter Kartini (1879–1904), who in her letters during her short life had advocated similar ideas. Progressives on both sides of the colonial divide, *priyayi* and Dutchmen, found themselves in a common programme on behalf of education and the family. Kartini's arguments were repeated in the Lesser Welfare Report by Javanese women and by Dutch colonialists like the Orientalist C. Snouck Hurgronje and the civil servant Steinmetz. Education for girls was considered 'the mighty lever for reinforcement of family life and hence of society as a whole' (Van Bemmelen 1982: 5).

An idealized Western family pattern served as the model. Snouck Hurgronje maintained in 1911 that 'educated Javanese women would cooperate with their *priyayi* husbands *to bring the Native family to an association with our family system*' (my italics). And referring to *priyayi* girls he continued:

> Whosoever wants to cooperate in the education of some hundred girls of Java in this vein, may flatter himself with the well-founded hope to see recognized later the monogamous life in Java as the normal lifestyle as the fruit of his work and to see Javanese parents work seriously at the edification of the life of their children (Snouck Hurgronje 1915: 94; my translation).

However, this identification of female education and Western family life resulted in piecemeal educational politics only. At the end of the nineteenth century, *priyayi* children of the highest class could attend education in Dutch at the European primary school and the co-educational so-called first-class native schools. In order to meet the larger demand for primary education in Dutch, the Dutch Native School (HIS, *Hollands-Inlandse School*) was installed in 1912. The government added secondary education for girls [so called *meisjesvervolgscholen*] and professional education (*nijverheidsscholen*) in the early 1920s. Both types were open to European, Chinese and *priyayi* girls. The fact that lessons were in Dutch popularized these types of education, especially among *priyayi*.

Separate education for girls, however, would remain largely restricted to private initiative. The colonial government, although in favour of education for girls, was happy to leave this to others: to the Christian missions and specific institutions, such as the Kartini Foundation and the Van Deventer Foundation. In 1939, only 4 of the 14 popular *nijverheidsscholen* in Java for girls were state institutions (Brugmans 1938: 344 and 352, Van Bemmelen 1982 Appendices: 40, Lelyveld 1992: 203 and 263–64).

As far as policies for stable marriages were concerned, the colonial government was even less successful. In 1936 it introduced a law, fixing the minimum marriage age at 15 years for women, and 18 for men. This measure was meant only for Christian Indonesians from Java, Ambon and the Minahasa, where the government could follow previous regulations of the missions. Although pressed by Dutch civil servants to do so, it had not forbidden child marriage. The matter was too sensitive. The government tried for some years around 1930 to collect more information and numbers about this Javanese custom. But since this had resulted in unreliable data and local abuses like medical examination of Javanese brides-to-be, it decided in 1932 to refer the subject to private initiatives. It was brought to the attention of Javanese regents and women's organizations (Locher-Scholten forthcoming).[7] Polygamy had never been a popular institution among Europeans. In 1914 Steinmetz, chair of the commission on Lesser Welfare research, had suggested a straightforward prohibition. It had been rejected by Indonesian and European members (*MWO* 1914a: 88–89). In 1937 the government tried again; it did circulate among Indonesian organizations a proposal of a marriage ordinance, introducing the registration of civil monogamous weddings for the Indonesian educated elite. A civil registration would categorically exclude the possibility of polygamy. Although the government stressed the voluntary character of the registration, it met fierce opposition from Islamic and nationalist parties and groups. The proposal was withdrawn that same year. Indonesian women's organizations were divided, but complied with the nearly all-Indonesian opposition (Vreede-de Stuers 1960: 76–83, Locher-Scholten forthcoming).

In conclusion we may state that, even if the colonial government adhered in theory to the reigning Western ideology of women in the household, it did little to propagate its practice among the Javanese elite. Its policies to reinforce *priyayi* family life in a Western sense were limited to co-ed primary education, to the financial support of other colonial groups (missions and educational foundations) and to (failing) attempts to reinforce Javanese family life through marriage regulations.

INFLUENCES OF PRIVATE INSTITUTIONS

It would be naive to attribute changes of Javanese mentality regarding family and household – however small – in the colonial period to government policies alone. There were other non-governmental organizations, which propagated the cult of domesticity. Private educational foundations and the Protestant and Roman Catholic missions formulated Western ideologies concerning marriage and the functions of women within the household. In the 1930s organizations of European women advocated a more professional household, in which the housewife would occupy a leading position. It remains doubtful whether they had more success in this respect than the colonial government. The Javanese groups, which they targeted, belonged either to the groups already reached by the government, to the elite, or to marginal Christian groups.

The Kartini Foundation – founded in 1912 and funded among others by the royalties of the publication of Kartini's letters – opened private primary schools (six by 1916) for *priyayi* daughters. Secondary education was provided by the Van Deventer Foundation. In the 1920s, the Kartini Foundation also provided three 'second-class native schools' for girls. These schools served two goals: preparation for a financially independent existence for girls and 'the cult of domesticity' (Gouda 1995: 97).[8] They prepared girls for 'the sphere of action, which will be opened for the large majority of the girls, that of housewife and mother' (Van Bemmelen 1982: 73). 'Second-class native schools' provided courses in home economics 'to prepare indigenous girls for their future role as housewives' (Gouda 1995: 86). *Meisjesvervolgscholen* and *nijverheidsscholen* focused on home economics (cooking, washing, ironing, embroidery, batik and lace-making) (Brugmans 1938: 355). They, however did not aim at clear-cut Westernization: Kartini schools, Van Deventer schools and *meisjesvervolgscholen* were meant to maintain the connection with the indigenous milieu, and thus expressed an 'Orientalist' orientation.

However, in spite of this ideal, this kind of education did lead unavoidably to Westernization. Courses in home economics referred to the 'professionalization' of the household, a twentieth-century process in Western countries, in which women had to fulfil certain duties along prescribed lines of training and performance. These courses thus reinforced Western family norms and practices among Javanese pupils.

To sum up, Western norms concerning the household only reached a very small sector of the Javanese female population: the daughters of the *priyayi*, the large majority of whom lived in cities. The peasant masses were (relatively) untouched, unless they lived in Christianized communities and had undergone the influence of the missions.

More than through formal education, the peasant population was affected by the messages of the Protestant and Catholic missions. These had recognized and popularized the important economic function of women within the Javanese household already at the beginning of the twentieth century. The missions had a special interest in women because they were considered 'the key to a Christian family life' (Van Bemmelen 1983). Rural women were thus not only instrumental in realizing the economic goals of the colonial government, but also in reaching missionary purposes. The missions' means to that end were similar to governmental goals for the *priyayi* girls: education and the striving for a monogamous Christian marriage. Child marriages, arranged marriages, the bride-price, divorce and polygamy should be abolished or countered as far as possible.

The missions were more successful than the colonial government in reaching the rural population. Their educational system for girls bore some fruit: in Christianized regions the literacy of girls was higher than elsewhere (Van Bemmelen 1983). Their education served first and foremost the purpose of creating proper housewives. Christian education stimulated Western middle-class values like cleanliness, hygiene and other qualities required of a mother of the house.[9] By providing sewing circles and by taking children into their own homes (the so-called *anak piara*, Schouten 1995), the missions laid the foundations for Western values in the Christian community. Especially the women's work, set up by wives of the Protestant missionaries, focused on home economics, sewing and cooking. In the inter-war years the missions also tried to raise a consciousness of the position of Christians in society. The cult of domesticity was certainly one goal of their education, but they wanted more than that. They also tried to include Javanese women in youth and women's work and to educate them as future female helpers of the missionaries (Van Bemmelen 1983).

Their measures in favour of stable marriages (age limits, prior personal notification by the marrying couple, discouragement of divorce) had some positive results in Christian communities like Mojowarno in East Java. But the missions achieved more through schooling and persuasion than through prohibiting. In the later years of colonial rule, for instance, the missions became more pragmatic and tolerant of polygamy (Van Bemmelen 1983).

The missions certainly were a factor in the propagation of Western family and household values. Their influence, however, was geographically local, socially marginal and numerically minimal. It remained restricted to certain areas in Java. In 1937 the Protestant mission and churches in Java and Madoera counted 96,000 Indonesian followers (both members and baptized). This was no more than 0.2% of all inhabitants of the region; half of them were found in East Java (Zendingsstatistiek 1937: opposite 572).[10] Catholic Indonesians were even less numerous: 15,500 in 1930 Bank 1983: 506). In the Islamized Sunda region of West Java, Christianity attracted the social outsiders, the landless and lonely, for which it functioned as an instrument of self-respect and group identity (Van den End 1991: 197, 253, 396, 473, 512). Their isolated position did not result in a quick popularization of new household values among the rural Javanese.

Neither can one attribute much influence to another representative of Western household values, the Association of Housewives in the Indies (*Vereeniging van Huisvrouwen in Nederlandsch-Indië*), one of the most important women's organizations in this respect. Established in 1931, the Association was one of the largest European organizations in the 1930s, counting more than 10,000 members, who mostly lived in the cities of Java and in North Sumatra. It focused on a professionalization of the European household, giving information on how to run a household, on food prices, cooking, fashion, etc. Its board and membership included some *priyayi* women – whom it may have provided with a role model concerning European manners and (formal) dinner style.[11] The content of its journal bore an apparently ethnic-neutral character: in practice it was highly Eurocentric. For the Association, the household in Java was the Dutch or European household. The Indonesian or the Chinese household fell outside its scope. The Association did not claim an educational task for itself as far as other groups or classes were concerned. At most, it provided cooking lessons for Javanese servants of European families, who had to learn the European menu (Locher-Scholten 1994: 26). One may presume that servants in the European households, often from a rural background or from the lower urban classes, acquired an intimate knowledge of European housekeeping. However, their influence cannot have been very strong, since their group was limited to 2% of the Indonesian population in 1930 (300,000 of the 40 million inhabitants of Java and Madura) (Volkstelling 1930 III Oost-Java: 126–27). Hence, if the Association of Housewives in the Indies exerted any influence on the Javanese household at all, it was on women in *priyayi* circles in urban communities only.

JAVANESE EXPERIENCES

The question remains as to how far these Western preoccupations with the Javanese household affected these households. Which reactions can we notice from Javanese women in this respect? To what extent did the European norms and values coincide with Javanese norms and values?

Javanese ideas of a woman's proper place were class-bound. Little data are available of a peasant ideology in this respect. From practices in daily life we may deduce that women were indeed held responsible for the economic well-being of their families and worked with their husband as 'two oxen before the household cart' (Locher-Scholten 1987: 92–93). In princely and *priyayi* circles, ideals about female submissiveness coincided with independence, providing economic activities in the batik and jewellery trade (Djajadiningrat-Nieuwenhuis 1992, Florida 1996). Western middle-class visions of maternal destiny intertwined with indigenous patriarchal norms or *adat*, revealing – as historian Frances Gouda has stated recently – 'a complex pattern of complicity between both cultural views of women's proper place' (Gouda 1995: 28). In the twentieth century, Western education and concomitant ideas gained ground among the modernizing *priyayi*. In its early years, Indonesian nationalism, like the Javanese *Boedi Oetomo* and the Islamic *Sarekat Islam*, expressed a longing for independent women, who would be prepared to fulfil their task as mothers and housewives according to Western norms and who would no longer act as the concubines (*nyais*) of European or Chinese men. The *Sarekat Islam* also protested against the immoral *selir* system, popular among *priyayi* (*MWO* 1914a: 20, Van Vollenhoven 1918: 568)).[12] The nationalist student group *Jong-Java* [Young Java] even organized marriage associations whose members adhered to a marriage age of 25 for men, 18 for women (*MWO* 1914a: 5).

These Western ideas also created female followers, as Kartini's letters show. In the Lesser Welfare Report of 1914 nine Western-educated *priyayi* women expressed their wishes with one voice: an extension of Western education for Javanese girls as well as total rejection of polygamy, of marriages against the will of the couple, and of child marriage. Their educational goals were directed to professional education (teaching, nursing and midwifery) and the cult of domesticity: girls' education should be a preparation 'for their earnest task: Mother as Educator of the coming generation'. This education should be given by European women; Javanese teachers were not to be trusted (*MWO* 1914a: 5, 9–10).

The European family served as the paradigm: it was an idealized model of harmony and well-being. One of the objections against the *selir* system of wife and co-wives was not only the suffering of women, but also that of the children. Javanese *priyayi* children lived in loveless (*liefde-arme*) surroundings. Their unequal status and the hierarchy within the family were a source of friction and made harmony impossible (*MWO* 1914a: 8).

To sum up, educated *priyayi* women in the 1910s followed their male family members in a longing for Western education as a means to achieve modernization. In its wake they accepted and propagated Western household ideals. These *priyayi* values remained. In 1932, a *priyayi* girl could write to her former Dutch teacher of the Kartini school, that she had formed a "girls study club", because we want to help each other with domestic training in sewing, cooking and hygiene, in short, we want to learn everything we need to know in order to fulfil our duty as housewife' (Gouda 1995: 103). In the same letter she wrote happily about her future plans of being a teacher and earning her own income. Whether schooling resulted in different household patterns within *priyayi* family remains unclear.[13] Of course, these selected quotes do not cover the total range of Indonesian norms and values concerning the family and household of the period. They do indicate though that Western ideas were gradually becoming assimilated by the elite. They were never taken up by the Muslim masses, as the heavy opposition to the proposed law on voluntary monogamy in 1937 shows.

CONCLUSION

Members of the European colonial elite (largely but not exclusively male) perceived the Javanese household through a bifocal, class-directed lens, set in a frame of Western household notions. They recognized two different types of household (the peasant and the *priyayi*); they appreciated two different functions of each household type (the productive and the socializing function); and they valued the position of women within each type in two different ways (as autonomous and as dependent). This bifurcatory view had far-reaching consequences with regard to policies. The colonial government did not favour 'the domestication' of women from the peasant class, but recognized and used their productive work as a cornerstone of economic life. They did not need to be 'Occidentalized'. Orientalism, the approach of the East as culturally static or even stagnant, dominated the vision of this class.

The *priyayi* household, and its little appreciated socializing function, resembled more that other stone: a stumbling-block. For women within this type of household, an education and marriage model along Western lines was proposed. The former, however, was left to a large extent to private initiative; the latter failed in the 1930s due to Indonesian opposition.

The privately run educational foundations, together with the Christian missions and the Indies Housewives' Association, definitely propagated 'the cult of domesticity' and tried to disseminate this through schooling and publications. However, their influence was limited to the women of the *priyayi* elite or to marginal groups in society, such as Indonesian Christians.

Colonialism thus popularized 'the cult of domesticity' but for a select group only: among Christian rural women and among women of the elite, who were socially closest and factually best known to the Dutch. This ideology was connected to so-called Javanese values which recognized women as wives and mothers, although traditionally the role of wife and mother in Java held other connotations than of being a proper housewife. In its education for *priyayi* girls, however, colonialism not only valued women as housewives, but also created professional possibilities for economic independence. Hence, the foundations of the ideology of 'the cult of domesticity' were laid in the colonial period, but this was not the only or strongest ideology. The elite groups that were reached had to develop the organizational, educational and communicational means to a far greater extent, before the ideal of a 'proper housewife' could 'trickle down' to the Javanese/Indonesian middle and lower classes. In the colonial period the PKK would have been an impossibility.

NOTES

1. This modesty was not without foundation: the illiteracy of the Javanese population demanded special provisions. The counting had been done during personal visits of the census takers, mostly volunteers recruited from the indigenous civil service, in one week in October 1930. During these visits the latter had to get information about the number of persons, houses, literacy, heads of family and labour.

2. Similarly, in 1936, budget indices of civil servants were calculated for a nuclear family with two children, one of them attending school (Hart 1936).

3 For our analysis of twentieth century perceptions of the household the *cacah* is only of theoretical importance: it had been abolished as a basic unit for tax collection in the early nineteenth century when land rent and Cultivation System were introduced.

4 The title was an acronym of the Dutch words *willen, doen* en *richten* (to want, to do and to focus) (Gouda 1995: 43).

5 *Selir* were unofficial wives of *priyayi* (co-wives/*bijvrouwen*), usually from lower descent and often taken for reasons of political alliance. They could be married temporarily in case of a child (Van Vollenhoven 1918 I: 567).

6 This was probably a daughter of Pakubuwono IX (r. 1862–93), who had two wives and 51 concubines (Florida 1996: 213).

7 Contrary to Vreede-de Stuers' remarks, these medical examinations were not ordered by the government (Vreede-de Stuers 1960: 75–76).

8 An analysis of school material would certainly confirm traditional images of 'a woman's place'. Although not yet researched, it is unlikely that school material diverges from the content of colonial children's fiction of the same period, which focused on cosy and harmonious family relations and on the traditional role of the mother. See, for colonial children's fiction, Locher-Scholten 1994: 32–38.

9 According to the *adat* regulation of the important Christian community of Mojowarno (East Java), the wife was obliged to follow and serve her husband as well as 'to keep the house proper and clean' (*MWO IXd* 1911: 50).

10 In 1915 only 0.1% (32,5000 of the 40 million inhabitants of Java and Madura) were so-called 'Christian Natives' ('Christen Inlanders' 1917: 488). In the Lesser Welfare Report on *adat* regulations for Native Christian (Protestant) communities in Java, only 15 of such communities were mentioned (*MWO IXd Adatregelingen*: 10). Both the Protestant and Catholic missions and churches had more adherents in the Outer Regions: Catholics more than 210,000 (1%); Protestants 1.6 million in 1937 (9% of the Indonesian population of the Outer Regions).

11 Personal communication of M. Dajadiningrat-Nieuwenhuis.

12 The nationalist organizations did not oppose mixed marriages, those of an Indonesian man with a European woman. Nationalist leaders themselves, for instance Sutan Sjahrir, would marry European women. See Mrázek 1994: 81 and 112.

13 In her children's book *Widijawati*, the Javanese author Arti Poerbani, pseudonym of Partini Djajadiningrat, daughter of the Central Javanese Prince Mangkoe Negoro VII, tells the informative story of a Javanese girl who becomes a teacher and a midwife. However, she does not portray this modern heroine in her household duties, for the story ends prior to marriage (Poerbani 1948).

4

Representations of Women's Roles in Household and Society in Indonesian Women's Writing of the 1930s

Barbara Hatley and Susan Blackburn

INTRODUCTION

In the complex discourse in contemporary Indonesia on issues concerning women, there is a sense of ongoing contestation and re-interpretation of gender roles. These issues include

- official assertions of the prevailing ideology of women's primary responsibility within the nuclear household
- reinforcement of this image through the media and in institutions such as schools
- seminars on women's roles in various fields of enterprise or on problems of sexual harassment in the workplace
- exposés of the plight of Indonesian women workers overseas
- popular treatises on topics such as hair care and the Muslim headcovering, in keeping with the current upsurge in Islamic religious expression

Though the prevailing ideology claims a time-honoured, religiously legitimated status in its doctrine of *kodrat wanita*, the predestined, inherent role of women (as wives and mothers), social practice suggests a greater plurality of views and behaviours.

Attention to and concern over the social roles of women have played an important part in the modernization process in Indonesia, as it has in other colonial and post-colonial countries. Discussion of such issues in the press and other media is in itself nothing new. What is perhaps unique is the purposeful, systematic promotion of a dominant ideology by state authorities and the paucity of explicitly asserted alternative views, despite a complex, rapidly changing social reality. The sources, perceived intentions and social effects of the dominant ideology are questions which have been discussed by others. Instead, what we would like to do in this chapter is to turn for comparative purposes to an earlier period in the history of twentieth-century Indonesia, when the debate over the 'woman question' ran hot. Our focus is the 1930s, a time of consolidation of the new concepts and organizational forms, which had sprung up in the early twentieth century in response to intensified colonial contact and modern social transformations. Expectations of the new, modern Indonesian society, including its implications for women, were widely articulated at this time, by individuals, organizations and in the press. Our aim in looking to women's writing of this period is to see what ideas were dominant then, whether these show continuity with or divergence from today's prevailing gender ideology, and to what extent women contributed with a distinctive voice to the discussion.

In 1930s Indonesia, images of and prescriptions concerning the 'modern woman' held a prominent place in discussions on modernity, progress and national identity among the educated elite. A paramount issue was that of the education for girls, publicly promulgated since Kartini, practised in a variety of vocational and other schools, but still very much a site of contestation between progressive and conservative positions. The logic of a socially progressive stance, committed to the creation of an Indonesian society incorporating many of the advancements of the West, demanded that women be educated in order to understand this new world, and to prepare their children for participation in it. Modern, progressive women were needed as wives and companions of modern men, as educators of future generations and as contributors to society. But at the same time feelings of ambivalence about the changing environment, a fear of a threat to the established social hierarchy and cultural values, found expression in dark predictions of moral decline and family breakdown as women were seduced away from their proper roles by new freedoms. As in other late colonial states, though apparently not with such sustained and systematic elaboration as in India, for example,[1] women were constructed as cultural boundary markers in a definition of self versus other; of authentic national identity. Excessive Westernization of Indonesian women, caricatured in images of shallow materialism and sexual promiscuity, was a sign of cultural degradation: the desired modern woman should be educated, progressive and able to maintain traditional cultural and spiritual values.

The emergent new media of communication – the newspapers, magazines and literary publications which had mushroomed with the social and political transformations of the early twentieth century – were vital for expressing these views. Ben Anderson (1991) has illuminated the role of the press in emerging nations in not only transmitting information but in forging a sense of community among readers. In the case of women readers, though their numbers would have been very small,[2] the role of such media may have been especially significant. In a magazine article in the late 1920s appealing for letters of support from readers for her idea of forming an association of female journalists, the woman author suggests that, in view of the very restricted social contact allowed women, letters constitute the most feasible medium of communication (Hong Le Koan 1928a: 495). Here one gets a glimpse of the vital importance of the written word, including magazines and other published material, in bringing knowledge of and connection to the outside world to women largely confined to the household.

In a brief chapter such as this, it is not possible to deal comprehensively with the whole body of women's writing during this period. We have chosen to focus on two particular areas; the magazines produced by the numerous women's organizations which represent various regions and classes and religious groupings, and several examples of fiction published by women authors. These two forms of writing clearly had different functions. The magazines were published by women's organizations as a source of practical information and edification for their (women) members; produced *by* women *for* women, they provided models for modern life. The novels, by contrast, were published for the 'open market', for readers of both sexes and unspecified backgrounds, portraying the individual consciousness and experience of their characters on the model of 'modern literature' rather than addressing practical issues. Yet their authors came from the same circles. Western-educated, often working as schoolteachers and journalists, they were involved in women's organizations and/or other types of social and political activity. Many of their readers would have shared features of this background, albeit at a less organizationally active level. Such readers clearly constituted only a small minority of Indonesian women of the time, given the very limited extent of female education and literacy. Hence these works can hardly be said to have depicted society-wide concerns or to have had mass public impact at their time of writing. Yet they document influential new ideas as they were conceptualized by writers, transmitted to readers and arguably then spread more broadly through society. The two fields of writing might be seen to represent complementary perspectives, that of publicly espoused social ideals and of private emotional reflection.

THE MAGAZINES

Seven periodicals published by Indonesian women's organizations in the 1930s have been selected for examination (see Table 4.1).

This is a varied collection, representing a cross-section of women's organizations of the time. *Isteri* [Woman] was the mouthpiece of the Indonesian women's federation, *Perkoempoelan Perhimpoenan Isteri Indonesia* [PPII – Federation of Indonesian Women's Organizations], founded in 1928. It brought together a number of women's organizations with a generally nationalist and moderate orientation, including *'Aisjijah*, the women's wing of the modernist Islamic organization *Moehammadijah*, which issued its own organ, *Soeara 'Aisjijah* [Voice of *'Aisjijah*]. All the other periodicals were produced by non-religious organizations. *Pedoman Isteri* [Woman's Bulletin] and *Keoetamaan Istri* [Women's Excellence] derived from organizations associated with what might be labelled a *priyayi* [Javanese upper class] viewpoint: the *Perkoempoelan Isteri Pegawai Bestuur* [PIPB – Association of Wives of Government Officials] and *Keoetamaan Istri*, which was closely associated with the Javanese organization *Boedi Oetomo*. It would, however, be a mistake to brand them as wholly Javanese in outlook since their members were also non-Javanese, and indeed *Pedoman Isteri* was the brainchild of, and edited by, a Minangkabau woman, Datoek Chairul Sjamsoe Toemenggoeng. However, their readers and contributors appear to have been largely from the colonial civil service, which was dominated by upper-class Javanese. *Soeara Iboe* [Voice of Women] was the product of a group of educated Tapanuli Batak women, and *Serikat Kaoem Iboe Soematera* [SKIS – League of Sumatran Women], which published *Soeara Kaoem Iboe Soematera* [SKIS – Voice of Sumatran Women] was an organization of West Sumatran women, the editors being a group of teachers in Padangpanjang. Finally, *Sedar* [Aware] was the mouthpiece of the radical women's organization *Isteri Sedar* [Aware Women] which was nationalist in orientation and refused to join the PPII because it despised the watering down of feminist and political views necessitated by the consensus rules of the federation. It was also openly contemptuous of women's organizations which aimed only at 'teaching women how to cook, embroider and sew' and to become 'perfect housewives' with no wider views (*Isteri Sedar*, December 1930).[3]

Table 4.1: Seven publications by Indonesian women's organizations of the 1930s

Name of Periodical	Place of Publication	Organization
Pedoman Isteri	Jakarta	*Perkoempoelan Isteri Pagawai Bestuur*
Isteri	Jakarta	*Perkoempoelan Perhimpoenan Isteri Indonesia*
Sedar	Jakarta	*Istri Sedar*
Soeara 'Aisjijah	Yogyakarta	*'Aisjijah*
Soera Kaoem Iboe Soematera	Bukittinggi	*Serikat Kaoem Iboe Soematera*
Soeara Iboe	Tapanuli	*Soeara Iboe Tapanoeli*
Keoetamaan Istri	Medan	*Keoetamaan Istri*

What do these journals have in common? First, they were all edited by Indonesian women for an audience of women, which differentiates them from publications of non-Indonesian women (e.g. Dutch, Eurasian and Chinese), and from men's publications. Although the earliest Indonesian papers for women were started by men in the 1910s, by the 1930s all these publications were written and edited by women.[4] It is interesting to speculate how far their format and preoccupations were still dictated by their origins and continued existence in a world of publications dominated by men. The seven periodicals display a range of formats, from the older-style, more naive and spontaneous effusions (often in verse) of contributors to SKIS, to the more polished and professional appearance of *Pedoman Isteri*. What they have in common is a strongly exhortatory, didactic style, which may relate as much to the strong impression of schooling as to the model of male publications. Second, their audience consisted primarily of the members of Indonesian women's organizations. These are far from the commercial women's magazines of later years: their circulation was restricted and their format mostly non-commercial in appearance, although most carried advertisements. At the time almost no commercial magazines for Indonesian women existed, largely because the number of educated women able to afford such magazines was extremely limited in the 1930s.[5] As will be explained below, some of these periodicals attempted to cater to some of the same needs fulfilled by commercial magazines in areas of fashion and 'feminine pursuits', but most had a predominantly serious, 'uplifting' tone related to the aims of their sponsoring organizations, which were all concerned with the betterment of Indonesian women. Third, they were all products of a 1930s Netherlands Indies. As such, they reflected the spread of western education and consumer goods, rising Indonesian nationalism and awareness of the presence of colonial rule. Contributors knew that they lived in a new age of *kemadjoean* [progress] and wrestled with the problems of living in a multiracial society struggling to establish a modern identity.

It is not the purpose of this chapter to canvas all the issues raised by these periodicals, but rather to examine how they reflect current notions of women and the household. What follows are some notes concerning the level of interest in the role of women in the household as compared with non-household responsibilities of women, the perceived tasks of women in the household, and current views of the nature and composition of the Indonesian household. The general context of these concerns is that of 'modern' Indonesian womanhood, and what it was seen to require of women in the household.

Writers in all these publications took very seriously the duties of women as wives, mothers and managers of households. For some contributors, the role was more restrictive than for others. Those most conscious of Islamic teachings had the narrowest viewpoint. In the Medan journal, *Keoetamaan Istri*, for instance, in January 1939 Roqayah Hasan Sjazly, an Indonesian woman teacher in Cairo, emphasized women's responsibility for bringing peace and happiness to the household: they must make great efforts to provide emotional support for husbands and children. 'It is certainly the duty of the wife to follow and obey the husband. God made man superior to woman ... Wives should not go out of the house without the husband's permission.' This was, however, at the extreme end of the spectrum of views presented in the pages of these journals.

In the same publication in April, Nj. Soenarjo walked a fine line between the old and the new. In the past, she wrote, it was considered enough for a girl to be pure and good at serving her husband and at running a household. Women were destined to be mothers, and had to be aware that they would later have responsibilities as wives, household managers and as educators and carers of children. These duties entailed acting as an equal partner to her husband, knowing how to keep a peaceful and prosperous household, moulding the characters of her children within the norms of Indonesian custom, and knowing the rudiments of hygiene. Significantly, she added: 'Girls must be prepared to seek their own livelihood, to protect their lives in times of crisis between husband and wife, and to support their families if their husbands cannot fulfil their responsibilities.' More nationalist writers emphasized the Indonesian woman's responsibility for fostering children conscious of their obligations to the nation.

In none of these periodicals were women seen to be restricted to the realm of the household, which is not surprising considering the wider ambit of the organizations that sponsored them. Indeed, some periodicals devoted little attention to matters concerning the household tasks of women. *Soeara 'Aisjijah* carried far more articles about Islam (replete with Arabic quotations) than it did about women's worldly responsibilities, although it proclaimed that these were important for women. Compared with the space devoted to instructing women about the glory of religion, there were few pages about mundane matters like child-rearing, although it was frequently emphasized that schooling was important for girls so as to train them for their role in raising the next generation of Indonesian Muslims. The predominant impression is of a very high-minded vocation for devout Islamic women. If religion preoccupied *Soeara 'Aisjijah*, the main concern of *Sedar* was secular nationalism: its image of the modern Indonesian woman was of a politically active one. For this periodical too, household tasks were of a very secondary nature. As one might expect, *Isteri* spent much of its time promoting the activities of the PPII and reflecting in an increasingly nationalist way on women's role in nationalist politics, allowing little space for reflections on household responsibilities.[6] *Soeara Iboe* tried to project the special concerns of Tapanuli Batak women, especially their resentment of being excluded by *adat* [customary law] from inheritance rights. An article in its issue of May 1932 was significantly headed, 'Should we only aim to manage a household?' to which the answer was, of course, 'definitely no'. As the product of a group of women teachers, SKIS was naturally preoccupied with the importance of education for girls. The periodicals that had most to say about household matters were those which most reflected *priyayi* women's concerns, namely *Pedoman Isteri* and *Keoetamaan Istri*. But they too emphasized that women's responsibilities reached well beyond the home into politics and social welfare activities.

That said, what did these periodicals convey about women in the household domain? Raising children was given high priority and respect, and most periodicals at some time carried articles instructing women how to care for children in the modern way. Hygiene, nutrition, character formation – all these concerns reflected Western ideas of the time, but most authors gave the subject a specifically nationalist twist: this was also Indonesian women's main contribution to the formation of the modern nation.

Few periodicals could omit catering to their readers' perceived desire for advice on modern household management. At the very least this usually involved giving information about nutrition[7] or recipes, which were of a remarkably multi-racial kind: European and Chinese food usually featured along with Indonesian dishes. Advertisements often portrayed small-scale household goods, soap being the most common and the most emblematic of the new desire for cleanliness.

In the 1930s Dutch women's periodicals like *De Huisvrouw in Indie* [the organ of the Indies Housewives' Association] were projecting the ideal of the modern European household in the Indies. Its impact on the thinking of the tiny Indonesian urban middle class of the 1930s is well illustrated in the two *priyayi* women's periodicals represented here. These journals carried extensive advertising and appeared altogether more substantial. Their readers were blossoming into avid consumers, to judge from the copious fashion-notes,[8] articles on beauty care featuring Western cosmetics, and the many advertisements for Western-style furnishings and kitchen implements. An advertisement in *Keoetamaan Istri* in March 1939 featured three models of perambulators, including one which was 'streamlined' [*bak stroomlijn*]. In a radio talk in February 1935, Njonja dokter Latip, a well-known editor of the women's magazine *Doenia Kita*, was reported in *Pedoman Isteri* as giving a long and definitive view of the middle-class housewife, which might have come straight out of the pages of *De Huisvrouw*. Most strikingly, she lists in detail the required contents of every room of what she describes as a small house, which amounts to a very large number of pieces of furniture, crockery, cutlery, linen, etc. *Pedoman Isteri* had in fact a sophisticated appreciation of the economic significance of the household. In 1936, along with a number of other Indonesian papers, it organized an exhibition of household needs (*Keperloean Roemahtangga*) along the lines of exhibitions held by the Dutch-dominated Housewives' Association, arguing:

> The Indies is at a turning-point in economic policy. Exports have declined and thus the Native consumer is increasingly of interest. The aim of *Keperloean Roemahtangga* is to cultivate in that consumer the significance of more and better nutrition, clothing, housing, childcare, hygiene, education, recreation, etc. (April 1936).

> The intention is to show importers and manufacturers that the world of the Indonesian wife exists and is as mature as the world of wives of other races. The manager of the Indonesian household uses furnishings and implements for her house according to the present-day progressive times ... No longer do all our housewives only cook *ikan asin* or *trassi* and cook in a fireplace or hearth (June 1936).

Keoetamaan Istri of November 1939 recounts a conversation between Intjek [Mrs] Rachman and her *baboe* [maid] on the subject of milk. The mistress tells her servant that the doctor has instructed her to drink a litre of milk a day, and when the *baboe* responds that milk makes *kampoeng* [lower-class Indonesian] people sick in the stomach, the mistress delivers a lecture about the nutritious qualities of milk. By the 1930s, the presence of milk in a women's journal was almost a definition of its westernized, middle-class nature: like *De Huisvrouw in Indie*, journals like *Keoetamaan Istri* were listing local dairies and the cost and quality of fresh milk, which was an expensive item and an acquired taste for Indonesian households. Women's organizations like *Persatoean Isteri Pegawai Bestuur* [the Civil Servants' Wives' Assocation, which was associated with *Pedoman Isteri*] and *Keoetamaan Istri* had also begun to offer the kind of services for members which the Housewives' Association provided, such as courses in cooking, handicrafts, and cake-, dress- and flower-making.

In the periodicals of the other women's organizations mentioned here, such ideas were, however, only faintly echoed, either because their readers could not afford such trappings of Western lifestyle and/or because they did not aspire to it. The poorest of these publications, *Soeara Kaoem Iboe Soematera*, mirrored a far more rural lifestyle, as might be expected in a paper from West Sumatra.

Finally, what do these periodicals tell us about Indonesian women's perceptions of the composition of their households? It is striking how little they have to say directly about this subject. Although they certainly acknowledge the centrality of mothers and children, there is almost no mention of other household members and little discussion about children other than infants, which may reflect the young age of the women contributors. Fathers seem to be presumed to be absent from the household, playing the role of wage-earner: at the very least, they appear to have little to do within the home. In fleeting recognition of the fact that the divorce rate in Islamic Indonesia was very high, writers sometimes admitted that divorce might lead to the need for women to support their children themselves, thus accounting for the complete absence of fathers. As noted above, even the relatively conservative Nj. Soenarjo, writing in *Keoetamaan Istri* in April 1930, acknowledged the fragility of marriage. Similarly a contributor to *Soeara Kaoem Iboe Soematera*, Delmie, wrote in December 1930:

> Most of our girls consider marriage, i.e. having their own household, as the sole aim in life which will bring them security. I shall not refute this idea, but marriage does not always bring security and tranquillity for us. We cannot guarantee that we will meet men who can bring us happiness and fulfil our trust. For this reason, do not make marriage the prime goal, rather attempt first to achieve another objective, such as pursuing knowledge, learning a craft, etc., but never sit with folded hands doing nothing.

Despite awareness of the possibility of divorce, however, no particular attention was devoted to what might happen to households in its wake. The problems of single-parent families were not addressed, nor were those of stepparenting, although re-marriage by divorced Indonesians was extremely common. A very rare allusion is found in to *Soeara Kaoem Iboe Soematera* in January 1930, in an article significantly entitled *Manakah Iboekoe?* [Where is my mother?] where the author, S.C. Odius (presumably a pseudonym) argued that a stepmother who loves and protects children like a mother should be treated as one.

A number of these periodicals discussed polygamy as an issue of burning interest to women's organizations, but none was prepared to broach the concrete reality of living in polygamous households. In a fleeting reference in *Soeara Kaoem Iboe Soematera* (December 1930), the outspoken writer Selegoeri roundly criticized polygamy for resulting in

> children in Minangkabau who do not know their father, who have never been supported financially by their father. I have never seen a happy woman who has been made a co-wife (*dipermadoekan*) and only people who are happy can be said to have achieved progress (*kemadjoean*).

The failure to discuss extended kin is also very striking, considering how important a part relatives play in Indonesian family life. In the pages of these periodicals parents-in-law, grandparents, aunts and uncles, nephews and nieces are remarkably absent, apart from a rare mention where they appear to be more problematic than helpful. The most likely reason for their absence is that these women's organizations could not work out how to accommodate extended kin in a 'modern' family which, according to Western dictates, must necessarily be nuclear and living a lifestyle different from that of the older generation. For some government officials' families it may also have been the case that transfers meant they had relatively little contact with extended kin. This first generation of women educated in schools may have felt, too, that their relatives knew little about the ways of 'modern' households, accounting for their willingness to seek the advice of 'experts'. (Whether or not they took that advice was another matter.)

Finally, the role of servants in the household was also a problematic one. In many ways it infringed on the perceived roles of housewives according to the Western middle-class image: after all, it was often the servants who did the bulk of the cooking, housework and childcare. Were servants members of the household or not? Some periodicals did not tackle the issue. Others mentioned servants in passing (as seen in the example from *Keoetamaan Istri* above), yet did not address the challenge they posed to the presumed intimacy of the nuclear family. The assumption that women could and should play a role outside the household was, however, implicitly based on the presence of these servants to relieve the housewife of some of her duties.[9] It may be significant, however, that there was no equivalent in these periodicals of the Western notion of housewife [*huisvrouw* in Dutch] with its implications of full-time vocation at home. The contemporary Indonesian term *iboe roemah tangga*, a literal translation of 'housewife' was not used in the 1930s; rather, these periodicals spoke of women as managers of households (*pengoeroes* or *pemegang roemah tanggah*), recognizing that servants might be doing the actual daily work, and permitting women to reflect more on their responsibilities for the formation of the character and morals of their children than on actually feeding and clothing them. The only periodical explicitly to discuss servants was, predictably, *Sedar*, which occasionally reminded its readers that servants were workers who deserved proper treatment as employees. A contribution by Moedinem in the June–July 1931 issue struck a jarring note:

> Those of us who have servants don't think of them as humans. They work [long hours] and earn very little ... Those who live in have to sleep just anywhere and are sexually exploited by the father of the household.

Another writer (November 1931) urged women to treat their servants like members of the household (*huisgenoot*). The term *orang seroemah* – apparently a literal translation of the Dutch term – was significantly added in brackets. Contributors to *Sedar* also often reminded readers that for most Indonesian women there was no question of staying at home: lack of money forced them out to work. In the ranks of women's periodicals these were anomalous voices.

In conclusion, these periodicals represent Indonesian women of the 1930s reflecting on their roles. As befitted members of organizations devoted to wider tasks, they were not preoccupied with women's role in the household. Insofar as they did cover that topic, they projected a desire to see women forming 'modern' households, which appeared to be nuclear in composition and concerned with raising children for a new world in many ways different from that of their forebears. In an article on baby care in *Isteri* (August 1932), for instance, mothers were warned that babies should not always be picked up and fed every time they cried, that they must always be put to sleep in their own sleeping place and that they should be inoculated against smallpox. Such specific instructions were often required for the management of modern urban households, and aspects of Indonesian life which did not fit the new pattern were frequently ignored.

Like all women's magazines, commercial or non-commercial, these Indonesian journals of the 1930s presented a construct of women in the household which did not so much mirror reality as project a desirable model for an age of *kemadjoean*. For readers and writers, living up to the ideal of the modern Indonesian woman was a demanding project, requiring much moral exhortation and some practical 'expert' advice. Many uncomfortable adaptations clearly needed to be made in adjusting expectations of the ideal household to life in a colonial, developing society. How could an image of the household derived from Western bourgeois society fit a poor, basically rural colony? How was women's new role to be reconciled with the equally strong expectation that they represented continuity and tradition in the household, as the guarantors of familial stability and harmony? The journals reveal, in their silences, their preaching and occasional emotional outpourings, the struggle going on in educated circles to resolve these issues.

Fictional Writing

If, in womens magazines of the 1930s, the new ideals for the modern age tended to work against straightforward description of real-life conditions, this was even truer for fictional writing, dominated as it was by certain standard themes and literary conventions through which reflection on social reality was necessarily filtered. For women authors this framework presumably was accepted along with the general parameters of literature as an overwhelmingly male field. For women are rare among pre-war literary writers: of those, many used pseudonyms since 'it just wasn't heard of for a woman to write'.[10] One might expect more constraint on the direct expression of women's voices in fiction than in the magazines. But an understanding of the conventions of the form to which these women contributed should allow insight into the potential expression within this framework of distinctive womanly perspectives.

Two categories of fiction are recognized for this time: the 'serious literature' published by the Dutch publishing house *Balai Pustaka*, distributed through its lending libraries and studied in schools, and popular fiction serialized in the press and published in small, pamphlet-like volumes. Though in official ideology a sharp distinction is drawn between the two, largely based on the reputedly cheap, shallow, sensational content of popular writing, in fact in both types of fiction romantic, sentimental plots are ubiquitous. Love and marriage are the predominant themes, set in the context of changing values and norms, and shaped significantly, through melodramatic twists of the plot, to the mysterious workings of Fate. A key trope is that of marriage as a site of conflict between the individual wishes of youthful protagonists and the pressures of family and society. Such love relationships frequently fail, and the novels end with the deaths of one or both of the protagonists. These gloomy plots have been seen to be variously related to social conditions of the time. One observer interprets these fictional deaths as reflective of the inability of writers to conceive of solutions to the social problems faced by their characters, 'problems which were the result of the excessive and oppressive power of customs derived from the past and the absence of guidelines for the present'. Writers appealed for support from their readers for the kind of positions adopted by their characters by stirring up emotions of pity and sorrow over their suffering.[11]

A feature of *Balai Pustaka* novels in their function as serious modern literature is one shared by popular fiction (self-defined as entertainment), namely to focus on the inner thoughts and moral concerns of the characters. There appear to be parallels here with the attitudes of writers of self-consciously 'modern' fiction in China, who are described by Rey Chow as eschewing the 'decadent' and 'feudal' attention to outward detail of traditional Chinese writing for 'morally-motivated naturalism' and detailed accounts of their characters' reflections and thoughts (Chow 1991: 87, 90, 106). In Indonesian fiction, a quintessential example of inward-directed writing might be seen in Armijn Pane's *Belenggu* [Shackles] (Pane 1964), where right from the opening sentences the text plunges into the interior consciousness of the protagonists, with minimal attention to physical description of people and scenes. Other novels of the period are less singular in focus. But here, too, descriptions of gardens, meal-tables and human figures mainly function to set the scene for the key narrative focus, personal feelings and social ideas, objectified in the private thoughts of the main characters. Both women and men are defined in terms of this 'humanistic' understanding of the modern self: the practical detail of their lives, in or outside the household, is of little concern.

Female characters in novels by male writers are frequent sites for expressing the competing ideological conceptions of the 'modern woman' mentioned earlier. In keeping with his own confidently socially progressive ideas, Takdir Alisjahbana celebrates a very positive model of the modern woman as active, successful champion of women's rights in *Lajar Terkembang* [With Sail Unfurled] (Takdir 1936). Armijn Pane, by contrast, envisages his fictional characters like his own generation of Indonesians, as culturally disoriented by the colonial experience. He portrays Tini, the aspiring emancipated woman in his novel *Belenggu*, struggling with her own dilemmas and the misunderstandings of others. In popular literature at an earlier period the *nyai* charcters [Indonesian concubines of Europeans] had allowed for reflection in various ways on race relations and political issues. Popular writing, which by the 1930s seems to have been a predominantly Chinese field, saw many male writers expressing conservative views in stories exposing 'the so-called "modern girls" who had left their Chinese identity as well as Chinese civility behind them' (Salmon 1984: 165).

How did women authors contribute to such discourse? As a practical way of exploring this question within the limited space available, we shall concentrate on a few representative works, with some comparative reference to the broader picture. Attention focuses chiefly on the three best-known and most accessible pre-war literary texts by women, *Kalau Tak Untung* [If Fortune Does Not Favour] by Selasih (1969), *Kehilangan Mestika* [Lost Jewels] by Hamidah (1935) and *Buiten het Gareel* [Out of Harness] by Soewarsih Djojopoespito, later published in Indonesian as *Manusia Bebas* [Free Human Beings] (Soewarsih 1975). The authors of these novels all come from social backgrounds similar to the writers of the women's magazines. All three novelists were teachers and actively involved in organizations. One of the authors, Selasih, also wrote for, and edited, the Minangkabau journal *Soeara Kaoem Iboe Soematera* discussed earlier: Selegoeri, author of the sharp critique of polygamy quoted earlier, is one of her many pen-names. Hence the magazines and novels taken together arguably constitute a coherent body of work representing the thought of educated, urban, indigenous Indonesian women.

Involved here is a concentration on the 'serious' rather than popular stream of pre-war writing. (Of the above-mentioned novels the first two were published by *Balai Pustaka*, the third submitted initially to *Balai Pustaka*, then published independently.) Indeed popular writing, with its strong Chinese connections, relates to a somewhat different field of women's issues, publications and organizations which we do not have the space to follow up here. This is not to suggest, however, of that it is of lesser interest or importance. In terms of readership, it was probably more widely read than more 'serious' writing. A very informative review of this field has been written by Claudine Salmon (1984); other works are in preparation. Here reference is limited to some comparative comments on particular stories from the popular press.

All three texts have a strong autobiographical flavour. Like the writers, the protagonists of these stories are women schoolteachers. Hamidah is reportedly the pen-name of Fatimah Hasan Delais, who was born in Bangka, like the protagonist of *Kehilangan Mestika*, and taught continuously until her death at the age of 40 in Palembang, also the key site of action in the novel (Jassin 1987: 163). Selasih (also a pen-name), like her heroine Rasmani in *Kalau Tak Untung*, was a Minangkabau schoolteacher who wrote much poetry as well as fiction from an early age (Teeuw 1979, vol. 1: 68; Prihatmi 1977: 21). As mentioned above, she was also an outspoken journalist and political activist: now in her nineties she was recently the subject of a documentary film. Soewarsih, meanwhile, like her protagonist Sulastri, taught together with her husband during the 1930s in independent, nationalist schools in Bandung and Semarang. She suffered poverty and alienation because of the Dutch repression of these schools, and she wrote a novel in Sundanese which was rejected for publication. Here one finds not just suggestion of autobiographical connection, but clear, sustained reflection on personal experience.[12]

All three narratives focus on issues of love and work, involving relationships between the protagonists and men from similar educated backgrounds. *Kalau Tak Untung* tells of the love of Rasmani, a young girl from a poor family, for her childhood companion and schoolmate, Masrul, who is posted as a government clerk to another city. Hamidah, the protagonist of *Kehilangan Mestika*, has two loves – first a childhood friend, Ridhan, who studied at a Dutch high school in Batavia and then become a trader; second (after Ridhan dies), a cousin, Idrus, who is a poet and intellectual who assists her with her teaching work. Sudarmo, the husband of Sulastri, the main figure in *Manusia Bebas*, is a teacher and activist modelled closely on Soewarsih's husband. In a documentary film about her life, Selasih states that *Kalau Tak Untung*, her first novel, the title of which she interprets in the sense of *tak jodoh* [not fated for one another] was written after her sweetheart left for Batavia, vowing that he would return only to marry her. When he returned, however, he married one of her classmates.

All this suggests considerable correspondence between the subject matter of these novels and the personal experiences of their authors. At the same time, the form in which the subject matter is presented shows strong influence from the conventions of pre-war fiction outlined above. *Kalau Tak Untung*, in particular, admirably fulfils the parameters of romantic fiction and humanistic, inward-focused modern writing described above. *Kehilangan Mestika* appears somewhat less smooth in its execution. Comparisons of the two describe Selasih's text as 'more smoothly written and composed' (Teeuw 1979, vol. 1: 68) and more unified and sophisticated (Prihatmi 1977: 17–22). *Manusia Bebas*, meanwhile, arguably fulfils the conventions more in the breach than the observance, as we shall see shortly.

The trajectory of the narrative of *Kalau Tak Untung* follows the relationship of Rasmani and Masrul through years of separation, as Rasmani remains loyal and supportive, constantly writing letters to her friend, despite his betrothal to one girl and marriage to another. Finally, as Masrul's unhappy marriage breaks down and he has to leave his job, he at last admits his love for Rasmani. He returns, they become engaged, and Masrul goes off to find a job. After a year, however, distressed by his failure to find appropriate work, he breaks off the relationship. Then, when his fortunes change, he writes happily to summon Rasmani. But Rasmani's heart is too weak to sustain these repeated shocks, and she falls ill and dies.

Much of the text consists of conversations between the various characters and letters, mostly between Masrul and Rasmani, expressed in flowing, eloquent sentences and heightened speech. Topics of discussion often concern marriage: the mistaken custom of early marriage; the rights and wrongs of formal schooling for prospective wives'; Masrul's parents' expectations that he will marry a girl of their choice and the pressures placed on him by a wealthy teacher's family to wed their beautiful daughter; family disruption as Masrul lets down his parents by choosing the latter course. Predominant themes are the saintly generosity of heart of Rasmani, the naive confusion and vulnerability of Masrul, and the destructive effects of the interference of families, who pressurize and manipulate young people into arranged marriages. In keeping with the weightiness of these topics, and the 'inwardness' of modern writing, everyday, material detail is included only as it provides the context for reflection on major themes. Rasmani's activities as a teacher, for example, receive only cursory reference, when a letter arrives from Masrul while she is playing with her pupils in the schoolyard.

The overarching theme, meanwhile, setting the framework within which action and discussion take place, is generally defined as that of the workings of inexorable fate. The title of the novel suggests this, as do statements by the protagonist Rasmani at several points in the narrative. When Masrul marries, for example, the broken-hearted Rasmani laments that this is her fate (*sudah nasibku*), as a plain girl of a poor family who should not have aspired 'to reach the moon' (Selasih 1969: 119). On her deathbed she writes to Masrul describing her dreams of their life together, but these, however, will not come about because 'God does not wish to fulfil my intentions' (Selasih 1969: 213). Commentators in turn describe the novel as a 'story of the unhappy love of two young people who apparently are not destined for each other' (Teeuw 1979: 68) and interpret the message of the ending as 'something that the writer wishes to express from the depths of her heart: that the fate of humans, the course of human life, is determined by fortune' (Prihatmi 1977: 23).

Certain aspects of the text, however, suggest a different reading. A key site of this suggestion is Rasmani's sister, Dalipah. For Dalipah, like the reader, is a direct witness to the pain suffered by Rasmani because of Masrul. Masrul's letters to Rasmani, presented in full to the reader, are also shared with Dalipah. Frequently she reacts with surprise: while the cause of this response is not made explicit, it generally reflects the reader's own startled indignation. For Masrul continuously displays a blithe insensitivity to Rasmani's feelings. At one point he writes to ask her help in overcoming a problem in the match his parents have arranged for him – would Rasmani be willing to teach his intended bride to read and write? Later, trying to decide whether to marry the wealthy, beautiful teacher's daughter or his 'faithful childhood companion' (i.e. Rasmani), he writes to Rasmani for advice, ostensibly on behalf of a friend experiencing this dilemma. When, even after they have finally acknowledged their love, Masrul again lets her down, the saintly Rasmani complains to herself 'Men!' 'Men!' But she says nothing of this to others. It is left to Dalipah to intimate to Masrul, after Rasmani's death, how deeply he has disappointed her sister. Masrul himself at the end of the novel expresses bitter regret for causing Rasmani's suffering and death. The graceful flowing sentences of the text break down on the final page into tortured, fragmented phrases as Masrul confesses to the dead Rasmani: 'I've killed you ... I've killed the one who loved me' and refers to his suffering as the 'punishment of one who did not value love' (Selasih 1969: 213–214).

Alongside the romantic trope of immutable fate as the cause of the tragic events of the novel, a counter-discourse implicates, though never explicitly identifies, male weakness, selfishness and insensitivity.[13] In much of women's fiction, a more forthright or worldly-wise female companion of the pure, innocent female protagonist is used to challenge accepted notions of the feminine. Here such a figure, the heroine's older sister, is able to voice criticism of male behaviour in love and marriage.

The less sophisticated text of *Kehilangan Mestika* does not fit quite so neatly within the model of the romantic novel. Written in the first person, it narrates the experiences of a female protagonist named, like the author, Hamidah. It follows the heroine from the time of her graduation from teachers' college in Padang Pajang, through her work as a teacher in Bangka and Palembang, her two unfulfilled love relationships and arranged marriage, to her eventual divorce and return to her home town. The conventional motif of family conflict over issues of love and marriage is very much the motor of the plot-twice the narrator is the victim of perfidious relatives with whom she is living who conceal her sweethearts' letters and in the second case even write fictitious letters to discourage her beloved, so that Hamidah will marry the man of their choice. The familiar devices of twists of fate and untimely deaths are also prominent in the narrative. Hamidah's first love, Ridhan, dies after an operation, and her second sweetheart, Idrus, who has remained single out of love for her, dies in her arms from an unexplained illness shortly after she comes home after her divorce. The novel, which has commenced with the question 'Fate ... Fate ... Can the things that happened to me be described as fate?' (Hamidah 1935: 3) ends with the words 'I remained living alone, apart from all the people I loved and those who loved me. What is the use of living like this?' (Hamidah 1935: 77).

Not all of the text, however, focuses on such lofty questions and melancholy reflection. In the course of the narrative there is much down-to-earth discussion of Hamidah's particular experiences and difficulties as a woman.[14] The issue of *freedom* for women, to work, to mix socially, even to talk to people outside the family, features prominently. As in *Kalau Tak Untung*, on the subject of marriage the main protagonist's own natal family displays enlightened, progressive views, while other relatives are conservative and repressive. When Hamidah first returns after graduation from school she receives several offers of teaching positions in Palembang, but family members forbid her to go because of the dangers of big city life for an inexperienced young girl. Fortunately her progressive-minded father encourages her to give lessons to relatives and neighbours, and eventually she is appointed to a local school. She also establishes a women's organization. As the first woman in her area to break the rule of social seclusion of adult girls, she and her family are vilified: her father, as religious official, is threatened with removal from office for supporting her, and she and her sisters are labelled heathens for not covering their heads. But gradually social acceptance grows. Then comes the news of her transfer to a school in Palembang, an appointment which her extended family uniformly condemns, but which, with her fathers support, she is able to take up.

Returning home ill after learning of her sweetheart Ridhan's death, Hamidah spends some time convalescing, then tries to look for a job. But here she faces great difficulties. An office position is not possible because all her coworkers would be male. Her father forbids shop work. 'How hard it is for a young woman to make a legitimate living while avoiding people's talk!' she laments. 'Sometimes when I think about all this I ask myself regretfully why God caused me to be born into this world as a woman' (Hamidah 1935: 37). Her plan to set up a school for girls fails because of the refusal of parents to allow their teenage daughters to leave the house. By giving lessons in people's homes she and her friends overcome this problem; under the influence of her ideas, girls begin to enjoy a little more freedom. But not all change in this area can be regarded as progress, it seems. Some young women who 'misunderstand' her intentions start abandoning traditional dress for short skirts, skimpy tops and make-up. In order to combat this disturbing Westernization, a special public meeting is held to stress the importance in these changing times of maintaining Eastern decorum and religion.

Her father's tragic death disrupts this challenging, interesting life, as Hamidah must move to Batavia to stay with relatives who have been entrusted with her welfare. They refuse to allow her to work or to have any social contacts beyond the family. Even responding to the greetings of men who are not family members is forbidden. When her pleas to her fiancé for assistance receive no response, because of her relatives' deceitful interference, Hamidah finally agrees to marry the man they have chosen as her husband. The early years of this arranged match are torture, even though her husband loves her and treats her well. How much worse it must be, she thinks, if both husband and wife have been forced into the marriage by their parents! Things improve as their business thrives, and she is finally able to move out of her husband's extended family home. Her views on the superiority of the nuclear family to the extended household are unequivocal. 'It seems that a husband and wife will never prosper', she states, 'if they must live together with their brothers- and sisters-in-law', and 'It was as if I had become queen of my own household. I was in charge of ensuring its peace and order. My dreams as a woman had been fulfilled' (Hamidah 1935: 70).

One central aspect of her womanly role, however, remains unfulfilled – after ten years of marriage, the narrator is still childless. By this time she has grown to love her husband, yet she allows him to marry a second wife in order to have a child. Things go well at first, but after the child is born her husband's attention shifts entirely to his new wife. Hamidah blames herself for this turn of events, for allowing her husband to marry again – for all their noble intentions over the child, her husband has been swept up by worldly passion. She asks for and obtains a divorce and sadly returns home. Comparing Hamidah's description of her experiences with the melodramatic, melancholy reflections which frame her story, it is tempting to impute an implied 'no' to the opening question as to whether 'fate' has been responsible for her plight. Her sufferings have their source, surely, not in the workings of a remote, supra-human 'fate', but in the everyday social repression of women in a patriarchal society.

The mixture of features observed in these two *Balai Pustaka* texts – the combination of reflection on the problems and aspirations of women with melodramatic, romantic plots and invocation of inexorable fate – appears also in popular fiction by women authors. Forced marriage, polygamy and parental interference in freely chosen love relationships are identified as unjust and lead frequently to the untimely death of the female protagonist. Positive outcomes seem elusive – even when the hurdles have been overcome, the unwanted arranged match aborted and the sweethearts permitted to marry, fate or divine intervention causes the death of the young heroine.[15] On occasion there is reference to more activist women's concerns. The protagonist of the short novel *Poeteri dari Salome*, for example, serialized in the weekly *Panorama*,[16] is a young woman who writes in the press under the pseudonym *Poeteri dari Salome*, just as the author of the story, using the name Hong Le Koan, wrote frequently in *Panorama* on women's issues and founded the Association for Women Journalists, mentioned earlier. The novel begins with a visit to the heroine from a journalist and feminist activist from Sulawesi, and a discussion of the role of the press in publicizing women's concerns. But this contact is broken off as the girl rushes to her father-figure and mentor who is ill in another city: the focus of the narrative then shifts to the girl's marriage to her mentor's adopted son, with many emotional revelations, mysterious letters and fateful illnesses, and no further mention of journalism or women's issues.

In Soewarsih Djojopoespito's text, by contrast, there is no talk of fate as a motor of events, no melodramatic speeches, romantic letters or untimely deaths: the narrative is set firmly and realistically in the world of nationalist education and political activity of the 1930s. This involves accounts of public meetings to attract pupils to the independent school run by the protagonist and her husband; accounts of police raids on their home; reflection on the government repression which has emptied political party rooms and caused many friends to languish in gaol; and frank revelations of personal and ideological conflicts between colleagues. Yet these political reflections are interspersed with lively, colourful descriptions of the everyday – the petty humiliations of enforced stays with relatives when the couple's teaching cannot sustain them; tensions between husband and wife over money; sharp-eyed observations of the physical features and personal foibles of fellow teachers, family members and friends; detailed accounts of memorable events such as Sulastri's first labour, 'assisted' by a maidservant who could only crouch under a table, sobbing with fright. In place of the one-sided, tendentious portrayals of the 'modern woman' of many male texts – the earnest, committed feminist (Takdir), the restless, idle wife (Armijn Pane) or the shallow vamp of much popular literature – Soewarsih's text presents a lively, complex, totally human figure. The heightened mood, language and plot development of the romantic novel, and the constraints of inwardly focused, self-consciously 'modern' writing are replaced by straightforward, diary-like reflection on everyday events and encounters.

Much explicit comment arises on issues of particular concern to women, on marriage and on household life. The suffering of women in polygamous marriages, for example, is graphically illustrated by the case of Sulastri's own parents. Her father announces casually, without warning, to his stunned wife while they are visiting their daughter after the birth of her child, that he has just married a young girl who has been living in their house. Sulastri expresses deep disappointment and shame over her father's behaviour, and discomfort at the self-sacrificing, self-effacing attitudes of her mother which have so long caused her own needs to be overlooked. Elsewhere in the text there is discussion of the political struggle against polygamy in which a colleague of Sulastri's, Juhariah, is actively involved. Like Hamidah, the protagonist of *Kehilangan Mestika*, the narrator of Soewarsih's text, firmly endorses the advantages of an independent household. She describes the discomforts and tensions of extended households, particularly where there are boarders as well, and at one point forces her husband to find money to rent a house of their own, unable to bear any longer the situation of staying with relatives.

One issue of contention within the extended family concerns the upbringing of children. Sulastri is critical of her sister-in-law's reliance on servants for the upbringing of her children: after staying for a time in her household, Sulastri's once-independent and active young daughter is becoming spoilt and passive. Evident here is Sulastri's commitment to a Western-influenced view of child-rearing as training in independence. Earlier, at the birth of her child, Sulastri describes being torn between her Western learning and instinctive beliefs in traditional customs. Here generational tensions come into play, for 'with the arrival of Sulastri's mother conflicts began between new methods and modern ones' (Soewarsih 1975: 136). Her mother uses herbs on the baby and plans traditional birth rituals, which her modern-minded husband rejects, while Sulastri wavers uncomfortably between the two.

Above all, Soewarsih's text is concerned with marriage – not the forced oppression of arranged marriage but the experience of modern, educated young people who have chosen their own partners. Here the focus is not only on the pleasures of intellectual and emotional companionship which such a union can bring, but also on the strains and tensions of accommodating two individual wills, and the frustration and disappointment caused by a partner's perceived insensitivity to one's needs. In the central relationship of the novel, that of Sulastri and Sudarmo, Sudarmo is described as harshly critical of his wife, disappointed in her failure to live up his inflated ideals, at her interest in 'trivial' things like clothes. Angry words between them are often followed by prolonged periods of tense silence. Both of them realise that they need affection but 'both are stubborn by nature'; Sulastri confesses to herself that she is heart-broken by their quarrels but feels 'too proud to lower myself and for the hundredth time apologize to him' (Soewarsih 1975: 47). Sudarmo, meanwhile, cannot accept her intransigence, for despite his modern belief in women's emancipation, at an unconscious level he still has traditional expectations of wifely subservience. Such feelings, it is suggested, exist on a different plane from conscious ideals, as 'something we receive with our mothers' milk' (Soewarsih 1975: 47).

Other unions, among Sulastri's and Sudarmo's relatives as well as their fellow teachers, all have their particular problems. Some experience difficulties similar to those of Sulastri and Sudarmo, as in the case of one husband's unrealistic expectations of his wife, but there is also much variation. Marriage to a good-hearted but pedestrian man is seen to have held back the potential intellectual development of a bright young former schoolmate of Sulastri: the latter's sister-in-law, Lurni, should have married a man of a higher social position who could have satisfied her need for luxuries and status, in the absence of which she seeks distraction in women's organizations(!). Meanwhile, Sulastri's sister, Marti, often quarrels with a husband whose stoic style, at odds with her own volatility, further exacerbates their conflicts. Women as well as men are shown to contribute to marital difficulties. Occasionally the dialogue explicitly addresses the problematic nature of the married state. A wife's assertion of suffocating boredom, living with a man who cannot converse, who simply agrees to whatever she does, prompts her husband's bitter response that marriage is indeed boring and painful, and should be done away with (Soewarsih 1975: 166).

What makes Soewarsih's text so different from the other novels we have been examining and indeed from pre-war fiction in general? How is it that she comes to include the mundane details of ordinary life which the other authors eschew, giving her text an everyday reality identified in more recent times as typical of women's writing? How does she come to deal so explicitly, even bluntly, with issues of gender tension which are only hinted at in other texts?

One must be wary of assuming that Soewarsih writes as other women novelists would have done if they had dared; that somehow she is giving unmediated expression to the voice of educated Indonesian women. For many factors are at work here. Soewarsih's text was produced under unique circumstances: when her original novel in Sundanese, *Marjanah*, was rejected by *Balai Pustaka*, she wrote a revised text in Dutch which was taken to Holland where it was published in 1940. Ironically for any would-be celebration of Soewarsih's novel as a reflection of pure womanly consciousness, she received much advice during the rewriting process from the progressive Dutch (male) intellectual Edgar du Perron, who was living in Bandung at the time. It was Du Perron, it seems, who urged her to write about her own experiences rather than following the format of romantic, didactic fiction. He even showed her several texts of his own as models of true-to-life, personal narration.[17] The work which resulted was very different from Soewarsih's original fictional story.

Yet, for all the guidance she may have received, the narrative voice in *Manusia Bebas* is clearly Soewarsih's own: the events she recounts are things that happened to her and the characters correspond to people she knew. The personal incidents and sentiments are surely also infused with her own voice. And inasmuch as these correspond with concerns of other women novelists, albeit expressed in a very different form, one can identify a shared body of experience and thought, which forms a useful point of comparison to women's writing in magazines.

CONCLUSION

Both magazines and fiction contribute to a picture of Indonesian women actively involved in redefining their roles in the household, in marriage and workplace according to the new ideals of modernity, while also struggling with the problematic aspects of this discourse. As anticipated, the novels reflect on the more personal, emotional aspects of women's experience while the magazines deal with public issues and practical, organizational strategies. The everyday issues of household management discussed in the magazines find little place in literary texts with their more abstract focus: the love relationships and marital experiences of the novels are presumably considered inappropriate fare for the magazines with their informative, didactic functions. Yet there are distinct commonalities and complementarities in the two bodies of writing. The reflection of wifely suffering in polygamous marriages presented in the novels augments the polemical discussion of the issues of polygamy in the magazines. The question as to why extended family relatives are absent from the households portrayed in the magazines finds an answer perhaps in the negative portrayal of the extended family in the novels. With their conservative, constraining attitudes and attempts to control individuals' lives, their presence is unlikely to be supportive of the modern ideals that the magazines are promoting.

In both fiction and magazines there is a celebration of the nuclear family household as a site of achievement and fulfilment for women. Both the individualistic focus of this ideal and the specific features defining the modern household show clear influence from Western models. There is an intriguing contrast here with the contemporary picture of the nuclear family as a site of *traditional*, ongoing wifely nurture and support for husband and children: in the 1930s the nuclear household was new, modern and provided opportunities for women to develop their own skills.

Yet this household is clearly far from a haven of contained domestic contentment. For within modern marriage come the pressures of the new psychological expectations of the husband–wife relationship so graphically documented in Soewarsih's text, along with the domestic demands of new methods of household management and child-rearing. Meanwhile there are many outside claims on women to contribute actively, in multiple ways, to the world beyond the home. For the protagonists of the novels, commitment to a teaching career is a central 'given' of the text: in the magazines women's roles in employment, political activity and social welfare are much discussed. At one point Soewarsih's protagonist Sulastri is described as feeling unable to breathe, so tightly is she constrained by multiple pressures – her responsibilities to her husband, Sudarmo; the expectations of other people; the demands of her teaching job. But at the same time, the text goes on to recount her feelings of happiness when she reminds herself that she was doing all this for her native land, 'an entity which at that moment had the face of Sudarmo and the school' (Soewarsih 1975: 46). Might this be a fitting general summation for the experience and consciousness of Indonesian women like Soewarsih in this period of history, struggling in their own ways, within their own particular spheres, to bring about the new Indonesia?

Authors' Note

This article had its origins in two separate papers presented at the 1995 workshop 'Indonesian Women in the Household and Beyond: Reconstructing the Boundaries'. Susan's focused on reflections on women and the household in the women's press of the colonial period; Barbara's on such reflections in fiction by women writers. Combining our efforts at the editors' suggestion, we have maintained our original responsibilities; Susan for discussion of the magazines, Barbara for the fictional writing, plus the formulation of some framing remarks.

NOTES

1. See, for example, Partha Chatterjee's discussion of the shaping of the concept of the 'modern woman' in late nineteenth century and early twentieth century India (Chatterjee 1993).

2. The 1930 census reported that only 2.2% of Indonesian women were literate (*Volkstelling*, 1930, vol. 8; p. 29).

3. It is notable from the titles of these periodicals and their organizations how many words for 'woman' existed in the 1930s. The most general word, *perempoean*, was not yet displaced by the current word *wanita*, which was not used in these publications. Terms like *iboe* and *isteri* could be used for 'mother' or 'wife' respectively, but also to refer to women more broadly.

4. For an excellent brief survey of the history of women's journals in Indonesia, see Salmon (1977).

5. One of the few Indonesian women's magazines of the times not issued by an organization was the monthly *Doenia Kita*, significantly published at the end of this era (1937–1941) and edited by Nj. A. Latip: it closely resembled the *priyayi* publications discussed here.

6. As one of its writers put it, 'Woman is the caretaker of the family. Let our women's movement ensure that it cares also for the big family of Indonesia' ('Teaching Girls', *Isteri*, February 1931).

7. Rather apologetically under the title 'A Little about Food', a contributor called Soekarmi in *Isteri* of March 1931 wrote: 'Some people may say, "What is the use of reading about cooking? After all, our ancestors knew how to eat without knowing about the science of nutrition ... and they lived healthily too ..." True, but this is to forget that some of us fall sick just because of a wrong choice of food. Every day we cook without considering what is good and bad to eat.'

8. 'As a civilized people we must raise our fashion level' wrote Iben*oe*, a female contributor, to *Keoetamaan Istri* in October 1937.

9. Hence, for instance, an article like that in the July 1932 issue of *Isteri* ('Teaching women to be equal to men in the movement') which claimed that many women had plenty of spare time on their hands, which needed to be spent in 'devoting ourselves to the good of the country' rather than doing handicrafts, going shopping, or gambling.

10. In the film about her life, the author Selasih makes this comment on her use of a pseudonym for the publication of her first novel, *Kalau Tak Untung* [If Fortune Does Not Favour].

11. The comments are from Armijn Pane, himself a famous novelist and literary critic of the 1930s, in the articles 'Figuren in de roman-literatuur' in *Bangoen* 1/4, 15 August 1937, pp. 51–56, and 'Mengapa Pengarang Modern Soeka Mematikan?' in *Poedjangga Baru* VIII/9 March 1941 pp. 225–231. These references appear in Keith Foulcher's sensitive and illuminating analysis of Armijn Pane's work (Foulcher, in press).

12 The account of Soewarsih's life by Gerard Termorshuizen (1991: 33–34) indicates quite specific reference in the novel to figures in Soewarsih's life. The depiction of Sulastri's overbearing sister Marti and her husband are modelled on Soewarsih's own sister Nining and her husband Abdoel Karim Pringodigdo; Sutrisno is Soejitno Mangoenkoesoemo, a brother of Tjipto Mangoenkoesoemo, etc.

13 An interesting comparison to *Kalau Tak Untung* can be seen in Selasih's other pre-war novel *Pengaroeh Keadaan* [The Influence of Circumstances], published in 1937. Here male weakness in marriage is explicitly identified as a major cause of the suffering of the female protagonist. But this weakness takes the form of failure by the young girl's father to curb the vicious persecution of her by his second wife, her stepmother. The girl's future husband, the young schoolteacher who takes pity on her, is a paragon of virtue. 'Circumstances' rather than fate constitute the motor of action, as confirmed several times in conversations between characters. The young girl's escape from the oppressive circumstances of her home cause her to lose her shyness and sense of inferiority, while her family's decline into poverty because of the stepmother's greed brings realization of wrong-doing and repentance. Again a measure of social critique, towards male weakness, female greed and the workings of the Minangkabau family system, is contained within the framework of a highly romantic plot.

14 The novel has in fact been faulted by critics for its inclusion of pedestrian description of everyday events. The protagonist's sea journey home from her school in Padang Panjang, in particular, is seen to be rendered in banal detail 'which has no connection at all with the theme' (Prihatmi 1977:18). But in fact on this trip and a later one from Bangka to Palembang to work, amid the artless reportage there occurs reference to incidents of considerable potential significance. Two instances of what would now be labelled 'sexual harassment' prompt the narrator's remark that such behaviour is probably commonplace, and the rueful words 'Truly you are weak creatures, my fellow-women, you become mere sport for cruel men' (Hamidah 1935:19). Nothing develops out of these events, the narrative simply proceeds on its way, but one feels the reference is not an idle one, that it arises out of a broader concern.

15 In the story '*Doenia Rasanja Antjoer*' [The World Seems Broken Apart] by Miss Kin, for example, which appeared in the monthly *Goedang Tjerita* in March 1931, the heroine dies suddenly on the very eve of her wedding to her true love, following her recovery from attempted suicide and life-threatening illness over a planned arranged marriage. The account of her death is introduced to the reader as 'an event which, if not regarded simply as Fate, can be identified as the will of almighty God' (p. 82). Note the similarities to the ending of the novel *Kalau Tak Untung*, and the comments by Armijn Pane on the prominence of deaths of the protagonists in writing of this time.

16 See *Panorama* 1928, May to July issues.

17 See Termorshuizen 1991.

5

Reconstructing Boundaries and Beyond

Sylvia Tiwon

> The task is to refigure this necessary 'outside' as a future horizon, one in which the violence of exclusion is perpetually in the process of being overcome (Judith Butler [1994] 'Bodies that Matter').

INTRODUCTION

This essay begins by juxtaposing elements from the title of this volume with a quote from Judith Butler in order to foreground the challenge implicit in the terms of the project of reconstruction. I am thinking not only of the feminist project of reconstructing conceptual boundaries about households to collapse the false dichotomy of private versus public spheres. The need to rethink the exclusion of the household from the discourse and practice of capitalist economics, and indeed the dichotomy of macro- and micro-spheres themselves, has already been signalled by White (1992: 21–22), who points out the difficulty of ascribing a fixed (thus exclusionary) definition to the household as a concept. The concept is, in his words, a 'catch-all minimal socio-economic unit' which may be understood in terms of separately and carefully delineated units engaging the entire economic process. In the particular context of rural Indonesia, the household may thus be approached as the economic foundation of social (agrarian) structures by which 'unpaid surplus labour' is extracted in a variety of ways. White offers an indication of how economics pervades even those relationships within the household and must include the possibility of surplus extraction mechanisms among household members based on hierarchies of age and gender. Seen in this way, it is possible to regard the household as at least a potential arm for exploitation, and particularly of the labour of women. The so-called reproductive functions, and particularly procreation – perhaps the core of the most socially and culturally sanctified of human activities centred on a particularized figuration of the female – may also be seen as being incorporated within and shaped by this network of economic relationships.

RECONSTRUCTING BOUNDARIES AND BEYOND

Most of the essays included in this volume already give a clear indication of the fluidity of 'household' as a term; some indeed show that the vagueness about the boundaries can in fact make of a household a strategic space from which a woman actively engages the socio-economic network, opening up opportunities for herself and perhaps winning a stronger position from which to negotiate internal household mechanisms of labour extraction. My own essay begins with a contemplation of the word 'beyond' in perhaps a more radical way than was the intention of the common project. By this I hope to provide a perspective on the interface of household, family and the post-colonial nation-state and to foreground the conceptual and political implications involved in the task of 'reconstructing' boundaries within what Butler terms the 'regime of truth' (1994: 165) in New Order Indonesia. I hope also to raise the question of whether strategies aimed at inclusion – giving women a voice by articulating their experiences – might in the short term at least, expose women to the risk of co-optation by the prevailing regime of truth.

While there is a general acceptance of the importance of deconstructionist analyses of discourse, there remains an underlying suspicion that the anti-foundationalist trajectory of post-modernist thinking actually sneaks in a new essentialism which privileges language itself and relegates 'reality' to a secondary, highly questionable position.[1] Gayatri Spivak's 'radical de-centering of the subject' provides but one example of the type of discourse analysis that undermines ideas about the possibility of recovering woman as a 'real' subject (Spivak 1988).[2] Saskia Wieringa's critique of discourse analysis is perhaps more immediately pertinent, for she sees its praxis – and particularly of such tangentially Lacanian French feminists as Kristeva and Irigaray – as belonging in the realm of the symbolic rather than being rooted in the socio-economic and political struggles, particularly of women in the South, 'whose praxis is much more related to socio-economic and political issues' (Wieringa 1995: 30). She thus highlights the crucial fissure in the facade of the international solidarity of women, a fissure that should serve as a warning of the potentially colonizing effects of scholarship as an enterprise itself already subsumed within the singularistic hierarchy of Western discourse. Even Butler's analysis of the 'materiality' of matter, a line of thinking that forms the basis for some of my own arguments here, may be seen as belonging squarely within the sphere of esoteric Western philosophy, which spends too much time on ancient, perhaps even questionable, texts. It might thus appear that using the techniques of discourse analysis implies the imposition of extraneous Western categories (and thus further violent exclusions) upon non-Western realities. The point I wish to make here is that the understanding of household as a concept is already entangled within the politics of signification of post-colonial Indonesia and that the project of reconstruction may be strengthened by a short prelude involving some deconstruction.

Two works are basic to my essay: the first is Benedict Anderson's thinking about 'nation', the second is Butler's deconstruction of the notion of 'matter'.

While Anderson's work focuses on nation as a historical construct (a collective creation) – and thus pushes such concepts as 'sovereignty' and 'community' into the realm of culture, Butler's essay serves to historicize the term 'matter' itself. Both works, though not necessarily interconnected, are useful to show how socio-economic praxis cannot easily be disconnected from the discourse within which it is constituted.

By defining nation as 'an imagined political community', Anderson (1991: 6) opens up an important avenue into an understanding of nation (and thus the nation-state), one that is especially useful for tracing the shaping of Indonesia as a post-colonial entity against the matrix of multiple cultures and languages. The nation is imagined 'because the members of even the smallest nation will never know most of their fellow-members, meet them, or even hear of them, yet in the minds of each lives the image of their communion' (p. 6). That the nation is thus imagined does not imply that it is somehow negative. In a sense, 'all communities larger than primordial face-to-face' ones are imagined. Thus, most importantly, 'the *style* in which they are imagined is what distinguishes them' (p. 6, emphasis mine) from other large entities such as the religious states and monarchies. In contradistinction to religious states, nations imagine themselves as limited (i.e. not encompassing all of humanity); by contrast with monarchies, nations are imagined as 'deeply horizontal' fraternities, as communities of equals. In brief, then, we might say that the modern nation is a particular style of political imagination, or a political construct in a particular style.[3]

In a more directly deconstructionist vein, Judith Butler questions prevailing assumptions underlying 'materiality', particularly as it is used in feminist critiques of post-structuralism/post-modernism that argue for the 'material irreducibility of sex' (1994: 142) in the face of theories that appear to reduce everything to language.[4] Rather than offering a space beyond language where 'real' lives are lived in 'real' bodies, 'matter' itself is a concept – indeed, one we cannot do without – which is 'bound up with signification from the start' (p. 144). In her complex analysis of the genealogy of the concept, she traces the association of the feminine and matter and shows that 'the figure that women become' within the 'metaphysical cosmogony' from which matter as a concept issues is 'one that remains largely inchoate in the constitution of matter' (p. 166).

I risk over-simplification of Butler's difficult philosophical critique but I wish to take 'matter' as a term already subjected to this questioning to consider how nation 'materializes' in a male imagination. Print (and print capitalism), education and mobility, the necessary vehicles in the shaping of this imagination, were largely beyond the grasp of women. In Indonesia, this was so particularly at the crucial early stages, when Kartini decried her inability to publish in print the experiences important to her. Her father, fearing that publishing the feelings she expressed so eloquently in her hand-written letters would bring shame upon the family, allowed her to publish articles only on indigenous crafts.[5] Few women received Western-style education and fewer still were politically active and able to take advantage of the new mobility afforded by modern means of transportation. Most of their contributions to the nationalist cause have been cast in terms of an extension of their 'natural' bent for housewifely duties. If the national fraternity may also be construed as a social contract to regulate access to women's bodies and to lend legitimacy to male 'sex right' in the name of social order beyond the natural state,[6] the absence of active feminine intervention in the nationalist imagination (thus not merely the feminine in the nationalist construction) may be understood not simply as a lack but as an exclusion. This line of thinking is elaborated in a thought-provoking article on state fatherhood in Singapore by Geraldine Heng and Janadas Devan, which concludes with the following statement: 'Women, and all signs of the feminine, are by definition always and already anti-national' (Heng and Devan 1992: 356).

The following passages in this essay represent an effort to delineate in broad strokes the processes by which women became anti-national: processes that depend not only on the evocation of specific cultural traits inherent in 'traditional' symbols of the feminine leading to the well-known construct of the *kodrat wanita* [women's essential nature] but also, and perhaps more directly, depend on the narrative of nation begun, somewhat ironically, in the discourse of colonial empire. I submit that it is this discourse – i.e. this 'style' of imagination – which in Indonesia shaped the concept of the indigenous households and that this stylization enabled its exclusion and legitimized the process of marginalization we now see taking place everywhere within the developmentalist pragmatism of the New Order.

MATERIALIZING STATE, HOUSEHOLD AND FAMILY

In 1995, the New Order government paid tribute to the family in a spectacular pageant on 'Family Day'. The parade, which included numerous floats and elaborate dances, was presided over by the 'first family', General (retired) and Mrs Soeharto, dressed in matching outfits in the 'indigenous' textiles that have become the New Order's outward sign of cultural identity, also incorporating the Western-style sign of gender difference (trousers for him; a skirt for her). The celebrations were auspiciously coordinated to commemorate, at the same time, the end of the revolution, when the Indonesian guerrillas returned from their bloody engagements in the outlying areas to the civilization of the city of Yogyakarta and the bosom of their families – their wives and mothers. Apart from the fact that this celebration might be seen as a not-so-subtle shift in the centre of heroics from Sukarno–Hatta (as civilian politicians) to Soeharto (as emblem of military power), it also staged the distant chaos of revolution as a finished event, underlining the importance of the return to the city as a return to order.[7]

This depiction of the end of what in Sukarno's time was termed the 'physical revolution' was, of course, nothing new. A 1949 publication entitled *Illustrations of the Revolution, Indonesia 1945–1950*[8] shows a photograph of soldiers filing into the city bearing arms, accompanied by a caption which reads thus:

> Meanwhile, in an atmosphere of a sinister quiet the first guerilla units of the Republic entered Jogjakarta city. A very moving moment indeed. Like a child who after roaming around for a long time at last comes back to the lap of its mother, so did our forces come back to the embrace of the capital city of Jogjakarta. They might still be filled with suspicion when they began to enter the city. Was it really true that the Dutch had left Jogjakarta, they might wonder.[9]

A significant difference between these two depictions lies in the fact that whereas the 1949 description uses the figure of a child returning to a mother, and uses it figuratively, the 1995 depiction, performed for television cameras – and thus aimed at the entire nation simultaneously – dispenses with overt metaphorical representation, and offers in its stead a depiction of a moment meant as history, in which the emphasis is on the courageous, active husband (Soeharto) returning to his faithfully waiting wife (Suhartinah). Both images activate a dichotomy of action–waiting, easily subsumed into the male–female hierarchy; yet there is a qualitative difference, and the two are not interchangeable. Although the return to the female in both depictions suggests the return to nurture and comfort, any attempt to superimpose the image of the child upon the image of the husband would render questionable – if not simply ludicrous – the heroic agency of military power not only over the enemy, but also over the female. Both depictions are replete with significant dichotomies: urban–rural, centre–periphery, history–tradition, to name the three most obvious ones. However, for the purposes of this analysis, I wish to foreground the important shift which has taken place in the power-laden dichotomy of male–female within changing notions of household and family. This shift may roughly be described as a shift away from perceived matrifocal household to male-headed (thus patriarchal) nuclear family.

Setting aside, for the moment, the 1949 depiction, I should like to point out the irony involved in the 1995 event. While evoking, in separate tableaux on wheeled floats and dances in the streets, the idea of the 1945–1947 revolution, the parade presented a revolution consigned to the past in contradistinction to Sukarno's refusal to declare the revolution over. It thus becomes a revolution domesticated in more ways than one, as it celebrates the originating moment of the true Indonesian foundation for family in the pairing of man and wife.[10] By locating it at the moment when the nation returns to the state of 'order' – a notion which finds its parallel in the 'return to civilization' in the earlier depiction of the same event – the performance identifies the nuclear family glorified on this day as the basis for the state and future greatness, a position also ascribed to it by numerous key government statements. In this event, the first family appropriates the revolution for itself, because Sukarno, with his series of wives and mistresses, can be paired only – on this family day – with Hatta. This male (and coincidentally, civilian) pair cannot be the progenitors of the (civilized) nation.

This public celebration of the nuclear family as the basis of nation finds its legal arm in the marriage laws of 1974, the first legislative product of the New Order's *MPR* (*Majelis Perwakilan Rakyat* or People's Consultative Assembly). While these marriage laws are generally taken as a signal of the victory of the long political struggle of most women's organizations, a victory denied them throughout the Sukarno years, they are now beginning to be questioned not only by orthodox Muslims for their restrictions on polygyny[11] but also by secular feminist voices who deplore the legislation of the subordinate position of the wife. Article 31 (3) of the 1974 marriage laws, for example, defines the husband as head of the family and the wife as the housewife (or, to be more precise, 'mother of the household': *Suami adalah kepala keluarga dan isteri ibu rumah tangga*). Article 1 of these laws defines family (*keluarga*) and household (*rumahtangga*) as one and the same: *Perkawinan ialah ikatan lahir bathin antara seorang pria dengan seorang wanita sebagai suami isteri dengan tujuan membentuk keluarga (rumah tangga) yang bahagia dan kekal berdasarkan Ketuhanan Yang Maha Esa*.[12] Article 32 further stipulates that husband and wife must have a permanent place of residence (1) in the form of a house (*rumah tempat kediaman*) which (2) they choose together. This may be interpreted as a stipulation for separate nuclear family housing.[13] We might conclude that the only type of household recognized as 'material' to the law is the nuclear family.[14]

GENERAL OUTLINES OF STATE POLICY

The 1993–1998 GBHN (*Garis-Garis Besar Haluan Negara*, or General Outlines of State Policy ratified by the People's Consultative Assembly in 1993), which also lays out the basis for development over the next 25 years, enshrines the *kodrat wanita* despite the fact that a draft of the document prepared by the Armed Forces fraction was circulated among women's organizations and was protested by several of them. In Section F.9.a, we find the following definition:

> Women, as citizens as well as a human resource for development (*sumber daya insani pembangunan*) have rights, responsibilities and opportunities which are the same as men in all aspects of development. The fostering (*pembinaan*) of the role of women as equal partners of men is aimed at increasing their active role in development activities, including efforts to materialize (*mewujudkan*) a healthy, prosperous and happy family, as well as the development (*pengembangan*) of children, adolescents and youths, within the framework of the development of the complete Indonesian human (*manusia Indonesia seutuhnya*). The position of women within the family and society and their role within development must be maintained and increasingly stepped up in order to provide the greatest possible contribution towards the development of the nation, while being mindful of their essential nature (*kodrat*) and dignity.

Disturbing as this statement might be, with its overtones of state control over all aspects of life and its insistence on the *kodrat* of women, it becomes even more disturbing when it is placed against the GBHN section on economics, which governs such apparently unrelated topics as transmigration and indigenous peoples under various headings, such as transmigration, forestry, mining, etc.: areas that have the greatest potential to impact upon those populations who do not register within the official duality of *masyarakat perkotaan* [urban population] or *masyarakat pedesaan* [rural population].

Despite the definition of women as *mitra sejajar* [equal partners] of men, women are still the producers and nurturers of the *sumber daya manusia* [human resources] within the confines of the family defined as the *wahana sosialisasi pertama* [first socializing receptacle] of the nation (see, e.g. Chapter IV. F Kesejahteraan Rakyat, Pendidikan dan Kebudayaan, 2.g; also, on the educating role of the family, E.3). Keluarga is defined more fully in Chapter IV. F. 5 Keluarga Sejahtera, point (a) as follows:

> The development (*pembangunan*) of the prosperous family is aimed at the materialization (*terwujudnya*) of family life as a seed-bed (*wahana persemaian*) for religious values and the high values (*nilai-nilai luhur*) of national culture in order to increase the welfare of families and to foster the perseverence of the family (in such a way) as to be able to support development activities. It is necessary to foster the growth of social consciousness as to the importance of the norm of the happy and prosperous small family resting on the foundation (*dilandasi*) of the sense of responsibility, volunteerism, religious values, and the high values of national culture.

Furthermore, point (d) reinforces the idea that this is no mere symbolic gesture (it is, after all, also the basis for population control, see point (b): *mengendalikan laju pertumbuhan penduduk*), for the concept is part of the small family movement (*gerakan keluarga kecil bahagia*) which must be spread throughout society and become the culture of the entire nation (*memasyarakat dan membudaya di seluruh tanah air*).

Under the section on transmigration (section 16), thus under the rubric *Ekonomi*, together with industry, agriculture, transportation, etc., we find references to the people who have been rendered invisible under the official duality (rural–urban populations): these are the *peladang berpindah* [shifting cultivators] and *penduduk yang hidup terpencar* [inhabitants who live scattered about].[15] These people, mostly thought of as parts of the forested outlying areas to which transmigrants are sent, are to be resettled (*pemukiman kembali*) in ways that will harmonize (*serasi*) with the lifestyles of the transmigrants. Point (e) of section 7, *Kehutanan* [Forestry] stresses the need to regulate the housing of forest communities (*masyarakat yang tinggal di hutan*) and shifting cultivators. Point (g) states the need for forestry information services, especially for those people in and around the forest, to teach them the ways of *perhutanan sosial* [social forestry].

These views pervade the entire document. The conclusion we may draw is that the culture and society of the nation rests on the *kodrat* of women as reproducers and nurturers within the nuclear family (men are given but brief mention under the general term *orangtua*) housed under its own separate roof, either in rural areas (*pedesaan*) or in the city (*perkotaan*). Anything that does not fall under either category is not recognized as being social or even civilized. As the section on Culture (*Kebudayaan*) suggests, national culture is shaped out of the 'high cultural values' and selected external values, in accordance with *peradaban* [civilization; see e.g. section (e), point 2].

The GBHN stipulates that national law must be uniform in its articulation and in its force. While this is clearly an important channel for the imposition of national norms regarding women, families and households, the ways of the law in Indonesia are not necessarily the primary channels for change. It is commonly known that the legislative procedure in Indonesia is dominated by the executive branch, a fact partly enabled by the 1945 Constitution which concentrates enormous power in the hands of the president. More serious implications arise through executive manipulation of the procedures for legislative change. In the area of labour legislation, for example, the process of change is initiated by ministerial decrees and regulations (the *PerMen, Peraturan Menteri* and the *KepMen, Keputusan Menteri*) often in direct conflict with existing labour laws. Once the practices have been generally implemented, they become the norm and the legislation process is then brought into the action to ratify what has already become 'common practice'.[16] A variety of sources indicates that the same is happening with the forced transformation of the multiple forms of household into the nuclear family.[17] The legislation imposing uniform village government throughout the nation thus serves to provide legal cover for an action already taking place, a crucial element of which is the family planning movement, which, in many of the outlying areas (including East Timor) is deeply felt as a means of keeping indigenous, non-Javanese communities small and marginalized.[18]

LAND RIGHTS

A further area in which government development policies severely undermine the existence of peripheral communities – and thus of traditional/alternative forms of household/family – is in land rights. In the *Undang-Undang Pokok Agraria* [Agrarian Laws], for example, the government (during the Sukarno era) describes its relation to the land mass of the nation in terms of the assumption by the national government of the *hak ulayat*: the traditional community right to the land it occupies. The 1960 legislative product is directed, of course, at the abolition of colonial land rights.[19] While the law recognizes the traditional *hak ulayat* of indigenous communities, it opens the way to bureaucratic interference through the procedures involved in documenting communal rights. It also opens the way for a thorough reinterpretation of precisely what constitutes *hak ulayat*. Present-day problems around such large-scale projects as the

Freeport mine in Irian and extensive forest exploitation in Kalimantan have much to do with the different interpretations of community land rights.[20] Transmigration and transportation are two other areas which have a direct and detrimental impact upon indigenous ideas of significant space.[21] These contesting – and increasingly marginalized – constructions of space should also be included in the understanding of alternative ideas of the household.

There are many more areas not generally covered by Women's Studies and it is not my intention here even to pretend to be comprehensive. My main intention is to offer an indication of the broad range of areas rapidly falling under direct government control (or in other cases, under the control of capital enterprise) which create an enormous network in which ideas of household and family – and thus the positioning of women – need to be understood.

I should like to return now to the depiction of family and revolution with which I began this section and to point out a further irony underlying the construction so interwoven with the construction of heroic (male/military) subjugation of both the colonial enemy and of woman. While the Dutch colonial regime was indeed ousted from Indonesian territory, its hold on the territory of the imagination remained. The community of nation was not imagined out of the blue but rather was reinscribed upon a map of dominion already assembled and disseminated in a variety of ways by the Dutch. A telling rehearsal of the discourse of nation is to be found in the pre-war novel, *Sitti Noerbaja* by Marah Roesli (1922: 272), in which the words so crucial to the nationalist imagination come from the mouth of the Dutch resident, who is instructing (in Minangkabau language) a gathering of *penghulu*s [lineage heads] in the merits of the Dutch system of taxation:

> All islands included in the territory of Hindia [i.e. the Dutch East Indies] must become one. Whether Malay ethnic groups, Javanese, Dayak or Papua, Dutch or Chinese, all the inhabitants of Hindia must become one and must work together to bring progress to our land.

This is the example he gives of the benefits (ibid.):

> Look at the School for Javanese Doctors [*Sekolah Dokter Djawa*]; it is only to be found in Java, but the Javanese are not the only ones to benefit from this school. People from Minangkabay, from Batak, Menado, Ambon and others are also able to study there to become doctors.

The listing of ethnic communities, narrated in the language of a larger, supralocal unity, is similar to the laudatory descriptions of the experiences at this same medical school for indigenous people which Sam (the hero) repeats to his sweetheart at home in Padang:

> Padang, Batak, Deli, Palembang, Batavia, Sunda, Java, Madura, Ambon, Menado and others, we heard many different songs, sung in many

different languages and many kinds of dances and martial arts did we see (p. 107).

The exhilaration evident in the hero's descriptions of a node in the 'pilgrimage' of nation[22] (his sojourn at the medical school in Batavia) belies the unhappiness with which the *penghulus* greet the resident's speech (behind his back, of course) and what we might call the 'failure of the imagination' of the *penghulus*, who represent to the colonial power the matrifocal communities in which the *rumah gadang* [family house] is the still centre of a network of expanding loyalties and commitments:

> The resident himself has said that we must not ask other people for things we need; why should not each *kampung* and each *negeri* fulfil its own needs? Why should we have to help people in Celebes, Timor and Papua? We haven't even seen their faces! And who is to guarantee that they will eventually help us should we find ourselves in need? (p. 274).

The taxes demanded by the faraway and alien government are a vehicle for the disruption of the local face-to-face community turning, in this case, upon the need to forge a sense of fraternity with peoples unknown and well-nigh unimaginable, under the paternal aegis of the colonial regime.

The system of taxation is a particularly significant force in the shaping of the supra-local imagination, for as Schrieke points out, the penetration of money into the rural communities itself does not necessarily bring about true economic change. If there is no consistent need to circulate money as money (in terms of discourse analysis, by retaining its function as sign, rather than understanding it merely as a signifier to be converted into what it signifies, as in, for example, barter economies), money becomes only 'a store of value, not a medium of exchange' (Schrieke 1960: 98).[23] It is in the exchange that money gains its status as sign, and local conversions which stop its circulation are merely misunderstandings of the discourse of cash, and quickly 'corrected' by the institution of a regular system of money taxation. There is, of course, an enormous array of colonial regulations which served to disrupt local discourse and opened these communities to the hegemony of colonial state (and capital) discourse.

An important part of colonial policy was the declaration of 'public domain' and, against that, private property. Here again, the *adat* of local communities worked against supra-local imagination. Local ideas of land tenure resisted classification into public and private. Land was, generally, inalienable and, as a result, could not enter into supra-local circulation. Land, in effect, was not sufficiently 'material'. Only through alienation could it gain status as a proper signified to be assumed into the supra-local circulation of signs, and thus 'materialize' in the sight of the law. Schrieke's analysis of the impact of capital penetration into local communities uses primarily the Minangkabau as an example; however, from this example he draws more generalized conclusions, as his citations from Adriani (pp. 122–123) on Toraja society would indicate.

There is much more to be said on the subject of the disruption of local communities, the abandoning of the *rumah gadang*, the cooptation of the *penghulu* and the entire *adat* community (partly to counter radical Islamic elements and, ironically, at the same time to counter a rising 'modern' communism) and the dislocation of household and women. However, for the purposes of this brief chapter, the above points must serve to highlight the problematic household–family–nation interface and its location in the history of colonial statecraft from which the modern, independent nation was wrested. Schrieke, supported by evidence offered by Adriani, brings up the notion of communities centred on matrifocal households as inimical to the required development of individual, alienable property.[24] This closely parallels ideas of matrifocal households ('matriarchies') as inimical to a proper (read: Western capitalist) process of individuation of males as property-holders and citizens who are able to engage in the common contractual relationships that form the basis of national societies – societies needed for a nation-state to exist. It is here that we may perceive the convergence of 'ideology' and socio-economic processes.

The following invocation of family is embedded in de Kat Angelino's work on colonial statecraft:

> The Silent Force of the faithful fulfilment of obligation towards unknown shareholders and savers, travellers, that is what makes everything possible and she is the daughter of the Spirit of the West. Not in the buzzing stockmarket, not in the droning factories, not in all the halls of teeming business life does one seek her cradle, but rather in the monogamous family, in the children's room of a million homes; from the care of the housewife and mother, from the example of heads of families, from the word of the teacher and religious instructor, from the inscription of our best, is born this 'Silent Force' (de Kat Angelino 1930: 457).

While the prose, bordering as it does on the panegyric, may seem florid, the way in which de Kat Angelino describes the nuclear family as the matrix from which the transformative capitalist drive springs is clear. Furthermore, in identifying the 'unknown' nature of the individuals who are yet organized in a unity, he provides a precedent for Anderson's imagined community of nation and reveals the subordination of woman within the conflation of family and household to the 'head of family' as originating principle. Moreover, by using the term 'Silent Force', he evokes his readers' familiarity with the idea of the silent (or hidden) force of the East so powerfully rendered by Couperus in his novel, *Stille Kracht*, and thus sets up a hierarchical dichotomy hinging upon the construction of the East as the place of magical powers beyond Western reason. In de Kat Angelino's Orientalist lexicon, the East has 'soul' while the West has 'spirit'. And, in order for the Easterner to comprehend and assume the spirit of the

West, he must 'learn to see the spiritual and moral matrix[25] of the Western family' (p. 457).

It is this monogamous family (with the woman firmly tethered within it in her role as reproducer and nurturer) which enables 'the hundreds of thousand drops of saved-up capital energy' issuing from all types of people, which, when brought together, create the 'enormous energy-ocean of capital' (pp. 456–457). This is then the family that enables true (capitalist/male) individuation, distancing from the matrix (under the guidance of the head of the family), and enables alienation as a necessary stage of development not only of the self but also, and more importantly, of matter as alienable property. Without the function of alienation, within the capitalist structure it is not possible to speak of property.

It is not surprising that de Kat Angelino should refer to Schrieke's work and sum it up as an indication of the inward-looking communities dominated by *moederrecht* [mother right] which is unable to differentiate human activity into public and private spheres. This defect of matriarchal *adat* (construed as the deficient equivalent of the law – the paradox is inevitable and shows the limits of the discourse of law) works against the possibility of contractual relationships and thus militates against the originary social contract that marks the superiority of Western states.[26]

Against this picture of the nuclear family, de Kat Angelino places a description of an extended household, quoted from material on India under the British Raj:

> The Hindu home is a source of endless distraction and embarrassment. It has crushed many a spark of native fire, buried many a noble project. Poverty is not the worst of its destructive agencies, but the agitation of feeling caused by the living together of a large number of men and women, very few of whom are in sympathy with each other, and almost every one of whom has some grievance as against the rest, cannot fail to deaden energies (p. 268).

Although he recognizes that this description, written by an Anglicized Indian, is somewhat exaggerated, he follows it with a further quote:

> In the joint family no obligation exists on any one member to stir a finger if one does not feel so disposed, either for his own benefit or for that of the family; if he does so, he incurs no responsibility, nor is any member restricted to the share which he is to enjoy prior to the division (pp. 268–269).

These observations coincide with Adriani's views of the 'matriarchal' communities in the Dutch East Indies: small, non-urban, inward-looking and static communities built upon the basis of the extended household, in which there is no possibility of proper differentiation between private and public, in which there is no possibility of capitalist individuation, and which absorbs into its inchoate 'matrix' all sparks of energy and spirit. Such a view of the 'matriarchal' sees it simply as the formless receptacle that refuses to give issue to that which becomes (capitalist-legal) material. Most importantly, the drive to proper statehood takes place through the penetration of this resistant matrix by the 'spirit' which thereby liberates the individual contained within it as mere potential, and activates the process of 'social birth' into nation.

It may perhaps seem an exaggeration to hear in these passages echoes of the 'great project' Daendels proclaimed as he began the construction of the great highway that was to penetrate indigenous communities, and even more so to hear these in the New Order glorification of nuclear family and household. However, the gendered perception, always in a tangential, problematic relation to the nationalist cause, can and must engage in a different archaeology of the imagination to contemplate the implications of what lies 'beyond'.

The aversion for traditional forms of household continues with little interruption into the nationalist imagination of the Sukarno era. His *Sarinah* (Sukarno 1947) presents Bachofen's premise of matriarchy as the first instance of human social organization to remind women of the power they once had – and to some extent still were seen to have – a power they must learn to harness for the sake of the nation. As Wieringa (1995) reminds us, however, the lesson of matriarchy is not intended to empower women as women. Rather, in Sukarno's (and the socialist) view, women must learn to understand that the fight for emancipation is not for liberation from the domination of men but rather for the victory of socialism, which will ensure that women will be able to contribute to the nation without sacrificing their innate yearnings to give birth and to nurture. The happy socialist family is one in which the wife and mother is freed from the drudgery of unpaid housework. But more than this, however, Sukarno makes clear that his idea is not to restore any kind of matriarchy, nor even to dismantle the patriarchy which defeated and replaced it, but rather, in the interests of helping the woman to heal the 'rent' (*scheur*) in her psyche caused by the exploitation of her labour within the family, to rid patriarchy of its 'excesses'.

The matriarchal household cannot be a viable form of social organization because it shows itself to be a problematic basis of property. In matriarchal communities, men have no way of verifying the identity of their offspring, and thus have no way of being sure that their property will indeed pass on to 'their' progeny. This line of thinking quite clearly echoes the colonial view of so-called matriarchal households and communities as being inchoate; it also introduces the 'feminine role' in nation-building as one excised from the inward-drawing, shapeless and essentially anti-national communities, and enshrines woman in the rosy cloud of the socialist family in which only one aspect of housewifely drudgery is recognized as appropriately economic. Her reproductive organs, meanwhile, and the work done there, remain enclosed in a mysterious process beyond economics. In a very real sense, the female body cannot be fully 'materialized' within economic thinking; it must remain 'beyond' economics precisely because it entails a primary subordination of the female by the male to guard paternity, which in the myth of private property becomes the originating point for the narrative of nation.

Conclusion

I should like to return now to the quotation with which I began this essay to further the discussion of the implications of invoking possibilities beyond the current configurations of household and family. Butler makes a very pertinent point when she writes:

> Of equal importance is the preservation of the outside, the site where discourse meets its limits, where the opacity of what is not included in a given regime of truth acts as a disruptive site of linguistic impropriety and unrepresentability, illuminating the violent and contingent boundaries of that normative regime precisely through the inability of the regime to represent that which might pose a fundamental threat to its continuity. [Moreover, she warns,] ... to include, to speak as, to bring in every marginal and excluded position within a given discourse is to claim that a singular discourse meets its limits nowhere, that it can and will domesticate all signs of difference (p. 165).

If we take this warning seriously, and I feel that we must, we might pause to consider the implications of this statement on the feminist project – academic and activist – in general, and in particular, its implications for Indonesia.

There are those, of course, who might simply wish to deny the validity of this question by pointing to the dangers implicit in the philosophical complications of post-structuralist/post-modernist discourse itself as a new dominant force, tending towards extreme fragmentation of knowledge and, especially in the case of so-called Third World societies, the imposition of *fin-de-siècle* over-industrialized (and perhaps losing it) Western *ennui* and fear, upon that part of the world towards which so much of the capital and the benefits accompanying the status of 'developed First World' seem to be turning. The dangers are there, of course. There is also a distinct threat in the disturbing tendency led especially by the ASEAN countries towards a sinister cultural relativism which, in its not-so-implicit repudiation of the concept of universal human rights, appears to lend support to the post-modernist/post-structuralist questioning of the universalism and essentialism underlying the concept of inalienable human rights.[27]

However, the very hesitation that any contesting project arouses – the self-censoring mechanism that kicks in to remind us of the risks we take, and perhaps more serious, the risks to which we put others – should serve as a reminder that in Indonesia, at least, the violence of exclusion at the same time creates a forgotten space, an underground beyond the reach of its powers. And that giving voice to this forgotten space may also mean bringing it into the field of vision of a regime that practises the violence of exclusion at a very literal level. It is not only women who suffer, of course; the New Order's trail of blood does not in itself distinguish gender. But, as Saskia Wieringa's work – and the case of Marsinah, to name but one recent example – shows us, women are vulnerable at yet another level. The apparently consistent use of what we might call a mediated rape, in which objects such as corn cobs and rods replace the male's physical penis, point to a particularly violent form of abuse enabled by the ideological and phallogocentric[28] construction of subordination being female and penetrable.

At the practical level, thus, we must ask, how do we deal with all this? For the sake of 'science' do we take the risk and tactically refuse to grant names, carefully deleting referents to real locations and real people? If the scientific project is the phallogocentric naming (representation) of the objects it materializes, does withholding names – papering-over identities – constitute a first insurgent act of feminist scholarship? Do we all need to renounce our 'own' names and thereby extricate ourselves from the network (and hierarchy) of names that inscribe identity? Of course, the ironies accompanying the scholarly enterprise deny us this possibility, although it may be worth considering. But beyond this practical level we might ask, is the representation of the 'beyond' itself a project to incorporate within the regime of truth that which it has forgotten? It would be dishonest to claim to have the answer. However, the question itself may serve to make us aware of the possibility of aiding the domestication of the 'beyond' and to risk subjecting it to a violent recuperation. Representation and reconstruction of boundaries are thus eminently political acts which, in New Order Indonesia, may well constitute insurgency.

Notes

1   See for example, Nicholson (1990).

2   Laurie Sears (1996) offers a possible response to this stance.

3   This is but a selective summary which cannot present the full range of Anderson's interpretation of what he calls the 'anomaly' of nationalism (Anderson 1991).

4   Cf. Wieringa's level of the symbolic (Wieringa 1995).

5   A somewhat more detailed discussion of this is found in Tiwon 1996.

6   See Pateman (1988) who distinguishes older paternalist hierarchical structures from modern patriarchy, which is a fraternity of sons who – as the story of social contract goes – have deposed the rule of the father.

7   My depiction is based on a live television broadcast.

8   I am using the 1954 edition.

9   Section 1949; the volume is unpaginated; the original is in English.

10 This complements the analysis of 'State Ibuism' by Djajadiningrat (1987), and the 'state mother' by Anderson and by Suryakusuma, both in Sears (1996).

11 Mme Soeharto's official obituary, carried by many newspapers in the US, conspicuously lists the fight against polygyny as one of the activities for which she is to be henceforward known.

12 'Marriage is a physical and spiritual tie between a man and a woman as husband and wife with the aim of forming a family (household) which is happy and eternal on the basis of the belief in One Almighty God.'

13 It is only now becoming clear that the marriage laws also, at least in some cases, make life more difficult for village women as their sexual activity has to be subjected to interference by the numerous levels of state bureaucracy. From interviews with Nursyahbani Katjasungkana; see also, Singarimbun and Sairin (1995).

14 It is necessary also to point out an area which this depiction of nuclear family as essential household excludes and renders invisible: the servants – most of whom are women – who so often complete the urban middle-class households and are administratively recognized as members of the family/household because they must be registered in the official *Kartu Keluarga* [Family Card]. This is an example of the conflicting needs of the government. At the same time, the invisibility of household servants, outside security concerns, makes possible a distinct type of internal household exploitation of female labour. There has been great resistance to the intrusion of labour regulation through employer–servant contracts; to this date all efforts at introducing such contracts have failed. I have benefited much from discussions with Nursyahbani Katjasungkana, now of APIK, on this and other topics.

15 Also, in other government documents, often referred to as *perambah hutan* [roamers in the forest].

16 See, e.g. Danu Rudiono (Prisma 1992). Further explanation of executive procedures behind labour legislation which essentially undermine the legal hierarchy was also provided by the former head of LBH Jakarta, Nursyahbani Katjasungkana and by Fauzi Abdullah, *Lembaga Informasi Perburuhan Semarak*.

17 See, for example, Anna Tsing, *In the Realm of the Diamond Queen*, for the impact of government '*pemukiman*' policy on the Dayak as they are forced to abandon their long houses. See also *National Geographic* (February 1996) on transmigration and the indigenous peoples of Irian. There is also a growing body of NGO reports on this issue.

18 In some cases, the movement is identified with a silent programme at least bordering on ethnic cleansing. There have been many instances of the forced use of Depo-Provera (a three-monthly injection to prevent pregnancies) on often unsuspecting women. Interviews with NGO activists indicate similar cases in Eastern Indonesia and Kalimantan. Some people have said,

for example, that it is the Javanese who need to control birth, not small communities, and that therefore the blanket nature of the family planning programme threatens to shrink and destabilize peripheral populations.

19 Its success in this has been questioned; see, e.g. Mubyarto (1987).

20 See also Tsing (1993) for different conceptions of space.

21 A review of cases, and interviews with LBH Jayapura staff in 1994, for example, revealed a number of cases in which indigenous communities found themselves in direct conflict with government forces, particularly in cases involving different interpretations of land-lease contracts made with the Dutch in the times before incorporation into Indonesia.

22 Anderson (1991) uses the term 'pilgrimage' for the movement from the periphery to the centre of power as analogous to the pilgrimages to sacred places that reinforce the sense of the community.

23 Schrieke is quoting from Henry Dodwell, 'Economic Transition in India.'

24 See especially the section on 'Communist Propaganda' beginning on page 111.

25 'Matrix' as that which gives form, i.e. that 'materializes' something without itself becoming material.

26 See particularly his discussion of *adat* law, which he refuses to recognize as a legitimate *rechtssystematiek*, pp. 110–116.

27 This despite the fact that Indonesia has ratified the UN charters on human rights and women's rights, and more blatantly, despite its own colonial heritage.

28 The term is Lucy Irigaray's.

6

Beyond Women and the Household in Java
Re-examining the Boundaries

Diane Wolf

INTRODUCTION

The household has constituted an important focus of study since the 1970s, appealing to those from multiple disciplines for different reasons. As a 'basic, communal, multi-purpose, social-economic unit' (White 1980:9), the household invited economists, both neo-classical and neo-Marxist alike, and anthropologists, sociologists and geographers, all of whom drew on economics, to test their different theories about utility, work, labour, production and reproduction. At the same time, the household allowed feminists to distance themselves from the family – that very construct within which the locus of women's subordination is located and from which they were attempting to free themselves. Additionally, the household was and still is very attractive from a methodological perspective (it is visible and concrete, enabling easy access to a physically contained unit.

Our theoretical models inform, enable and also limit our ways of thinking, doing research and understanding the processes we observe. I wish to illustrate how theories of household behaviour present an excellent example of how theoretical constructs have limited our vision. In this chapter I shall highlight certain problematic assumptions that have been made in household studies generally and in Javanese household studies specifically, delineate some of the findings on women and households in Java, and examine some of the important entities beyond the household which connect with women's position within the household. I shall conclude by articulating some theoretical and empirical questions and methodological challenges to the gender and household literature.

MODELLING THE HOUSEHOLD

Neo-classical household economists have developed models that are simple and parsimonious (Hart 1992; Kabeer 1994) and in doing so, they produce a reductionist and unrealistic view of how people interact and households function. Neo-Marxist household economic models share many of these problems.

Neo-classical household economic models and the studies that drew on them conceptualized households as an undifferentiated entity that operates as a unit, with one joint utility function. This suggests that the household has its own goals, which are the same for all those within it, and that everyone faces the same fate. It assumes an 'all-for-one and one-for-all' mentality which itself is based upon a kind of selflessness and communalism. This vision of the household overrides any contemporary Western notion of autonomy, the self, or multiple selves: it merges the individual with the household as though they are synonymous, particularly in the case of women; and it reifies the household as an animate being. Individuals, particularly women, were thought to carry a household welfare gene which meant that it was simply assumed that any and every action was done with the household's welfare in mind. (To 'test' this assumption, simply think about how unfamiliar 'men and the household' sounds.)

In more Marxist approaches to household studies, there were certain similarities with assumptions found in neo-classical approaches. Households were seen as victims of structural change (e.g., erosion of subsistence agriculture to wage labour, capitalist relations, industrialization) as they struggled to survive. This predominant image again suggests a corporate unit with members sharing similar fates. Furthermore, studies of households in changing modes of production and reproduction portrayed peasants or workers as devoid of agency, or any ability to make any kind of decision or impact.

Both approaches generally missed intra-household relations of power, conflict, acquiescence, resistance and coercion. Both missed inequalities and hierarchies, disagreements, fights, violence, blow-ups, disruptions, fissures and breakdowns. The kind of intra-household cooperation and complementaries assumed in such models would mean that the harsh relations that dominate the marketplace are parked at the front door, shielding family relations from the cold winds of capitalist calculation. This romantic notion of a moral economy at home where everyone pools goods and income reflects an unrealistic utopian socialist image (Folbre 1986: 6). This image begins to fade, however, when power and the kinds of hierarchies, dynamics and conflicts that accompany it are factored in.

In the New Household Economics, the household is assumed to have one decision-maker, the paternalistic and wise father. This benevolent dictator has incorporated the interests and needs of different family members and makes just decisions with the collective good in mind (Hart 1978: 35). This assumption builds upon the problems of the previous set of assumptions. Domestic inequality, power and conflict are simply assumed away for the sake of simplicity. Father-deciders seem to have a kind of self-interest that incorporates everyone's self-interest, a dynamic not borne out by the health and nutritional data from South Asia and other highly patriarchal societies. Kenneth Galbraith points out that in mainstream economics, 'the household ... is essentially a disguise for the exercise of male authority' (quoted in Kabeer 1994: 101).

Some economists have turned to a bargaining model of the household which does not assume or require altruism or consensus in intra-household dynamics (Kabeer 1994: 109). Long-term contractual rights and obligations along with economic incentives affect decisions and outcomes. Decisions occur as the

> resolution of potentially conflicting preferences through a process of negotiation between unequals. ... The bargaining process thus generates intersecting contractual relationships between different household members, specifying their rights and obligations to each other, as the basis of household cooperation ... Attempts to renegotiate – and achieve success at renegotiation – will reflect changes in individual circumstances which in turn impinge on relative bargaining power within the household (Kabeer 1994: 109).

Thus, these models allow for unequal power within the household. The model is limited, however, by its view of 'intra-household processes in terms of strategic actions by self-interested individuals' (Hart 1992: 117).[1] Criticized by new household economists as too complex, others may find such models too limiting and confined.

Household decisions within economic models are assumed to be rational, reflecting local constraints and a calculus of household labour and capital endowments. This notion of rationality has been further reinforced by the notion of household strategies, which suggests that households are guided by a strategic rationality in their decision-making. This image inverts the previous predominant image of a more passive unit that treads water until the next wave of structural change presents challenges. Yet, it still harbours assumptions of communalism and cooperation.

Lest we dismiss these models and the unrealistic images they project as irrelevant, it is important to acknowledge the power of the field of economics and its influence on development policies. Furthermore, drawing on Naila Kabeer's work, the connection between 'ways of thinking and ways of doing' (1994: ix) are highly relevant in household studies since certain theoretical approaches have played a dominant role in development policy and programme formation in ways that privilege men and marginalize women within house-holds. The World Bank does not turn to cutting-edge anthropologists or feminist scholars for their insights on households when formulating a country project – they turn to economists or those inspired by economics, most of whom ignore the contributions of feminist studies (Deere 1995). The policy implications of the New Household Economics suggest that development programmes serve the household's interests by aiming goods and services to the household head. Since he is assumed to be altruistic and benevolent, it can be assumed that he will distribute these goods wisely if not fairly. Therefore, development programmes aimed at benefiting the household head, usually a male, or at least distributing the goods to him would, under this model, be sufficient. The definition of the household utilized by most aid organizations reflects a rigid preconception, usually based upon a nuclear family model (World Bank 1996). This image converges nicely with Indonesian state ideology concerning male and female roles within the family, particularly the notion of the male head of household and the mother-housewife.

We know from development practice that such a model ends up serving male interests while ignoring and marginalizing women. Gaynor Dawson (1995) provides an excellent example of how these economic models affect development discourse and programmes for transmigrants in Indonesia. Men are considered to be the transmigrants, the farmers, while the heads of households and household members are assumed to share common interests. The nuclear family household is the basic model and it is thought to have a wife who takes charge of the household realm. Family structure is conceptualized statically and inadequately due to male labour migration, which leaves women heading the household for periods of time.

Anthropologists, particularly feminist anthropologists, kept household studies in line, questioning the natural conflation of family with household and presenting diverse and complex forms of households. Anthropologists encouraged questions about sites of residence, production, consumption, reproduction and income-pooling, stimulating a more flexible approach to the household and a view beyond individual households as sites of primary economic functions (Wilk and McC. Netting 1984).

Feminists have also played an important role in theoretically and empirically shaking up household studies (Deere 1995). While feminist economists have problematized the unrealistic and sexist nature of household economic models (Folbre 1986), others have opened up the households' windows and doors to deconstruct it, to analyse internal processes focusing on economic contracts or transactions (Carney and Watts 1991; Whitehead 1981; Guyer 1988; Fapohunda 1988; Moore 1994). These studies have challenged certain images of automatic economic cooperation and factored in more dynamic and conflictual behaviours. They have shown that not all are equally treated or equally considered. How then do women in Javanese households fare?

Household Studies in Java

Some of the advantages and disadvantages of household studies can be seen in research done in the 1970s and 1980s in Java. Economists, anthropologists and demographers fastidiously counted and documented the labour time of household members, both children and adults in poor rural households (Hull, T. 1975; Hart 1986; White 1976), producing some very exciting material on the relationship between poverty and work, between poverty and different trajectories of childhood, and between male and female work lives within poor households. In such research, work, labour and income were the main foci and 'the household' remained the cornerstone unit, unaffected by the possibility of power differentials or conflict, as it was often limited to reacting to difficult circumstances, or calculating its labour and capital resources (Guest 1989). The ways in which Javanese culture might mediate some of these decisions within households was largely missing because households were portrayed primarily as economic actors.

Contemporary rural Javanese studies have continued the sensitivity to class differences (Peluso 1992; Sullivan 1994; Saptari 1995) but it is usually a more feminist analysis that takes the researcher inside the household. Norma Sullivan's (1994) study of gender relations among lower-class women in an urban *kampung* in Central Java is sensitive to differences between family, household and hearth hold as well as intra-household differences. And Juliette Koning (this volume) points to the increasing ideological and material 'nuclearization' of nuclear families in Central Java, helping us question internal household processes.

Contemporary studies of Javanese women also have been more sensitive to the contradictory influences of culture and ideology, upon women. Norma Sullivan (1994) carefully looks at the role of the state and other gendered ideologies in shaping urban Javanese women's beliefs and practices. Although state ideology encourages an image of the ideal woman as basically a wife and mother first rather than a worker, material needs dictate that most Indonesian women work. Although this follows a long tradition of female economic activity, such contradictions between ideology and practice are important to explore and understand (see Saptari, this volume).

In my own research, I initially followed the more economistic tradition of the peasant studies that preceded me. I had a difficult time letting go of the idea of a household strategy and listening to the discordant views I was hearing (Wolf 1992). Parents criticized daughters who did what they wanted to do, including pooling very little of their income. In my research, two factory workers complained of *tuyuls* [little gremlin, childlike spirits] stealing the money they had saved at home. They were absolutely sure that their siblings had not stolen the money due to the amount that had been stolen but I am fairly sure that some family member did take the money. These relationships do not easily add up to a united action and common goals or strategies. They suggest the kinds of turmoil that we expect in our own families but do not seem to fathom in poor Third World ones.

WOMEN AND THE HOUSEHOLD

There is clearly disagreement about Javanese women's status, their autonomy, or agency within the household. Generally, post-independence ethnographies are more sanguine about women's position and present a somewhat unidimensional image of high female status and autonomy. The 'baseline' typically used when referring to women's position or gender relations in Java comes from Hildred Geertz's (1961) *The Javanese Family* and Robert Jay's (1969) *Javanese Villagers*, whose post-independence research has had a profound (and perhaps misleading) effect on shaping conceptions of Javanese women and the family.

Their strong statements about female domination of the domestic realm and their focus on women as primary nurturers has influenced research – and as Branson and Miller (1988) argue, state policy – for the past 25 years.[2]

On the other hand, those influenced by feminist approaches to social science have approached the generally accepted view of high female status and relatively egalitarian relationships within the family more critically, questioning earlier assumptions and arguing that Javanese women are not as autonomous or powerful as was commonly accepted. While Javanese women may enjoy some economic autonomy, they may enjoy less than was previously thought, since patriarchal controls may co-exist simultaneously. Additionally, the constraints of class and poverty further limit women's lives, tainting terms used more frequently by the first two groups such as 'autonomy', 'freedom', and 'choice' (Saefullah 1979; White and Hastuti 1980; Mather 1982; Manderson 1983; Smyth 1986; Wieringa 1988;).

There appears to be little difference between male and female scholars' analyses of Javanese women in Geertz's and Jay's generation. However, contemporary female scholars tend to be influenced by feminist scholarship and thus question earlier assumptions about women's high status more than do male scholars. Female scholars today are also much less likely than male scholars to assume household cohesion and consensus and more likely to analyse intra-household conflict (MacDonald nd; Hull, V. 1975; Stoler 1976; Mather 1982; Pyle 1985; Hart 1986; Wieringa 1988; Guest 1989; Williams 1990; Wolf 1990) with few exceptions (White 1976; White and Hastuti 1980). Yet, Barbara Hatley (this volume) questions certain feminist assumptions such as the restrictiveness of the household, wondering whether Indonesian women wish for more than they have. Clearly, this argument ties into more complex issues of ideology and of questioning First World feminist notions of self and fulfilment.

Women's position within Javanese households has been examined in multiple studies, beginning with the 'classics': Hildred Geertz's (1961) and Robert Jay's (1969) study in Central Java in the early 1950s. In their books, they acknowledged women's relatively equal if not dominant position in household decision-making, particularly when compared with other parts of Asia. Although neither focused on power differentials within the family, both were struck by women's strength, their autonomy in household financial decisions, and by women's networks. Reflecting the social sciences in the 1950s and 1960s, labour, work, income or class differences did not constitute their main concerns. However they did put forth an image of domineering Javanese, if not Indonesian, women which has influenced scholarship for decades (Branson and Miller 1988) and has only recently been questioned and rethought (Errington 1990).

Such research portrays Javanese women as independent, economically autonomous, and equal if not superior to their husbands, emphasizing their freedom (Alisjahabana and Takdir 1961; Geertz 1961; Jay 1969; Koentjaraningrat 1967; Meyer 1981). A slightly different but related portrayal is that Javanese women are neither superior nor subordinate to their husbands; instead, they have hidden or different powers, and exert their influence indirectly (Koentjaraningrat 1967: 260; White and Hastuti 1980; Willner 1980; Reid 1988). A corollary to this last argument is that women's status in Java may not be equal to men's, but it is certainly better than women's status elsewhere (Wertheim 1964; Koentjaraningrat 1967).

While Hildred Geertz's useful and important book has yet to be replaced with a more comprehensive one, both she and Jay may have overemphasized somewhat the level of independence or autonomy Javanese women enjoy. I am not arguing that Geertz and Jay were somehow 'wrong', but rather, that the approach they utilized tends to ignore key points of tension in Javanese women's lives. Their approach tends to obscure such issues as women's lack of control over sexuality, women's lack of power within and beyond the household, the constraints of poverty upon women's lives, the minuscule amount of financial resources they might control, and the contradictions in expectations over women's economic market behaviour versus 'feminine' behaviour.

WOMEN, INCOME, AND HOUSEHOLD DECISION-MAKING

Both Hildred Geertz and Robert Jay point to the dominant if not domineering role of Javanese women in financial household decision-making: 'There is an astonishing degree of female dominance to be observed in everyday village life' (Jay 1969: 92; see also 61, 45, 124; Geertz H. 1961: 123(125). Jay's analysis of Javanese gender relations may reflect American gender and family ideology during a time when patriarchal relationships were the norm inasmuch as it reflects Javanese ideology, which portrays images of strong, domineering women who rule their husbands and the roost.

Researchers have pointed to control over income as an indicator of Javanese female autonomy and high status (Geertz, H. 1961; Jay 1969; Blumberg 1984). Yet while control over money is equated with power in Western culture, Javanese cultural forms of power emanate from other sources (Geertz, C. 1960; Anderson 1972; Djajadiningrat-Nieuwenhuis 1987). In fact, from an elite perspective, dealing and bargaining in the marketplace for daily necessities with the small amount of money most Javanese women have to spend is considered to be a low-status activity. Seeking refinement or being *halus* is an indication of power in Javanese culture, and it is limited to males, elite males in particular (Djajadiningrat-Nieuwenhuis 1987; Sullivan 1994: 142). A refined person would seek inner peace and harmony and not concern himself with the earthy and earthly activity of exchanging money, an activity seen as more crude and coarse (*kasar*). Indeed, Errington points out, while Westerners identify power with activity, forcefulness and effectiveness, in Southeast Asia, exerting such force or engaging in such activities demonstrates the very opposite ('a lack of spiritual power and effective potency, and consequently diminished prestige' (Errington 1990: 5). As Errington emphasizes, such economic 'power' may in fact represent the opposite of power in cultural terms, accruing lower rather than higher prestige.

However, while Errington's points are well taken, the question of power, decision-making and dominance must be further considered. Since these notions of power and refinement apply more to the elite (*priyayi*), it does not mean that all non-elite Javanese men and women are completely powerless. Micro-level power relations do exist within households and families and other groups. A rural Javanese woman from a poor household may never become *halus* within a particular Javanese cultural framework; however, she may still have the ability to control her own actions and perhaps the actions of those around her.

What then do we know about women's control over income or the household finances and how might this connect to autonomy or household power? In Central Java, Valerie Hull found that 80% of the wives she interviewed said that they tend to keep household money but a majority said that both husband and wife decide how to spend it, meaning that managing money does not mean deciding how to spend it. Like Geertz and Jay, Hull also observed that most household financial dealings are performed by the wife. Either the wife alone makes financial decisions or she does so jointly with her husband (Hull, V. 1975: 120), however, Hull also notes that in poor rural households, there is little money over which the wife can make decisions.

White and Hastuti's (1980) detailed study of household-decision making in West Javanese villages broke away from the tendency to look at inequality between households and began to look within the walls and under the roofs of these corporate units, finding inequality and perhaps disagreement among couples. They did *not* demonstrate female control of the domestic realm and showed little female input in production-related decisions. Women influenced decisions concerning food but did not dominate decisions about clothing or household utensils (p. 39). Thus while according to husbands, women controlled the household purse, they did not necessarily do so in reality. Anke Niehof's (1995) study, also in West Java, encourages us to question our assumptions that women's access to greater financial resources automatically leads to a strengthened position within the household. In the households she studied, only half of the women decided on their own how to spend the money they brought in.

Central Java is much less Islamic and patriarchal than West Java, and women may be able to make more decisions that affect other household members. In her Central Javanese research, Stoler (1976) found that women in landed households were able to control part of the production process, especially decisions regarding whom to invite to the harvest; but again, those who own sufficient land such that they can hire labourers represent an increasingly tiny minority in rural Java. In my own research in Central Java (Wolf 1992), I was surprised by the relatively autonomous economic behaviour of young village women who worked in factories. I found that young women who were not from the poorest households sought factory employment, often without parental permission, and controlled how they spent their meagre incomes. Indeed, much of their discretionary albeit tiny income was spent on themselves unless there was a family emergency. Furthermore, those factory daughters who wished to were able to have more of a say in choosing their own spouse. These young women seemed to be perpetuating and pushing at the boundaries of the traditional economic autonomy that Javanese women have experienced.

Additionally, different research methodologies may also contribute to the discrepancy in findings between West and Central Java. When respondents are asked to describe household financial arrangements in the abstract, it is much more likely that they will offer a normative account of how they think it should be. This may lead to both men and women stating that women dominate in 'holding the purse strings' (Papanek and Schwede 1988). If, however, respondents are asked about a specific financial decision, as they were in White and Hastuti's (1980) study – i.e., 'who decided the last time you bought a pair of shoes?' – they are more likely to describe the actual workings of the household.

White and Hastuti's findings suggest that caution be exercised in fully accepting Geertz's and Jay's generalizations about high levels of female control over household income. While Geertz's and Jay's views may in part reflect Javanese ideological notions of domineering women, the actual day-to-day inner workings of a household may, in fact, be more complex. This is not to say that Javanese women are powerless within their households, but rather, that they are not necessarily the all-powerful henpeckers that Jay suggests.

Popular conceptions of domineering women then may be grounded in a somewhat different reality. Women may *manage* or *budget* household income but this needs to be distinguished from *controlling* decisions about household expenditures – differences that research needs more fully to substantiate.[3] It is possible that these different financial roles may have been conflated in some research findings or that there are substantial differences between Central and West Javanese household practices. Additionally, research suggests that women are forced to earn much of what they then can manage or control. Thus images of domineering women and henpecked husbands take a different form when compared with the more likely reality that many husbands shirk or may not be able to meet financial responsibilities, leaving the question of daily income, food, and other needs to their wives (see also Saptari, this volume).

Notions of female dominance may not only mask men's sometimes shaky contributions but also, women's heavy workloads. Javanese women carry a disproportionate burden of household concerns compared with men. While Javanese men do engage in childcare, women are expected to perform almost all the household work in addition to earning income outside the household (Mather 1985: 160; Hart 1986: 129). In addition, they are responsible for procuring and preparing food daily. White and Hastuti suggest that the ideology of female dominance is but one way to keep women controlled and to justify their enormous domestic burden. Ultimately, Norma Sullivan argues (1994), Javanese women accept and perpetuate male dominance. However, such notions of agency must be understood within the context of patriarchal ideology.

Going beyond purely economic decisions, we have little information on household dynamics in general. Although individuals and families may desire *rukun*, a state that women often mediate (Cooley 1992), those of us who have done research are aware of family fights, of stories about someone running away from home temporarily to protest against an action or inaction. Do intra-household relations in Indonesian cultures and classes reflect more the complementarity assumed by some economists and propagated by the state, or the conflict depicted by feminists?

Clearly, one need not choose one side of a limited binary opposition since both (and other dynamics) may be fully operating simultaneously. Studying household relations with attention to both sources of support and conflict would be useful and also a challenge, since in some areas of Indonesia conflict and opposition are not demonstrated in a direct manner. Although most Western feminist research has focused on household conflict, it is again important to consider that households are arenas for multiple dynamics, some of which are non-conflictual, supportive, and extremely important for our research subjects. Thus, while understanding that household conflict can help us deconstruct academic notions of how households operate, we should attempt to go beyond our limited notions of what is important and include some of our subjects' priorities.

BEYOND THE HOUSEHOLD

I wish to consider also the kinds of relevant institutions, groups or resources that exist beyond the household, which affect women's position within the household; or how this position is reflected in ideology, organizations and practices beyond its boundaries. Starting from the macro-level, the state and its propagation of certain notions of womanhood have been the focus of some research. State ideology of proper womanhood projects an image of an intact nuclear family in which the father is the head while the wife and mother is a housewife, fulfilling those roles as part of fulfilling herself as a woman.

This image is very class-based, since only well-off families can afford to have the wife out of the labour force, and it is in dire opposition to the realities of most Indonesian women's lives. This image portrays a particular family structure and ignores the substantial percentage of households headed by females owing to death, divorce, desertion or migration (Hetler 1984; Guest 1989; Smyth 1993). Finally, it projects a very submissive image of women which is contrary to traditional practices in many parts of Indonesia. Indeed, this kind of submission would create an economic disaster for a woman who trades in the market, but perhaps it is also a message to the new and young industrial labour force in an effort to quell their energies.

Research has focused on how state ideology of women and the family has been enacted in various women's organizations, particularly the *Dharma Wanita* and the PKK, examining both the hierarchies in the organization, how members are recruited into the organization and the degree of coercion involved, organizational activities and the message transmitted to members (Suryakusama 1988; Wieringa 1988; Sullivan 1994). While some activities in PKK focus on increasing household welfare, they are, for the most part, housewifely and highly apolitical in orientation. The inequalities and heavy burdens borne by women in poor households are not addressed or acknowledged, in part because men and women are seen as equal and complementary.

Indeed, the realities of daily life for poorer Javanese women are that labour and work occupy most of their time. Some of this includes domestic work and other activities for household reproduction. Although patron–client ties among rural households have been explored, researchers have not yet focused on the dynamics between workers and supervisors/owners in agriculture (e.g., among kin, harvesting teams or other work groups) or in other rural-based, non-agricultural entities. For example, how family relations may intermingle with work hierarchies on a harvest work team, or in small factories (see Weix 1990). In the Taiwanese factory workshops where sociologist Ping-Chun Hsiung (1996) laboured and observed, she found that workers and managers were often related. These family relations fed into exploitative relations which workers did not feel empowered to resist or protest. Although we are aware of the longer hours rural Javanese women spend at work, at home, in the fields and in the marketplace, we have less sense of family dynamics around the question of labour allocation and self-exploitation – e.g., how sons and daughters are treated and socialized concerning such work; whether they resist, and if so, how.

In larger factories, labour relations reflect a constellation of state policies and capitalist practices accented with the flavour of particular Indonesian family relationships that get replayed between managers and workers. The reproduction of these familial hierarchies between the manager-father and his children-workers acts as a form of labour control, exploitation and quiescence. But being a father in Java means taking a protective stand towards one's daughters. When one personnel manager in my study (Wolf 1992) forced piece-workers to work into the night without providing transportation home during the rainy season, he crossed a moral line, exposing his workers to danger. They reacted as daughters might do – by withdrawing rather than speaking, by staying away rather than confronting him. Indeed, their 'stay-out' constituted a strike and forced him to change his demands. Although these kinds of relationships may be logistically difficult to observe, it is useful to push this line of questioning further, to better understand industrial work relations

Women's organizations constitute an extra-household realm that can both reflect and affect women's position within their households. Unlike *Dharma Wanita* and the PKK, which are state-run women's organizations, the *arisan* [rotating savings association] is voluntary and constitutes a rare entity in Indonesia. While villagers and workers may use it to accumulate sums of capital they could otherwise not save up; the urban elite utilizes the *arisan* to buy cars and other expensive commodities. In my research, I found that the *arisan* was the most important outcome of factory employment. It allowed workers to save substantial amounts of capital, which not only helped them accrue prestige at home as gift-givers, but also allowed them to help out during family emergencies and crises, providing a social security net. It also allowed some recently married women to save enough capital to build their homes, expediting their move out of their parents' homes. Thus, employees' use of this particular organization changed family structure. Over time, the *arisan* became the main attraction of factory employment. In my view, however, the *arisan*, as a means to an end, reflected an anti-household strategy as it kept small amounts of money out of circulation. Older sisters with money in their possession found it hard to turn down their younger siblings' requests for snacks or pencils; daughters found it difficult to turn down their fathers' requests for cigarettes. The *arisan* simply removed some of their money from household circulation, at least temporarily, giving workers more control over expending it once they had saved it up. This ability to save sums of capital also gave them more prestige than doling out small sums of money since they were able to buy larger and more visible gifts and investments. Research analysing *arisan*s among both the middle class and elite would provide a much-needed view from above.

Javanese women greatly rely on informal and formal networks, including and beyond the *arisan*. Ratna Saptari's focus on factory women (in this volume), their households and kin networks in East Java demonstrates the importance of looking beyond the four walls of a house or of a production unit in order to understand how Javanese households function socially and economically and how Javanese women combine factory work with domestic exigencies. She found that factory income supported the domestic unit but these inter-household ties also worked to strengthen women's position in the labour market. G.G. Weix (in this volume) deftly portrays how elite Javanese women negotiate their positions and resources and how networks are strategically created and maintained through complex arrangements based on 'social debts', thus ensuring and perpetuating their status and prestige as '*Ibu*'. Joke van Reenen (this volume) focuses on kinswomen's networks among the Minangkabau in Sumatra, who function within a matriarchal and matrilocal system. In her research and in that of Carol Davis (1995), it is clear that networks rather than households constitute a more useful focus when analysing Minangkabau social structure. In Flores, Willemijn de Jong (in this volume) examined the network of exchange among weavers which, she found, enhanced their standing both within and beyond the household.

Women consolidate their position within the household through the support and resources of extra-household relations; extra-household networks may also strengthen women's position in other realms such as the labour force. However, in order to further network analysis, we also must critically approach the concept and delineation of 'networks' as carefully as we have approached the household – how it is defined, constituted, and practised.

Along similar lines, friendship is a much-understudied topic, one that becomes more relevant as young women spend more time in schools or in large factories away from home. While extra-household organizations may provide the mechanisms for gaining status within the household, friendships provide the support women may need to encourage or sustain certain decisions. In my study, friendships encouraged and supported young women in their attempt to leave home and migrate, to seek factory employment, to purchase new forms of attire, to engage in romantic behaviour unbeknownst to their parents; basically, to push at the limits of what parents might have felt was acceptable. Through the support of peers, many of whom worked in the same factory but did not live in the same village, young women behaved in a more assertive, decisive, and forthright manner.

Clearly, there are other forms of extra-household relations or organization that are highly relevant to the lives of many Indonesian women, such as religion, the media, performance, and other topics. This list could continue, but it is perhaps more fitting to conclude with some thoughts about how to rethink the household and its boundaries.

REFIGURING HOUSEHOLD STUDIES

Although we might reject the simplicity and rigidity of certain household economic models, this does not mean that we should reject the concept and workings of households themselves. Households remain important sites of subsistence, social reproduction and daily practices, affected by the broader structures in which they are embedded. Households engage in the 'daily management of resource entitlements (Kabeer 1994: 114) and 'organize a large part of women's domestic/reproductive labour' (Moore 1988: 55). Kabeer encourages us to abandon the 'ideological baggage of the new household economics and to seek instead generalizable approaches to economic interactions between kin' (Kabeer 1994: 114).

Household studies by non-economists have been greatly influenced by household economic models and their language, if only because researchers build their work upon previous studies, many of which are grounded in household economic discourse. In recent years, the emphasis may have shifted to some extent from production and reproduction to contracts and negotiation, remaining firmly embedded in economistic assumptions, foci, and discourses, adding a legalistic twist. Additionally, the agency of poor people has been discovered, and terms such as 'negotiation' or 'renegotiation' demonstrate recognition of this agency and of poor people as social actors.

It would better reflect lived realities if we attempt to move away from the naturalized and normalized language of economics, law and politics when studying the household. I am not arguing that economic resources, labour or power are irrelevant in household constellations, but rather, that we should loosen our assumptions that they are the only or most important organizing principles for our subjects. It is important to find out what bases our subjects use for defining and understanding their households. (In that regard, it would also be useful to understand what bases we use for defining our own households.)

Does the more politicized view of intra-household relations held by academics reflect in any way our subjects' experiences of household life or the changes they have experienced therein? How do householders view their intra-household relations? Can we deduce from our observations and their descriptions, that they are in fact pursuing their self-interest, renegotiating intra-household contracts, and calculating their benefits? We know what negotiation looks like when we observe or engage with Indonesian market women but what does it look like in the household? Is the household a battlefield and what does that look like? These are the kinds of questions that must be asked by critically minded scholars before adopting these laden concepts at face value.

Going beyond Kabeer's argument for focusing on economic flows, the task at hand is to observe better and track intra-household relations from multiple perspectives so that we can develop an adequate and useful conceptual vocabulary. How do poor, middle-class or elite Javanese, Sundanese or Dayak women – and here I would further differentiate by age and status between generations – deal with individual (theirs or others') or household decisions, individual needs or desires, or demands? Turning the focus to studying the 'center', the dominating classes – middle-class and elite households – or 'studying up', helps us understand social class relations and the context of poor households. We need to try and understand the meaning of decisions and changes for those involved so that we can choose and develop more fitting vocabulary to describe these interactions.

Although critical social scientists have finally granted agency to our subjects, we still do not let their priorities or their understandings of these units overly influence our conceptual and methodological apparatus. The factory workers that I studied enjoyed talking about the factory with me, but they also enjoyed talking about their friends, their boyfriends, their families, and any recent lurid stories that were circulating in the factory or the village. Making, having and spending their wage income was very important to them and eventually underwrote their families' survival. But being a factory worker was not the sole definition of their existence, of their concerns, of their hopes. Clearly, such analyses must include the role of ideology in our subjects' priorities and discourse, which can be somewhat tricky, as we take a position of knowing what they really think or really want or what is superimposed on them.

Moving towards an analysis of what our respondents find important may take us down a curious path – it may very well bring the family and kin back into focus and bring friendships into focus. Economic relationships, interactions and wages are very central and I am not suggesting they are unimportant to Javanese women or men within households. However, economic considerations may at times be much less significant to them than the nature of family relations, friendships, and other interactions and networks. In other words, researchers may be placing undue emphasis on the financial issues at the expense of social factors. Although 'the family' was abandoned for ideological and disciplinary reasons, it may figure more importantly than household studies have allowed.

Traditionally we have asked questions about how structural changes (e.g. agricultural transformations, industrialization) affect households or women (or both). A more interactive approach 'beyond the household' would encourage questioning how households or particular household relations affect extra-household configurations and processes, reversing the conventional uni-linear direction of academic questions. In my study of industrialization, I found that the presence of rural-based families in which young women workers lived affected, subsidized and fuelled industrial capitalism. It is possible that the increasingly *berani* [assertive] behaviour which young women workers displayed at home towards parents encouraged them to try it out at work and stand up to the managers. The economic support of families offered these non-migrant workers enough security to encourage them to engage in labour protests, as they dared to challenge the managers and working conditions. While this less-travelled path of questioning reverses the conventional gaze of causality, we must tread cautiously so as not to over-imbue our subjects with the agency and power greatly to change the robust and hegemonic forces of capitalism.

We need to bring the researchers' voices into our methods and writings as well. Household studies in Java (and in Indonesia more generally) tend to exclude the researchers and the importance of their adopted positions *vis à vis* those they researched. Many of us come from countries whose colonialist and/or imperialist influence in Asia affects our own desire to carry out research in Indonesia. I think that those complicated relationships need to be voiced and explored. Excluding our own voices, conflicts about research, and our own insertion into the research process creates a silent author who is transparent but has the power of knowing (Bhavnani 1988). I am not suggesting, however, that we turn our focus to ourselves, putting ourselves in the centre and further marginalizing the women we study (Wolf 1996). Bringing ourselves into the process as researchers and authors will help demystify the research and the text, a fitting task for those engaged in demystifying the household and beyond.

NOTES

1   See Kabeer (1994, chapter 5).

2   For example, Meyer (1981), in his study of the value of children in Sunda (West Java), wholeheartedly accepts Geertz's, Jay's and Koentjaraningrat's views that Javanese women hold a strong position within the household and 'verifies' that this is also true in Sunda, by speaking with some colleagues who support the view that women are the 'minister of the interior' in the family in Sunda as well. He writes 'it is quite plausible that women there [in Sunda] have a powerful voice in household matters' (Meyer 1982: 100). By using this methodology – speaking with a few colleagues, probably male –

he received similarly ideological responses which are then taken as social facts, a method that would not be acceptable for most topics in sociology or demography without some data or critical analysis.

3   Morris (1990: 106) explains that *control* involves decisions about the distribution of income and the way in which it is allocated within the household. *Management* refers to the process of implementing financial decisions. *Budgeting* refers to spending within particular expenditure categories and attempting to expend as little as possible. Thus, Javanese women may be more involved in the budgeting and management of household income rather than control over it.

SECTION III: CHALLENGING THE HOUSEHOLD CONCEPT

The three chapters in this section unequivocally contest the notion that the household is the most suitable unit of analysis when trying to analyse and understand gender relations and the dynamics that underlie them. Studies from respectively the Moluccas, Northern Bali and Sumatra demonstrate that this holds true not only for the relations between men and women, but also for the relations women have *vis-à-vis* other women.

The study of Franz and Keebet von Benda-Beckmann on 'Houses, People and Residence: the Fluidity of Ambonese Living Arrangements', shows that in Ambon co-residence is a just another strand to already multi-stranded relationships, leading to cooperation in some spheres but also functioning as a potential source of tension and conflict. Actually the demarcation principles according to which care and cooperation are given to others are not so much sharing a roof or common cooking pot, but rather dependent on status, age and gender. It is, for example, largely on the basis of patrilineal kin relationships and the principle of patrilocality that individuals are brought together as co-residential units. But once living under one roof, it depends mainly on the women who spend much time together in the house, whether this situation is to continue or not.

In her study 'Bitter Honey: Female Agency and the Polygynous Household, North Bali', Jennaway shows that women engaged in polygynous marriages usually prefer to live in separate dwellings (a place with a separate kitchen or *kuren*), but for economic reasons may be compelled to live together under one roof. If we are to understand the nature of gender relations and understand what motivates the wives and the husband, we have to look beyond the various spatial arrangements – at the different interests that Balinese women may have in the establishment or termination of such an arrangement. First wives greatly lose out when their spouses marry another woman and they will usually try to prevent this from happening. (Potential) co-wives on the other hand benefit in terms of economic security and social status. In contrast to what is often assumed, it is not so much the spouse then, but co-wives whose initiatives lead to the ongoing establishment of polygynous marriages on Bali.

As Joke van Reenen's contribution on 'The Salty Mouth of a Senior Woman: Gender and the House in Minangkabau' reveals, in the Minangkabau situation too, individual women are figuratively and literally at the centre of the so-called *rumah gadang* (or 'big house', so characteristic for this matrilineal society). This in particular applies to senior women, who continue to be pivotal in shaping domestic and kin structures in and outside the *rumah gadang*. Analysing the personal networks of women and men, then, reveals more about gender relations within Minangkabau society than studying the *pariuak* [cooking pot unit], 'household' or 'family'.

7

Houses, People and Residence
The Fluidity of Ambonese Living Arrangements

Keebet and Franz von Benda-Beckmann

INTRODUCTION

Over the past 15 years the debates about 'the household' have reached a high level of sophistication. The 'black box', as the household has been described, has been opened (Niehof 1994). Its contents have proved to be a rich variety of diverse relationships, undermining the explicit or implicit assumptions that households were so uniform and homogeneous in relevant social and economic aspects that they could serve as a useful basis for scientific analysis and comparison as well as for planning. From the side of women's studies it has been pointed out that women hold a different position in households than men. There is also general consensus now that households cannot be easily separated from the social world outside because household members have diverse relationships with persons living in other houses which may be more intensive and important than contacts with the persons within the same house. The internal and external relationships of persons living together in a house thus have been submitted to intensive scrutiny.

One of the virtues of the critique of the household concept has been to show how much variation is subsumed under this term, how varied the patterns of internal and external cooperation are, and how these change over time and throughout the life-cycle. This variation is captured by distinguishing types of households in terms of composition and authority or representational structure (male- or female-headed). The explanation of the variation in the social and economic functions of households then is usually sought in the composition of the household – or the hearthhold – and in economic and practical considerations (see e.g. Finch 1989: 25). However, the conditions under which people live together in houses and which underlie the variation in the composition of households as co-resident units, have rarely been analysed systematically.

In this chapter we shall argue that for such an analysis it is not enough to open the 'black box' and look to see what is inside; we also have to look at the black box itself, examine its physical structure and social meaning, and question the reasons for the structure and composition of co-residing people. The physical structure and social meaning of a house itself are important explanatory factors of variation in the composition of and cooperation among inhabitants. The purpose of this chapter is to examine the relationships between houses, common accommodation and cooperation in the most important aspects of social and economic life. In particular we are interested to see the extent to which residence affects gender differences. As will become clear, residence is not merely a way of locating persons and identifying them with a certain space and house as a place of accommodation. Residence also localizes economic activities, or at least the profits of economic activities; and it is a way of localizing people's political positions, rights and obligations.[1] By shifting the focus from households as the basic social unit to co-residence, we hope to contribute to the further unravelling of the concept of the household. This perspective allows for a widening of the explanations that might account for cooperation and network formation and maintenance through shared accommodation. After a discussion of the current household critiques and the implication these critiques should have for the study of residence, we shall demonstrate our approach with an analysis of residence in the village of Hila, a Muslim village on the north coast of the island of Ambon.[2] We shall address three sets of issues which together provide an analysis of residence that takes houses as such into account.

1. *Variation in the association between people and houses.* We shall start by describing the variation in residential arrangements, their stability or fluidity. We shall trace groups of people through the various houses in which they live during their lifetime. And we shall also look at different types of houses, and at their social history (Appadurai 1986; Kopytoff 1986).

2. *The conditions of co-residence.* We shall then examine the conditions under which co-residence comes about. We shall look at the legal regulations structuring co-residential arrangements, at the social structure and social relationships which lead to the formation, or termination of such arrangements, and at the strategies developed to deal with these factors.

3. *The significance of co-residence for social, economic, political, religious and ritual cooperation and organization.* Finally we approach the question of what co-residing means: In what ways is the fact that people live together in one house important to the organization of their lives? What do they do that people not living in one house do not do? What variation do we encounter here, and what are the social, legal, cultural and ecological factors that underlie these variations?

Household Critiques and Their Implications

In the recent debates about households a pragmatic-political and a theoretical line can be discerned. The pragmatic line comes first of all from politicians and administrators, from census and tax officials. The more involved the state administration became in controlling village life, the smaller the administrative units with which it dealt became. Sometimes these units had to be created in order to facilitate administration. These units were narrowed down from villages, via clans and lineages to households, i.e. a unit formed by houses and the people living in them. Like all the other units, households were seen, or deemed to be represented by a head who was typically a male, the presumed authority in the household. Indirect rule was thereby brought to the lowest level of social organization. Officials may not always have chosen the most relevant or enduring form of social organization for their administrative system. The unity of people co-residing in a house, created by this household concept, may not everywhere have been functionally very important in other social, economic, political or ritual spheres of life. Yet it was a practical choice. Households have the advantage that they tie people to territorially fixed and bounded space – thus getting rid of more or less vaguely localized and bounded units such as the family or the clan, while avoiding having to deal with each individual separately. The administrators therefore should not be reproached. They had no pretensions to elevate their pragmatic administrative unit to the analytical level. They were not concerned with theories on tribal subsistence or peasant economies or comparative analyses of co-residential units across time and space. Their task was simply to count people and to levy taxes, and the household served these purposes well. Only when they started to design economic and social policies based on the assumption of homogeneous households did they run into trouble.

Pragmatic considerations also undoubtedly played a part in the increasing popularity of the household unit for social scientists. Houses are a convenient location to gather data. Besides, the economic and political significance of more encompassing social units or categories (like lineages, clans and tribes) seemed to have faded with the increasing incorporation of local social organizations into wider political and economic networks and institutions. Rather than drawing intricate genealogical diagrams or tracing spatially dispersed members of lineages or extended families, social scientists found it easier to map households, which were more readily identifiable, if only because these had been identified by the state administration as the new building-blocks of social organization. To some extent, research – and in particular development and action-oriented research carried out under time constraints of rapid rural appraisals and oriented at the objectives of development projects – simply had to adapt to such constraints, often against better judgement.

More important, however, seems to have been the other, theoretical descent line of the household. For social anthropologists, development sociologists and economic theorists of subsistence or peasant production, the household provided a recurring frame of reference and challenge, as evidenced in Sahlins' ideas of the domestic mode of production (1974), the 'classical battle line Lenin vs. Chayanov' (Wong 1987: 15), and the assumptions and propositions of the new household economics (Ellis 1988). Although the concepts of 'peasants', 'domestic group', 'family farm' and 'household' had different connotations, the household was regarded as *the* social unit of income pooling and consumption sharing, of production and reproduction, and of joint decision-making. So strong was this functional unity of the household that it became reified and personalized: the household became an actor in that it allocated labour, it had needs and utility functions, and it pursued strategies (see Whitehead 1990).

These theories form the background against which much contemporary critical research in rural areas in developing countries has been carried out. It has given researchers concepts and propositions to test. Over the past 15 years an impressive body of ethnographical evidence and theoretical argument has been built up by social scientists and economists; researchers of gender relations in particular having made important contributions. The evidence shows convincingly that the concept of the household and the assumptions built into it were rarely empirically supported and were theoretically misleading, at best superficial. Many authors have shown that in the societies they studied, the people co-residing in a house did not always form units of income pooling, consumption and production, and they pointed at the methodological consequences for the study of production and reproduction of rural people (E.g. Cohen 1976, Elwert 1980, Evers 1984, Wong 1984, Fapohunda 1988, Wolf 1990, 1992). The assumptions of new household economics based on the household as an 'actor' have been convincingly criticized (E.g. Guyer and Peters 1987, Dwyer and Bruce 1988, Folbre 1988, Guyer 1988).

Gender studies in particular have questioned these propositions and have pointed to the divisions of labour and the power relationships within households, the differential power, needs, wishes and strategies of members of a household (Whitehead 1990; Moore 1994). The external relationships of persons living together in a house thus have been submitted to intensive scrutiny. Furthermore, the relations between (members of different) households were shown to play an important role in the economic and social organization (see Elwert 1980; Wong 1984). Consequently, it was argued, researchers must pay attention to intra-household differences and differentiation, as well as to inter-household relations and networks.[3]

What were the implications to be drawn from these critiques? One way out has been the continued search for 'fundamental' social units. If earlier understandings and definitions of the household could not be substantiated empirically and consequently flawed theories in which these understandings figured prominently, then perhaps a more narrowly defined social unit would do: the household redefined as a hearthhold, as universal social unit in which at least the most important social functions for consumption and reproduction converged (van den Berg 1997). Others have adopted a fresh perspective on social and economic organization in which households, however defined, would not a priori play a major analytical role, but would be just one, potentially important, unit within and among the wider sets of supra-individual relationships and social institutions. As Wong has argued 'the fundamental fallacy of this approach lies in its methodology – that of an analysis built around a unit defined a priori rather than analytically derived concepts that would focus on attention on processes' (Wong 1984; see also Guyer and Peters 1987). Already in 1979 Yanagisako concluded in her review that

> it seems to be more analytically strategic to begin with the investigation of the activities that are central to the domestic relationships in each particular society, rather than with its domestic groups. If we start with identifying the important productive, ritual, political and exchange transactions in a society and only then proceed to ask what kinds of kinship or locality-based units engage in these activities, and in what manner, we decrease the likelihood of overlooking some of these salient units, particularly those that do not fit our conventional notion of household (Yanagisako 1979: 186).

We certainly subscribe to such a functional approach. However, we feel that the further implications of these critiques have not been fully drawn. Despite these new approaches, the concept has shown remarkable tenacity and the most severe critics have been reluctant to discard it altogether. Through a lack of alternatives, it still seems to be taken for granted too easily that households, however generally defined, are somehow the basic units of living, however open, dynamic and stratified these units may be. They are still used as 'counting units' to forming the basis of comparisons, which begs the question of whether they are indeed the basic units or not. As long as the concept remains the point of departure for the description and analysis of social and economic life, the concept, and the empirical variations that it captures, are not made subject to systematic analysis itself.

A Residence Perspective

In the critical discussions demonstrating what households are *not*, too little attention has been given to what they *are*, namely co-residential units. While there have been many excellent studies showing the variation in co-residential units, and consequently the quite different positions which such units assume in social and economic organizations, few if any have seriously looked into the nature of the association between people and houses and asked how people find shelter, and why and under what conditions they share accommodation. To be fair, various aspects are discussed in many studies,[4] but the box itself – its size and quality, value, location and its symbolic and legal status – has remained surprisingly unproblematic. The question is what difference these characteristics could make for the constellation of people living in or moving out of the box. The house, as a spatial physical unit, is usually directly tied to and made dependent on the social boundary created by it. In most approaches, this connection is constitutive of the household as a unit of analysis, rather than becoming subject to analysis.

However, in order to study the association between people and houses, we need the analytical dissociation of houses and the people living in them. Houses are physical structures and social spaces. Houses vary in size, degree of comfort, building materials, and the amount and kind of labour required for building and maintenance. They may vary from small temporary dwellings made exclusively from local materials to large modern buildings, and from individual houses to family houses. In most societies, both physical structures and the constellations of people living within them are highly variable, synchronically and diachronically. The composition of co-residing units, their stability and social and economic functions are likely to be strongly influenced by these factors. A residence perspective, moreover, should not be confined to those aspects of residence concerned with domestic and economic life. It should also take into account the socio-political aspects of residence, e.g. residence in areas with higher or lower social status, and the localization of political rights, which may be important in the residential strategies of people as motivation or constraint (F. and K. von Benda-Beckmann 1978).

These issues have to be clarified before other questions can be addressed, for example: What is the significance of co-residential groups in different domains of social organization and in comparison with other important social units? What difference does co-residence make to social organization? From this perspective, the focus is not on a predefined unit, but on variation in co-resident groups and on the explanation of this variation: on the dynamics of residential arrangements; and on the constraining and enabling conditions under which people start or stop living together, move into other houses or build new houses – conditions which also largely structure whatever social and economic significance co-residing groups have. Finally this perspective allows us to look at the problem of housing (in)security, notably of people who are particularly constrained in their access to shelter due to social, economic or physical characteristics.

VARIATION IN RESIDENCE

1. Houses and Co-residing People in Hila

Variation in Houses

The village (*negeri*) of Hila is a conglomeration of settlements. Coming from the city of Ambon by road, and approaching Hila by the border with the neighbouring village of Wakal, one first passes through three Butonese settlements, the *kampung* of Mamua, Waitomu and Tahoku. At the western edge of Tahoku there is a complex of new government buildings since Hila became the sub-district capital in 1980, as well as the buildings of the local clinic (PUSKESMAS), the village cooperative (KUD), a post office, and a research institute on fisheries established in the 1990s. Approaching Hila proper, the residential pattern becomes increasingly dense, particularly in the village core area. The variety of housing within and between these residential areas is striking, each type of housing providing living space of different quality and embodying different construction materials and labour processes. The following categories can be distinguished (see Figure 7.1):

1. Houses made more or less completely from sago palm leafstalks, called *gaba-gaba*, and thatched with sago leaves called *atap*, varying considerably in size. Most separate kitchens are also of this type. Such buildings have an earthen floor, and rarely have glass windows. Sago material is available from the sago forests of Hila. Most adult men have the skills required to build this type of house, and it can be done by a small number of persons, though the erection of the building is usually done in large working parties (*masohi*).

2. Houses made from timber and thatched with sago leaves. These are also very simple houses with earthen floors, timbered walls and without glass windows. All the materials are available nearby. This housing type can be built with the same relatively small amount of labour as the first category. Wooden planks are usually sawed by local specialists.

3. Traditional permanent houses built upon a foundation of (coral) stones and plastered with *kapur*, a mixture of burnt coral stone and sand. The lower part of the walls are made from the same material, the higher parts of the walls are made from sago leafstalks. The roof is thatched with sago leaves. These houses usually have an open verandah, with wooden pillars supporting the roof. The materials for these houses are usually available locally: from the sea, the beach, and the forest of Hila or neighbouring villages. *Kapur*-making requires a large amount of collective labour.

4. Semi-modern houses built from coral stone and half-timbered walls. Some of those have zinc plate roofs, others are thatched with sago leaves. The construction of such houses is similar to the traditional houses; zinc roofing, however, requires money.

5. Modern houses built from bricks and cement, large structures with zinc plate roofs, representing the most modern constructions. These have glass windows and often tiled floors. The materials for these buildings have to be bought and brought in from the outside. The construction of these houses also needs construction/building specialists (*tukang*), who work with three to five assistants. But many activities can be, and usually are done by unskilled labour.

HOUSES, PEOPLE AND RESIDENCE

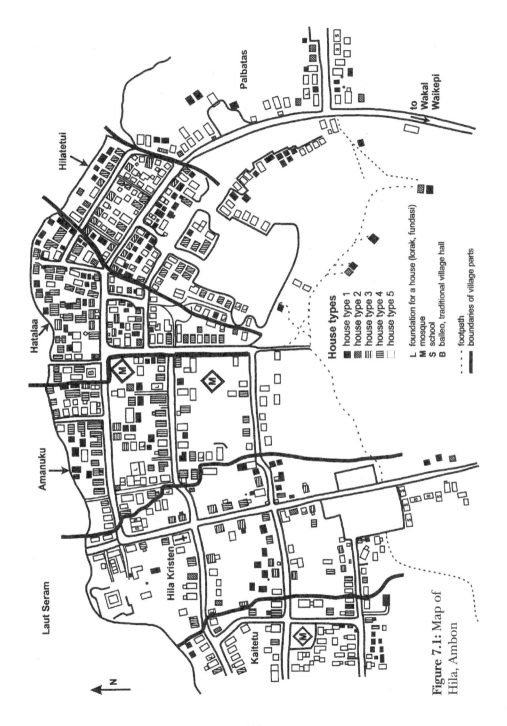

Figure 7.1: Map of Hila, Ambon

Houses of the last three categories are designed as *permanent houses*, to provide enduring residential space. It is expected that they can be repaired or partially rebuilt if the physical structure should become too weak. In contrast, most houses in categories 1 and 2, built from sago and wood, are designed to be temporary or provisional houses, serving as living quarters for a limited period of time. There may be different reasons for building a temporary dwelling. A house can serve as an intermediate home, until one's new permanent house is finished, or as a temporary additional residence for an overcrowded house. A kitchen sometimes also serves as an overflow accommodation when houses are overcrowded. An entirely different category of temporary houses are the houses for 'newcomers', such as Butonese immigrants. To emphasize that residence and resident rights are provisional, and that it is still unclear whether they will be allowed to stay permanently at that site, these immigrants are not allowed to build a concrete or stone house. This explains the high percentage of sago houses in the Butonese settlements.

The distribution of house types varies considerably between and within the four settlement areas. The core village of Hila, inhabited almost exclusively by ethnic Ambonese, was in 1985 dominated by modern stone houses or modernized half-timbered houses with zinc roofs. Some 55% of all (355) houses are of this type. 15% of the living quarters and all (71) separate kitchens are wholly constructed from sago, while 45% of the houses and all kitchen buildings are thatched with sago leaves.[5] The housing situation in the Butonese *kampung* is strikingly different: 55% of the 305 residential dwellings are solely made from sago materials, and nearly 75% are thatched with sago leaves (see Figure 7.1 above) (F. von Benda-Beckmann 1990a).[7]

Variation in the Constellation of Co-residing People

According to our sample, Ambonese houses have an average of 7.35 persons, while the Butonese average is 7.23, both ranging from 2 to 17 inhabitants for Ambonese houses, and from 2 to 14 for Butonese ones. The official statistics, however, mention an average of 8.9 for Ambonese and 4.9 for Butonese houses, but the difference is almost certainly not as large as the official statistics show.[8] There is, however, a striking difference in composition between Ambonese and Butonese houses. As Table 7.1 shows, Butonese live in two- or three-generation families, while married siblings or cousins do not live in the same house. Among Ambonese this is not uncommon: 20% of the houses in our sample are inhabited by more than one married couple of the same generation.

Nine out of the 22 Ambonese houses with more than one married couple have one kitchen. Of the houses with more than one kitchen, there are two kitchens in six houses, and three kitchens in two houses. All Butonese houses have one kitchen only (see Table 7.1).

2. The Dynamics of Residential Arrangements

The data of section 1 provide a static picture which only gives a general indication of house composition and kitchen structure. However, house composition, kitchen structure and the structure of consumptive units are flexible and change with the developmental cycle of the family members. We shall first give a brief overview of the general residence patterns during the stages of the life-cycle and then present the residential history of the family of Haji Sudin Patti and his wife Siti Manusia. If we look at individual people and families and at houses in more detail, we see considerable movement and impressive flexibility. Many people live consecutively in three or four houses in the course of their life, but may move back and forth many more times. Houses, on the other hand, see people flow through them, and in the process may change ownership and control, as will become clear from the residential history of a house described in the part entitled 'the significance of co-residence' later in this chapter.

Table 7.1: Compostition of Ambonese and Butonese houses

Composition of residents	**Ambonese** N=48	**Butonese** N=13
One couple (with unmarried children)	26	8
Three generations (max. one couple per generation)	12	5
More than one couple, same generation	3	0
Three generations (more than one couple per generation)	7	0

Life-Cycle Residence Pattern

Young children. The residence of young children is determined by adults. Most young children live with their parents, but quite a few live with foster or adoptive parents. One of the reasons for the adoption or fostering of children is that they help to take care of childless old people. The child, a granddaughter or niece, may start living with the couple long before they become needy, in anticipation of future needs. Eventually the foster child may take over the house, temporarily or permanently. Orphans are usually taken in by an aunt or uncle, or come to live with the grandparents of either side. Another reason for fostering or adoption is to take away the threat of grave sickness and death from the child. It is believed that the child will thus escape the magic and spiritual danger that surround its parents and their house. Sometimes the child stays only for a few weeks with the foster parents, but it may last much longer, and there are examples where the child stayed and was ultimately adopted. Once they get older, the children are quite free to decide whether to stay or go back to their own families, and some children happily move back and forth between the families, belonging to both. Only formally adopted children stay with their adopted family, but formal adoption sometimes takes place many years after a child has started to live with the foster parents, and thus may be a conclusion of a long-established practice. Fostering and adoption are very common. In two-thirds of all houses included in our survey it had occurred at one time. Half of all houses had at one time had one or more close relatives from the village living in as a foster child. Almost one-third of the houses had accommodated one or more high school students.

Adolescence. Adolescent children may leave their parents' home when there is too much conflict at home and stay with grandparents, other relatives or friends. Boys move around more freely than girls at that age. Sometimes it is not clear at all where an adolescent boy lives, for he may move between two or three houses. This free period ends upon marriage. If a youngster has to move out of the home village for further education, the choice has to be made between renting a room in student housing or living with relatives. Girls expressed a far stronger preference for renting a room to living with relatives than boys, because they feared being overburdened with household chores. In practice, girls did seem to do much more chores than boys.[9] In Hila many children from surrounding villages live in foster-like arrangements with Hila families (often distant relatives) during their secondary education.

Marriage. Post-marital virilocal residence after an official bride-price marriage is the culturally and statistically dominant residence pattern. But in the case of a 'take-in marriage' (*kawin masuk*) the son-in-law is more or less incorporated into his wife's clan, and post-marital residence is uxorilocal (see Cooley 1962; Van Fraassen 1972). However, residence rules and arrangements are rather flexible. It also occurs in the more common marriage form that sons-in-law move in with their wives' parents, in the expectation that they will eventually build a house of their own or move into a house of their own clan. Though polygamy does not occur frequently, there are several men in Hila with more than one wife. One of them lives with his two wives in one house, but each of the women has her own section of the house and they cook separately, their husband taking his meals and sleeping in turn with each wife. All other polygamously married women live in separate houses. Some husbands rotate among their wives, others live with one and only visit the others. For polygamous men, residence cannot always unequivocally be established.

A young couple usually starts out sharing a kitchen with the parents they live with. Slowly they become more independent. Depending on the relationship between the women, they may continue to share a kitchen, or split up. But it is not uncommon that at a later stage they may combine their kitchens again. Children may eat in either kitchen.

Divorce, widowhood and remarriage. Divorce is a reason to change living quarters for at least one of the partners. The inheritance system, though basically patrilineal, has strong bilateral features allowing for considerable independence for women. A woman may move into a family fall-back house, or go back to her parents. Sometimes she has equally strong claims to the house and it happens frequently that she stays while her husband moves out. Most younger widowed and divorced persons marry again and start a new family.

Although the tradition is for children of a first marriage to remain with the father, in practice they often stay with the mother. Step-parents often have a strained relationship with their step-children.

After the age of about 40 years, remarriage is no longer frequent, and a divorced or widowed person may move in with a widowed or divorced sibling, preferably of the opposite gender. The extent and mode of cooperation in such an arrangement vary widely. Generally it is valued that one is able to perform all tasks which a more conventional family also performs, while adhering to the gender-specific division of labour where necessary or convenient.

Old age. Most people expect to grow old in their own houses. For older people the amount and quality of help and care that they need and are able to mobilize is the main motivation for their decision to stay or move in with others. In order to secure minimal requirements of assistance in cooking and washing, they may take in relatives as foster children. Alternatively, though still controlling housing space, they will move voluntarily to another house if there is more congenial companionship, with a child or a younger sibling. When people get really old, they become increasingly dependent on others. Residence then follows their dependence, and they may not have much choice.

Case Study 7.1: A Residential History of a Family[10]

> Sudin's parents, Daud and his wife, lived in the Patti family house (*lumaela*) of the Patti sub-clan to which Daud belonged. The oldest sons Rahmad, Bail and Abdul were born there. Daud and his wife built a new house in 1928–1930, where their younger children Sudin and Aida were born. Rahmad and Abdul lived in Daud's house until they moved away from Ambon, Rahmad joining the KNIL and later moving to the Netherlands, while Abdul as a young man migrated to Jakarta. Bail remained in Daud's house, and still lives there. But he had it rebuilt after Daud's death. Sudin and Siti Manusia married in 1950. Their oldest son Gani was born in Daud's house. But Siti did not get along with her mother-in-law, and the young couple moved out into the family house where all their other children were born. Their first two sons married there and brought their wives into the family house (see Figure 7.2).
>
> Daud himself also moved for some time into the family house, while his wife lived in the new house with Bail and Aida. But later he moved back again into his own new house, where he died in 1967. When Aida wanted to marry, and her father opposed her marriage because she was to become the second wife of the (then) village head, she fled to the family house. She married nevertheless, and continued to live in the family house with her daughter. Her husband, who continued to live with his first wife, only visited her occasionally. After his first wife died, however, he moved in with Aida.

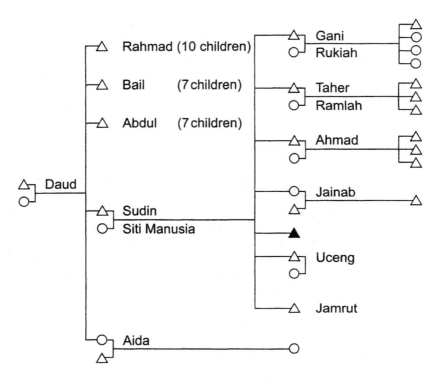

Figure 7.2: Kinship diagram of the Patti family

Sudin and Siti with all their children and two daughters-in-law moved from the family house in 1977 into their new house, built in 1977–1978. The third son Ahmad married and his wife moved in with him. The relationship between his wife and his mother was bad and in 1983 Ahmad and his wife moved into the family house where they lived until 1994. But Ahmad's eldest son frequently visited his grandparents and at times would practically live there.

In the early years in the new house, all women shared one common kitchen, Gani's wife Rukiah and Taher's (the second son's) wife Ramlah helped in the common household. Around 1980, when the first children were born, Rukiah and Ramlah established their own kitchen, built on the premises by Gani and Taher, with a separate fireplace for each of the women. Siti and her unmarried daughter Jainab continued to use the old kitchen building and cooked for Siti, Sudin and their three unmarried children. Siti and Sudin together with all their children and daughters-in-law and grandchildren slept in the main house, with the exception of Ahmad and his family. In 1986, a new, bigger kitchen was built for the daughters-in-law with one compartment for each woman.

Later that year Taher and Ramlah with their three children moved out into the house of a distant kinsman. Taher had helped much in the construction of the house and was asked to live there as long as the owner Dullah, a high civil servant, lived elsewhere (see F. von Benda-Beckmann 1987; F. and K. von Benda-Beckmann 1996).

In the early 1980s Gani and Taher had made plans to build their own houses. Gani had already selected a place to build a house of his own. But when he wanted to start building, his younger brother, a promising student at the teachers' training college, died, and all the money that had been saved was spent on the funeral. In 1986 Taher and Gani had again selected sites for their houses and thought of laying a foundation. The urge was temporarily toned down when Taher and his family moved into Dullah's house. Their departure made living in the house of Siti and Sudin more comfortable, because it had become less crowded. But a few years later, an aunt of Dullah's wife's moved into Dullah's house. Eventually the relationship between them was troubled, and Taher together with Ramlah and their children eventually moved back to Siti and Sudin.

After early retirement in the Netherlands Rahmad, Sudin's migrant brother, and his wife frequently visited Hila. They contributed to the improvement of the house of Sudin and Siti, so that it was enlarged with a kitchen and a bathroom. However, relations between the families soon deteriorated. The 'Dutch' relatives tolerated only Sudin and Ahmad, the son who had moved into the family house. Relations with Siti and her other daughters-in-law were particularly bad. Gani was ordered to take away the kitchen he had built in 1986, and a high fence was erected between the two houses. Rukiah from then on used Siti's old kitchen. When Taher and Ramlah returned to the house, they also started using the old kitchen and for some time she and Rukiah shared one.

In 1994 the only daughter Jainab married and moved to another village, but she visited her family frequently. Her son was born in Hila. After separation, she moved back to her parents and shares a kitchen with her mother. The fourth son, Uceng, also married and lived with his wife Fitria and their child in the house of his parents-in-law where more space was available. They had hoped to move into a house belonging to Fitria's family, but for some reason it did not happen. For quite some time they moved back and forth between the houses of the respective parents and in 1996 moved in with Siti and Haji Sudin more permanently. Fitria had a separate kitchen but sometimes shared one with her mother-in-law. Jamrut, the only yet unmarried son, lived in the main house. Ahmad, the favourite of their 'Dutch' uncle and aunt, built a house with their financial support, and moved out. But he maintained good relationship with his own siblings, and his brothers and brothers-in-law and other close male relatives and affines participated in the communal work (*masohi*) to help build the house, while the female relatives prepared food for the workers. In 1994 Gani also started to build a house and moved out. The foundation was laid and a simple wooden structure was erected which was to become the kitchen but served as living quarters until they had saved enough to pay for the construction of the house.

So in a period of about 15 years, at one time the whole family lived in the same house with one kitchen; at another time they were distributed over five houses, each with a separate kitchen. Mother Siti's unit consisted of eight people in the beginning, increased to 14, then reduced to five (Sudin, Siti and three unmarried children), and then was expanded again to seven or eight, and contracted to a smaller size again. Individuals may live in three or four different houses in the course of their lives, sometimes at quite different locations in the village. Daud had moved back and forth between the family house and the house he had built himself. Gani was born in his grandfather Daud's house, moved to the family house, then to his father's house, and into his own house, which may not be his last residence either. Brother Taher was born in the family house, moved into his father's house, then lived in the house of their distant kinsman Dullah, went back to live with his parents, and now eagerly waits to move into his own house. For many people it is not possible to establish unequivocally where they live during certain periods of their lives, nor is it always possible to say how many kitchens there are and who shares which kitchen. This is in particular the case for children and adolescents, but adults may also go through periods of unclear residence patterns. Polygamous men live in two or more houses. Young couples may for a considerable time move between the houses of the parents. And old widowed persons may move among relatives.

THE CONDITIONS OF (CO-)RESIDENCE

1. Introduction

The variation in houses and residential arrangements is conditioned by a number of quite different factors which together influence the formation or termination of co-residential arrangements (see also Niehof 1985: 158). Access to houses and land for house sites has its basis in *social relationships* such as kinship, friendship, foster and child–parent relationships, often created and reinforced through marriages, in the present or earlier generations. Kinship is structured by the two overlapping principles of patrilinearity and bilaterality. The patrilineal principle is the dominant one determining membership in a clan (*rumah tau* or *fam*), a landholding clan segment (*dati*), a clan association (*soa*) and the village. For most other purposes, however, villagers' kinship relations are bilateral. Also important, if less extended, are affinal relationships. The spouse's parents and their descendants are considered to be close kin. Nuclear families are called *keluarga*; this refers to parents and their children, but is also used to refer to three-generation families. These relationships, and the potential that they have for establishing residence, also have a legal basis in the *adat* of property and inheritance. Apart from membership in *dati*, which is based on patrilineal descent and ceases for women upon marriage, inheritance is bilateral. Actual access to houses and house sites is also influenced by the material and economic basis of social relationships and rights or obligations. Access rights to houses fail where houses are overcrowded; plans to build new houses are unfulfilled if one cannot acquire land or the necessary money, or mobilize the labour.

In the following sections we shall go more into the details of these different constraining and enabling factors that condition residence and variation in residence. We shall first describe the legal conditions, and then discuss the social relationships and the residential strategies of people during the various phases in the life-cycle. We then deal with the economic constraints which people may face, which also contribute to variation in residence. First the situation of Ambonese villagers will be discussed, followed by the conditions under which strangers acquire access to housing.

2. The Property Basis of Residence

Access to Residential Space

The possibilities for access to houses and rooms in houses is structured by property relationships.[11] Houses and land on which houses are to be built may have differing legal status. The legal status of houses and land defines the circle of potential claimants to housing and the circle of persons who must partake in the decisions as to who may live in an existing house, or who will be allowed to build a house and where the house will be erected. Actual access to existing housing space is largely a matter of acceptance by those living in the house. Generally speaking, upon marriage Ambonese villagers move in with close relatives. Kinship, good personal relationships with the inhabitants, as well as available space are factors that are taken into consideration. Empty houses are inherited by the descendants of the builder. If there are no immediate descendants, empty houses may also be given to more distant kin. When wanting to build a new house, people are confronted with other problems: the need to obtain the legal right to build a house on land and the need for the materials and labour for its construction. Such land can be inherited, given or bought. Less than one-fifth of all houses and house sites in the Ambonese settlement are bought, as most are either given or inherited.

The old clan houses (*rumah pusaka*) in the village centre have been clan property for many generations, often for centuries. Important decisions as to who may live in these houses are theoretically made by all members of the clan or clan-segment, but are in practice predominantly made by the male members of the oldest living generation and the residents of the house, if there are any, in particular the women of the oldest generation. Since women do more work in the house than men, and men have more possibilities to avoid each other in a house than women, the question of whether co-residing women get along with each other is more important than whether the men get along well.

A new house will obtain the status of self-made property (*perusa*) of the man or the couple for whom it is made, even though the land may be inherited property (*pusaka*). The couple may then decide who will live in the house. After their death their descendants will hold it as inherited property.

Claims to house sites depend on the status of the land. Patrilineal descent is the strongest legitimation to request allocation of a plot of land as a house site or to move into an existing occupied or empty house, but also matrifilial links are often needed to obtain permission to live in a house, as well as more distant kinship. Land and houses that have been *pusaka* for many generations have a larger circle of potential claimants than newly built houses or recently cultivated land. Usually land that is to be converted is *pusaka* of the descendants of the person who originally had brought the land under cultivation. They have to decide on such conversion and allocation. In practice the decision is taken by the men of the oldest generation. In case of *dati* land, the oldest generation male members of the *dati* group decide on actual allocation of a particular plot. Often there are trees on land envisaged as house sites. Trees may have a different legal status from the land itself; they may be the personal property of the planter (*perusa, tatanaman*) or the inherited property of a group of heirs. For example, a much valued durian tree may have been planted by the grandfather and is now *pusaka* of his male and female descendants, whereas the *pusaka* holding group of the land may go back further and is therefore much larger. As a consequence, different groups of persons may have to be involved in the decision-making process (F. von Benda-Beckmann and Taale 1996).

Conversion of agricultural land into a housing site will inevitably mean some economic loss to (some of) the larger circle of persons entitled to the proceeds of that land and the trees on it. If land is scarce in a particular lineage, permission will be given to close male relatives only. But if there is abundant land available, female lineage members and their husbands may also get permission to build a house. Conversion of home gardens in the village centre into house sites is in particular problematic for elderly women, for whom the alternative of a garden outside the residential area is too burdensome. These women have an important say in the decision about conversion, but usually they consent to the request.

In the village centre another motive for selecting a place to build a house may play a role. In former times there was a rather strict spatial division of the residential area according to the rank of clans. Members of the highest-ranking clans still consider it important to live in their section of the village, in Amanuku or Hatalaa (see Figure 7.1 above). Moving out would mean living among lower-ranking people and would cause some loss of status. In order to avoid this, the village centre has become very densely populated. However, the old status differences have lost much of their former strength, which may have made it easier for people to move out. At the same time, more people moving out, and being forced to move out, may have helped to weaken the old status differences between the areas. Many persons prefer more space, quietness and privacy, and will gladly move into an individual house in another village section, even at the cost of a slight loss of status. Besides, new criteria for residential value compete with the old status criteria. Living closer to one's gardens, to fishing places, to new economic opportunities, the road to the newly opened Higher Secondary School (SMA) and to the administrative centre and new public facilities like the Village Cooperative (KUD), the Medical Post (Puskesmas) and the post office have become more important and valued than the old criteria. Besides, new sites mostly make it possible to have a home garden close by.

Sales of housing sites among Ambonese villagers are rare in Hila, and have only started with the rapid expansion of the residential area outside the old village core and occur mainly among distant relatives.[6] Land is only sold when the buyer intends to build a *permanent* home. The sales by Ambonese which we could record involve areas in the old settlement core, which also became more crowded during the residential expansion. It involves further land which did not have *kintal* status before and was used as vegetable or tree gardens, planted with sago palms, coconut palms or clove trees. In that area, buying becomes more frequent. The area close to the road is the most desirable, and is gradually becoming very scarce (see F. von Benda-Beckmann and Taale 1996).

An important way to gain access to residential quarters is by being 'given' (*kasih*) a house or a housing site. 'Giving' can have different meanings, and includes allocations out of a common property stock. When clans become extinct, the last living members may give the land and/or house to another person or clan. In these cases land is given on a permanent basis and cannot be withdrawn. Also newcomers are often given land for houses in perpetuity. These last type of gifts create a special relationship between receiver (and descendants) and recipient (and descendants) which has many elements of a patron–client relationship. It entails the obligation of help towards the givers in a variety of circumstances: to come when one is called for communal labour, e.g. when houses are built and rebuilt, when roofs are thatched and when marriage or funeral meals have to be cooked and served. Such help is consciously seen and valued as recognition of the fact that 'they' have received their land/house from 'us'. It also calls for political loyalty – a loyalty often stronger than common clan membership.

Giving can also be for temporary use. The temporary character may be underlined by the fact that a house of a temporary type is built on the site. As long as people *numpang saja* [reside only temporarily in a sago house], the land can be used and usually no monetary compensation is asked. But temporariness may last a lifetime and such land may even be inherited. Transfers of given land or houses lie at the basis of many conflicts and uncertainties about its precise status (see F. von Benda-Beckmann and Taale 1996).

The Residential History of Houses

Houses and house sites therefore may have a varied property history. Successive occupants may live in a house on different legal bases. Inherited houses usually pass from the builders into *pusaka* of the descendants along patrilineal lines, but daughters are frequently allowed to remain in the house with their husbands, to be used by them and their descendants. This happens especially when there are already many ties with the family of the husband, because of earlier marriages between members of the respective families. The house is given to the couple, but it is not always made clear whether this is done only temporarily or on a permanent basis. Gradually, the house will be associated with the clan of the husband and eventually house and control over the house site pass on to his clan. In case of disagreement, the disputing families negotiate a settlement. Often such a settlement is reached by letting a boy and girl from the disputing families marry and live in the house. A brief summary of a house history may illustrate this.

Case Study 7.2: History of a House

> The Manusia house was on old house, built early in this century. It was located on a piece of land which had originally belonged to the Sama clan. When this clan was about to become extinct, the last living male clan member gave it to his foster child, a women from the Latu clan. She, together with her husband from a different village, lived in a house on the same site. Her daughter married Mesir Patti (Haji Sudin's father's father's brother's sister), who moved out of his father's house, and was allowed to build a house there. His wife being a Latu, he had good relations to the Latus who controlled the land. His wife, in an earlier marriage, had been married to a man from the Manusia clan and had had several children who grew up in the house of their step-father. After Mesir's death, the Patti relatives claimed the house as a Patti house. The Manusia children, adults by that time and led by Mahmud Manusia, the eldest son, refused to yield it. A compromise was reached, as is not uncommon, through marriage. Mahmud and his family would continue to live in the house, now a Manusia house. But one of his daughters would marry Haji Jamil Patti, a direct nephew (FBS) of Mesir and the major claimant. For an additional confirmation of the new relationship, Mahmud Manusia's younger daughter Siti would marry (later Haji) Sudin Patti, Haji Jamil's first cousin. The house is now considered 'a Manusia house' – it went from Sama to Latu, from Latu to Patti, from Patti to Manusia.

With the changing numbers of occupants, the social meaning of a house may also change from a regular one-family house to the family house in the sense of the centre of a larger family group. Over the years, the nuclear family for whom it was built expands and contracts, while new generations are born and start a family of their own. Sometimes the house may serve as a fall-back residence for quite distantly related individuals or nuclear families, who have not yet built their own houses, or who are unwilling to live with their parents. Sometimes temporary houses are left behind after the occupants have found a more permanent house in which to live. But house sites are becoming scarce and are not lightly given up any more. What starts out as a simple temporary house made of sago, may over time be rebuilt in wood and eventually in concrete. It may be enlarged and embellished. This process often takes decades.

3. Social Relationships and Residential Strategies

Apart from the rights to housing space or land, there are also obligations and standard preferences concerning residence, which vary according to gender and the phase in the life-cycle. In principle small children live with their parents; post-marital residence is viri- or neolocal in principle. But there are many examples in which these principles are not followed. Neither property rights nor residence rules and principles *determine* residence practices: moving in and out of houses, or building new houses, is also influenced by the nature and quality of the social relationships between people. Rules merely exclude certain options and facilitate others, leaving much room for individual choice and to negotiate agreeable living conditions.

For instance, it is an *adat* principle that the youngest son stay with his parents and take the house over eventually, but this is not always the case. In the Patti history, the older brothers often retained or took over the house. It also depends on the status of the house. While youngest sons are supposed to take over the house, it is the task of oldest sons to represent the lineage and the lineage (segment's) property, and therefore retain control over the future of the house. As far as moving out of the house also means moving out of the area in which the clan is located (in terms of the old political system), it may be the younger sons who have to move out while the oldest remain. On the other hand, old women usually prefer to stay with a daughter.

Marriage is an important event, which makes people think of moving out. But who stays and who moves out, and when, strongly depends on the quality of the relationships between the co-residing persons, on the availability and attractiveness of living space under the control of both spouses' families, and on the possibilities to build their own house. One common problem, and perhaps the greatest potential for tensions leading to young couples moving out, is the relationship between the mother and her daughters-in-law, or between daughters-in-law. It depends very much on individual personalities and their interaction whether a mother shares one kitchen with her daughters-in-law for a long period, whether some pressure is relieved by establishing separate kitchens, or whether the relationships get so intensely conflictive that the young couple moves out. It happened twice in the case of Haji Sudin.

The decision to move out depends also on the availability of space. This is not just a matter of the size of the house which they share with their parents, but also of the availability of alternative housing, such as clan houses or 'under-populated' or temporarily empty houses. As we have seen in the residential history of Siti and Haji Sudin, old clan houses function as a residential safety-valve if tensions within a house reach boiling-point, or if the parents' house becomes overcrowded. They also function as residential safety-net for people who have no normal family relationships, for example widowed or divorced old people. Such houses provide people with a temporary, interim residence; although they may end up living in the interim residence permanently until their death. Moving and building new houses not only occur when housing needs are imminent: people who have voluntarily emigrated to other parts of Indonesia or who have to live and work outside Hila as part of their professional tasks may build a house to live in after retirement. Plans to return are often rather vague and houses are in the first place built to keep open the option of returning to a comfortable house. The house of Taher's kinsmen mentioned earlier is such a case.

4. Economic Constraints for House-Building

Establishing new residence not only requires property rights to a house site; it also depends on economic possibilities and constraints. The people who build new houses are not very young and are often parents themselves. To acquire sufficient money for married couples to build a house is primarily the responsibility of the couple themselves. The cost of materials is paid either from a regular salary or wage labour such as bus driving, or from a series of good clove or nutmeg harvests. Some manage to save enough from fishing or baking bread, or from some other kind of trade. Parents will often see it as part of their obligation to help their children build a house, especially for sons. But they will usually wait until the young couple makes its own provisions, earnings and savings; then they will help (see also Hospes 1996). In families with several married sons, who are expected eventually to establish their own houses, the policy is usually that older children go before younger ones, males have priority before females, and sons before daughters. But policies may change when new circumstances call for it, for instance in the case of Taher who had the opportunity to move out to another house, or Ahmad who was supported by his Dutch relatives.

People who have selected and acquired a site for a permanent house will generally start by making the foundation upon which the later building is erected (*lorak* or *fundasi*). If there are reasons to move out quickly or before enough money is accumulated for a permanent house, a temporary house will be erected on the site. Others will wait until a permanent house can be built. There may be a period of years between laying a *fundasi* and reaching the state whereby the house is habitable. Recent increases in the price of building materials, and the drop in clove prices have greatly increased the waiting and saving period. With the village expansion well underway, people have become aware that land by the road is rapidly becoming scarcer. Many villagers secure a site by building the foundations and waiting until their financial situation improves enough to allow them to build a house. If needed, they can always, without much cost, build a temporary sago house. But for those who are absent, even a *fundasi* may not be sufficient; a complete house has to be built and some have even started to buy land to secure their position.

Temporary and permanent houses require different combinations of materials and labour. In the case of temporary houses, made from sago materials, wood and bamboo, both materials and labour can, if necessary, be acquired on a non-monetary basis. To build a temporary house, the house owner brings in his own labour force (*sendiri*), and often that of close relatives (*keluarga dekat*). Together they will prepare the required materials, sago leaf-stalks of various size, wooden poles or beams, sago-leaf roof elements, etc. To erect the house, they call in *masohi* labour, which is unpaid labour on the basis of mutual help from friends, neighbours and kinsmen, in exchange for food and cigarettes. Skilled labour is usually not needed, except perhaps for inserting wooden beams in the front wall for door and windows. Such a professional builder (*tukang*) will be paid in cash.

In the case of permanent stone houses, most building materials have to be acquired on the open market. The construction itself requires a large amount of skilled labour which also has to be paid for. The major problem thus is acquiring sufficient money to buy materials and, to a lesser extent, paying the labour. Usually a professional builder from the village is hired to construct the building and/or to supervise and direct the building process. He has usually three or four helpers. He may build the whole house with perhaps some additional help: this is called *kontrak*. But more often, he supervises unmonetized *masohi* labour. The payment which a *tukang* receives for his services varies according to his involvement in the construction process, and according to the relationship he has with the house builders. If he is a kinsman, he will usually demand less money than otherwise.

It is rare for houses to be fully built by paid labour, but it is equally rare for houses to be built without paying any money whatsoever in labour costs. Those who can afford to have a house built entirely by professionals often hesitate to do so and make sure some *masohi* is involved to show that they take social relationships in the village seriously. Teachers and other civil servants regard physical work as incompatible with their status and also rely on *masohi* labour to some extent. Both male and female relatives are invited to help: men help with the building, while the women prepare food and drinks. All buildings thus require some money to be paid for labour services, but paid labour can to a large extent be substituted by unpaid labour – one's own and that of close friends and kinsmen. *Masohi* labour, though unpaid, does require a substantial amount of cash for food and cigarettes. It is because of the expenses involved in providing food and cigarettes that the poorest cannot afford *masohi* and prefer to build a house alone or with one or two brothers or friends only.

5. The Situation of 'Strangers'

These situations and conditions pertain to villagers who have been born into the village and its web of social and economic relationships, notably property relationships. It is quite different for newcomers. As has been described in more detail elsewhere (F. von Benda-Beckmann and Taale 1992), the notion of newcomer (*pendatang*) is relative, since it is recognized that more or less all people living in the coastal village have come from somewhere else in the course of history. An important distinction is whether or not newcomers are fully incorporated into the social-political *adat* constitution of Hila through membership in the clan association (*soa*), either by individually joining a clan belonging to a *soa*, through marriage, or through acceptance of their own clan as *soa* member. In case of incorporation, land, including residential land, was in principle given for permanent use to an individual and his clan (segment). But not everybody is fully incorporated. 'Giving' of land to people not incorporated was in principle temporary and revocable, should the land need to be put to other uses. These practices continue to the present day.

An important category of newcomers is that of the civil servants. Hila, which became the sub-district capital in 1980, has seen a considerable inflow of civil servants, mainly school teachers and officials of the Puskesmas. They are in an especially precarious situation as they are usually young, often unmarried, and have a job that takes up most of their time and yet brings in little money. The government is expected to provide official housing for its civil servants, but does not live up to these expectations. Official housing is usually inadequate and building may take years. Civil servants therefore are largely dependent on villagers for living space. At the SMA in 1985, for instance, 23 of the 30 teachers were outsiders. Three married Hila spouses. They and three others have been incorporated into a clan association in Hila or the neighbouring village of Kaitetu, on the basis of their own or their father's marriage. Of the 30 teachers, 11 live in their own house and five live in an old school building which is no longer used. Six people live in with other families as foster children (*anak piara*, see F. and K. von Benda-Beckmann 1998). Two have acquired new housing, two have been given housing land, and four have rented a room. The difference between being a foster child and renting a room appears to lie in the degree to which the people can form an independent domestic unit. Single people are usually taken in as foster children, while married couples rather rent living space.

The situation is different for those newcomers who do not look for, or do not succeed in establishing residence on the basis of family or clan relationships. For them, there is no access to existing housing space; they need a site to build a house for themselves. Although there are some such cases in the residential area of Hila proper, by far the largest category of such newcomers are the Butonese living in the Butonese settlements as distinct residential and social groups. The early Butonese coming to live in Hila received land for temporary housing from the Ambonese landowners without a problem. Granting of temporary housing usually includes access to garden land (see F. von Benda-Beckmann and Taale 1992). Butonese may also acquire sites for permanent stone houses, in which case the land has to be bought from the Ambonese owners. The number of stone houses in the Butonese *kampung* is therefore an indication of how much housing land has been sold to Butonese. In all cases, there developed patron–client relationships between the Ambonese landlords/ sellers and the Butonese renters/buyers. But there is considerable variation in these relationships. The older the settlements are, and the more distant their location, the better and closer are the relationships. Not surprisingly, the oldest *kampung* Mamua has the largest number of modern stone houses on sold land (see note 8).

THE SIGNIFICANCE OF CO-RESIDENCE

In the previous sections of this chapter we gave an account of the variation in houses and co-residing people, and of the legal, social and economic conditions that underlie these variations. On that basis we want to address several questions: What is the significance of co-residence in the economic, reproductive, ceremonial and political organization? To what extent can co-residents (or 'the household') be regarded as a stable and basic unit within these domains of social organization? In what ways and how greatly does cooperation between co-residing persons vary? In dealing with these questions, we shall roughly distinguish between different functions of social organization: the production of food and other earnings; the preparation of meals, child-rearing and care of the aged; and the ceremonial activities and the position in political and administrative organization. However crude such a categorization may be, we prefer it to the conceptual straitjacket of the conventional dichotomies such as domestic/non-domestic or domestic/public, which raise more questions than they answer.[12] We shall first give a general account of economic life and organization, and illustrate this with a picture of the family whose residential history we have described earlier. We then deal more generally with different food production and income-generating activities, horticulture, commercial fishing and sago rasping, petty trade or other business, shops and wage labour. We examine how co-residence is conducive to cooperation in each of these types of economic activities. We shall then turn to more 'domestic' activities such as food preparation and consumption, child-rearing and the care of the aged. The final part of this section deals with the public sphere, notably the socio-political organization of the village and state administration at the lowest level on the one hand, and the public celebration of religious ceremonies on the other hand. We shall see how and to what extent co-residence is important in the public and political representation within the village community, as it is defined by the public administration and by local terms.

1. The Economy of *Cari*

The Moluccan rural population earns an income from many different sources. For centuries the rural economy has been a mixed one, combining subsistence production based on sago and fish with the production of cash-crops (cloves, nutmeg, coconuts) for regional, national and international markets (Van Fraassen 1972, Krause-Katerla 1986, Knaap 1987, F. von Benda-Beckmann 1990a, Taale

1991, Hospes 1996). Most people make a living from a combination of any of the following activities: horticulture (involving sago, vegetables, tubers and root crops, fruit, coconut, cloves and nutmeg), fishing, gathering and petty trade, and miscellaneous state projects or projects set up by Moluccan migrants in The Netherlands and Java. The range of activities open to individuals is great. None of these activities alone provides for a secure and dependable income, due to fluctuations on the world market for products such as cloves, nutmeg and coconut. It also has to do with seasonal characteristics of some crops, especially of sago (Brouwer 1990, F. von Benda-Beckmann 1990a). And it has increasingly to do with the unpredictable and intermittent flow of governmental projects for infrastructure and other development programmes that come and go (see F. and K. von Benda-Beckmann 1998).

These new forms of income, at times substantial but never enduring, seem to fit perfectly into the already existing economic pattern. People speak of *cari* [searching] when going to the forest to look for forest products, as well as when looking for a temporary job in a project, or selling products to the market in order to earn some cash income. This principle permeates the whole range of economic life (see Taale 1991). We therefore propose to speak of a *cari* economy. The stable incomes of the few relatives who earn a fixed salary, as well as the relationships in which relatives in the civil service may mediate, are also an important part of the *cari* system. The result is a highly volatile economic system, in which every individual kind of activity is highly insecure, but in which a certain stability and security are sought by combining many different activities, by keeping open as many options as possible, and by seizing an opportunity whenever it presents itself (see F. and K. von Benda-Beckmann 1995). Individual persons, more than families or households, search for and develop their own set of opportunities and possibilities. In order to keep options open it is important to sustain a wide range of relationships, for it is often through relationships that opportunities come up. People in general spend considerable time and energy in maintaining social relationships. Both men and women have to find a balance between individual *cari* behaviour and cooperation that is necessary or conducive to *cari*. Husband and wife develop their own network of cooperation, of which some but not all strands overlap (see K. von Benda-Beckmann 1992). They both have a fair amount of independence. As we mentioned earlier, this is enhanced by a land tenure and inheritance system that, though basically patrilineal, has strong bilateral features. As a result, both men and women have access to land of their family on their own account. As a result of the economic system of *cari* and the bilateral features in the kinship and inheritance patterns, men and women are rather autonomous and keep open many options both for cooperation and for freedom of movement and economic behaviour. To illustrate *cari* behaviour, we shall present a case history from the family that was introduced above.

Case Study 7.3: An Illustration of *Cari* Behaviour within the Family

Like many other women, Rukiah and Ramlah made and sold snacks at the roadside throughout most of the year. But during the fruit season, when *langsat* and *mangistan* were ripe, Ramlah took the opportunity to make more money than usual. In 1985 she made snacks to sell in the forest to those who were harvesting their trees and who were too busy to cook. From the money earned she bought fruit to sell in the market in Ambon city. However, she did not go to the market herself, for that would take at least half a day if not more and she could not spare the time, because she had to cook, do some cleaning and take care of her children when she came home. In the evening she would start making new snacks and leave in the morning for the forest on a new round of selling and buying fruit. Rukiah, who was pregnant at that time and who did not like to go to the forest as much as her sister-in-law anyway, also made snacks, but far less than Ramlah. She sold these along the roadside, to people on their way to or from the forest, and bought some fruit. She could also keep an eye on her own small children. The children of Ramlah stayed around the house under the supervision of Nurya, a niece who lived next door. Ramlah's husband Taher could not look after the children, for he was busy building a house. Besides, he had little patience and was not very dependable with his children. His sister Jainab worked for us and was not available either. Otherwise she would have taken the children under her care. Mother-in-law Siti was not available either, because she went to town to sell the fruit.

Siti liked to go to town and was clever at negotiating a good price, so she usually went to the market. Rukiah, who did not like to go to Ambon at all, never went, but Ramlah did occasionally, sometimes taking along fruit for her sister as well. Usually Siti would sell the fruits she had collected plus those of her daughters-in-law. She would spend the night outside on the terrace in order not to miss the first minibus that left between 1 and 2 o'clock in the morning. If she arrived at the market before 4 o'clock, she would be able to sell the whole lot to a retailer and be back by noon. If she arrived later, she would have to spend the whole day at the market and sell the fruit herself. That would be much more tiresome and get her home by the end of the afternoon, where a hungry son would be waiting for her to prepare an evening meal. Sometimes she would again go to the market the next day, but the regular work at home also had to be fitted into her schedule and she was not as strong as she used to be.

Ahmad, who was a good tree climber, helped his mother to pick her trees. This is men's work, although a few women claimed they could and sometimes did climb trees as well. If trees, planted by an ancestor and thus owned by the whole family, were ready to be harvested, men and women of each of the branches of descendants would go to the forest together and harvest jointly. This was always a fun occasion with a lot of laughing and screaming. Children were very keen on joining this family outing, because they were allowed to gather and sell their own fruit and keep the money. Parents would carefully keep their children's fruit apart. Rukiah, for example, sold the fruit gathered by her eldest son, together with her own, and made sure he got his money.

Men hardly participated in this fruit-selling business. They did not usually bring fruit to the market, but left this to the women. The profits were kept by the women, who were in charge of the money anyway. These weeks of harvest were extremely busy and women would only get a few hours of sleep a night. But they all felt they should not miss this opportunity, for one was never sure when the next good harvest would be, as *mangistan* and *langsat* have a cycle of three years. Though there was some variation in the season throughout the island, in the peak period the market was flooded with the same fruit, and prices would drop accordingly. The best period was when fruits were not yet ripe elsewhere or had already been harvested. In the main period, a hard day's work brought Siti a profit of no more than 2,000–3,000 *rupiah*, which represented 10–15% of the turnover. The fruit trade was relatively new, for it had only become possible to sell fruit at the market of Ambon after the road had been constructed in the 1970s and buses served as transport. Women had profited in particular from this road, since it meant they no longer had to rely on men to carry the fruit to the market. It had opened a new source of income for them.

Members of the family cooperated in various ways on other occasions as well. For example, the brothers sometimes went out to fish together. When the men caught so much fish that they could not eat or sell all of it the same day, the fish would have to be fried or smoked, so that it could be sold the next day or the day after that. The men would provide banana leaves and the sticks to spear the fish, while all women would sit together, usually with two fires, one for Siti and one for the two daughters-in-law and do the cooking. The next day each woman would sell her own portion. The times when the men would catch a great amount of fish were rare and when this occurred, everything else was put aside to prepare the fish. Ramlah, who at that time had more energy that the others, would still make her snacks at night and sell both fish and snacks the next day. These decisions are made individually, and depend on personal preferences, energy and need for cash.

Rukiah and her husband Gani together kept a vegetable garden on her family land. Her brother and sister-in-law, from the same clan as her husband, who lived next door, had a garden bordering on their garden. The men had fenced their gardens together and the women often went together to work in it or to fetch some vegetables or tubers. Ramlah and

Taher did not enjoy gardening and did not have one. Siti and Haji Sudin worked a plot of land next to the house of the 'Dutch' brother, and kept a garden with ground-nuts a few kilometres further down the main road to Ambon, where Haji Sudin's family owned land.

After Ramlah and Taher moved to the house of their distant cousin Dullah, which Taher had helped to build, Ramlah stopped cooperating with her mother- and sister-in-law. From then on, Ramlah and Taher started to sell ice-sticks which they made in a refrigerator bought by Dullah (F. von Benda-Beckmann 1987). Living in the house of Dullah meant that they were to cooperate mostly with his family, several of whom came to fetch a bucket of ice-sticks every day to sell to schoolchildren. Rukiah's eldest son Mahmud, aged 6, was also among the sellers. He was allowed to keep the money but it was agreed that he would use it for school utensils.

The example shows the variety of *cari* behaviour and the cooperation it involves. Ramlah took the opportunity to earn more than usual during the fruit season, by selling snacks and buying fruits to be resold at the market in Ambon. She did this in some form of collaboration with her mother-in-law. Building the house of Dullah had been a good opportunity for Taher to earn extra income. It also secured living quarters for him, his wife and children. But when she moved into Dullah's house, Ramlah ceased, temporarily, to cooperate closely with her mother-in-law.

The three elder brothers often processed sago together, but would take their sago into their respective kitchens. Whom they worked with largely depended on the property rights to the sago palms and the labour and sharing arrangements. They would sometimes give sago to other people living in their house, but also to relatives, friends or neighbours living in other houses (see F. von Benda-Beckmann 1990a). They would go fishing either individually, or together with friends, or join a fishing team for one or more seasons. They and their parents had separate cassava and vegetable gardens but helped each other occasionally. They helped their father with his clove trees, but had recently started to plant their own trees. Each of the sons and the father engaged separately in various other income-generating activities, working occasionally in construction, etc. The women, too, helped each other occasionally in economic activities, but usually they acted separately or together with sisters and other kin, close friends, or as in the case of Rukiah, with a befriended neighbour, baking and selling sago bread, producing sweets, or making and selling coconut-rice lunches. Each picked their own inherited clove and fruit trees together with their relatives and co-owners.

The example suggests that there is a clear tendency to have stronger and more multi-stranded relationships with persons within the same house. The example also suggests that individuals have webs of relationships with people within and outside their houses with whom they cooperate, depending on the particular kind of activity. In the section below we shall discuss briefly and more systematically the main economic activities in which men and women engage and see how cooperation is structured and to what extent living in one house is important.

2. *Cari* and Cooperation

Horticulture and silviculture.

These involve a high degree of cooperation between husband and wife. Couples who have a garden usually maintain it together. The work is highly seasonal and most of the year this is not intensive. Gardens may be made on family land of either the husband's or the wife's family. Property rights to land therefore shape cooperation to some extent. The garden itself has the status of *perusa* [self-acquired] of the couple. As case study 7.3 illustrates, siblings or in-laws may make a garden on adjacent plots of land and help each other to fence or harvest it. The proximity of persons living together in one house or next door is conducive to such cooperation, but is not a necessary condition; personal preferences play as much a role here.

Harvesting trees may be done by husband and wife if the tree has been planted by them, but it has to be done in larger working parties if property rights in trees are vested in *pusaka*-owning units who will harvest together. Fruit trees, cloves and nutmeg may be harvested by men and women, but sago harvesting is an exclusively male job. Usually sago is rasped on an ad hoc basis. There are only a few professional raspers who work in stable working parties over longer periods of time (F. von Benda-Beckmann 1990a; Brouwer 1996, 1998). Co-residence, other than as husband and wife, does not establish the primary social units through which this type of work is shared, but living together in one house tends to lead to increased cooperation.

Butonese, who do not own land and are not allowed to own trees, engage in a far more intensive mode of horticulture. Most of them do not have permanent houses and, as a result, they usually live in two-generation families. Cooperation in horticulture beyond that family is rarer, since they are not forced into cooperation by property relationships.

House-building

As we have seen before, the amount and quality of cooperation in house-building depend on the type of house to be erected. If *masohi* is involved, which is the case for the great majority of houses at some stage, the husband invites the men to come and work, while his wife will invite women to help cook. Each spouse thus mobilizes his or her own network. This means that there will be a core group of couples of which both spouses will come and work, but there are also persons who are invited alone, because he or she does not belong to the network of the other partner. Selection is made on the basis of several principles. In the first place, people who share rights to the land on which a house is erected are usually invited. Property rights therefore also structure cooperation in house-building. Selection is further based on services given in the past by the hosts, or expected services in the future. A person who plans to build his or her own house in the near future or who received help in the past will be much more interested in participating in *masohi* than others. Likewise, a civil servant or wealthy person who has done someone a favour in the past will call upon that person for *masohi* when building a house. Poorer relatives will gladly participate in the hope of some service from their wealthy relatives in the future. *Masohi* is thus a means to strengthen social relationships, and to widen the scope of *cari* opportunities. In the case of house-building, all persons living in the house of the hosts participate in *masohi*. The men usually also help the house builder with other work in the house as well.

Other traders
Only very few persons live from horti- and silviculture alone, because that does not cover all cash needs. To earn the necessary cash, people engage in all kinds of other economic activities. Here cooperation is not so much structured by property relations and other considerations dominate. Only a few have permanent specialized enterprises. There are a few shops which are all run by husband and wife, one by two brothers and their respective wives. Shopkeepers have little time for other activities. Professional builders and busdrivers also have little time for other economic activities. Apart from that there are some fishing groups, with a professional fisherman as the leader, an all-male activity. Participants are selected on the basis of kinship and friendship.

Quite a few women make snacks and sell these along the roadside. This is exclusively done by women and there is considerable cooperation among co-residing women, especially mothers with unmarried adult daughters, but also among sisters-in-law. Many women prefer to cooperate with friends who live close by, but almost invariably on an ad hoc basis. And women from one house usually do not sit on the same spot in order to avoid competition, unless they are very close and enjoy each other's company.

Working as driver or ticket collector on buses, or with a professional builder, and road building and other government building projects provide men with cash-earning opportunities, on an ad hoc or more permanent basis. Many work on such jobs for a short time, until better opportunities come up. If a working party is to be formed, one often finds men who live in one house or close friends participating. They hear of the opportunity from each other more easily than a brother who lives in another part of the village.

Civil servants
These people have a special position in the *cari* economy. For them status and, in the case of non-villagers, the contractual basis of their living arrangements determine the extent and mode of cooperation. Status prevents them from going to the forest to rasp sago or do agricultural work, but they need more cash than ordinary villagers and salaries are often not high enough to cover all expenses. Therefore, they depend on having a set of clients who may provide them with services. Female civil servants and wives of civil servants often trade in cloth and clothing, the wealthier ones in gold as well. Though the salary is used to create and maintain a stock of trading goods by the wife, her husband

is reluctant to mix with her business and often has only a vague idea of the actual income of his wife. But there are examples of extremely successful economic cooperation between husbands and wives (K. von Benda-Beckmann 1992). The situation of married senior couples and young unmarried civil servants at the beginning of their career differs considerably. Senior civil servants who have no relatives in a village usually rent a house and live there with just their immediate family. But they will enter into patron–client relationships with neighbours in order to secure the necessary services and food (F. and K. von Benda-Beckmann 1995, 1998). As we have seen, young unmarried civil servants often live as foster children with the family. They are expected to contribute financially in exchange for food and laundry and other services. Such relationships often form a curious mixture of fostering and patronage, in which the higher status of civil servant is balanced by the status of an unmarried foster child.

Household income management

Generally speaking, a person who earns cash is allowed to keep it for her- or himself. There is considerable but ambivalent income-pooling between husband and wife, the wife being the keeper of the couple's income. Husbands keep their money to themselves as much as they can, which is a cause of considerable tension. It is extremely rare that the husband keeps the money of the family and to do so is regarded as a ground for divorce. Husband and wife may borrow money from each other, but this is not easily done and is always a source of tension. Children who earn money often are allowed and encouraged to keep it for themselves. Adolescents keep the money they earn for themselves as much as possible, though girls find it a bit more difficult to do so.

3. Food Preparation, Child-Rearing and Care of the Aged

Food preparation and consumption is not necessarily done together by all persons living in one house. This section will deal with private consumption only. There are many occasions in which food is consumed in larger groups, for example when large working parties are engaged to do a major piece of work, such as house building, thatching a roof, or during wedding and funeral ceremonies. These will below be dealt with in section 6.

Almost all of the houses in which more than one adult couple live have separate kitchens. Even in those cases where, for example, sago has been rasped by co-residing men, it will often be divided when the food is prepared for consumption or storage. In the example discussed above, the three married brothers who went out to rasp sago each brought their share home and gave the main part to their spouses and a small part to needy close relatives. The processing of sago for consumption or storage is sometimes but not always done together by both husband and wife, depending on whether the individual wife sees further opportunities to make money. A woman who goes to her garden sometimes brings some vegetables for her sister-in-law or mother-in-law. The most stable consumptive units are married couples with their unmarried children, or with young married children with whom they share a kitchen, but we have seen that there is much ambiguity and fluctuation as to the precise composition of such a unit.

Cooperation in childcare has its own constraints and tensions. While economic cooperation of the type that Siti, Rukiah and Ramlah engaged in is quite common, wives of brothers do not interfere with the raising of each other's children. It is considered highly inappropriate to comment on the manners of the children of one's husband's brother and to do so would cause considerable stress in the relationships among the wives of brothers. On the other hand it is quite common and acceptable that blood relatives take an active part in the upbringing of the children in their wider family. Thus a niece, and not the sister-in-law, was assigned with the task of baby-sitting Ramlah's children. And Siti's son had to wait until Siti came back from town before he was fed. His sisters-in-law would not feed him. Though it is quite common and accepted that the relatives of the husband's side engage actively in the upbringing of their nieces and nephews, this can at the same time be a serious cause for tension and ultimate disruption. Much of the disagreement between Siti and Ahmad's wife had to do with the upbringing of their children, as well as with Siti's bossiness and her constant complaints about the laziness of her daughter-in-law (see K. von Benda-Beckmann 1996).

When a person falls ill or becomes old, the first persons to engage in care are those living together under one roof. But relatives, neighbours and friends frequently pay visits, so that part of the caring work is shared by others who live in other houses.

As we have mentioned before, divorced and widowed men and women past the age of 40 often remain unmarried and continue to have their own garden and kitchen. If they do so, there is a tendency to live together with another widowed or divorced relative, if possible of the opposite gender. It does not necessarily mean that these families will then form one economic consumer unit. Rather, living together under one roof increases cooperation in many respects. They come to a pragmatic arrangement in which they share what is convenient and keep other things separate.

The situation becomes different when such people get old. If they have been living with married children, they will continue to do so. Otherwise they will come to live with one or more children who live nearby. If there are no married children in the village, women especially will live on their own as long as they are physically able to cook. They depend on the whims of their more distant relatives for care and food. Elderly men are more easily taken up, because they are not expected to cook for themselves, even though they may be physically capable of doing so. Some elderly people visit different relatives for meals on a rotational basis, anxiously avoiding the danger that their relatives would tire of taking care of them. They belong to no single consumer unit.

4. Types of Houses and Economic Cooperation

We have seen that economic cooperation and the provision of care vary greatly. The question is now how this varies with the type of houses. The example of the house of Siti and Sudin is typical for larger houses in which three generations live: a (grand)parent couple with unmarried children, one or two married children with spouse and (grand)children. There is a clear division of labour and cooperation along gender lines, but married status also plays a role. For instance, the unmarried adult children of Siti and Sudin are part of Siti's kitchen, while only married couples may contemplate establishing their own kitchen. Furthermore, in-laws cooperate economically in a way that allows for maximum independence.

The situation is different in a fall-back house such as the family house (*lumaela*), the main reason being that those living together there are more distantly related. Ahmad and his wife Jainab, and Aida and her husband live together, but each couple has its own kitchen. But Ahmad likes his aunt Aida a lot and he sometimes would pick fruit for her or coconuts to make oil. Whenever he rasps sago she gets a basket. Only in case of special affective ties may adult inhabitants decide to cooperate closely. Otherwise, each couple or single adult keeps its own kitchen, takes care of its own children, and tries to earn money on his or her own.

The extent and intensity of cooperation among people living under one roof further depend on whether close relatives and good friends live close by or not. Thus, Gani often works closely together with the brother of Rukiah, who is married to his cousin and who lives next door. They go fishing and sago rasping together and have a garden next to each other, which they fenced together. We have also seen that Taher and Gani, and Rukiah and Ramlah, worked closely together as long as they lived in one house. Moving out to a house 300 metres further down the main road ended much of this cooperation; the distance had become too great.

Temporary houses made of sago leafstalks are not meant for large families. Typically a one- or two-generation family lives there and operates rather autonomously. At the same time, cooperation between husband and wife is closer and more intensive than in larger families and larger houses. In general Butonese live in small temporary houses and cooperate mainly with co-residents. Because of their status as strangers, they have no direct access to land and houses. They need an Ambonese patron with whom they maintain relationships by various forms of cooperation and services (see F. von Benda-Beckmann 1990b; F. von Benda-Beckmann and Taale 1992).

Thus, for ordinary purposes, the type of house, as well as the contractual and property relationships to a house are important factors which shape the form, intensity and extent of cooperation. People who share a house tend to have more multi-stranded relationships and tend to cooperate more intensively than with persons living in another house. Property relationships to agricultural land induce cooperation in larger (in case of *pusaka*) or smaller (in case of *perusa*) social units. Furthermore, the *cari* economy encourages men and women alike to entertain individual networks of social relationships. There is considerable individual freedom of choice regarding whom one may cooperate with: there are constraints of property relationships; there is division of labour along gender lines; and the status of civil servants poses its own constraints on cooperation. On the other hand we have seen that the type of house poses its own constraints or possibilities upon cooperation: larger houses make more diverse forms of cooperation with persons sharing the same house possible; smaller houses lead to more exclusive, multi-stranded relations among the co-residents.

5. Political and Administrative Organization

The political organization of Ambonese villages is based on a complex mixture of Indonesian local government principles and *adat* elements. The political structure today is a combination of state government and local political organization which, in itself, has been continuously shaped by, but is distinct from, state government. *Adat* constitutional principles for centuries have been influenced by state regulation of local government and over the centuries have incorporated many regulations emanating from the colonial government.

In terms of the *adat* constitutional principles, individuals are members of socio-political groups, the clan association (*soa*), the clan (*rumah tau*) or the *dati* group. Though these groups have lost much of their earlier political significance, they still are important principles of political organization at the village level. These groups transcend or cross-cut co-residential groups, such as the village itself, the clan association and the patri-clan or clan segment (*rumah tau* or *famili*). At the lower level of decision-making within a *soa*, clan or clan segment, the family head, *kepala keluarga*, represents his dependants in deliberations and decision-making processes within these larger units. 'Family' here usually means the family of a person in the grandfather generation. Whether he and his descendants live in one house does not matter; the responsibility remains the same. If, on the other hand, two such family heads co-reside, each is the head of his family.

According to Indonesian constitutional and administrative law, people participate in political life as individual citizens, and are also represented as individual citizens through public elections at the village, provincial and national level. But for many administrative purposes, the government deals with what it considers the fundamental social unit between individuals and villages, and that is *rumah tangga* [literally 'household']. Most planning is based on statistical data of households, meaning houses and the persons living together in houses. Census officers, whose task it is to carry out census and aggregate data for the sub-district (*kecamatan*) statistics, count houses and inhabitants of houses, irrespective of internal relationships among the persons living in one house, and irrespective of systematic differences between the Butonese and Ambonese population. No distinction is made between co-residents sharing a kitchen or having separate kitchens.

In matters of land tax (IPEDA), the situation is different. Though the exact ways in which people or groups find themselves entered in the tax register cannot always be followed, the rationale is to have tax paid by persons responsible for land-holding complexes, if possible also heads of households. Property of married women and daughters-in-law is considered household property of their husbands or fathers-in-law. Sons regarded as not yet 'fully independent' are counted as members of the tax-paying unit of their fathers, whether they co-reside with their fathers or not. According to the tax register there were 132 IPEDA paying units in Hila; in the Butonese *kampung* there were altogehter 178 units; while according to the census of 1984, Hila, including the Butonese settlements, had 636 households. The tax household therefore is larger than the census household,[13] but neither corresponds with the local terms *keluarga* or *famili*.

6. Ceremonial Organization

The organization in the sphere of ceremonies differs both from the relatively rigid political-administrative structures and from the highly flexible, everyday life with its seasonally determined fluctuations and its many ad hoc forms of economic cooperation.

Ceremonies are always celebrated with meals and prayers. There is a general obligation for all villagers to come and help, and each house is summoned. There is a clear division of labour according to age and gender. At funerals, for instance, it is the task of young men to dig the grave and to gather the wood-blocks and stones required to close the grave. They also fetch water and firewood and erect the temporary shelters. Several men are sent out to rasp sufficient amounts of sago. Though it is said that all should come and help, there is some idea of representation by family, in the sense that it is acceptable if only one or two sons of a (grand)father come. Co-residence is not crucial, though co-residing children may be more readily induced to come and help than a child living separately. The men regarded as heads of a family are expected to accompany the corpse to the grave and attend the burial. In the evening (and on the third, seventh and ninth days after the burial) they are invited to partake in the prayers and ceremonial meal. Family heads here means men in the oldest living generation, irrespective of whether they live together with their children or not.

Women have to contribute food, cook and bake. There is a division of labour according to status (married/widowed/divorced or unmarried) and to age. Old women who are too weak to do the hard labour are especially valued guests, not so much because they represent their house or family, but because they represent the village community as such and add to the sense of being a community. They make the intricate dishes of glutinous rice and sit and chew betel and they are the first to be served food, before anyone else is served. Healthy old women do the bulk of the work and also represent their nuclear family and house. They usually stay long and do not eat before the male heads of families have been served during the ceremonial evening meal and prayers.

The obligations to come and work are stronger, the closer people are related to the deceased and his or her family, in terms of kinship, neighbourhood, friendship or patron or clientship. Co-resident people usually have quite different relations with a deceased person. Co-residence unites ceremonial obligations only to some extent, as those of a nuclear family or of a grandfather-headed family. Thus, in ordinary cases a man and a woman of the oldest generation both represent the house, each in their gender-specific way. Depending on the personal relationships of each individual, the input of labour and cash of specific members of the house may be greater or smaller. The plate with food that each man and woman who came to help receives as a representative of a nuclear or extended family underlines this in a ceremonial manner. But in case of doubt whether or not to go to a specific ceremony, living together in a house will tip the balance in favour of going if one co-resident has a special relationship with the hosts. In general, living in a small one- or two-generation house entails fewer ceremonial obligations than living in a larger house with more than two generations.

Conclusions

We have seen that there is considerable variation, at one particular moment and over time, in the composition of the membership of houses. We have shown that this primarily has to do with a combination of the kinship and property system and the nature of social relations among family members. To some extent, variation in the composition of co-residential units also depends on the type and size of a house, and whether it is suitable for a small family only or for more than a two-generation family. As we have shown with the histories of houses and of families, co-residence rarely establishes long-term (or structural) social, economic or political units. Co-residential units thus are not necessarily economic units, nor units of production, nor even units of income pooling. In the agro-ecological and economic conditions of Hila, with a high degree of seasonality and ad hoc cooperation in specific economic activities, the economic principle of *cari* forces and allows each individual to keep as many options open as possible. Cooperation is largely based on good relationships rather than on structural lines of authority and dependence. In ceremonial and political respects, houses do not form a unit either. To some extent, social and economic cooperation is structured by property relationships. But even property relationships do not unite co-resident family members into one property-holding unit, although tax officials would be happy if they did. Concrete property rights come into existence as a consequence of individual economic activities (*perusa*) and are not automatically extended to other persons living in the house. Or they pertain to the shared inherited property of groups of heirs who usually live in several different houses. Individual residents of a house may be, and usually are, members of various productive enterprises, participating in a wide range of social and economic activities together with persons living in other houses.

This does not mean that co-residence would not shape the ways and the extent to which people living together cooperate in different spheres. There is cooperation among some co-residents, a frequent pooling of resources and mutual help arrangements. However, the nature of cooperative arrangements are rarely equally divided among all co-residents, and may be no greater than cooperation and pooling with persons with whom one does not co-reside. Gender, status and age are demarcation principles along which care and co-operation are extended. While cooperation depends on familial or other obligations, co-residence adds another strand to already multi-stranded relationships. Co-residence leads to feelings of belonging which are likely to strengthen bonds and make the intensity of their relations greater than if the same persons had not lived together. These cannot be reduced to the feelings arising from kinship relations. Also, there are constraints evolving from a stronger interdependence of the co-residents, forcing them, perhaps often against their wills, to do things together which they otherwise would not have done. People living together within one house tend to share more social strands than others, but this does not mean that these strands are the same and equally intensive for all co-residents. And each individual has more or less intensive social, economic and ceremonial relationships with people in other houses. Distance in terms of time, space and kinship are important determining factors for the intensity of each of these strands.

The very same factors, living together in multi-stranded relations in a bounded space, also have a considerable potential for tension and conflict, which may explode any existing form of cooperation of co-residents and ultimately lead to the termination of this residence pattern. Then adolescent children move out, wives go back to their families and young married couples move into temporary houses. Gender relations play an interesting role here. We have seen that individuals largely come to live together on the basis of patrilineal kin relationships and patri- and virilocal residence. But once people live under one roof, it depends mainly on the women, and the relationships between women, whether this continues or not. One of the reasons is that adult women have less opportunity to avoid each other than men because of the gender-specific division of labour, while their relationship is already more vulnerable since they are not closely related by kin and live in a house as in-laws. Their work, notably food preparation and childcare, is more directly tied to the house than that of men, whose social and economic activities take place more often outside the house, kitchen or house yard, and who more easily can find things to do away from the house if relationships at home become strained. Thus the actual place where core activities are carried out greatly influences the potential for cooperation or conflict in relationships. The spatial dimension and the ways in which relationships and activities are spatially 'grounded' thus are important aspects to consider. This is not only a matter of 'in-door' and 'out-door' activities and frequency of contact between persons. Also the physical structure of a house provides social boundaries, and within the house it makes a difference whether or not house and kitchen are in the same building. Outside the house there are also gradations of 'social spaces', the house yard, the neighbourhood,[14] the (*adat*) village section, etc.[15]

The Ambonese situation thus shows us that a description and analysis of social and economic organization can be made without taking 'households' as the point of departure. The term 'household' does not necessarily capture the most relevant property-holding units nor units of production, redistribution, care or ceremonial organization. Even at the level of government administration, household (*rumah tangga*) means different social units. The term suggests more stability and unity than is warranted. Households may be handy for aggregating population statistics, but not for more. Policies that take the household as the central unit therefore are not likely to reach the really relevant social and economic units. The emphasis which earlier household critiques have placed on the need to study inter-household relationships besides looking into internal household relationships cannot compensate for the shortcomings of the household approach. For as we have seen in the Ambonese situation, it is rarely possible, necessary or useful to speak of inter-household relationships in the sense of a relationship connecting two whole social units. Rather it is persons living in different houses, who enter into and maintain more or less intensive relationships.

Rather than giving households, which are single abstract social units, a priori a central place in one's analytical framework, it is more fruitful to ask what the relevant social units are, and what significance co-residence and co-resident units have in social and economic organization. Approaching these questions from a residence perspective and looking into the relationships between people and houses helps us to gain more insight into the conditions under which co-residing units are formed and the variable and changing significance they have. An analysis in terms of networks of relationships, in which some strands are more closely knit than others and some relationships involve more strands than others, and of which the spatial aspect, including co-residence, is one of these strands, is more appropriate for the highly volatile economic and social system we find in Hila. Of course, there may be societies with social units which can properly be labelled households. But a general methodology must be able to capture and explain cooperation in a *cari* economy. This is all the more pressing, because a *cari*-like economy may not be an idiosyncrasy of the island of Ambon, but instead quite common for poor peasants who stand with one foot in the market economy and with the other in subsistence, and who are faced with increasing government involvement and migration.

NOTES

1   In some societies, an individual's residence in these different senses may be located in different houses or different parts of the village territory. See K. and F. von Benda-Beckmann (1978) and F. von Benda-Beckmann (1979) for these different aspects of residence in Minangkabau *nagari* [village state, village].

2   We carried out field research on rural (in)security in the Central Moluccas during 11 months in 1985 and 1986. The research was sponsored by the Faculty of Law of Universitas Pattimura and the Indonesian Institute for Scientific Research (LIPI). See for earlier publications K. von Benda-Beckmann (1988, 1991, 1992, 1996); F. von Benda-Beckmann (1987, 1990a, b); F. and K. von Benda-Beckmann (1994, 1995, 1998); F. von Benda-Beckmann and Taale (1992, 1996).

3   The extensional character of network ties, Wong argued, is as crucial to the reproduction of the individual as the inclusion principle of bounded units (1984: 61). Alderson-Smith (1984) introduced the term 'confederation of households' to indicate the spreading of sources of livelihood over several households. In addition, it has been pointed out that households, in the sense of people with a common residence who share food and a kitchen, do not form static entities, but evolve throughout the life-cycle of its members and change in composition. See Kloek (1981: 25ff), Niehof (1985: 158), Freiberg-Strauss and Jung (1988), Wolf (1990: 40ff).

4   See Bender (1967). Niehof (1985: 184), for example, has touched upon this subject, when discussing the reasons that may influence the decision of whether a young couple on Madura will live patri-, matri- or neolocally.

5   For a more detailed description of house-types, see F. von Benda-Beckmann (1990a: 170).

6   The house types were not equally distributed over the Butonese settlements. In Mamua, the oldest *kampung*, the houses of types 4 and 5 constituted 33.6% of all residences; in Waitomu 21.8%, and in Tahoku only 18.8%. On the variation of the relationships between the Ambonese and Butonese in these three *kampung*, see F. von Benda-Beckmann (1990b), F. von Benda-Beckmann and Taale (1992).

7   Official statistics are notoriously unreliable. They mention 271 Ambonese houses, while we counted 355. But they mention 365 Butonese houses, while we counted only 305. The difference between the official statistics and our findings of Ambonese houses can probably in part be explained by the fact that many temporary buildings were not included in the official statistics, though they were used as separate living quarters. We may have missed some of the illegal Butonese houses in the hills, but that probably does not account for the total difference of 60 houses.

8   This information is based on two surveys among third grade Lower Secondary School (SMP) students in two consecutive years. For more details, see K. and F. von Benda-Beckmann (1987).

9   All names of individual persons and their clans mentioned in this chapter have been made anonymous.

10   For accounts of Ambonese land law, see Van Hoëvell (1875), Holleman (1923), F. von Benda-Beckmann and Taale (1996).

11 The standard size was in the mid-1980s 15 x 20 m. The sale's agreement (*jual-beli*) is usually laid down in a document and sometimes the village government writes its acknowledgement on the document. Formal written sales contracts (*akte jual beli*) are rare and we have not come across one single example of a house site registered with a certificate (*sertipikat*) by the Agrarian Office. Prices vary according to the relationships between buyer and seller, and according to the location and what grows on the site. Usually, land to be converted into a housing site is cultivated with coconut palms, clove trees or sago. Trees are always compensated, but land may or may not be paid for.

12 For an excellent analysis of the multiple meanings of the public/private distinction, including the distinction between the domestic (private) and public spheres in feminist scholarship, see Weintraub (1997).

13 Though having a population twice as large as the Butonese, the Ambonese have less IPEDA paying units. On the one hand, this could be explained by the relatively large families and landowning units among the Ambonese when compared to the Butonese. On the other hand, however, it may indicate the Butonese need for government support against political domination by the Ambonese. The first are, therefore, more inclined to cooperate in paying tax.

14 Ambonese *adat* has rather elaborate notions about the obligations of 'neighbours' (*ahli jirah*) towards one another, and about who neighbours are.

15 As we have shown elsewhere, this is also relevant for the relationships between Ambonese landlords and immigrant Butonese villagers which vary with spatial distance, and with the settlement pattern, depending on whether Butonese live dispersed among Ambonese or, as in Hila, in spatially segregated *kampung* (F. and K. von Benda-Beckmann 1991; F. von Benda-Beckmann and Taale 1992).

8

Bitter Honey
Female Agency and the Polygynous Household, North Bali

Megan Jennaway

A thousand moustaches can live together, but not four breasts (Mandelbaum, quoted in Stephens 1963: 56).

INTRODUCTION

Analyses of 'the household' in gender and development discourse have tended to assume monogamy (Krishnaraj & Chanana 1989; Hetler 1990). This has enabled notional boundaries to be erected around the nuclear family with its occupation of a discrete physical structure defining the household space. However, many of the world's societies practise polygyny. Members of polygynous households do not always share the same physical space; separate dwellings for each co-wife are a common feature. In such circumstances, the nuclear-family-based definition of a 'household' is subverted, with implications for how terms like household 'composition', 'form' and 'structure' are to be interpreted.

This chapter does not aim to find a universally consistent definition of the household. It concentrates instead on examining the social dynamics between members of polygynous households in North Bali. The focus is upon relations between co-wives, and the importance of the household in mediating these relations. I argue that the internal social dynamics of polygynous households are inherently volatile and may threaten the household's viability. This volatility may be somewhat ameliorated by modifications to the household's physical form; specifically, by locating each co-wife in separate, independent dwellings. The form and composition of the household is thus often a critical determinant of the way women perceive and experience their polygynous situation.

While polygyny has long been an object of anthropological fascination, theoretical understandings of the phenomenon are defective in at least two significant respects. First, anthropology has generally failed to take account of the diversity of empirically informed, indigenous perspectives on the issue (cf. Rabinow 1986; Clifford and Marcus 1986). Second, it has consistently failed to acknowledge women's agency in the formation and viability of polygynous unions, particularly the initiative of junior co-wives in effecting polygynous marriages (cf. Hiatt 1980). The approach taken in both this chapter and the empirical study upon which it is based[1] is an attempt to go some way towards redressing these two deficiencies.

One consequence of failing to consider female agency, either as potential informants or as initiators of polygynous practice, has been that women's subjective experiences of polygyny, as reflected in the discourses which they construct around it, have also been neglected (Bell 1993; Connor 1995). This discussion therefore adopts an alternative approach: it seeks to explore a variety of female perspectives on polygyny in North Bali through an examination of a) the cultural construction of marriage in relation to women, and b) the personal narratives of several co-wives from the village of Punyanwangi, North Bali.

THEORETICAL OVERVIEW

In his paper on polyandry in Sri Lanka, Hiatt (1980: 583, 588) observes that the dominant theoretical perspectives on polyandry fail to consider the importance of *female initiative*. This insight is equally pertinent to much of the anthropological theorizing on polygyny to date. To redress this deficiency, I shall highlight the significance of female initiative in the formation of polygynous unions in this paper.

Polygyny is defined as marriage that involves more than one wife simultaneously. It can be contrasted with its logical antithesis, polyandry, which involves more than one husband simultaneously (Leach 1991: 95–101). Both constitute forms of polygamy (multiple marriage).

In his *Ethnographic Atlas*, Murdoch states that 87% of societies world-wide are polygynous (1967, quoted in Goody 1973: 177).[2] Anthropological theories regarding polygyny are as wide-ranging and prolific as polygyny itself. Some emphasize the presence of social indicators such as sorcery (Stephens 1963: 57; cf. Bledsoe 1993: 178) or post-partum sexual taboos (Stephens 1963: 57; Clignet 1971: 174). Others invoke demographic perspectives which stress sex ratio imbalances (Leach 1991: 97; cf. Clignet 1971: 170),[3] low fertility (see Goody 1973: 179) or migration labour (Clignet 1971: 171, 175) as possible determinants of polygyny.

Typically, anthropology has attempted to explain polygyny in terms of class or kinship. Lévi-Strauss's view (1969: 44; cf. Leach 1991) of polygyny as 'the privilege of the chief ... both the instrument and the reward of power', strongly informed the structural-functionalist orientation of anthropology of his day. Subsequent researchers tend to confirm this view of polygyny as an attribute of either powerful leaders or privileged elites (Clignet 1970: 133, 1971; Musisi 1991).

An alternative and somewhat competing view of polygyny invoked classical kinship theory. Polygyny was thought to arise in social contexts where descent is patrilineal. The corollary to this was the notion that such societies are organized around the male reproductive imperative (Leach 1971, 1991; Goody

1973; Almagor 1971 and Hiatt 1980). These kinship-based explanations for polygyny thus amounted to what Hiatt has called 'kin selection theory' (1980: 584) and comfortably intersected, as he points out, with 'parental investment theory' as advocated by the sociobiologists of the 1960/1970s.[4] What both anthropological and sociobiological theories of polygyny had in common was the desire to explain the empirical phenomenon of male wife accrual without resorting to the scientifically dubious notion of a 'male sex drive' presumed by psychoanalysis (Pasternak 1976: 63; Leach 1991: 98).

None of these theories would seem to provide a satisfactory explanation for polygynous behaviour, however, since they rely on universal models for which the empirical evidence is complex and contradictory. The class explanation for polygyny cannot be sustained, given the substantial body of evidence to show that polygyny, like polyandry, is dispersed throughout societies, rather than being confined to their uppermost strata (Hiatt 1980: 586–587). Second, neither social (the kinship argument) nor biological reproductive imperatives account for the many instances in which polygyny is not a strategy to have more children, male or otherwise. Finally, the resort to biologist constructions of male sexuality is not justified when polygyny can be readily explained in terms of the cultural construction of marriage and its alternatives, as is the case for the society around which this study is focused.

Early feminist theory tended to regard polygyny as a manifestation of the so-called universal subordination of women (Rosaldo and Lamphere 1974; Reiter 1975). The anthropological corollary to this alleged an association between polygyny and societies in which women have low social status (eg. Stephens 1963: 50–51; Krulfeld 1986). However, substantial cross-cultural evidence indicated the opposite, that 'polygyny is most frequent among cultures which invest high values in their female members' (Stephens 1963: 50; Clignet 1971: 169).

Caroline Bledsoe's study (1993) of polygynous marriages in Sierra Leone underlines the ubiquity of conflict as an element in these unions. Her analysis of the competition between Mende co-wives regarding educational opportunities for their offspring shows that 'acute social differences can flourish within a single polygynous household' (Bledsoe 1993: 188). My North Balinese data overwhelmingly affirm the importance of co-wife conflict as a key variable of the polygynous situation. In order to ameliorate conflict, Balinese husbands will try, wherever possible, to accommodate each co-wife in a separate residence. Although Bledsoe does not specify the physical positioning of co-wives and its bearing on the conflicts she describes, her work is of great value in analysing the social bases of co-wife conflict. She demonstrates that attempts to explain polygyny in terms of class alone cannot be sustained; both gender relations and co-wife hierarchies within households are equally if not more significant than social relations between households.

Asian Versus African Polygyny

British structural-functionalist approaches towards the study of polygyny attempted to distinguish degrees of polygyny among different societies. Murdoch's

1967 typology of polygyny (see Goody 1973: 177) was influential during the 1960s. According to this model, African societies are characterized by 'general polygyny', defined as a more than 20% prevalence (Clignet 1970: 17), while those of 'Eastern Eurasia' – a rather dubious analytic category covering Eastern Europe and Asia – appear to practise 'limited polygyny', defined as a prevalence of less than 20%. While these data are probably confounded by the fact that the rates of polygyny for Eastern Europe and Asia are unlikely to be assimilable, the general point nonetheless holds that polygyny is more prevalent in Africa than in Asia (Goody 1973: 176). This contrast is particularly marked in the context of Muslim cultures. Hence most systematic studies of polygyny to date have focused upon the Islamic societies of Africa (for example Dorjahn 1959; Clignet 1970, 1971; Van de Walle and Kekovole 1984; Steady 1987; Musisi 1991; Bledsdoe 1993).

Nonetheless, the prevalence of a low level of polygyny for Southeast Asian states has often been observed in the literature. Rather than attempting to account for this disparity between African and Southeast Asian societies, this chapter focuses on Balinese polygynous practice and how its impact upon women is strongly mediated by household structure, both social and material.

An Indonesian Comparison: Polygyny in Lombok

Krulfeld's study (1986) of polygyny among Sasak peasant communities on Lombok provides a useful comparison with my Balinese data. Krulfeld contrasts villages classified along a continuum ranging from traditional (*waktu telu* - Ind.) to modern (*waktu lima* - Ind.). On the basis of observed differences in a number of criteria, she argues that women enjoyed relatively high social status in traditional Sasak society, while the Islamicization of modern Sasak communities has progressively eroded women's autonomy (Krulfeld 1986: 196–97). In particular, Krulfeld notes a sharp contrast between the increasing frequency of polygyny in modern Sasak villages and its comparative rarity in traditional communities (1986: 202). She concludes by asserting a strong association between polygyny and low female status among the Lombok Sasakese (Krulfeld 1986: 206).

Polygyny in Bali

Direct comparison of this Sasak data with Balinese polygyny is not straightforward, especially since Bali is predominantly Hindu rather than Islamic. Moreover, my preliminary impressions (as yet untested) are that in Bali polygyny is on the wane among educated communities[5] (which roughly correspond to Krulfeld's *waktu lima*/modern category) and is more pronounced in rural areas (corresponding perhaps to the *waktu telu*/traditional category).[6]

Anthropologists in Bali have tended to emphasize polygyny as it occurs among the nobility (*triwangsa*)[7] (Geertz and Geertz 1975: 131–38; van der Kraan 1985; see also Streatfield 1986: 22 and Covarrubias 1989: 157), owing perhaps to its more spectacular expressions in the practice of *mesatia* [royal widow burning]. In Bali, the historical evidence indicates that polygyny was common in Bali during the Majapahit era (from the sixteenth to the nineteenth centuries) among the ruling elite. Scholars have usually explained this by pointing out that only kings and some members of the caste-bearing nobility had the economic resources (and political incentive) to support a large retinue of wives and concubines (cf. Goody 1973: 182).[8] Thus the Balinese historical record would appear to affirm the general axiom that polygyny is a function of class and/or status. However, the lack of equivalent historical evidence regarding the marital practices of the non-caste (*jaba*) peasantry for the period does not imply that it was not practised by them. The observation that the aristocracy had greater economic means to support polygyny can equally explain why the peasantry failed to produce permanent records of their own marital practices, polygynous or otherwise. I suggest that the sustained incidence of polygyny among both the contemporary commoners in my study, and their forebears, implies its origins in the more distant past.

Conflict and Hierarchy among Balinese Co-Wives

Among the aristocracy, senior co-wives were distinguished by the title *Padmi* while subsequent wives were known as *Penawing* (Geertz and Geertz 1975: 131). According to Stephens (1963: 63), it is characteristic of polygynous societies generally that the rights of co-wives are clearly defined. Within the Balinese courts (*puri*), the children of the *Padmi* (senior wife) were socially superior to those of the *Penawing*; they inherited their father's wealth and title. To ensure against any conflict of authority that might arise in the event of their mother's death, the *Padmi*'s children were attributed higher rank than that of any of their stepmothers, the *Penawing*.[9] In relation to Bali's caste-bearing aristocracy, therefore, the general ideal that senior wives retain status superiority is borne out (Stephens 1963: 63; cf. Bledsdoe 1993: 172–73).

In contrast to the nobility, co-wives are not differentiated by status terms among Bali's commoners; all co-wives are referred to as *madu*. A brief look at how the term *madu* is linguistically applied permits an insight into the ways polygyny is constructed in Balinese discourse. (*Nga*)*maduang* means 'to bestow a co-wife upon one's wife' implying a gift or a boon (cf. Clignet 1970: 292; Bledsdoe 1993: 170–72). Yet in the absence of a tradition of economic cooperation between co-wives such as has been documented for parts of Africa (Bowen 1954: 118–21; Boserup 1970), this expression appears to constitute the kind of ideological fiction – albeit indigenous – that husbands wishing to persuade unwilling wives to accept a co-wife might find useful. Punyanwangi women's discourses on polygyny do not imply that co-wives are perceived as a gift or even as a resource that enhances the quality of a woman's life. If co-wives saw each other as a boon, it might be expected that senior wives would actively encourage their husbands to acquire junior wives, which is decidedly not the case from my data. In reality, as Duff-Cooper (1985: 409) has observed for the Balinese on Lombok, 'most [senior] wives are presented with a *fait accompli*'. In other words, they neither participate in the husband's decision to take another wife, nor in her selection. This view is supported by the fact that village women usually refer to their polygynous status as *kamaduang* [being made into a co-wife], which hardly implies their support for the decision and may even suggest their outright coercion. Ironically, senior wives in Punyanwangi are usually active players in their husbands' plans to take on another wife, however their activities are invariably directed towards preventing, not facilitating, the union.

'Honey-wives': Madu

Another translation for *madu* is honey, and the analogy of extra wives with honey is often made (eg. Mershon 1937: 55). This is consistent with the many references that abound in both the *kawi* classical literature and in popular discourse likening girls to honey or flowers and men to the bees that drink of their nectar (Parker 1993; Creese 1995). This association of polygyny with sweetness, however, would seem to represent a male perspective; for many co-wives the term *madu* parodies the bitterness that it almost invariably entails.

POLYGYNY IN *DESA* PUNYANWANGI

> The Balinese are naturally polygamous and it is common for men to have lovers and for women to take the extra-marital relations of their husbands as natural (Covarrubias 1989: 157).

The data for this discussion come from the pseudonymously named rural village of Punyanwangi in North Bali.[10] *Desa* Punyanwangi is an Indonesian administrative village (*desa dinas*) incorporating two customary villages (*desa adat*),[11] *desa adat* Punyanwangi and *desa adat* Senggigi, and a third community, *banjar* Banyusing, not ritually linked with either of the *desa adat*, nor constituting one of its own.[12] My analysis mainly concentrates on data provided by the larger of the two customary villages, *desa adat* Punyanwangi, however supporting quantitative data is drawn from the entire administrative village. In 1992 *desa adat* Punyanwangi had an economy primarily dependent upon the cash-crop production of cloves, coffee and tobacco. Religious affiliation was unanimously Hindu and only two households claimed caste (*triwangsa*) status.

Methodology

A combination of three methods was employed to obtain the data. The first of these was a household census taken across the whole administrative village of *desa* Punyanwangi (population 3,577). The second method consisted in genealogical records and was confined to the customary village of *desa adat* Punyanwangi (population 2,198). Third, qualitative ethnographic data were supplied by informants from both *desa adat*. I describe each briefly below.

The household census involved 139 households, representing an approximate 20% sample of the 706 households contained in the administrative village, thus including *desa adat* Punyanwangi (450 households), *desa adat* Senggigi (140 households) and *banjar* Banyusing (116 households). This provided information on the current marital status of household members as well as the number and status of spouses they had ever had. The survey showed the prevalence of polygyny to be 10.7% (15 out of the 139 households surveyed), which is significantly larger than the average prevalence of 3% quoted for non-caste [*jaba*] communities throughout Bali overall (Streatfield 1986: 22).

The second source of data consists of 45 genealogies that I collected in the course of my research. From these it is possible to get a sense of the frequency with which plural marriages have occurred in Punyanwangi over the past three to four generations. Of the 1,350 marriages recorded, 132 were multiple in nature, i.e. involving either serial spouses or polygamy. Hence multiple (i.e. whether serial or concurrent) marriages constituted approximately 10% of the total listed in the genealogies (Table 8.1). It should be noted, however, that only 60 of these 132 multiple marriages, or less than 45%, are actually polygynous, the others being serial. This finding is thus significantly lower than the results indicated by my household survey.[13] However, ascertaining the precise demographic frequency of polygyny in Punyanwangi is not my concern here: it is sufficient simply to note that polygyny occurs frequently enough for it to constitute a genuine marital possibility for village women.

Table 8.1: Comparison between male and female marriage destinies in *desa adat* Punyanwangi (genealogical data)

Type of marriage	Serial	Polygamous	Total
Women	57	0	57
Men	15	60	75
Total	72	60	132

Given the statistical overlapping between different but related families, the genealogical data cannot claim quantitative rigour. What they do provide is abundant direct evidence of the occurrence of polygyny within the village community, both now and in the past.[14]

The third and most important source of data for this discussion – ethnographic observations and accounts supplied by first-hand informants – again makes no claims to representativeness. However, by dint of anthropological serendipity, I was closely associated with several women who themselves were co-wives in polygynous unions. From this privileged proximity, polygyny – or the threat thereof – loomed large in village women's lives.

Defining the 'Household'

In order to incorporate the largest number of possible married couples (or triples etc. in the case of polygynous marriages), the Indonesian definition of household (*rumah keluarga* – Ind.) was used. According to this definition, a household consists of no more than one household head (*kepala keluarga* – Ind.) (defined as male) and is thus nuclear-family oriented. By contrast, the Balinese *adat* definition of a household head (also *kepala keluarga*) is the senior male within a household compound (*pakarangan*). Since a *pakarangan* normally includes several married men, it was not suitable for the purposes of this analysis. An alternative definition was suggested by the Balinese term, *kuren*. The *kuren* is the symbolic kitchen or hearth; in an abstract sense, it refers to the household set up by any single married couple, independently of in-laws (*matua*). It corresponds in physical terms to a kitchen (*paon*) and possibly to separate sleeping quarters as well. However, many married couples, particularly newly weds, have no claim to an independent *kuren*; in-marrying wives must share the affinal kitchen controlled by their mothers-in-law (*meme matua*), thereby signifying their lack of social autonomy. To use this definition would therefore be likely to give rise to significant omissions in the data.

In the case of polygynous households, most junior wives must initially share the senior wife's kitchen, thereby providing scope for the senior wife to inflict various little indignities upon the new wife (such as serving her last, or giving her inferior portions of food, or even denying food to her altogether, as happened in several of my case studies). On the other hand, they may be provided with their own kitchen *paon*-cum-residence, so that they essentially constitute a separate *kuren*. However, in this discussion I have deliberately adopted the Indonesian state's administrative definition of the household as that containing a sole married male, since this definition is most pertinent to the consideration of polygyny. To the extent that individual *kuren* may cut across polygynous households, representing them as separate households rather than compound households organized around one shared husband, it was not a suitable unit of analysis for my purposes here.

Personal Narratives from Polygynous Wives

Three of the various theoretical issues mentioned above deserve special consideration here: first, women's agency; second, co-wife initiatives in the formation of polygynous unions; and third, the importance of residential autonomy in ameliorating co-wife conflict. These are best illustrated by the personal testimonies of several of the women involved in polgynous marriages in Punyanwangi during 1992–1993.

Case Study 8.1: Ni Nengah Nasih/Ni Ketut Mariani: I Ketut Redika[15]

Informant: Ni Ng Nasih

Ni Nengah Nakti's story demonstrates all three of the above principles, viz. junior co-wife initiative, and co-wife hostility exacerbated by a lack of residential separation. It was related to me by Nasih herself over several months of friendship. I did not seek the perspectives of either of the other two in order not to compromise Nasih's confidentiality.

Nengah Nasih married her childhood sweetheart, Ketut Redika, a boy from her own descent group (*tunggalan*). Four years after the birth of their second child and son – Kadek Suryasa – Redika married Ketut Mariani. Although Nasih expressed her opposition to the marriage, she was unable to deter Redika because their own marriage was not registered.[16] Mariani moved in to live with them in the family home. This lasted for two years. Then Redika divorced Mariani.

But Mariani refused to give Redika up. She sought him out and tormented him. She would intercept him on his way from one home to the other or bewitch him with black magic. After three months Redika and Mariani remarried. Three months later they divorced again. Four months later Mariani and Redika remarried again, and the three cohabited bitterly for a further five months. Then Redika decided to transmigrate to East Timor. Well aware that Nasih would not come, he invited both wives along. Nasih was convinced that in the absence of her village relatives her *madu* Mariani would kill her: she saw herself as too gentle and soft (*magelohan*) to stand up to her co-wife. Accordingly Nasih remained behind to care for Redika's elderly widower father, cooking for him and attending to his needs.

After three and a half years Redika returned with Mariani and they all tried living together in the house again. Eighteen months later Mariani and Redika once more divorced. Four months after that Mariani was back. This time Nasih's patience snapped; she accused the couple of torturing (*menyiksakan* – Ind.) her. Redika responded by hitting her across the face so hard she fell over unconscious, cutting her face on the flagstone floor. She came to and he hit her again. She fell down again. Mariani stood by. It was 9.00 pm and her children were away. No one came to help. The next day Nasih packed her bags and went home to live with her father.

Having left Redika, Nasih was compelled to surrender Suryasa to her husband's custody, even though she and Redika belong to the same patrilineage. Suryasa wants to live with his mother but his father won't allow it. His mother misses him terribly, although he visits her every day. At Redika's home, Mariani persecutes Suryasa, denying him food. Often he comes to his mother for meals. Nasih finds this cruelty towards her son the hardest thing of all to bear.

Case Study 8.2: Ni Wayan Restiki/ Ni Kadek Ratiani: I Ketut Laken
Informants: Ni Kadek Ratiani, I Ketut Laken

Ni Kadek Ratiani's story again illustrates a clear junior co-wife initiative and a strong initial co-wife hostility ameliorated by residential separation.

Kadek Ratiani's brother opposed her first nine engagements. At 27, she was still a spinster. She was beginning to be seen around the village as not only 'past it' (*kadong telanjur*) but also as a rejected woman, a hand-me-down (*tweedehands* – Dutch/Ind.) – almost as worthless and soiled as a divorcee (*remeh cara balu*). Moreover, with so many failed public betrothals behind her, her chastity was now in question. The longer this situation persisted, the harder it would be to find a mate.

Then Ketut Laken, intermittently her sweetheart since childhood, took up work as a motorbike chauffeur (*tukang ojek*). He now had to ride past Ratiani's parents' house every day. Work was often slack and he took to dropping in on her for coffee. Before long the two had fallen in love again (*buin saling mademenan*), but now he was married to someone else and already had two children.

Despite this, Ratiani and Laken decided they wanted to marry. They knew the main obstacle would be Ratiani's brother, Nengah Nasa. Together they concocted a strategy designed to force Nasa's hand. If Ratiani were to fall pregnant out of wedlock, they reasoned, her brother would have to sanction marriage (*nganten maksa*). Ratiani soon fell pregnant but the strategy backfired: Nasa opposed the union anyway and the two married in the face of his extraordinarily sustained and strenuous opposition. After the wedding, Ratiani went to live with Laken at his paternal home.

Laken's first wife, Wayan Restiki, however, was no less outraged by Laken and Ratiani's liaison. She gave vent to her anger by denying her husband access to their two children and refusing to perform any domestic chores whatsoever, other than to prepare meals for herself and the children. She took to attacking Ratiani with a broom, literally sweeping her out of the house. Although Restiki refused to sleep with Laken herself, she made a point of sabotaging his attempted intimacies with his new wife, finding all manner of excuses to interrupt them in the act of sexual intercourse. To pacify Restiki, Laken ended up getting Ratiani to sleep on the floor next to his bed, where she slept for the next two months.

In response to Restiki's overt hostility, Ratiani adopted the posture of a submissive and docile wife, refusing to fight with Restiki and cheerfully carrying out all the chores neglected by her. Her mother in law (*meme matua*) was so impressed that soon Ratiani had the support of Laken's whole family. By contrast, Restiki's *galak-galak* [rebellious, fierce –Ind.] behaviour won her no sympathy from them. After several months of domestic acrimony the family finally conceded that, despite their poverty, Ratiani needed a house of her own. Laken had to sell a small parcel of land from his father's inheritance to finance it. Once the house was built, Laken commenced a system of spending alternate nights with each wife and slowly Ratiani's life began to improve.

Unfortunately, however, this was not the end of Ratiani's tribulations. Shortly after the birth of their daughter, Putu, Laken stopped visiting Ratiani. He avoided her for three whole months, during which period she sought advice from a spiritual therapist (*balian ketakson*). The *balian* said that Restiki had cast a spell on Laken so that he had 'forgotten' (*ngengsap*) about her. When Laken eventually returned to Ratiani, he denied that the separation had ever transpired. This convinced Ratiani that the *balian* had been correct in his surmise that Restiki had bewitched Laken into losing his memory.

From then on Laken became scrupulously conscientious about his obligations to each wife, alternating between their respective households each night. During that time Ratiani was convinced that her husband's affection for her was stronger than his affection for Restiki, and that he only returned to his first wife out of a sense of duty. An incident in which Restiki was caught having a flagrant affair with a neighbour, a couple of years later, affirmed Ratiani's confidence that she was Laken's favourite wife. Upon being discovered, Restiki fled to her parents for sanctuary, but in view of her disgrace they refused to take her in. They told her to return to her husband. She had no alternative but to do so.

When Putu was 5 years old, Ratiani fell pregnant again. She had no sooner given birth to her son than Laken abandoned her once again, this time for good. Laken and Restiki permitted the infant to suckle from his mother's breasts for just one month before forcing Ratiani to surrender it to Laken's patriline. Effectively, Restiki was now adopting the baby. Ratiani is still dealing with her grief.

Case Study 8.3: Ni Putu Kirimi/Ni Luh Teliti: I Nengah Mangku

Informants: Ni Putu Kirimi, Ni Luh Teliti

Ni Luh Teliti's story further exemplifies the elements of female agency and residential separation. However, here the co-wife initiative is evident not only in the formation of polygynous unions but also in their destruction. Moreover, separate homes in this case served less to reduce internal conflict than to exacerbate it to the point of destruction of the polygynous unit.

> Ni Putu Kirimi is a former divorcee who, upon deserting her first husband, was forced to surrender her three children to him. Her second husband, I Nengah Mangku, was a widower whose first wife died in childbirth. Kirimi and Mangku had a further four children, among whom were two sons. When after almost two decades of marriage, Mangku suddenly decided to take another wife, Kirimi was furious. Mangku went ahead and married Luh Teliti, building her a separate residence on land he owned some distance away from the main household.
>
> Teliti, herself a divorcee, was still young and pretty at the time. She had divorced her first husband after one year because she no longer loved him – they were not suited (*cocok*). For this she was heavily censured by her parents-in-law (*matua*). After surrendering her baby daughter to her husband's family, Teliti was then denied all access to the child.
>
> Teliti's second marriage was polygynous. It ended abruptly when her senior co-wife threatened divorce. Rather than be denigrated for having

driven out her (senior) *madu*, Teliti divorced again. With her third marriage also polygynous Teliti enjoyed strong solidarity with all three of her co-wives, but her third husband was an obsessively jealous man who took to following Teliti around and interrogating her about her encounters with those she had met or visited. On several occasions he even raped her. After suffering repeated beatings from him, she ran away to Denpasar where she worked as a maid for a few years. Upon her return to Punyanwangi, Mangku began to take an interest in her. They married and he built her a home of her own.

Kirimi was stung by Mangku's betrayal and told him so. He responded to her recriminations by going to live permanently with Teliti. Kirimi had long been providing for her family's material needs out her earnings from Mangku's small plot of riceland, her meagrely stocked *warung* and her main work as a banana-trader. Hence her husband's disappearance did not represent a great financial loss to her. However, she was incensed that in abandoning her, Mangku had also abandoned his children. Yet despite all, Kirimi refused to divorce her husband: she was not prepared to give up her children a second time.

For Teliti, marriage with Mangku has been the happiest phase of her life, although he is old enough to be her father. After several false starts, she is three months' pregnant and looks forward to having his child. She would like to be on better terms with Kirimi, but senses that the latter bears too much malice towards her.

ANALYSIS OF THE CASE STUDIES: PERVASIVE THEMES IN PUNYANWANGI POLYGYNOUS MARRIAGES

These narratives enable closer consideration of the three themes isolated above, briefly, the question of female agency and initiative in relation to polygyny, and the significance of household structures in mediating co-wife conflicts. It is clear from the case studies that co-wife conflicts in polygnyous contexts are almost inevitable.

Household Arrangements and Co-Wife Autonomy

The polygynous marriages in the foregoing case studies that lasted the longest – those of Ratiani/Laken and Teliti/Mangku – were those in which co-wives had separate dwellings. Polygynous husbands are aware that relations between co-wives sharing a *kuren* may be volatile. Hence in the interests of co-wife harmony they usually try to provide a new wife with her own *kuren* as soon as possible after marriage. Yet since this entails considerable expense, in the construction of a discrete building on a discrete parcel of land (preferably well away from the main household) the ideal of separate dwellings for each co-wife is not always realized.

Even where co-wives do have the luxury of living apart, polygynous unions are marked by instability. Ratiani and Restiki managed to come to terms with each other once Ratiani was physically removed from the main household, Restiki's domain. For over five years subsequently, the two maintained a superficial amicability that even extended to dropping in on each other for coffee and a chat or reciprocally minding each other's children from time to time. On the other hand, relations between Mariani and Nasih, who failed to achieve residential autonomy, were constantly acrimonious.

Stephens (1963: 65) states that the ideal that all wives should have separate households is almost universal in polygynous societies. While this ideal represents the aspiration of all the polygynous marriages that I studied in Punyanwangi, in practice it does not always materialize. Polygynous husbands are often poor and, in the absence of any real economic power, polygyny itself may become the instrument of their acquiring social status.[17] Thus despite the acknowledged desirability of residential separation, husbands such as Redika, as described above, were financially unable to deliver this outcome for their junior wives.

Co-wife Agency and Relative Status

In Punyanwangi, female agency in the context of polygyny is abundantly apparent. Both senior and junior co-wives are actively involved in manipulating the situation to their own advantage, but whether they are acting in favour of the polygynous marriage or against it depends upon their structural position in the co-wife hierarchy. Senior co-wives are stereotyped as rebellious and angry (*galak-galak*) while junior wives are seen as soft and submissive (*magelohan, lakar ngalah*), as demonstrated in the second case study. This is not surprising given that senior and junior wives have very different interests at stake. Senior wives have already achieved the monogamous cultural ideal, and in the absence of a tradition of co-wife cooperation in production (cf. Bowen 1954: 118–21; Boserup 1970), they do not stand to gain by 'the gift' of a co-wife (*ngamaduang*). Junior wives, on the other hand, often have everything to gain and very little to lose by seeking a polygynous outcome. While both categories of co-wife are distinguished by their active agency, therefore, only junior co-wives have an interest in initiating a polygynous marriage.

Senior Wives

All three senior wives in the case studies opposed their husbands' remarriage: what varied was the ferocity and nature of their responses to it. Nengah Nasih attempted to resign herself to being made a co-wife (*kamaduang*), although she did voice a mild protest which became increasingly vehement over time. On the other hand, Wayan Restiki conforms to the stereotype of the outraged senior wife, using every resource at her disposal to communicate her fury to her husband and to alienate her co-wife in a strategy that only bore fruit after many years. Putu Kirimi, an economically independent businesswoman, was successfully able to prevent her co-wife, Luh Teliti, from even entering the family compound. However, she was unable to effect a reversal of the marriage, and ultimately alienated her husband along with the wife that she had striven to repel. In all the other cases of polygyny for which I have data, the senior wife vigorously resisted the imposition of a junior wife in ways comparable to those already discussed.

However, it is unwise to assume that women's structural position in the co-wife hierarchy actually *determined* the response of senior or junior wives to polygyny. The case of Nasih and Teliti, for instance, inverts the stereotypes of rebellious senior wife/submissive junior wife: in this instance Nasih as senior wife was manifestly the more docile personality and it was her junior co-wife Mariani who seemed intent on driving her competitor out of the house. Hence in practice, wives' behavioural responses to polygyny are still very much contingent upon individual personality and cannot simply be stereotyped.

Although rebellion transgresses the polite codes of North Balinese society and flouts behavioural ideals of submissiveness which are particularly incumbent upon women (cf. Wikan 1990), senior wives clearly see it as a strategic alternative in circumstances where a co-wife is imposed upon them.[18] The strategy is not always effective, however: in Punyanwangi overt rebellion occasionally achieves the immediate reversal of the offending marriage, but this is rare. More frequently, conflict is protracted and the victory – should there be one – may take years.

Junior Wives

Irrespective of their lower status within the co-wife hierarchy, junior co-wives are in a very different structural position from senior wives. Although they come from a range of backgrounds, the one thing junior wives invariably have in common is that their prospects for marriage have been compromised in some way by their past life experiences. While candidate junior co-wives may include older unmarried women (e.g. Ratiani), widows, or naive young girls (Jennaway 1996), the vast majority of them are divorcees (e.g. Mariani, Teliti).

Both divorcees (*balu*) and ageing maidens (*daa tua*) are heavily stigmatized in North Balinese society (see below), and widows fare little better (as indicated by their identical designation to that of divorcees, namely, *balu*). Hence women whose reputations have been damaged presumably are motivated to secure remarriage and thereby restore their respectability as soon as possible (Jennaway 1996). In North Bali generally, male promiscuity is seen as 'natural' and premarital sexual adventurism in young males is affectionately indulged. After marriage, male infidelity is regarded as undesirable, but it is tolerated. It goes without saying that no equivalent sexual licence exists for women. In such a context therefore, where male promiscuity is culturally indulged as 'natural' (cf. Goody 1973: 189; Pasternak 1976: 63; Leach 1991: 98), it is hard to see how polygyny serves male interests, unless a man's first marriage has failed to provide him with an heir. The cultural logic of polygyny in North Bali therefore implies that it is potential co-wives who are most active in effecting polygynous marriages, rather than either their lovers or their lover's spouses (cf.

Hiatt 1980: 583, 588–590). Such women clearly have more at stake in securing a polygynous marriage, and therefore are presumably more inclined than their already married lovers to make wedlock – albeit polygynous – a condition of any amorous liaison.

'Luungen Nganten': the Value of Marriage

There is common saying among women in Punyanwangi that 'it is better to marry' (*luungan nganten*), meaning that marriage is preferable to the alternatives, which in Punyanwangi are spinsterhood, widowhood or divorce. Even those in unsatisfactory marriages or whose marriages had repeatedly failed often declared this view.

Descent in Punyanwangi is patrilineal and, traditionally, youngest sons inherited the family estate according to ideals of ultimogeniture (Geertz and Geertz 1975: 54).[19] It is rare but not unprecedented for daughters to inherit wealth. In the past, this usually occurred where there was no male heir. However, nowadays new ideologies of gender equality promoted by the Indonesian state are beginning to have an impact on inheritance patterns. Despite this trend, in North Bali there is still no clear obligation for brothers to consider their sisters' welfare in regard to the allocation of the patrimony. Indeed, unmarried sisters are sometimes even evicted from the family home upon the death of their parents.[20]

In practice, of course, many women retain the love and support of their parents and siblings throughout their lives. In the event of a marital crisis, the first place a woman turns to for help is her natal home. But there is no social contract that guarantees this safety net (witness Restiki's experience above). Hence it is not surprising that women strive so hard to marry monogamously, and failing this, even polygynously, to avoid the perils of relying upon the vagaries of the natal environment.

In cultural terms, even apart from the economic and social vulnerability of unmarried daughters, village women do not perceive spinsterhood as a viable alternative to marriage. Women who fail to marry are stigmatized as virgins (*daa*)[21] throughout their life. In 1992 there were only three spinsters in the village, and two of these were regarded as mad. The third was an unmarried mother who had been ostracized by her brother and consequently lived alone with her son.[22]

Thus from women's perspective a major motivation for marriage is to guarantee themselves in their old age security through their children. Given the insecurity of natal support, several junior wives voiced the fear of not having children (*takut sing ngelah panake*) as their reason for marrying polygynously. Children rather than husbands, it seems, are perceived as a woman's best guarantee of material security.

Divorce as the Inverse of Polygyny

Several scholars have commented that divorce is rare in Bali (Geertz and Geertz 1975: 56; Streatfield 1986: 22–23). But such a view entails considerable gender bias, for it defines marriage in terms of the fate of male egos. In my genealogical data, women evinced a rate of divorce up to four times as high as men (Table 8.2).[23]

Table 8.2: Number of men contracting plural marriages, *desa adat* Punyanwangi.

No. of concurrent wives	Concurrent (polygyny)	Serial (widowhood, divorce)	Total
1	-	15	15
2	53	0	53
3	4	0	4
4	2	0	2
>4	1	0	1
Total	60	15	75

This is consistent with the fact that in Punyanwangi, men in unsatisfactory marriages have the option of polygyny, while women lack the equivalent alternative of polyandry. The discrepancy arises because of cultural restrictions upon female polyandry: women who engage in plural marriage therefore tend to marry serially, thus necessitating divorce,[24] while men who engage in plural marriage do so concurrently, in the form of polygyny.

Divorce often represents both the structural and the practical inverse of polygyny: either a woman divorces her husband because she is threatened with polygyny, or as a divorcee she is only able to secure remarriage as someone else's co-wife. For the majority of my divorced female informants, polygyny (or the threat thereof) was the immediate cause. Nyoman Marini's case is instructive. Marini divorced two husbands before settling down with her third. She came from a wealthy landowning household and saw no reason why she should put up with a first husband who wanted more wives and a second who was an inveterate gambler.

Deterrents to Divorce

The deterrents to divorce in North Bali are considerable. Divorcees (*balu*) are stigmatized as little better than used, worn-out merchandise (*barang rosokan* – Ind.) who have already 'been dipped' (*suba macelebang*) and who are hence 'past it' or 'too late' (*kadong telanjur*). The one positive construction of a divorcee is that she will be resigned and give in easily to avoid arguments (*pasrah menghindari cekcok* – Ind.). Significantly, both constructions – the negative image of her as a used consumer item and the positive image of her as submissive and meek – are formulated in terms of a divorcee's potential for remarriage.

Notwithstanding the undesirability of such social stigma, property rights appeared to constitute a greater deterrent to divorce in the minds of my female informants. The deterrent is twofold. The first pertains to material property. Women who initiate divorce with their husbands forfeit their claim to any of his material wealth, other than that which they themselves have brought to the marriage. Should the husband initiate divorce, however, a woman's position is slightly better: she may be awarded half his property, particularly if he is intending to abandon their children. However, this applies to only a minority of cases: most husbands have little interest in ending a marriage when the alternative of polygyny is available to them.

The second deterrent to divorce pertains to biological property: children. In Balinese Hinduism, spiritual and social identity is conceived as being transmitted through the father's line. Hence children are regarded, in both a spiritual and a juridical sense, as belonging to their father's lineage. Moreover, the perpetuation of the father's patrilineage therefore depends upon his offspring. This explains why a woman is required to surrender custody of her children to her husband's kin in the event of divorce (and, in some circumstances, widowhood). Those divorcees who had forfeited their children appeared to suffer immense personal grief. Avoiding the loss of their children was for most unhappy co-wives the major, often the only, factor deterring them from divorce.

Ideological Legitimations for Polygyny

In North Bali, the ideological legitimations for polygyny emphasize a husband's right to seek a male heir. As mentioned above, sons are essential to the spiritual and biological continuity of the patrilineage. Daughters are unreliable bearers of patrilineal identity since they relinquish it upon marriage. Not only are sons more valuable to a man in a social sense, but also they are arguably more valuable in an economic sense. In a rural community such as that of Punyanwangi, sons can be expected to contribute agricultural labour throughout their youth and then, upon their inheritance of part or all of the family estate, to direct their earnings back into the family home. This translates in everyday discourse as the idea that it is natural and normal for a man to have a son. Wives who fail to produce sons are therefore highly vulnerable to polygyny – at least in theory.

But the empirical evidence from Punyanwangi does not support this argument. Of the 15 polygynous marriages detected in my household survey, only four of the original monogamous marriages had failed to produce male offspring (see Table 8.3).

In this sample, 11 out of 15 polygynous marriages were entered into *even though the first wife had already produced a son.* Indeed, the number of first marriages failing to produce a son is outstripped by the number failing to produce a daughter. For those wishing to argue that reproduction is the major incentive for polygyny, a stronger case could be made based on lack of a daughter. But the empirical evidence tabled above implies that in actual practice, very few polygynous unions in Punyanwangi are contracted on the basis of some alleged male reproductive imperative. Rather, the quest for a male heir would seem to constitute an ideological fiction which serves to obscure the real motivations underlying polygynous associations. I suggest that these have more to do with *female* imperatives to secure conjugal respectability than with the husband's presumed need to have a male heir.

Table 8.3: Number and sex of children of first marriages of polygynous men

Sons	Daughters (No. of)					Total
	0	1	2	3	4	
0	2	1	1	0	0	4
1	2	3	1	1	0	7
2	0	1	0	2	0	3
3	0	0	0	0	0	0
4	1	0	0	0	0	1
Total	**5**	**5**	**2**	**3**	**0**	**15**

Senior wives, even those with sons, frequently become insecure about the claim upon the patrimony of any offspring to the union between the junior wife and the polygynous husband. In a context of ultimogeniture, such insecurity arises from the threat of the senior wife's children being deprived of family resources while the husband remains alive, and of the family estate upon his death (cf. Bledsoe 1993: 174–175). This would certainly jeopardize a senior wife's old age security. In several cases, for instance that of Restiki/Ratiani detailed above, the senior wife took the precautionary measure of adopting the junior wife's children. This practice is also reported for other parts of Bali (Mershon 1971: 159). Such a strategy is designed to shore up a woman's long-term interests against the assault of a competing polygynous claim upon her original monogamous wealth base.

Conclusion

In Punyanwangi, the institution of polygyny serves as a mirror in which several features of the social system can be discerned. First, it exposes fundamental gender inequalities which deprive women of any positive life alternatives outside of marriage. Second, as an inferior category of marriage, it serves both as the threat underpinning the maintenance of monogamy and as a safety-net for those marginal women whose conjugal interests have been seriously compromised. Finally, it drives still other women to divorce: a gamble which may pay off in terms of allowing them a second chance at monogamy, but which often backfires in that usually they are reincorporated into the conjugal economy in the inferior role of junior wife. Punyanwangi women's various discourses regarding marriage, divorce, and remarriage as a co-wife, reveal a sharp awareness of their limited life-choices in a rural community and their active agency in trying to effect the best outcomes for themselves. These discourses suggest that while both senior and junior co-wives actively engage in the attempt to influence their marital destinies, it is largely due to the initiative of potential junior co-wives – rather than their spouses – that polygynous households continue to be established in Punyanwangi.

The personal testimonies of polygynous wives in Punyanwangi collectively constitute a subjective female discourse which highlights the non-pertinence of universalizing male-dominated theories of polygyny. For village women who are involved in polygynous transactions, assuming the role of a 'honey-wife' (Mershon 1971:55) is often experienced as an unhappy, if not bitter, fate. Individual women's experiences of polygyny are different and often antithetical, depending upon their position in the co-wife hierarchy, their success in establishing an autonomous household for themselves and their offspring, and their psychological ability to survive protracted or intermittent domestic conflict. While senior wives perceive their husbands' remarriage as an acute blow to their self-esteem and economic security, junior wives – coming from a position of stigma – are likely to feel it as an elevation of their material prospects and as a personal boost to their self-image. What is common to both groups of wives is the disharmony and conflict which they differently experience within the polygynous household setting. While these may be somewhat vitiated by the provision of separate dwellings, co-wives' feelings of mutual insecurity and jealousy may still be expressed from afar in the form of witchcraft accusations (as in Ratiani's case). Where co-wives are compelled to live together, however, domestic tensions may surface in explosive and destructive ways. For some women polygyny may have tragic consequences, in the deprivation of their children, or in economic or social destitution. Awareness of such anguished alternative destinies constitutes a powerful incentive to adapt to polygynous household arrangements – however bitter – and to endeavour to maintain them as long as possible.

Jack Goody (1973: 189) has suggested that, in view of the world-wide prevalence of polygyny, it is 'not the absence of monogamy that needs to be explained, but that of polygyny'. I suggest the reverse, that in societies in which male promiscuity is tolerated and even positively evaluated, as in North Bali, it is still polygyny which needs to be explained. Incorporating women into the account serves to do precisely this, by highlighting the fact that unmarried women have less of an interest in being party to male extramarital sexual escapades than in translating these into firm conjugal commitment. It also provides an alternative perspective on the nature of the Balinese household, by highlighting a range of different structural forms that they may take. It would seem from this North Balinese evidence that the notion of the 'household' may have limited utility as analytic construct, given that it tends to mask the different specific domestic arrangements which polygynous marriages often entail.

Notes

1. This chapter is based upon 12 months ethnographic fieldwork conducted in the village of Punyanwangi, North Bali, in 1992. The research was funded by an Award for Postgraduate Research on AIDS (APRA), administered by the then Commonwealth Department of Health and Community Services, and

BITTER HONEY

      an Australian Award for Research in Asia (AARA), administered by the Commonwealth Vice-Chancellors' Committee.

2. These statistics must be interpreted with caution: although polygyny occurs in a majority of societies, this is not the same as saying that a majority of marriages which take place within a given society are polygynous.

3. See also Pasternak (1976: 63).

4. According to parental investment theory, humans are genetically programmed to maximize their reproductive fitness (see Mayr 1963; Trivers 1972; Wilson 1975).

5. Indonesian development ideology, for reasons that probably have much to do with maintaining the support of its various Western sponsors, discourages the practice of polygyny. For instance, male public servants – comprising an educated bureaucratic elite – are bound by legislation which compels them to gain the consent of their wife before taking on any extra spouses. Defaulters face dismissal. Likewise, Indonesia's rapidly expanding middle classes appear to disdain polygyny as inconsistent with their adoption of 'modern' and 'progressive' Western values.

6. See Clignet (1970: 33; 1971: 177), Goody (1973: 178) and Bledsoe (1993: 188) on the question of the relationship between education and polygyny.

7. All foreign terms are Balinese unless otherwise indicated.

8. For instance, Friederich (1959: 92) mentions the precedent set by Prince Ngurah Sakti Pam'chutan, who is recorded as having had 500 wives. More usually, a prince's wives numbered around 45–50 (van der Kraan 1985; cf. Streatfield 1986: 22).

9. A bizarre consequence of this was that a low-born junior wife (*Penawing, Jero*) was often accorded lower social rank than that of her own children, by virtue of their mixed descent from a noble father (Geertz and Geertz 1975: 131).

10. To protect informants' identities, all place names encompassed by Punyanwangi village and all Balinese personal names are pseudonymous.

11. 14 See Warren (1993) on the differences between Indonesian administrative villages [*desa dinas*] and customary villages [*desa adat*] in the Balinese context.

12. *Desa adat* boundaries are cross-cut by local communities known as *banjar*. In *desa* Punyanwangi *banjar* boundaries did not conflict with *desa adat* boundaries: *desa adat* Punyanwangi was coterminous with two conjoined *banjar*; *desa adat* Senggigi was coterminous with one; while the fourth *banjar*, *banjar* Banyusing, was entirely independent of any local *desa adat* boundaries.

13. Informants' accounts are likely to be biased towards a lower perceived incidence of polygyny, due to the vulnerability of human memory in recalling with precision the marital arrangements of distant or deceased relatives.

14. The incidence of polygyny appears to have been higher in past generations, thereby lifting the overall average. Superficially, it would therefore seem that the practice of polygyny is declining in the present day. However, its slightly lower incidence among the middle generation (30–50 year olds) is

somewhat offset by a higher rate of divorce and remarriage (i.e. serial marriage), possibly implying greater female self-determination. The relative absence of polygyny among the younger newly-wed generation (15–30 year olds) may simply indicate that young males at the beginning of their marital careers have not had sufficient time or resources to acquire additional wives.

15 *Ni* is equivalent to the Western 'Ms', *I* (pronounced 'ee') to the Western 'Mr'. To avoid ambiguities in the text, I refer to people by their personal names, rather than their birth-order names – Wayan, Ketut and so on – which would be more polite. In normal daily interaction it is quite offensive to address a person by their personal name, other than a contraction of it (and even this privilege is reserved for familiars).

16 Since the 1978 review of the 1974 Marriage Act, it has become possible to register marriages at the Registry of Births, Deaths and Marriages (*Kantor Kelahiran, Kematian, dan Perkawinan*) (Streatfield 1986: 21). This enables wives to take advantage of their right to apply legal sanctions if their husband remarries without their consent. In 1992, however, very few rural couples had bothered to obtain this insurance, although among younger-generation women I discerned a greater motivation to avail themselves of this juridical right.

17 There is a clear status increment in having more than one wife; such men usually held or aspired to influential positions in the village community (Jennaway 1996; cf. Musisi 1991).

18 Such extreme expressions of senior wife hostility are not confined to the study area: in the nearby island of Alor outbursts of violence between co-wives can include street-brawling, punching and kicking (Stephens 1963: 59–60).

19 Increasingly this is shifting to a pattern whereby one (any) son volunteers to take over management of the land, while his brothers either help him farm it or receive a payout representing their equity in the land. Now, however, new ways of favouring the last-born son have emerged, such as providing them with the best educational opportunities that the family can afford, at the expense of their siblings' educations (cf. Bledsdoe 1993).

20 This undermines the claim by some researchers that unmarried daughters are highly valued (Suryani and Jensen 1992: 149).

21 Although in certain ritual contexts, such as the role of temple medium (*paramas*), female virginity is a highly valued prerequisite of office.

22 Her parents were both deceased and her brother had inherited the patrimonial estate.

23 For instance, of 75 polygynous or serially marrying males, only 15 marriages had ended in divorce. By contrast, of 31 serially married women (polyandry not being an option), 23 marriages had ended in divorce; the remaining eight had been widowed (genealogical data).

24 The striking imperative for either divorced and widowed women seems to be secure remarriage. Of the 31 women detected whose marriages had been terminated, 30 eventually remarried, underlining the high premium placed on matrimony by the women of *desa* Punyanwangi.

9

The Salty Mouth of a Senior Woman
Gender and the House in Minangkabau

Joke van Reenen

INTRODUCTION

Anthropologists who investigate Minangkabau society often do so because they are interested in a particular problem relating to matriliny. As a reaction to this, others have pointed out that the differences between matrilineal (or unilineal) and cognatic systems are generally overdrawn (cf. Stivens 1991, Watson 1991, Peletz 1994). Irrespective of the kinship system there are many correspondences between various societies in Indonesia or Southeast Asia; one of the recurring themes is a certain degree of female-centredness in household organization and close kin ties (e.g.: Vreede-De Stuers 1959, Tanner 1974, Stivens 1991, Peletz 1994).

Although I fully agree with the view that matricentrality is a widespread phenomenon in Southeast Asia, in this chapter I intend to demonstrate that matriliny does make a difference to gender relations in the domestic sphere. However, we are faced with a conceptual problem if 'household' is taken as the unit of analysis. In the highlands of West Sumatra it is hard if not impossible to distinguish the household as a separate social category. Both men and women retain strong ties to their own kin group after marriage and the conjugal unit is not independent nor very corporate. Women are 'central pillars of the house' (van Reenen 1996), men's position *vis-à-vis* the house is relatively peripheral: the male domain is outside and men have dual responsibilities in the houses of their wife or wives and those of their own matrikin. In my view gender relations will be better understood if one starts from the individual man or woman in his or her network of family and kin relations, rather than investigating internal relations among or external relations of 'household members'. This point will be illustrated by the case of a 60-year- old village woman, who gives her view on certain aspects of gender relations in her own house, family and kin during various stages of her life.

Conceptual Issues

The 'household' has been defined in many ways.[1] In much of the anthropological literature a distinction is made between household and family, whereby the household (domestic group) is used to refer to the residential unit, while the concept of family is based on kinship (cf. Keesing 1976, Yanagisako 1979, Schwede 1991). In contrast, in neo-classical economic analyses the household has been considered as a unified entity of production, consumption and residence. Other authors define the household as a production and consumption unit (e.g. Rodenburg 1993); an income-pooling unit (e.g. Wallerstein and Smith 1991); a production unit (e.g. Fapohunda 1988) or a group of people who share food and common shelter (e.g. Hetler 1986; Wolf 1991). This last approach – 'persons who share food and shelter' – is the one most recommended by the United Nations. Perhaps the simplest way of identifying a household in this approach has been to inquire whether a group of persons share a 'common cooking pot' (cf. Hetler 1986).

Each of these definitions has drawbacks when applied to specific empirical cases. Kabeer argues that the challenge is 'to find generalisable approaches to kinship-mediated economic flows, which can accommodate the empirical diversity of household forms' (Kabeer 1991: 8). Others take a more radical stance and dismiss the usefulness of the household analysis. Pittin, for instance, who conducted research among the secluded Muslim women of northern Nigeria, criticizes household analysis on grounds that 'the domestic group is often seen as monolithic, clearly bounded, and unchanging, except in so far as the domestic cycle produces changes in personnel' (Pittin 1987: 26). She argues that findings from micro-studies show a much more fluid structure and a wide system of networks cross-cutting domestic units and uniting women of different households.

In Minangkabau rural communities we are faced with similar fundamental conceptual problems. At first sight the definition of household as a 'group of people with a common cooking pot' might seem appropriate. The Minangkabau concept of *periuak* designates 'cooking pot' as well as 'a group of people who share a cooking pot'. However, to what extent can this 'cooking pot unit' be considered as a significant and relatively independent social unit? In order to answer this question, we shall examine first what it is not. The *periuak* is not a housing unit. Persons who are out of the village much of the time – as migrants who work or study elsewhere – will usually be counted as members of the *periuak* of the women who cook for them whenever they come home. Besides, several *periuak* – cooking pot units – may share one house. For instance, two adult sisters and their conjugal families may live together in the same house, yet as a rule cook and eat separately. Second, the cooking pot unit does not necessarily have its own 'head'. One senior woman may wield ultimate authority in the house, even if it is inhabited by several groups with their own cooking pot. Third, the cooking pot unit is not a separate production or income-pooling unit either. Members of several cooking pot units may have important economic resources in common, such as land and houses; members of one unit may provide considerable material contributions to those of another unit; and various members of one unit keep separate purses. In other words, it is not very fruitful to distinguish the group of persons who share a cooking pot as a unit of analysis, since it is by no means a bounded, independent or corporate socio-economic entity.

The boundaries of the domestic unit in Minangkabau village communities are obscured by the way it is integrated into the matrilineal kinship organization. The building blocks of each *nagari* (Minangkabau village community)[2] are a number of matrilineal groupings of varying order of inclusion. The largest groupings are named clans, which incorporate smaller groupings such as lineages and lineage segments. The smallest unit is that of a mother and her children, called *samande*. The matrilineal groupings are of great importance to the lives of individual men and women. They cross-cut the cooking pot unit. Every person, man or woman, has strong ties with his/her own matrilineage. A man may live in his wife's house and belong to the same cooking pot unit as she does, yet he will continue to have important rights and duties among his own matrikin, who belong to different cooking pot units. In the following sections this problem will be clarified by depicting the position of men and women in relation to the Minangkabau house, the *rumah gadang*.

WOMEN: STABLE CENTRE OF THE *RUMAH GADANG*[3]

For many centuries the 'traditional' Minangkabau house, the so-called *rumah gadang* [big house], has dominated the highlands of the west coast of central Sumatra. Although more and more 'modern' houses are being built, the *rumah gadang* continues to retain great ideological value; it has become a major symbol of Minangkabau matriliny and ethnicity.

The *rumah gadang* is a big construction made of wood, sometimes supplemented by split bamboo. It stands high on poles and is entered via a wooden or concrete staircase. Its roof – formerly made of palm fibre but nowadays of corrugated iron – is horn-shaped, with two or more pairs of curved ridge beams. Formerly a rice barn stood opposite each *rumah gadang*, but today the rice is stored elsewhere and most of the barns have fallen into disrepair or been pulled down. The *rumah gadang* belongs to a matrilineage or a segment thereof: a group of three to four generations of people who are related in the matrilineal line. Apart from the house, these people have also common rights to other ancestral property such as land and valuable goods.

The *rumah gadang*, or 'inside', represents the female domain, while the public sphere, or 'outside', is male-dominated. In Minangkabau these spheres are overlapping entities and neither sphere (domestic or public) is valued more highly than the other. The conceptualization of gender relations depends on the standpoint of the observer: seen from the outside – from the village and the most inclusive matrilineal groupings inwards in the direction of smaller descent units – traditional rural Minangkabau society will appear as a male-dominated society. Conversely, seen from the perspective of the house looking outward - with the house as the centre within circles of ever wider and more inclusive matrilineal groupings – Minangkabau society will appear as female-dominated; some would even say 'matriarchal'.

In Minangkabau *adat*, women constitute the stable core of the *rumah gadang*, socially and economically. Adult or senior women (*bundo kanduang*)[4] are likened to 'central pillars of the house' (*limpapeh rumah nan gadang*) (i.a. Dt. Rajo Penghulu 1986a, 1986b). They are protected socially and economically due to matrilineal descent, matrilineal patterns of inheritance and matrilocal patterns of residence. Senior women are highly respected. Mak Rahmah, one of our informants whose case will be discussed below, explains that when she was living with her extended family in the *rumah gadang*, the oldest woman was the most influential; 'her mouth was the most salty'.

Historically the common pattern of residence was matrilocal. In village communities matrilaterally related women remained together in the same *rumah gadang* or in adjoining houses. All adult daughters had their own room [*bilik*] in the *rumah gadang* where they received their husband at night. Little children slept with the mother; young girls could sleep in the big front space. Elderly women often moved out of the rooms to a place close to the kitchen. A new *rumah gadang* was built next to the old one as soon as the first house was 'full', meaning that all rooms were occupied by adult women. The oldest daughter or one of the senior women was the first to move out.

Women not only constitute the residential core of the house, they are also considered the custodians of the ancestral property: they 'hold the key to the treasure chest'. In Minangkabau society land is the common property of a lineage, but as a rule the use rights are passed on to the female offspring.

The Dual Place of Men in the *Rumah Gadang*

In contrast to women, who formed the stable core of the house as a social and residential unit, the men's place in relation to the house was peripheral. In the past a married man came to his wife's house in the evenings and left early in the morning. When he had more than one wife – as many men did – each of the wives stayed in the house of their own mother and he took turns to visit them, at least this was the ideal. During daytime a man spent most of his time outside, at work or in a coffee-house, and he returned to the house of his mother and sisters regularly to sit down and chat and inquire about the situation in their house. This pattern of residence for married men has often been called duolocal.[5]

Bachelors and widowers did not have a real home either. Adolescent boys used to sleep in the prayer house (*surau*) and eat at home; frequently old widowers or divorced men returned to the house of their sisters or were forced to spend the night in the prayer house, among the boys.

A married man was entitled to respectful behaviour in his wife's house. He was designated as *sumando*, a title used for all in-married males to a house or lineage. The *sumando* was considered to be an honoured guest in the house of his wife, who should be served and treated with deference. There were many taboos observed in the demeanour of 'people of the house' (his in-laws) towards the *sumando*, and their association with him was carried on in a highly formalized and subdued manner. However, being a guest, the *sumando* was not free in his actions and he did not have much power over his wife and children. Divorce was very common, as the *sumando* could easily have his toes trodden on by the demeanour of his wife and her kin.

A man did not have much authority over his own wife and children. Instead he did have authority over his sisters' children in his role of *mamak* [real or classificatory maternal uncle]. The *mamak*, more particularly the senior male members of the house (*tungganai rumah*), represented the *rumah gadang* in the outside world.

Economically speaking, a man was also more attached to his sisters and sisters' children than to his wife or wives and his own children. There was a time when males cultivated the land of their mothers and sisters rather than their wives' land. And a good *mamak* was a man who managed to increase the common property of his own matrilineage.

Briefly, in the past a man had a marginal position as husband and father in the sense that he was not expected to spend too much time with his wife and children, had little power over them, and few economic obligations towards them. By contrast, as a *mamak* [mother's brother] a man wielded authority over his sisters' children; the *mamak* came to see his mother and sisters frequently, cultivated their land and had economic duties towards them.

DEVELOPMENTS IN MATRILINEAL *ADAT*

Minangkabau matrilineal *adat* has undergone rapid modifications since the second half of the nineteenth century due to a combination of factors. Population pressure has led to land scarcity. Increasing educational opportunities and new professional opportunities outside the agrarian sector have made it easier for men to earn a private income which, in turn, is used increasingly to the benefit of their wives and children rather than their sisters' children. Externally, colonial and later on Indonesian national policy has contributed to a strengthening of the position of the conjugal family and of the husband/father. The mounting influence of Islam has reinforced this government policy. All in all the position of the husband/father has become stronger and concomitantly the role of the *mamak* has become less important. Today many men build separate houses for their wives and children, where they live as a conjugal family, if the man is not in the *rantau* [destination of migration]. A man has become more attached to the land of his wife than that of his mother or sisters. Economically and socially he is now closer and feels more responsible towards his wife and children.

Nevertheless, in rural areas a man continues to play the dual role of husband/father and *mamak*. After marriage he retains his social and economic duties towards his sisters and sisters' children, with whom he shares clan and lineage membership. He still plays a role in the management of the ancestral property of his kin group, including land and houses. When a man stays in the house of his wife's mother, he is still considered a guest there. If he builds a separate house for his wife and children, it is usually located on the land of the lineage of his wife, in the proximity of his wife's matrikin. The house will be inherited by his daughters and in the next generation it will become part of the ancestral property of his wife's kin. In this house, which he built himself, a man may act more as a head of the family, but his authority will remain restricted. Some wives are strong and dominant and in any case their kin groups remain responsible for all matters concerning the kin group, including the management of the ancestral property.

One implication of the peripheral place of men in the house and the village is a strong centrifugal tendency among males: many men leave their villages and the regions in search of work, experience or education – sometimes to run away from the confines of kinship. Migration makes it possible for men to intensify their bonds with wife and children, either by sending them remittances or by taking them to the *rantau* in order to establish a more clearly defined conjugal family (See e.g. Kato 1982, Naim 1984, 1985).

As far as women are concerned, in spite of the fact that they are beginning to migrate in growing numbers – either individually or, more frequently, to join their husband – they have a much stronger foothold in the village and many women actually prefer to remain behind. Their place in the village is more stable and secure than that of men. Descent is traced through women, matrilocality has remained the norm in rural areas, and the use rights to land are still passed on from a mother to her daughters. Yet the gender relations are changing. Gradually women are becoming more dependent on their husbands, partly due to mounting land shortage and the growing importance of education and the market economy for economic success, from which men profit in a more direct way than women. The following argument serves as an illustration.

RAO-RAO, A VILLAGE COMMUNITY[6]

In 1990 we conducted research in Nagari Rao-Rao, a village community located in the highlands of Bukit Barisan, in the cultural heartland of the Minangkabau.[7] The village is situated between three towns which form a triangle: Batusangkar is located south, Bukittinggi northwest, and Payakumbuh northeast of Rao-Rao. The village is connected to these three towns by a provincial road.

The centre of the village consists of densely populated living quarters. During the time of our research numerous *rumah gadang* still survived in this area. The north corner of the *nagari* contained rice-fields with dispersed simple dwellings, while the southwestern part consisted of woods and gardens, with scattered houses. To a large extent the geographical pattern corresponded to a socio-economic cleavage: the vast majority of the women and their families who occupied the centre of the village controlled rice-fields and gardens, whereas the inhabitants of the outer areas (a relatively small minority) controlled little or no land.

Most villagers made a living from one or a combination of the following sources:

- agriculture (wet-rice cultivation for private consumption and the cultivation of cash crops in gardens);
- circular trade;
- remittances sent back home by emigrant relatives;
- farm labour or share-cropping.

The provincial road that runs through the village was used by private cars, trucks, buses, and other kinds of public transportation during the day but lessened by evening. A sand road leading into the gardens was used regularly by small trucks for the transportation of farm products. Although it was not impossible to enter other parts of the village by car as well, this was a rare occurrence. Very few villagers owned a motorized vehicle, and the village itself is a maze of undulating roads and paths, some of them constructed in the form of stairways.

In 1990 most houses in Desa Rao-Rao were supplied with electricity. Desa Lumbuang Bapereang, located in the garden area at some distance from the main road, was not yet connected to the electricity grid. In this *desa* the houses were lit by petrol lamps. There were only few television sets in the village then, but when I came back in 1993, their number had increased considerably. The vast majority of the houses had no private water supply or sanitary facilities. To obtain water to drink, to clean dishes, and for washing, bathing and sanitary purposes, the villagers made use of public bathing places which had been constructed in various areas of the village. These bathing places were supplied with water from a river conveyed through large pipes. They were screened or surrounded by walls; the sexes remained separated.

The village had a beautiful new mosque, which had been built several years previously with money from villagers who had migrated and become rich. There were also many *surau* [prayer houses], of which some were still in use, others had fallen into decay. There were four elementary schools in the village and one kindergarten. There was a Puskesmas [centre for community health]. And there was a post office, which had been opened in 1987. Twice a week a market was held in the centre of the village. In other words, during the time we carried out our fieldwork, Rao-Rao was by no means an isolated village, but neither was it urbanized.

BACKGROUND TO CASE STUDIES 9.1 AND 9.2: MAK RAHMAH[8]

Among the many women from Rao-Rao whom we interviewed in depth was Mak Rahmah, a woman approximately 60 years old. Her perception and views on social relations in her own *rumah gadang* and family at various stages of her life will be presented below. Her story is a good illustration of the complexity of kinship networks and the difficulties one encounters in trying to identify a 'domestic unit'. It also shows the actual functioning of – and the recent developments in – the contrasting association of woman with 'centre' and 'stability', and of man with 'outside' and 'ambiguous roles'. The 'I' form will be used in presenting Mak Rahmah's story, since it is largely a translation of parts of her account, albeit with minor stylistic adjustments. However, the various elements of her story have been put in such a way that the contrast between 'female/centre/house' and 'male/periphery/outside' comes out most clearly.

Biographical Data

Mak Rahmah was born in Nagari Rao-Rao around 1930. She had two brothers, who lived with their wives and families elsewhere in the village.

Mak Rahmah had been married twice. She was divorced from the first husband and widowed from the second. She had four children. In 1990 her two sons lived in the *rantau* [destination of migration], in places elsewhere in Sumatra. Both of them were married to women from Rao-Rao, who had joined them in the *rantau*. Mak Rahmah's two daughters were also married, but they had stayed in Rao-Rao. One of them lived in a house not far away, which had been built by her husband. The other one, her elder daughter, remained in the *rumah gadang* that belonged to Mak Rahmah and her matrikin. Mak Rahmah herself slept in the adjacent *kedai*, a small grocery of which she was the owner.

Case Study 9.1: Mak Rahmah's Account of Women, Family and the House

> As a small girl I used to live in the *rumah gadang*. The other people who lived in this house were my *datuk* [mother's mother; hereafter referred to as 'grandmother' or 'MM'] with her husband,[9] the younger sister of my grandmother [MMZ] with her husband and her four children, my own mother with my father and their four children, including myself. My grandmother had only one child, namely my mother. There were five rooms in the house. One room was occupied by my grandmother, one by her younger sister, another by my mother and two rooms were used by the children.
>
> When I was small, I was brought up by all people in the house, but most of all by my grandmother [MM] and her younger sister [MMZ], because these two women were most often at home. When my grandmother was still alive, she was the one who controlled everything; that is, she had power in matters concerning our corporate property (*harato pusako*) and other matters, because she was the oldest woman in the house. Whatever she said or whatever she ordered us to do, we always obeyed. After she died it was her younger sister who decided on everything, and this is how it went on: whoever was the oldest woman in the house, she

was the one who was most influential – as we say, 'her mouth was the most salty'.

When I was a young girl I was never involved in deliberations, whether it concerned marital partners, corporate property (*pusako*) or other things. After I got married, actually not much changed, because there were still so many older people in the house who could discuss matters. It was only when I was going to have a son-in-law that my opinion was asked about the possible candidate. Why was my opinion never asked on anything? Perhaps it was because I was staying in the *rumah gadang* and in those days there were so many older people who were wiser than me, since I was still young. Perhaps it would have been different had I lived in my own house.

When I was a young girl our *rumah gadang* was very peaceful; there were absolutely no tensions. Perhaps there were tensions, but I was not aware of them; from the outside the tensions were not visible so that we little children obviously did not know about them. It was only when I grew older that I found out that actually there were tensions and conflicts, but these were always solved and the outside world did not hear about it. My grandmother was very wise in solving problems; as far as I know no conflict ever erupted and there was no resentment between us.

In the old days my mother used to cook together with my grandmother [MM] but not with grandmother's younger sister [MMZ] and her daughter [MMZD]. And after I had a family myself I cooked together with my mother until I had a son-in-law. Before that time my grandmother and her husband had passed away.

After I got married I kept on living in the *rumah gadang* and I occupied one of the rooms. I did not join my husband in the *rantau* because I had to take care of my parents who were old and I had to cultivate the *sawah* and the gardens, because I was my mother's only daughter.

When I was to have a son-in-law, I moved out of the *rumah gadang*. My husband built a new house nearby, because the *rumah gadang* was full. My old room was then occupied by my daughter who had a husband; and even now she still occupies this room. I was the one who moved out from the *rumah gadang*, because I was the oldest of the granddaughters of my grandmother and I was the first to have a son-in-law.[10]

At present, I live with one of my daughters though not in the same house. My daughter remains in the *rumah gadang* with her children and I myself live in the shop near this house. I do not stay in the *rumah gadang* because all the rooms are full there, since the daughter of my mother's sister lives there too with her family. But although I live separately from my daughter – albeit not far away – I always eat with her and sometimes one of my grandchildren sleeps with me in the shop.

As far as I know our ancestral land (*tanah pusako*) had already been divided when I was still a small child. It had been divided after the death of the mother of my grandmother [MMM]. Later on, after the death of my grandmother, my mother inherited the part of my *datuak* as a whole because she did not have any sisters, and now I am in control myself.[11] The one who is in control of the land disposes of its yields.

At present my daily work consists only of petty trade in the shop next to our *rumah gadang*. Actually I trade just in order to do something with my free time, because I am no longer capable of going to the rice-fields. Nowadays these are cultivated by my daughter. I eat with my daughter so I do not have to worry about that. For my daily needs I take commodities from my own shop, and my sons who have migrated send me remittances.

Analysis

When Mak Rahmah was young, she lived in a *rumah gadang*. When household is defined in terms of residence, her household was of a joint type. A number of matrilaterally related women – two elderly sisters with their adult daughters – lived together with their eventual husbands and unmarried children. It was 'joint' in certain other respects too. The children were brought up by all the adult women in the house, in particular the two oldest women who were at home most of the time. Moreover, just one woman was considered as the 'head of the household' for all matters internal to that 'household' in the sense of the entire *rumah gadang*, namely the most senior woman. In this case Mak Rahmah's grandmother [MM] used to be the most powerful woman; after her death, her position was taken over by her younger sister [MMZ].

After Mak Rahmah got her first son-in-law she moved out of the *rumah gadang* while her newly-wed daughter stayed behind. Later on Mak Rahmah's second daughter moved out of her house to go to live in a new house that was built by her husband. In the meantime the other branch of the family – consisting of the offspring of the sister of Mak Rahmah's grandmother [MMZ] – stayed behind in the *rumah gadang*. In other words, in 1990 the *rumah gadang* continued to accommodate a joint family in terms of residence. Mak Rahmah reckoned herself as an occupant of this house – where she took her meals – even though she slept in her *kedai*.

However, apart from residence and power, Mak Rahmah's household has never been joint. If control over primary economic resources is taken as the decisive criterion to define the boundaries of a household, her house comprised two separate extended families. The land was owned corporately by Mak Rahmah's lineage, but the use rights had been divided among smaller units a long time ago. Mak Rahmah's great-grandmother [MMM] had decided to divide it between her two daughters: Mak Rahmah's grandmother [MM] and grandmother's sister [MMZ]. These two women had each transmitted their own parts to their own female descendants. The two family branches in the house (descendants of respectively Mak Rahmah's grandmother and her grandmother's sister) controlled land separately and disposed of its yields independently. As far as Mak Rahmah is concerned, the fact that neither her mother nor she herself had had sisters, was advantageous with respect to the availability of land. Due to the limited number of female offspring, the land had not been split up since her grandmother's death.[12] Hence, in Mak Rahmah's *rumah gadang* there were two extended families, each of which cultivated their own part of the lineage land.[13]

Above all, when the household is defined as 'a group of people who share a cooking pot' – the *periuak* unit – then this family has never been joint since the day Mak Rahmah was born. In all instances a senior woman and an adult daughter would cook together, but adult sisters or cousins cooked apart. This means that in Mak Rahmah's *rumah gadang* there had always been two cooking pot units. Each of these units has comprised a senior woman with an adult daughter plus their eventual husbands and unmarried children.

Case Study 9.2: Mak Rahmah's Account of Men, Family and the House

> I had no sisters but I did have three brothers. When they were young, they came home during the daytime to eat; in the evenings they went to the prayer house to recite the Qur'an. They spent the night in the prayer house. When they grew up they started to trade at the markets and sometimes they went far away, for instance to Aceh. After my brothers got married, of course they went to live with their wives. But they were often away to the *rantau* and did not spend much time in the village. When they came home to the village, they would sometimes come to our house during the day. And if by chance they were in the village while we had work to do in the *sawah*, they would certainly help us, unless their wives' kin were busy in the *sawah* too.
>
> My parents were farmers and when I was young I enjoyed helping them in the *sawah*. From the age of 15 onwards I no longer went to the *sawah*; my work consisted mainly of household tasks such as sewing, cooking and so on, because in the old days a girl had to stay at home and she was not allowed to leave the house often. It was my *mamak* who would forbid me to go out.[14] This *mamak* was very strict and would not stand any protest, but admittedly he always took good care of all the needs of his *kemenakan* [sisters' children], in particular his nieces. In those days a *mamak* always guarded the behaviour of his nieces jealously, because should anything happen, the shame would reflect on the *mamak* as well as on the whole family.
>
> Formerly, when cultivating the land we were helped by all members of the *rumah gadang*, joined by other relatives. For instance, when it was time to harvest we would notify our brothers (as *mamak*), then the *mamak* would tell their wives and the wives would come to our *sawah* to help. But today these things no longer happen; it is as though the people do not want to know about it any more. In the old days, after the paddy was taken into

the house, we would give several baskets full of rice to the *mamak*, not as a wage but as a sign of our relationship.

The heavy work in cultivating the *sawah*, such as hoeing, was done by farm labourers.[15] We used to pay them wages in the form of paddy. This does not mean that our brothers did not want to help us: if they happened to be around they would also join in and assist the labourers. But our brothers did not help if they had work to do in the house of their wives or if they were away, for instance trading. For the light work, such as cutting the rice, threshing and weeding, we usually did not hire paid labourers, because this is women's work and we had many female relatives.

In the past, a mother-in-law did not want to eat with her son-in-law; when he was in she even acted as though she was not aware of his presence. She would say no more to him than was absolutely necessary and when he wanted to give household money to his mother-in-law he would give it through his wife. It was the same with us young girls. We had a tremendous feeling of respect for the husbands of our sisters; we would hardly ever greet them, let alone chat with them. It was not like today, when young girls chatter away freely to their sister's husband. As young girls we were also forbidden to talk casually to our own brother; this too was considered awkward.

I got married twice. By now both my husbands have died. I was married off by my *mamak* with the consent of the entire kin group. Both husbands were from Rao-Rao. Both husbands used to migrate to places elsewhere in Sumatra. I never joined them because I did not want to leave my old mother alone; so I stayed behind in the *kampung* and took care of my children and I went to the *sawah*.

I did not stay long with my first husband because we did not have much in common; finally we got divorced after he had left me with three children. My first husband was not a good man. He had been sought by my *mamak*, the son of my *datuk ketek* [mother's mother's younger sister: MMZS]. During the first years of our marriage, he behaved well; perhaps he tried to win the sympathy of his mother-in-law, so that the whole family would like him and trust him. But after he left for the *rantau* – when my children were still small – he never came home, and finally we divorced, and thereafter he never contributed anything towards the upkeep of his children.

When I was divorced I was very happy. I felt free because I was no longer humiliated; even though we had financial hardships, I did not complain because I had brothers and a rice-field and gardens, which provided a livelihood for me and my children. The villagers did not call me bad names, because even as a divorced woman I did not enjoy parading around; I was increasingly busy with my work, because I knew that my children had to eat and live.

Two years after the divorce, I remarried. By this husband I had one more child, a boy. Although I had three children already, he was very fond of all the children. He did not make any difference between the children;

that is what made me like him so much. This second husband of mine also traded in the *rantau*, like the first one, but he always sent letters. Once he sent news that he could not come home because he did not have any money; his business had not been very profitable, so I sent him money from here just to come home. But he did not want to accept it and not long thereafter he came home and said that he had recently been successful in the *rantau*. This was the way he was, my second husband: he had a great sense of responsibility towards his family and he respected my relatives, so that I would have felt sinful had I not respected his relatives too.

I love all my children very much, my sons as well as my daughters, because we have all suffered together. After my first husband left us they were still small; I made a living for them. Before I had my shop, I went to the *sawah* as a farmer, besides which I cultivated other people's *sawah* in order to eke out our income, and in addition I made snacks early in the morning, which were sold by my son. Now that they are married themselves, they always remember their mother; every month they send me a letter and frequently they send money. Of course, they do not send remittances every month because they have a hard life themselves. The main thing is that they are happy; if they do not send money it does not matter. To me all my children are the same, because however far away a child is, and however bad he is, it is still my child. As far as my old age is concerned, I do not have to worry because my daughter lives here in the *rumah gadang*; so I am very happy about that.

Analysis

In a previous section we tried to define Mak Rahmah's 'household' from a female perspective. We have seen that her *rumah gadang* constituted a joint household in terms of residence and authority, but it comprised two extended households if economic resources such as land are taken into account, or if household is defined as a unit with a common cooking pot.

The situation appears even more complicated when one tries to determine which men in Mak Rahmah's family belong to which household. In Mak Rahmah's story her own father and her mother's father play a very subordinate role. Actually they are just mentioned in passing; their place in the house as well as the way in which they related to other people in the house remain obscure. Mak Rahmah's brothers and her respective husbands play a more important, albeit an ambiguous, role in her story. Physically her brothers as well as husbands were absent much of the time: from an early age her brothers slept in the *surau*; when they grew up they often left for the *rantau* and so did her two husbands. As symbols of authority the men are not very visible either: the only time Mak Rahmah mentions a man in connection with power is when she talks about her *mamak* who used to watch the behaviour of his young nieces. Indeed, the chastity of a young girl is the concern of her matrikin, and her *mamak* will be held responsible. Yet one may presume – although this remains implicit in Mak Rahmah's story – that her 'powerful' *mamak* was rarely at home:

he would sleep in his wife's house, and come back to his mother's house regularly to supervise the situation.

Where do the men come in? Mak Rahmah speaks about her two husbands in affectionate terms. She did not like the first husband; in contrast she did like/love the second husband. But apart from this, the males enter her story primarily in their roles of provider. Her account exposes the dual economic responsibilities of men towards their wives and children on the one hand and their sisters and sisters' children on the other. Mak Rahmah's *mamak* took good care of the needs of his sisters' children. Her first husband was a bad man who failed to take care of his own children; her second husband was a good man who felt responsible and took care of all her children. After the divorce from her first husband she had financial problems but she did not complain because she 'had brothers' (and rice-fields). However, the dual economic roles of men are expressed most clearly in Mak Rahmah's discussion of the cultivation of her rice-fields during the 1950s or 1960s. She describes a transitional phase, when men had started to have primary duties and rights towards their wives and their wives' land but were still strongly attached to their mother's and sisters' land.[16] In those years Mak Rahmah's brothers were in the *rantau* much of the time; when they were in the village they would assist either their wives or their sister in cultivating the rice-fields. They would give priority to helping their wives, but if there was not much work to do in their wives' fields, they would lend a hand to their sister (Mak Rahmah), if necessary. As an acknowledgement of their 'relationship', Mak Rahmah gave her brothers several baskets of rice in return. Today her kinsmen and kinswomen no longer cooperate like they used to; this means, for example, that brothers will not help their sisters in the rice-fields.

In short, when Mak Rahmah was a young woman, married men were involved in two houses: the house of their wives and those of their mother and sisters, with partly overlapping social and economic obligations and rights in both houses. In none of the houses were they full residents. This sort of situation is certainly changing, and men are becoming more attached to the house of their wives, as can be seen from the fact that a brother is no longer inclined to assist his sisters in cultivating her rice-fields. Yet the dualism has not entirely faded away. The importance of the male role of *mamak* is, among other things, well illustrated by the fact that men who were born in poor families with little or no land, and therefore unable to perform the economic duties of a *mamak* properly, take a pride in supporting their sisters' children as soon as their wealth increases through personal effort.

The words of another middle-aged woman from Rao-Rao are illuminating. This woman was asked what kind of man would be a good husband. Her answer is a clear illustration of the dual expectations that women have towards husbands and brothers:

> A good husband is a man who keeps the balance between the family of his wife and his own family. In other words: he feels responsible to his wife's family but also to his own family. ... Formerly a husband did not spend much time in his wife's house, but he had to present himself as a

good *sumando* [in-married male]. A *sumando* has to respect the *mamak* of the house, his mother-in-law and his wife's kin; he is also needed to make suggestions when a decision is to be taken. At the same time a man has to be a good *mamak* in his mother's family and he has to take responsibility for his sisters' children, because the demeanour of a husband in his mother's family is of tremendous importance for the evaluation of a mother-in-law towards the wife. If a man does not pay sufficient attention to the family of his mother [his matrikin], his mother will say that he is henpecked by his wife, and then of course she will take a dislike to her daughter-in-law.

At the same time this quotation indicates that even at present senior women still think of their own position as pivotal and influential within the kin group and between kin groups.

Concluding Remarks

In this chapter I have tried to demonstrate that the household is not a very fruitful unit of analysis for Minangkabau rural communities. Even if one defines the household as a group of persons who share a cooking pot, this definition appears problematic. Although there is a 'common cooking pot unit' – the *periuak* – this group is not in the least independent or corporate. Instead, the individual stands in the centre of a network of kin relations, each of which has its own significance for specific domains of social and economic life. An analysis of personal networks of men and women will probably lead to a deeper understanding of gender relations than the analysis of relations within the 'household' or 'family', whatever this may mean. Married men remain strongly attached to their own matrikin; they are expected to fulfil a dual role as *mamak* [mother's brother] and as husband/father or *sumando* [in-married male]. Although their position as husband/father has become stronger over the past decades, the integration of conjugal families is far from complete. A man's place continues to be fairly peripheral: his children belong to his wife's clan and lineage; usually he has access to ancestral property only through his wife; he has limited authority over wife and children.

Women – in particular senior women – continue to be pivotal within the domestic and kin structure. The line of descent is continued through women; use rights to land and houses are inherited from mother to daughter; matrilocality is still a norm and senior women continue to be influential persons in circles of the family and kin, and hence indirectly in wider society too. In addition, increasing rates of migration of males out of rural areas have strengthened certain 'matriarchal' features in the village community (see also Naim 1984, 1985): the more dynamic and clever men leave the village and search for success in the *rantau*; as a result the rural areas are tending to become more and more dominated by women both numerically and in terms of power.

A few comments are called for. Living in the village is becoming difficult, owing among other things to population pressure and shortage of land. Men have better opportunities than women to earn a private income (*pancarian*), and much of their income nowadays is spent on behalf of their own wives and children. Hence, it may be said that women are gradually becoming more dependent on men, in particular on their husbands. Nonetheless, most Minangkabau women do have other resources at hand in case of need. If the husband is no longer there, or if he is not capable of providing for his wife and children, many women fall back on their land and their kin (grown-up children, men in their role as *mamak*, or others).

What about the increasing numbers of women who are leaving the village and, with their husbands, are establishing a more nuclearized family in the *rantau*? Although this was outside the scope of my research, a few hypotheses may be adduced. First of all, migration does not automatically mean that a woman loses her rights to the ancestral property (land, houses); hence, in case of failure or a reverse of fortune in the *rantau*, the road back to the village is usually not entirely closed. Often bonds between a woman and her kin in the village are maintained through letters (two-way traffic), remittances (from *rantau* to village) and through consignments of rice (from village to *rantau*). Despite this, a woman in the *rantau* will be more dependent on her conjugal family for emotional, social and economic support; at the same time there will be less immediate social control from kin than is the case in the village.

Some authors have suggested that extended unilateral kinship systems in themselves imply a weaker bargaining position for women than do bilateral kinship systems. Papanek and Schwede, for instance, state that in (Asian) societies where households are composed of several generations - or where this is the unattained cultural ideal - it is much more likely that individual action is constrained by the limits set by specific social roles (1988: 97).

I do not know and, moreover, it is not up to me to judge whether living in a nuclear family (away from the village; usually in big cities) is better or worse for Minangkabau women. Anyway, whether a woman does or does not join her husband can be either a personal choice or the result of pressure from the side of the husband or that of her own kin. It is certainly true that limits are set on individual action in extended families, as Papanek and Schwede say, but it should be noted that men as well as women are subject to these limits. Moral or social restrictions do not always and everywhere work merely to the disadvantage of women. What is more, living in the village has certain definite advantages for many Minangkabau women: in their own village communities they are assured of a minimum of social and economic security among their kin, land and houses. At the same time they enjoy a relative autonomy in their daily lives, mainly owing to the fact that they have their own sources of income (from land or otherwise) and that the men are away from home much of the time. In a matrilineal and matrilocal setting, extended families are no doubt beneficial to women, in more than one respect.

NOTES

1   For critical reviews of definitions, see Pittin (1987), Fapohunda (1988), Blumberg (1991), Kabeer (1991), Wallerstein and Smith (1991).
2   The boundaries of the *nagari* do not always correspond to those of the *desa*, which is the smallest unit in the Indonesian administrative system.
3   A considerable amount of literature has been dedicated to the specific socio-economic position of Minangkabau women within the house or family, e.g.: Korn (1941), Alisyahbana (1983), Navis (1985), Postel-Coster (1985), Prindiville (1985), Tanner and Thomas (1985), Pak (1986), Sanday (1990), Blackwood (1993).
4   'Adult women': women who are or have been married.
5   For a critical review of this concept see i.a. K. and F. von Benda-Beckmann (1978), and F. von Benda-Beckmann (1979).
6   'Village community' is used here in the sense of *nagari*; Nagari Rao-Rao consisted of two *desa* (see also footnote 2).
7   The research was on changing gender and kin relations, from a female perspective. It was carried out together with assistants from the Department of Sociology and Anthropology of the Andalas University. It has resulted in a PhD thesis (van Reenen 1996).
8   Mak Rahmah [Mother or Mrs Rahmah] is not her real name
9   In most literature on Minangkabau the concept *datuk* (or *datuak*) is identified with the (male) title for *penghulu* [head of lineage or clan]. In Rao-Rao *datuk* had a wider meaning; it was used for senior women as well as senior men, namely: a person's MM, MF, FM, FF, MMB, FMB. The *penghulu*s in the village were generally called *datuk* too, but particular kinsmen/kinswomen used different titles. When Mak Rahmah speaks of her *datuk*, what she means is her mother's mother (MM).
10 Granddaughter (*cucu*) is used in the classificatory sense here. Mak Rahmah's mother's mother has only one granddaughter in the straight line. However, her sister's daughter's daughters [ZDD] are also her granddaughters.
11 Just like her mother, Mak Rahmah does not have sisters; therefore all of her mother's land has been transmitted to her.
12 This situation might change in the next generation, since Mak Rahmah has two daughters who are both entitled to the land.
13 Other economic resources will be discussed briefly below.
14 This was a classificatory *mamak*, namely: a son of Mak Rahmah's mother's mother's sister (MMZS). (Mak Rahmah's own mother did not have any brothers.) The *mamak* used to be responsible for a girl's chastity.
15 The 'heavy work' to which Mak Rahmah refers is the part of the labour normally carried out by males.
16 We are here speaking of Nagari Rao-Rao; in other places this transitional phase took place at an earlier or even later stage.

SECTION IV: MOBILITY, DOMESTIC ARRANGEMENTS AND FAMILY LIFE

The following three chapters are detailed micro-studies of New Order Indonesia showing the effect of a wide range of mobility patterns (daily commuting practices, rural–urban migration as well as transmigration) on the form and function of domestic arrangements. In particular in migrant communities where spatial divisions by definition defy conventional physical and social boundaries, traditional definitions of the household are not longer tenable.

It will also be shown that women are active agents in the process, either in their position as migrants or as those who stay behind. The economic independence of women may even form the very basis for male migration. However, whether it is true that costs eventually match benefits for women is another story

In her study entitled 'Different Times, Different Orientations: Family Life in a Javanese Village', Juliette Koning combines the time-lag argument with attention to kinship and 'life of the outside' experiences, as they pattern interaction between family members and family formation behaviour. She focuses on how physical mobility redefines social mobility and intra- as well as inter-household relations of family life in Central Java, where the predominant form of domestic arrangements has become the nuclear family. The effects of this process on members of the various generations, as well as women, appear to be very different

Becky Elmhirst focuses in her case study called 'Negotiating Gender, Kinship and Livelihood Practices in an Indonesian Transmigration Area' on the tension between intra-household relations and external forces and the different outcomes that this process has for the daughters of respectively local and Javanese migrant communities in South Sumatra. Different cultural notions about a daughter's economic role in the household have resulted in different patterns of women's migration and job search. Despite their history of migration, daughters of Javanese migrant households were only allowed to work in the village and thus live up to ideological ideals. Daughters of local households were allowed to migrate to financially rewarding factory work on Java, although this was considered to be ideologically less pure.

Patrilineal kinship systems and patriarchal family values are generally speaking constraining for women. Also among the Toba Batak of North Sumatra patrilineal kinship rules present serious constraints to female agency. Yet in 'Staying Behind: Conflict and Compromise in Toba Batak Migration' Jane Rodenburg argues that women are important actors in facilitating men's migration by managing family and farm. This in turn also enhances their own manoeuvring space and so makes them far from passive victims. Thus, the study is a sound analysis of, on the one hand, the complex ways in which gender relationships are constituted and reconstituted within the household and in the wider society; and, on the other hand, the ways in which women negotiate accommodate and resist the organizing power of these gender relations in their everyday lives.

10

Different Times, Different Orientations
Family Life in a Javanese Village

Juliette Koning

INTRODUCTION

The household or family often functions in the social sciences as the basic unit of analysis by which to study social, cultural, economic, political or historical changes. The fact that the family and household are often so used substantiates their considered theoretical importance and, what is more, their considered universality. At the same time this choice expresses a kind of functionality of physical boundaries within which the social scientist has a grip on what is taking place. Although in many societies, like Java, the family or household is one of the major networks in which people are engaged, it is certainly not the *only* one; indeed, in some societies a household or family in such terms does not even exist. Furthermore, family and household as terms are often used interchangeably, while obviously they are not necessarily one and the same.

What stands out in any analysis of family and household studies are the controversies over what in fact constitutes a family or household: whether the family and household exist at all or whether relationships and roles are more important manifestations; whether the family and household are a given fact or more a process with cyclical developments; and whether their form and function change in sequence. None of these questions has been solved yet and probably never will be, especially not if the aim is to come to general and cross-cultural conclusions or definitions. As expressed by Netting, Wilk and Arnould (1984: xxvi), 'arriving at a clear-cut, cross-culturally valid definition of the household is as problematic as the blind man's description of the elephant'. Moreover, the household or the family as an analytical construct is also subject to corporate assumptions (Kemp 1988); households in particular are easily 'reified and personalized: the household became an actor, it allocated labour, it had needs, utility functions and pursued strategies' (F. and K. von Benda-Beckmann, this volume).

It is not as if nothing has been attained, though. Our knowledge of the manifold features of family and household life has increased enormously over the last few decades. Not only is it recognized that there is enormous cross-cultural variation in residential arrangements, but the move away from perceptions of the household and family as closed, harmonious units and as homogeneous and altruistic connotations, has lent new meaning and importance to the study of family and household life. The work of gender-oriented social scientists which opened up the household especially stands out among the more recent attainments.[1] By observing and studying family and household life in terms of the interactions between people and with broader societal processes, we can reveal more about family and household life and relationships than has hitherto been the case, especially where Southeast Asia is concerned.[2]

This chapter focuses on a Javanese village, Rikmokèri, in order to shed light on the shifts that are taking place in both the meanings and practices among the various generations *vis-à-vis* family life. The reason for focusing on family life is twofold. First of all there is an intriguing lack of interest in this realm in its own right in rural Java studies as they have appeared since the early 1970s. Although 'the family' as such is often seen as a meaningful and important domain, in most studies it plays a peripheral or marginal role subordinate to the specific topic under scrutiny. After the influential works by Clifford and Hildred Geertz, Robert Jay and Koentjaraningrat in the late 1950s and early 1960s on socio-cultural life in Java, major interest in this theme has waned. This neglect is all the more surprising since life in rural Java has been anything but static. In fact it is precisely the transformations since the advent of the New Order government which have attracted the attention of quite a few social scientists, producing a great many important and interesting studies on rural differentiation, demographic transitions, rural-urban migration, resource control, rural industrialization, and local leadership, to mention just a few. Second, by 1990 Indonesia had attained impressive economic growth, had undergone rapid demographic change, and had achieved an unsurpassed increase in communications and transportation networks, especially in Java.[3] All this makes one wonder what this signifies for ordinary people leading their everyday family lives, especially in a village where a growing group of young villagers seek a livelihood and cultural ideals in Jakarta as circular migrants. This latter phenomenon has, as I shall show, had quite an impact on family life. The fact that 43% of all households have at least one family member engaged in this circular labour migration to Jakarta, shows the magnitude.[4] Although there are no reliable statistical records, it appears that the move to Jakarta started on a very small scale in the mid-1970s to reach the highest out-migration so far in the 1990s. Most of the labour migration (*mboro*) before the 1970s was of a rural–rural based character and involved following the rice harvest from area to area. This chapter will show that labour migration not only redefines intra-household relationships and with it family life, but that it also imbues social mobility, which affects both the village and the family.

I pointed out above that in the literature household and family are often used interchangeably as terms, even though they are rarely one and the same. Here I shall explain what I mean by family life and why I prefer to talk of families instead of households.

Family life in the present chapter refers to the interactions between people who are related by blood or marriage on matters of common concern (marriage, childbirth, financial matters, roles and responsibilities) and which usually take place within the realm that they share daily, i.e. the house or household. In the village under study, which also stands for Java in general, the majority of domestic arrangements concern nuclear families (61%), followed by augmented (17%) and multiple nuclear (14%) families, and female-headed households (8%).[5] In all but one case in Rikmokèri those residing under one roof are related and take part in discussions on how daily life as a family – husband, wife, child, grandparent, parent – should be lived. Since I am mainly concerned here with *interactions* along generational lines, the term 'family life' signifies this best. There is one more danger in this intricate web of concepts and their meanings, namely that not all family members live under the same roof. Family ties usually extend to other houses in the village and also to other villages (sons marry out) or even to other islands, if sons or daughters migrate. Therefore, family life as used here is confined to those family members who live under the same roof and interact on a daily basis.

A final note needs to be made on the generational approach which I have used in the study. Without arguing that generations are homogeneous groups, which they obviously are not, the locus of orientation of the generations in Rikmokèri turned out to be rather divergent. This is related to the quite different socio-historical contexts they grew up in, which subsequently set the background for their lives. The older generations lived through war, revolts and recessions, whereas the middle generations experienced the coming of the New Order. The younger generations are the product of the latter and saw life getting better, at least until the mid-1990s. I have argued elsewhere that as a result, the generations in the village are ranged back-to-back and are looking in opposite directions at what they each deem important and valuable (Koning 1997: 14). I have defined the generations/households according to the age of the women in the households: younger-generation households are households in which the female head is younger than 35 years; in the middle-generation households the female head is between 35 and 50 years old; and the older-generation households have a female head who is 50 years or older. For the in-depth interviews on the visions of the various generations on the topics discussed below, I worked with a sample of 62 households which included 18 younger-generation households, 23 middle-generation households and 21 older-generation households.

In the following section I shall look at various debates on the family and the household to point out the studies that inspired me and to see what lessons can be drawn from these debates for the Javanese case and for this kind of studies more in general. Thereafter I shall shift my focus to the New Order family ideology as propagated by the state to detect whether or not this doctrine has any association with the way Rikmokèri family life is evolving. Having set the stage, I shall proceed by delineating who lives with whom under one roof as this gives an initial insight into age and gender positions in families on the basis of which we can inquire in more detail about certain roles and responsibilities. The phenomenon of absentee (migrant) family members, for instance, affects the content and tasks within a nuclear family to a large extent. After this I shall address the theme of marriage and children, which are both central features in Rikmokèri family life. The focus will be on possible changes in local customs. A fairly recent phenomenon in Rikmokèri family life is the question of remittances, and I shall pay special attention to this topic because it is one very distinct realm where (grand)parents and children, and husbands and wives confront each other with changing patterns of demands and behaviour. In the final section some conclusions on Rikmokèri family life across generations will be drawn.

The Household and Family Debate: Any Lessons to be Learned?

On the face of it, it seems quite dangerous to opt for a topic pertaining to family life because of the ambivalence surrounding household and family studies. Statements that we face a 'theoretical crisis' and that 'strictly speaking we do not know what changes we are talking about when dealing with family issues' (De Oliveira 1992: 202) lead to rather a grim picture. The question that I would like to pose is whether there are any lessons to be learned from the engagement of social scientists in this topic over the last few decades. In order to reach a conclusion, I shall first look at what family studies have to bring us before examining the more household-oriented studies.

For a study on changing family life, a first lesson lies in the discussion within historical sociology about changing family forms in Europe under the processes of industrialization and urbanization. Of central concern was whether the change in family forms was related to modernization processes, and whether the nuclear family was becoming the dominant form or not. Many thought it was. Goode (1963), for instance, asserted the link between the conjugal family and modernization, while Parsons and Bales (1955) saw processes of differentiation in modernizing societies as the main instigator of the rise of the nuclear family. The nuclear family with its 'structural isolation and role segregation of husband and wife' was considered best equipped to operate in the 'modern world' (McDonald 1992: 15–16). This presupposed functional relation between the nuclear family and industrial society has been criticized among others by Laslett (1972). From the mid-1960s onwards he accumulated evidence resulting in the statement that the nuclear family form may have in fact been one of the enduring and fundamental characteristics of the Western family system (Anderson 1980: 23–25). Although the information brought forward by Laslett severely undermined the old hypothesis of the 'unilinear development from pre-industrial extended family households to industrial family nuclearization', this hypothesis was replaced by a new, but equally unbalanced, one 'stressing continuity in family form and structure over many centuries' (Janssens 1991: 13). Hence, any attempt to link the prevalence of certain types of family forms (the nuclear one) to the functional requirements of society (the industrialized urbanized one) is fruitless. Such one-way causal explanations are highly problematic.

This point is taken up by Janssens, who in her study of family and social change in the Dutch town of Tilburg for the period 1840–1920, shows that the relationship between changing family systems and industrialization is far more complex. Where the structural-functionalist reasoning stresses the direct link between structural, ideological and behavioural change, a 'time-lag' argument holds that structural change does not *immediately* result in changes in attitudinal and behavioural patterns. This is best demonstrated by Tilly and Scott (1978). They show that the process of industrialization in Britain and France meant that an increasing number of women and girls started to work for wages. In the initial phase of this process, the existing routine of the family economy continued but in a new setting. Even though many girls left their rural homes to work in the cities, 'ties of family and the sense of obligation to one's parents long persisted among working girls' (Tilly and Scott 1978: 111). Gradually, however, family ties changed. Since these young girls started earning their own wages, which augmented their autonomy, they gained more influence over the allocation of family resources. The individualization of income also disrupted the supposedly common interests of the household or family. This 'time-lag' argument offers a promising framework (and second lesson) as it indicates that the ideas and attitudes that people already hold are used as tools to adapt to changing social and economic structures. This approach also leaves open the (very likely) possibility that different social groups adopt different strategies in an attempt to adapt to changing circumstances (Janssens 1991: 20–26). The young girls in the work of Tilly and Scott very much resemble in their behaviour the young villagers of Rikmokèri several decades later. Although Java undergoes rapid change and transformation, it does not automatically lead to a complete collapse of, in this case, family life the way it was practised before. People as participants try to find ways to react to the impact of the changes and although certain networks (such as the family) weaken or nuclearize, others (re)appear (friendship bonds).

Where in sociology and historical sociology the attention was often on the 'changing family' in tandem with societal processes as we saw above, in economic and feminist anthropology it was especially the household that became central in debates on consumption and reproduction. The more economic approach focuses on the allocational behaviour of the household as unit of production and consumption within which the reproduction of human labour is secured (Wong 1984: 56). Although this approach has brought important information concerning income pooling and resource distribution to the fore, it harbours many shortcomings: the third lesson. The problem is that the economic approach perceives the household as a social entity where a unity of interests, cohesion and solidarity rule. Such an outlook 'submerges important information about variation in household composition – by gender, age, and kinship – and intra- and inter-household resource allocation and distribution' (Evans 1991: 54). Feminist anthropologists pointed out the necessity of opening up the household and of studying intra-household relationships. They refuted the idea of the altruist because it ignores domestic conflicts about intra-household distribution of tasks, goods and entitlements. As a result the idea that differences of concern and gain among household members are part and parcel of family life slowly gained ground (Hartmann 1981). In order to understand the different position and authority of genders and generations within households, we have to look at who makes decisions, what kind of decisions, on whose behalf, and how other family or household members are submitted to them (Wolf 1990: 61): the fourth lesson.

Apart from arguing in favour of analysing the nature of intra-household relationships, anthropologists revealed the surprising neglect of kinship and gender in household studies. These are all-important organizing principles in everyday life, especially in the realms of family and household. Gender 'as a crucial parameter in social and economic analysis is complementary to, rather than competitive with, the variables of class, ownership, occupations, incomes, and family status' (Sen 1990: 123). Javanese society, although often perceived as embodying equality and complementarity between females and males, still accomodates differences between 'official' and 'practical' portrayals of gender (cf. Peletz 1994). There can be little doubt that women and men in the same household or family can and at times do have dissimilar objectives and desires. Guyer and Peters emphasize that households and families are not solely task-oriented units or places to live, eat, work and reproduce; they are also sources of identity, situated in 'structures of cultural meaning' (Guyer and Peters 1987: 209). The extent to which kinship and/or family ideology determine the room for manoeuvre of household and family members needs to be examined, especially where the ideals of the younger generation on subjects such as marriage and family conflict with ruling family ideologies: the last lesson so far.

To conclude then, the picture is not as grim as portrayed above. The lessons demonstrate that attention to kinship and ideology and the links to wider societal realms and processes give the necessary insights into family life (or intra-household spheres). We also need to regard the different powers and entitlements of both the genders and generations within families and households. Furthermore, the family is a realm where kinship principles are socialized and manipulated and where identity formation takes place. However, since late-twentieth-century Java is very much in motion, this greatly affects family life and these related personal and family attributes.

FAMILY LIFE IN RIKMOKÈRI

In this chapter the relationships and issues within the home are of major importance because they highlight generational and gender positions and views. Cogently, the family is neither fixed nor bounded, nor is it isolated from the wider society within and beyond Rikmokèri. With a younger generation that is inspired in their life choices by their experiences in the wider world (like formal education and working in Jakarta), the family is the place where existing patterns of (grand)parent–child and husband–wife relationships and interactions are no longer self-evident to the extent they once were.[6] In fact, such relationships and the concomitant expectations and behaviour patterns are increasingly being challenged. Those children who earn cash, live away from home, and contribute to the household economy at a young age expect a certain autonomy not accorded them previously. These young villagers talk of the freedom and feelings of independence related to living away from home, and being able to earn cash on their own account. The same is the case with husbands who work in Jakarta. Whereas spending money, especially on more expensive goods or investments, used to be a topic of consultation between husband and wife, the husbands now often spend the remittances on goods and items which the wives have not been consulted about and may, for instance, have disagreed with. These are just a few examples where existing patterns and the behaviour and actions of family and household members have become less predictable to the others.

Apart from daily family life in Rikmokèri, there is also a specific New Order ideology on family life.[7] The state not only prefers families with only two children, and thus tries to interfere directly in the family formation behaviour of its citizens, it also promulgates the family as the cornerstone of society. In order to safeguard that society and the achievements reached so far, the state has formulated specific roles for fathers, mothers and children. During various village meetings, Rikmokèri villagers are instructed on these roles and the lifestyles they are supposed to uphold. Even speeches by local religious teachers glorify the family and point out, just as the village officials do, the need to preserve family and community values. Held high among these ideals is the obedience of children to their elders, the serving role of the mother and wife, and the economic provider role of the father. The state obviously tries to manoeuvre its citizens into a prescribed way of life, but whether Rikmokèri villagers adhere to this New Order ideology is a moot point.

THE NEW ORDER CONTEXT

Since the New Order state has very outspoken views about what family life in Indonesia should entail, it is worth taking a closer look at how these views are propagated. Although the New Order family ideology is in essence directed at the civil servants as the direct representatives of the state, the latter are saddled with the task of promoting these messages in their local communities and of setting a good example themselves, as in Rikmokèri.

The most persistent message concerning family life over the last two decades has been the message of the small and happy family. This is disseminated via all possible channels, most predictably by the family planning fieldworkers who have become part and parcel of daily village life in Rikmokèri because of their regular presence in the village. Recently a new phase in the family planning programme was initiated with the passing of a new law (UU 10/1992) on Population and Prosperous Family Development (*Perkembangan Kepen-*

dudukan dan Pembangunan Keluarga Sejahtera).[8] The most interesting aspect of this new law is the shift from a family planning focus to a more purely family focus. In this latter approach the family is the vehicle for national development, or in the words of former President Suharto at the opening ceremony of the first National Family Day, 29 June 1993: 'Let us build a prosperous family as the vehicle for our people's development' (*marilah kita bangun keluarga sejahtera sebagai wahana pembangunan bangsa*). In order to encourage the goal of development (*pembangunan*) and prosperity, the family is now assigned several functions: one is to ensure that all its members will worship one God (religious function); another is that it should become an independent economic unit which achieves prosperity on its own merits (Haryono Suyono 1994a: 7–9). The final goal is the realization of the 'quality family' (*keluarga yang berkualitas*) (Haryono Suyono 1994b: 17). As such, this smallest unit in society consists of husband and wife, or of a husband and wife and their children, or of a mother and her children, or of a father and his children (Haryono Suyono 1993: 1).

In the meantime 22 requirements have been drawn up in order to decide whether a family is still stuck in a pre-prosperous state (*keluarga pra sejahtera*) or has already attained maximum prosperity (*keluarga sejahtera plus*). Checking through all these 22 requirements (which include having three meals a day and having different sets of clothing for indoor and outdoor activities), it can be concluded that Rikmokèri village is in a state of pre-prosperity, but this would be missing the target by a mile. It is fairly obvious that many of these requirements are specifically urban, middle-class inspired. In short, these yardsticks of prosperity are fairly illusory, at least for the situation in Rikmokèri.

Although this new family prosperity programme was not yet fully functional in Rikmokèri during the research, the outlines themselves speak volumes about the New Order family ideal, which can be summed up as the small, nuclear, self-supporting, urban, middle-class family. Admittedly this ideal may be far from the reality in Rikmokèri, but among the younger, so-called New Order generation, several fascinating similarities in ideals are noticeable. Young couples espouse the ideal of the nuclear family. Although it is not a new ideal, as I shall show below, it is much closer to the grasp of this generation than it ever was for former generations. What is more, with work histories in Jakarta behind them, these young villagers have witnessed the sort of urban, middle-class family life being propagated and they confess to being attracted by it. This is not the same as being able to achieve it or even to pursue it; nor should it be forgotten that obviously not all the situations they have witnessed reflect the image of that urban middle-class ideal. What it boils down to is that the sorts of family ideals disseminated by the Suharto government to some extent converge with the ideals of the young in Rikmokèri. But Rikmokèri is not yet Jakarta, nor is it solely inhabited by the young: the generations have their own ideals and lifestyles.

LIVING UNDER ONE ROOF

In order to reveal the arrangements of family life in Rikmokèri, it is instructive first to look at who lives with whom under one roof. Alas, here the focus is on family life as it takes place within the household. We have to be careful though, since the differing configurations of people living under one roof may very well be variations of one and the same family type. Households only exist by dint of the people residing in them, who pass through various phases during their life-cycle (birth, adolescence, marriage, divorce, death). The household is thus a 'moving target in terms of composition, structure, overall productive capability, and consumption requirements' (White 1980: 21). The household's inception is couched in the marriage of the initial couple and childbirth: the phase of 'expansion'. This is followed by the phase in which the children grow up, marry, and move out of the parental home to set up their own household: the phase of 'dispersion or fission'. And finally the initial couple dies and is 'replaced' in the community by the families of its children (Fortes 1966: 4–5). Although in essence correct, it has been pointed out by many anthropologists since Fortes that this developmental cycle of households is too simplistic a concept to describe what really happens. This is certainly valid for Rikmokèri families. The idea that the children grow up and remain in the parental home until they marry is no longer valid, since many children work and live away from home. The day-to-day running of such a nuclear household might very well diverge from what this ideal type suggests, namely the living together of parents and children.

As stated in the introduction, Rikmokèri has some 60% nuclear families. But data on migrant and non-migrant families reveal that more than 35% of the nuclear families have either no husband or no children at home most of the time. So what then does 'nuclear' mean? In fact, one could argue that these nuclear families are *de facto* female-headed. Some 58 nuclear migrant families (of a total of 138 nuclear migrant families) have a husband working in Jakarta. With a pattern of returning to the village once every three months or so for a few days, this has implications for the daily household affairs. Of these 58 husband-absent households, the majority (47 households) belong to the younger-generation households. This implies that a fair number of young women in fact run their households and families on their own and that there is a tendency towards the feminization of family life. This does not imply that women previously never had a major role in family life, but rather that nowadays they tend to have greater responsibility for handling these affairs. The following case is an example.

Case Study 10.1: *Mbak*[9] Yatim

> *Mbak* Yatim is 32 years old. Her husband works as bricklayer (*tukang batu*) in Jakarta. He does not work for the big construction projects in which most labourers are engaged, but for private clients. This way he earns a fairly steady Rp. 10,000 a day including meals. He rents a room in Jakarta

with a friend for Rp. 50,000 a month which is paid in three-monthly instalments. There is no regular pattern to his coming home; sometimes he comes home once a month, sometimes Yatim only sees him again after three months. Yatim explains that she is already used to having a husband who is away most of the time (*merasa sudah biasa ditinggal suami*), that now it has become a way of life. Of course she wishes that he could work in the village and be home all the time, but as she herself asks, 'what can he do in the village?' She adds that if the truth be told, her husband would also prefer to work in the village, which is after all where his roots lie. But returning to the village implies coming back to become a farmer or farm labourer, which is not his cup of tea. Yatim avers that never in his life has he worked as a farm labourer on the *sawah* of others, only on that of his parents and what is now partly their own *sawah*. They inherited 0.16 ha *sawah* and in practice its cultivation falls on Yatim's shoulders. Should her husband be home while there is work to be done in the *sawah*, he certainly assists, but he does not come home expressly to do so. Besides having the *sawah* and household to manage, Yatim also has a young child, Sri. It is her only daughter, whom she adopted as a two-month-old baby from a young woman whose husband had left for Jakarta but never returned. So most of the time it is just Yatim and her daughter at home and her days consist of managing the house, the *sawah*, taking care of Sri, and visiting her parents who live nearby.

For many young married women whose husbands work away from home, female friendships are becoming more important. In these friendships they share what it means to have a husband in Jakarta: they often have one or two young children at home, and some also share a history of work in Jakarta. Although these families live in so-called nuclear households, for this group the nature of the family is obviously not the same as for those where the husband is around every day. In this light, their seeking out of other networks to fulfil certain needs, not only in practical terms (as in taking care of each other's children in turns so that they can go and work in the *sawah*) but also in emotional terms (to go back in story-telling to the times they themselves were migrant workers in Jakarta) is all too understandable. What this means is that although the household composition can indicate certain patterns of family life, the actual day-to-day situation can vary greatly from that generally considered to be the prevalent form.

Young widows and divorcees have several other problems to cope with, especially in those cases where the children work away from home. It is an incontrovertible fact that these children generally contribute more than their peers to the household of their single mother. Although in many cases the mother acknowledges that such supplements are crucial to the family economy, it is also an additional burden for her, since she is already on her own and now sees her children maybe only once a year. Then again, human nature being as it is, not in every instance do these children hand over their earnings to their mother, which only aggravates the feelings of loss and loneliness.

Hence, the point to make is that it makes a difference whether a household consists of a single parent, of a conjugal couple with their young children, or of a conjugal couple with their children and with a married daughter whose husband has joined this household and their young baby. These very different formations influence intra-household contacts, authority patterns, as well as the division of labour for household tasks. With more adults present there are also more potential workers who can support the family economically or share in certain tasks. In reality, as we shall see below, this is rarely the case. It is not common practice in Rikmokèri for everything to be pooled or shared in augmented nuclear or multiple nuclear families. This is also the case with *Mbak* Kari, who as a married daughter with her husband and young child, lives with her parents in a multiple nuclear household and who has a history as migrant worker in Jakarta.

Case Study 10.2: *Mbak* **Kari**

> *Mbak* Kari married in 1992 at the age of 20 after a long period of working in Jakarta. Bitterly upset that she was not allowed to continue her education, at the age of 14 she decided to join a friend in Jakarta where she worked several years in a garments factory. Hence she cut cloth for Rp. 70,000 a month, including two meals and a bed in one of the two large dormitories for the women next to the factory. During the years she worked in the factory she returned to Rikmokèri only once or twice a year. She vividly remembers her arrival in Jakarta. The city was bursting with life (*ramai-ramai*), but she also remembers that she needed some time to adjust to city life and to the work in the factory. There were so many unfamiliar faces in the huge factory that it scared her. Looking back she concludes that in fact she never really felt at home (*nggak betah*) there. The woman who supervised the female workers was very strict and did not allow the girls to chat during their work.
>
> After several years, having saved a fair amount of money, she thought 'enough is enough' and returned to Rikmokèri. She did not experience great difficulties in returning to village life after her Jakarta years. The simple fact is she never really did anything exciting in Jakarta. In her spare time she usually visited some friends from the same subdistrict and the most they ever did was to go to a zoo. Upon her return to the village there was some gossip about the goods she brought with her such as a television set and a sewing machine. She thinks that maybe some people were a bit jealous. Once back in the village she returned to her parental home and worked side by side with her mother in the household and in their *sawah*. She also took a sewing course in a nearby town. Having finished the course, she started a dress-making business at home for a while. Four months

after she and her future husband met in the nearby town, they were married and the new husband moved in with Kari's parents. He keeps ducks but at times he works in construction in Jakarta for several months.

The parental home is now quite crowded with Kari, her husband (when at home) and their 2-year-old daughter Miai. Then there are her parents and their two youngest children. Kari and her husband have a room at the back to themselves. Although they live in the same house, the two couples manage their own finances and in principle cook for their own families. Of course, at times the two women take over from each other and also at times make one meal for the whole family, but then one woman buys the vegetables and the other the *tempe*. After having lived like this for about two years, Kari is growing anxious to move out. The house is just too crowded and there is no privacy at all. She feels annoyed that she cannot even quarrel with her husband because her parents will overhear them and make comments. To top it all, she has had enough of her parents' interference with her upbringing of Miai. With the savings from Jakarta she bought a buffalo, which she sold after the animal grew into an adult and with that money she bought a plot of land not far from her parents' house. Now the building can start soon. She feels it is high time to start her own household.

The organization in houses where two couples reside under one roof (as with *Mbak* Kari) or where a parent is living in, has its own dynamics. The case of Kari is representative of many other similar cases in which married children live with their parents for a while or where other adult relatives are living in. As the case indicates, there is not much pooling of resources. The couples keep separate budgets and there is also not much change in the more general pattern of the division of household labour: the laundry is done by the women separately and the cooking is done in principle for their own families. Turning to the authority patterns, more often than not people start to get on each other's nerves and conflict frequently arises because people are not able to act and behave as they want, as Kari clearly pointed out. Authority patterns are also subjected to undue stress, especially when parents interfere in the affairs pertaining to the young couple and when the frames of reference are rather divergent as a result of their having inhabited different spaces, as is the case for *Mbak* Kari.

The conclusion is that household type or living under one roof cannot be disconnected from other features of family life, such as: the development cycle; whether or not there are migrating family members; whether or not the household is headed by a woman; and whether there are married children in the parental home. In the following section I turn to marriage patterns in Rikmokèri, which is the initial basis of family formation and a major fulfilment of family life. There have been some incisive changes in these realms and family life has not been left untouched.

Marriage and Children: Changing Local Customs

Marriage and having children are among the most important events in personal and family life. Not complying with the 'ideal' age for marriage or not being able to have children are therefore deemed to be quite disastrous. Not marrying actually never happens. Not being able to have children does occur and is in most cases a ground for men to divorce their wives. For the women trapped in such a situation their misfortune often leads to a flurry of gossip and social ostracism. One woman expressed her feelings saying: 'There is nothing I can share with the other women of my age, they do not want to talk to me.' But before we can continue on the topic of children we need to address that of marriage.

Marriage

One of the most important transitions in the prevailing local marriage patterns across generations is the change from arranged marriages (*dijodohkan*) to self-selection of marriage partner. Another is the rising age at first marriage for girls which in the village rose from 11.7 to 16.7 years when the three generations (i.e. grandparents, parents and children) were compared.

As for marriage and age at first marriage, of the 62 sample households, 21 are older-generation households. Of the women who head these families, only 10% married just once, 45% married twice, 25% married three times, and 15% married four times. One woman married six times. For all these women, both the first and the second marriages were arranged. Even in the cases of a third marriage, all but one were arranged. The average age at first marriage for this group was 11.7 years. Two women have been in so-called second-wife marriages, but both made plain that they had asked for a divorce not long after the marriage. Of the 23 middle-generation households, the majority of the women married once (68%), several married twice (18%), and a few three times (9%). One woman married four times. Of all first marriages, 82% were arranged and 18% were based on own choice (in one case no information was obtained). The average age at first marriage for this group was 15.8 years. Interestingly enough, among the 18 younger-generation households, the number of female heads who married once (44%) and those who married twice (39%) is almost equal. In three cases (17%), a third marriage has taken place. The number of self-selected marriage partners grew: for this group 34% chose their own partner in the first marriage (and almost in all cases of a second marriage). Also the average age at first marriage rose a little to 16.7 years.

Since women of the older generation were often married off at the age of 10 or 12 years, often before their first period, it was at times a really traumatic experience for them. Several women still remember the panic of not knowing what was going to happen to them and some talk about the shame of crying during the ceremony. Taking account of their extreme youth, it is not so strange that these were arranged affairs: this also explains why these marriages were almost never consummated. There are differing reasons given why marriages were arranged at such young ages. However, both the older men and women said they just followed their parents' wishes (*manut saja*). Some suggested that for parents, especially mothers, marrying off a daughter or son was a token of being a good and competent mother. Others mentioned the transfer of responsibilities for a daughter from the parents to a husband, and for the more elite families it was often a question of securing wealth and *sawah* by making sure the children of these families married each other. Since divorce was nearly as common as marriage, it seemed more important to have a child married off at least once. The most common reaction was that this was just the way things were done in former days. As an older man explains:

> Parents used the Javanese calendar to arrange a marriage. Such matchmaking was not based on wealth as it was believed that happiness and good fortune (*rejeki*) can only be achieved by the joint endeavours of a couple, not by inherited wealth. Still, it seldom happened that a child from a rich family married a member of a poor family. The less wealthy partner would always feel inferior (*minder*) from the start. So, it is better to bring together two children of the same status.

His wife adds:

> Having a daughter not married by the age of 12 or 14 would severely stigmatize the parents as not being able (*mampu*) to marry off their daughter properly, either in terms of money or according to the customs. The stigma also taints the daughter. Not being married by such an age in fact automatically implied that she had committed an impropriety (*kelakuannya tidak baik*), as a result of which no potential groom would dare to marry the girl in question. It was not like today when young girls are given the chance to grow up first (*gadis-gadis dibiarkan dewasa dulu*).

Although the practice of arranged marriages, and indeed of marrying more than once, is becoming less common, this does not mean that it has been completely discarded as hopelessly outdated custom now devoid of any value. Quite a few (grand)parents rate the chance of success of an arranged marriage as being much higher than of a marriage based on mutual emotions or something called love. Precisely because the emotions are involved, they argue, it is more difficult to act rationally. The young tend to disagree, as is shown by their expressed preference for someone they really 'like'. The majority of the married couples in the village either married someone from within Rikmokèri or found a husband in one of the surrounding areas. The general residence pattern is that a young couple starts to live in with the parents of the bride for a while and then set up their own house close or next to the bride's parents' house or at another location in the same hamlet (the principle of the uxorilocal residence pattern flowing into a neo-local one). Among the younger couples, however, the husband now often comes from a more distant part of Java, even from outside Java. This is related to the fact that a growing number of daughters seek work in Jakarta. Now this city, instead of the village and its surroundings, is deemed the place to meet future partners. Jakarta obviously has an appeal, in terms of looking for work and as the place where the action is, for young people from all over Indonesia.

The husbands who come from other parts of Java or from other islands altogether, have a difficult time adjusting to the life in Rikmokèri. It takes a long time for the young men from 'faraway', who often continue to work in Jakarta but of course come to visit their wives regularly, to feel 'at home' in Rikmokèri. Even more than the husbands who originate from the area, they exhibit the tendency to stay indoors while in Rikmokèri for a short visit. In a situation where the local men who migrate lose touch with what goes on in the village and their families, the situation is far worse for these new husbands. This adds to a mounting local detachment of the younger groups.

For girls in their early twenties, marriage is an intricate and dominant issue in life. Those who work in Jakarta are often summoned back home because the parents think it is time for them to get married. For many of these young girls this leads to confusion. It is not that they do not want to get married, but getting married means the end of working in Jakarta, and this is not an easy choice. Obviously the idea of having one's daughter married before she is considered too old, or shames her parents, or is gossiped about, still rules the roost locally. In view of the wider networks in which many of the young are engaged, and the other spaces that inform their lives, plus their enjoyment of a fairly independent lifestyle at a young age, it is no surprise that marriage has become a site of tension between them and their parents.

Children

Writing about Javanese culture, Koentjaraningrat argues that 'in rural as well as in urban Javanese families children are much desired' (1985: 100). With the birth of children, parents are assured of support in their old age. Moreover, children bring peace or status to a family, and from an early age children are involved in the household economy (they fetch water, firewood and fodder or clean the house). They are also wanted for economic reasons. Hildred Geertz states that 'a woman with many children is envied; a barren woman is pitied' (1961: 83). The situation in Rikmokèri certainly proves that children are very much wanted for a variety of reasons, including the obvious emotional ones. The old age security rationale is still important among the older generations, but once the children move out it is a question whether one of them will return to the village to take care of the parents. The joy children bring certainly holds true most of the time and is among the main reasons cited. That they bring warmth to the family and that warmth in the family leads to peace in the heart, as Koentjaraningrat argues, is not particularly conspicuous in Rikmokèri nowadays. Without suggesting that this was never the case in earlier days, it can be argued that the conflicts that children have nowadays with their parents over such issues as household tasks, age of marriage, or upbringing are more common and more outspoken. It is not for nothing that the following saying has become commonplace in the village: 'In former days children followed their parents' wishes, but these days parents have to follow their children's wishes.' This is related to the fact that children spend more time in school or away from the village and so are more in touch with the wider world, which serves to provide them with a variety of other interests and ideas about how to spend time or express certain ideas and wishes. It seems that parents also allow children to play more, making this a greater part of childhood than possibly was the case before, when each and every available hand was needed to secure a livelihood. In some families this is of course still true, but life has progressed for all families in the village, allowing more time for playing and simply being a child than ever before.

The involvement of young children (below the age of 12) in the household economy seems to have declined with the necessity to spend more time in school. Children still help to fetch firewood, sweep the garden, and at an older age seek wage labour in Jakarta. It has already emerged that there is no fixed rule that those who earn money in Jakarta must support the household economy. But no matter how good or bad the parental circumstances, most migrating children do hand over some of their earnings and with that probably contribute more to the household in financial terms than children their age ever did before. By so doing they gain a position or a certain authority never before assigned to children. This gives them more power over their own life choices, and also allows them to go against the wishes of their parents at times. Again there is absolutely no question that the situation has been completely reversed. Children still respect their parents as much as ever and that is where the problems start, because opting to go one's own way or going one's parents' way is like walking a tightrope.

Approaching the delicate matter of having many children (as argued by both Geertz and Koentjaraningrat), it seems at least in Rikmokèri that this never was the case, and with the ideal of the small family propagated by the government since the 1970s, it has become even less so. The older generation has an average of 6.5 children ever born and 4.0 children living. Among these older women there are only 3 women who have not lost a child (one woman is childless). The middle generation has an average of 4.6 children ever born and 3.2 living children. And the younger generation so far has an average of 2.2 children ever born and 1.8 children living. Comparing the generations: of the younger-generation women in the sample, 71% has never lost a child; of the middle generation 48% has never lost a child; and among the older generation, only 15% has never lost a child. As the information shows, both the number of children ever born and the number of children not making it through their first years are much higher among the older-generation women and declines considerably for the middle and younger generations. This can be traced back to better health and nutrition and to the availability of more effective contraceptives since the 1970s. It cannot be reasoned that in 'the old days' people wanted more children than they do now or that they were ignorant in family planning matters; at least, I did not find the evidence for this. Older women gave birth up to 12 times and although this was often interpreted to have been the will of God, the women of that generation also knew how to massage a womb in order to stimulate an early abortion. The fact that ever since modern family planning became available, women in Rikmokèri generally do use either one of the so-called modern family planning methods (although with intervals and change of methods), indicates that women in Rikmokèri have a fairly persistent record of wanting to space births and also to restrict the number of children.

Comparing the experiences of various generations, it is safe to say that family life in Rikmokèri has been (and is) influenced by the changes and shifts in the realms of marriage and children couched by outward mobility and by more general developments in health services. We have seen that the age at first marriage for women has risen; that there is more self-selection of marriage partners; that the number of children that women bear and who die in their first years has dropped quite substantially; and that there is an increasing use of modern family planning methods. All these changes have engendered their own response within family life as we saw. One consequence is the growing ideal among younger Rikmokèri villagers to marry at the age of 20 to someone whom they like and with whom they can start an independent household as soon as possible, preferably with the prospect of two children in the future. Couched in these terms, it sounds almost like the New Order ideal. So, when and where do young couples start their family life and how does this relate to the existing patterns?

WHERE TO LIVE?

As a rule in Rikmokèri daughters stay in the village upon marriage and sons move out to their wife's village. Newly weds either move directly into a house of their own, still a fairly rare event, or they live with the parents of the wife for a while. When and where the new couple finally sets up a home of their own depends both on the economic means and on the space available. Up to the present time it has been common practice that the parents of the girl supply their daughters with a piece of their property on which to build a house. Following this pattern, daughters often end up building a house next door to the parents' house, space permitting. This residential pattern is common for Rikmokèri and consequently often large parts or blocks in a hamlet or neighbourhood are inhabited by people who are related (as consanguines or affines). The residential areas are becoming more scarce however because many young people move out of the parental home earlier in their married life than was the case among the older generations. Taking into account that they often have an overwhelming preference to do so, especially if they have led fairly independent lives in Jakarta and in the long run find it difficult to pick up the threads of their lives in the parental home (as we saw with *Mbak* Kari), in many cases they have also been able to assemble the economic means to achieve their dreams and often have acquired the expertise to do so themselves. The younger generation has a definite preference for neo-local nuclear family life. Having one's own house and running one's own household independently both in financial terms and, very importantly, in terms of authority – that is without any of the parents around – are ideals shared by most young men and women. One young woman declared:

> Once we have a husband and children we do not set off for Jakarta again. We all want to start our own household. We want to arrange and organize our own household ourselves and no longer to have to share the house with our parents.

A glance into the past shows that these are not completely new ideals. The older generations only had to overcome more obstacles to achieve them. They faced the obstacles of purely economic aspects and the bundle of local customs. Looking first at the economic reason, in the past young couples were more dependent on their parents' contribution to the building or setting up of separate household quarters. Nowadays, as the examples have shown, many young couples can finance the transition themselves, using their earnings from Jakarta. The other reason which pertains to the local belief is that a couple has to be ready to undertake such an endeavour. As an older villager put it: 'A couple is not supposed to build a house if they are not yet mature (*mateng*), economically and mentally.' Or as Koentjanaringrat states: 'A young couple is usually considered unable to manage their own household. Consequently they reside in the house of one of the parents *until they are considered to be able to manage their own affairs*' (1985: 133, italics mine). It is possible to adduce the argument that this process of attaining a state of 'being ready' (the couple should have secured access to *sawah* and understand what is involved in raising children) took longer in former days than it takes now. If children nowadays often go to work in Jakarta at the age of 13, they reach the point of being 'able to manage their own affairs' sooner, at least in their own eyes. Of course the rising age at first marriage plays a role as well. Since the first marriages of the older generation took place at the age of 10 or 12, after the official marriage the youthful spouses stayed in their own parental homes and usually a divorce followed soon after. The same can be said for many of the middle generation. Those who were married at the age of 15 often returned to their parents' homes. *Bu* Rasban who was married at the age of 12 recalls:

> One day I was told that the next week I would get married to Rasban. Although he is from the same village, I had never seen him before. It was a big wedding celebration with a *wayang* [shadow play] performance and Rasban gave a buffalo as bride-price, as well as some jewellery. All I could do was cry. After the wedding I continued to go to

school until I finished primary school. After a while Rasban came to live in our house too but we did not share a room. It was only after several years that my parents decided that we should move out and they built a house for us.

Among the younger generation we have seen that being 16 or 17 upon marriage has become the average, and among those not yet married there is a preference for marriage at the age of 20.

So the present-day newly weds are older and they try to have their own house as quickly as possible. Together with the increase in out-migration since 1990, this has led to an increasing activity in house-building in the village, which lends certain parts of Rikmokèri a truly semi-urban ambience. The remaining sites are either being bought up by young people working in Jakarta or are already being built on. Many of the young opt to buy a plot of land as soon as possible, worrying about building a house only later. Their priority lies in securing a place for themselves in the village because Rikmokèri is not becoming a deserted village. Nothing could be farther from the truth: it is not yet a suburb but it is certainly assuming the status of a residential locality more than it ever was, especially so for the migrants who are seldom 'at home'.[10]

Reviewing the evidence, it seems that there has not really been a change in the ideal of setting up a neo-local nuclear household among the various generations of young couples. What has changed though is that the capacity and authority to do so among the present-day young generation comes at an earlier moment in their lives than was the case for older generations. Apart from the fact that the building projects give the village a completely different look, a change of appearance which derives from the new fashion in house styles and the materials used, it also means that family life is undergoing some changes. Whereas it was more common to share a house (but not necessarily more than that) for a good number of years, this is rapidly changing. Living under the same roof implies that people live in each other's pockets. Although a house next door might be as open or closed as the room of a married daughter in one and the same house, there is still more freedom, privacy and nuclearization of family life than if there is co-habitation.

REMITTANCES

Of all the various issues that are part and parcel of family life, one is of a more recent date and is becoming predominant with the rising number of families who have a family member in labour migration; this is the issue of access to and use of remittances. Obviously it is difficult to generalize about and to arrive at some common pattern describing how this money is used. Especially since it is a topic that tends to be swathed in secrecy. When it comes to remittances, factors like who is making the money (a husband or a daughter, a married or an unmarried young man) coupled with such aspects as the home situation (e.g.: Are there other resources available? Is the migrant in an independent household or still living with parents? Are other household members also in migration?) play a role. Common sense decrees that not everybody must be making the same cash in Jakarta and certainly not everybody displays the same spending behaviour. Despite these drawbacks, in this section I shall try to shed some light on this issue because of its impact on family life.

In quite a few cases it is the husbands of the young nuclear families who migrate. This means that their young wives find that family and daily livelihood are very much their responsibility. In these situations cash comes into the household on the return of the husband, which may be once a month but more generally once every two or three months.[11] The cash brought back home by men who work in construction varies from Rp. 100,000 to Rp. 200,000. This money is often used to repay debts. Debts are incurred because the women often have had hardly any other access to cash (apart from their sporadic farm labour) to pay for daily necessities, *arisan* [rotating savings association] participation, school costs or electricity. In many cases the young husbands work especially with their own nuclear families in mind. Since they are at the beginning of their marriage and family lives, a fair amount of cash goes to the house and family as such. These men display a far less extravagant spending behaviour than do the unmarried men. But these patterns are generalizations and there are also young husbands who spend all their earnings on things they like as we shall see below.

Mbak Kari's circumstances explained in case study 10.2 (two households under one roof) show that separate budgeting is the rule, making the remittances either a husband–wife affair (where the son-in-law or husband migrates) or a parent–child affair (where the sons and daughters migrate).[12] This accords with the argument that, although various household compositions can be found in Rikmokèri, the majority in practice function as nuclear families, at least as far as finances and daily family affairs are concerned. The issue of remittances underlines this again. Notwithstanding this nuclear practice, where more generations live under one roof or where two couples share the same dwelling, there are more opportunities to turn to each other for support (this being either cash, rice, or emotional support). But for the young couples who now have their so desired own roof, there is an unspoken rule that once a child has his or her own home, he or she has to cope alone. So what about the issue of remittances? A few features can be summarized.

Where the circular out-migration involves parents and unmarried children, the parents foster an outspoken expectation that the children will hand over some of their cash earnings to them. Broadly speaking, this expectation counts more for the daughters who migrate than for the sons. A more active spending behaviour is tolerated for the latter or shrugged off as 'boys will be boys'. A young widow whose son and daughter both work in Jakarta commented on her son, who had come back without any money from Jakarta because he had been 'ill', that she did not believe him. Despite her admission she did not make too much fuss about it, while she was scathing about the behaviour of her daughter who had used her money to buy clothes, lamenting how unfortunate she was to have a daughter who spends money on things for herself. Conversely, the children certainly display a combination of on the one hand wanting to help their parents, which they do for compassionate reasons in response to family needs and to answer the expectations they know their parents have, but on the other also wanting to use the money they earn for their own pleasure. They all confess that they want to feel what it means to spend their hard-earned money on things that would otherwise be difficult to come by, such as make-up, new music tapes, a wristwatch and so on. These are considered luxury goods, with which they can impress others back home.

Very often the girls tend to think of their future and invest in more practical items for their post-migration lives back in the village, such as a bicycle or sewing machine (the latter being one of the items *Mbak* Kari bought) or by investing money in a buffalo which can be sold later on. Obviously these various expectations, wishes and demands fostered by both parents and children do lead to family conflicts over the use of and access to remittances. It presents a whole new topic in which parents and children are ranged on opposite sides. Remittances, and especially the power represented by this cash, play an important role here fermenting conflicts of a different magnitude and content from other conflicts, which are generally part and parcel of the parent–child relationship. The general tendency referred to by the villagers is summed up in the oft-repeated saying that the youth of today have far more of their own way than ever before. This is certainly also related to the growing authority of children, built up on the basis of the remittances of those who migrate and bolstered by rising formal education and the wider experiences to which these young villagers are exposed. Finally, the migrating youth are witnesses of urban life to its fullest as well as seeing the behaviour of the urban youth, which inspires them to branch out on their own to explore new prospects.

Seen in this light, remittances generate a new relationship between parents and children. First of all, the latter have become the members of the family who bring a very important contribution into the family (cash). Second, the children have been in touch with (and participants in) wider networks that lie outside the village, such as the factories in which they work or the middle-class households which they serve. This assertion is also valid for those children who have not migrated but are continuing their education. The cash and the new environment outside of the village provide them with new experiences that shape their (widened) frames of reference. These are quite different experiences than those of their parents and grandparents whose frames of reference were built more on local village affairs and war times. Therefore the content of and the way in which conflicts are dealt with have also altered because the position of the actors towards one another has shifted.

I want to conclude this section with a case on the issue of remittances as it impresses the lives of Yati and Wono, in order to show that the general patterns are at times too general.

Case Study 10.3: 'I Want a Sony'

Apart from Yati's father, all other male family members work in Jakarta or Bandung. They come home irregularly, but at least once every two to three months. Even Yati's adopted daughter, Asih, who is now 9, seems to accept the situation without much difficulty: she is happy when her father, Wono, is at home, but not reduced to floods of tears when he leaves again. The kitchen at the back, the scene of such activities as the daily cooking, is the central meeting site. Every day Yati and her sister and neighbouring female friends gather there, talking about daily events, problems, their husbands in Jakarta, the amount of remittances hoped and expected, or just chatting and joking while eating their favourite raw vegetable salad with a spicy sauce (*lotek*).

With their husbands away the sisters themselves take care of the *sawah* which they have already inherited from their parents. It is very common in Rikmokèri that the men leave this task to their wives. Daily life for the sisters involves taking care of the *sawah* and of their separate households. They also help out in the little shop next door which is owned by their father and mother. In return they have access to this *warung* for their daily needs (except rice). Asih is the only young child in the family and according to Yati, Yati's mother interferes too much in her upbringing. But because Yati is in fact dependent on her parents for cash, which is needed to pay school and electricity bills and the like (being a farmer she does not really have access to cash because the harvest sold is used either to pay for the new cultivation costs or for paying off debts), she often feels trapped. This situation is not made any easier by the fact that Wono usually spends his city earnings in exactly the way he wants. Interestingly enough, it was a colour television set that became a true issue of conflict.

Wono had already repeatedly expressed his wish to be able to relax when at home. He decided that having a television set would be the solution. Prestige-wise, a Sony colour television is also a great asset, and this aspect is very important to him. Wono complies in many respects with the rush to buy consumer goods which he witnesses in Jakarta and Bandung, the places where he works. Mesmerized by this he spends most of his remittances on the things he fancies. The struggle over cash has become an important aspect of the couple's family life. Yati is someone who is not very interested in such luxury goods. She is first and foremost a farmer and has also experienced periods of *paceklik* [time of food scarcity before the harvest] more than once. Haunted by such memories, she considers attaining food security and cultivating her *sawah* more important than buying assets.

On one of his visits home, Wono and his brother-in-law went on a shopping spree. He had Rp. 200,000 from his work and upon their return Wono informed Yati he had bought a Sony colour television set and that he would go back later that day to pick it up. The down payment had already been made but that only covered half the cost. Yati was asked for the rest. Eventually she gave him the money left over from selling part of her standing rice crop. When Yati's father found out about this he was furious, pointing out to his daughter that spending so much money on a television set is very irresponsible. Later that day when Yati discussed her father's reaction with her sister in the kitchen, complaining that she did not like her father interfering in her personal affairs, her father overheard and reacted: 'Children should not gossip about their parents, that's not right.'

Although Yati was very much against using her money for a television set, in the end she went along with it because, as she related later, if she did not agree the atmosphere at home would be far from pleasant. Wono would certainly have behaved as if she did not exist. But more importantly, if the money had not been used to buy a television set, it would have slipped through their fingers (*habis*) as well. When there is cash in the house, the neighbours know it and will take the opportunity to come and ask for a loan, returning it only in small amounts (*akan habis sendiri*). If they borrow Rp. 10,000 they repay it with Rp. 1,000 every week and what can one do with Rp. 1,000?

Yati certainly does not always comply with her husband's wishes. She explained that she had a choice to make and, having looked at the various options, she chose to give him the money for the reasons mentioned above. In situations where husbands working in Jakarta have become the main breadwinners, their wives have become dependent on this cash inflow. The same goes for parents in cases where it is the children who bring in the cash. This almost automatically gives those supplying the cash a degree of power: the power either to hand over the remittances or to refrain from doing so; the power to decide how much they will submit to the family; and the power to decide what to do with the money in the first place.

As the case study shows, Yati has hardly any access to or say over Wono's remittances and, even more telling, he has the power to ask money from her to fulfil his consumer needs (and prestige because the Sony really made an impression on all the neighbours). Yati, as a farmer, usually does not have much ready cash and so when she fails to receive much from her husband, she resorts to selling some of her rice stock which is needed for their daily consumption and for her social obligations. Some cash contributions are therefore necessary, if only to pay the larger expenses such as new shoes for Asih or tax. In this case it is Yati's parents who help out with the cash. Yati is in fact in a rather privileged position having parents who have ready cash around daily because of their little shop. Most other families find themselves in a more complicated situation, not having any access to cash at all unless their husbands, sons or daughters supply it. Yati's dependence on her parents for cash, however, combined with the local custom of showing respect to her parents, complicates her life since she can hardly raise her voice when her parents interfere with the upbringing of Asih, for instance. She is 'cash dependent'.

CONCLUSION: FAMILY LIFE ACROSS GENERATIONS

In this chapter I have combined the time-lag argument (how a process of change, in this case out-migration, gradually affects family life) with attention to kinship and 'life-of-the-outside' experiences (Liechty 1995) as they pattern interactions between family members and family formation behaviour. This should help us arrive at a better understanding of why family life in Rikmokèri is changing and how exactly it is changing. Hence, what can be concluded about family life in this village as it impinges on the various generations?

The expansion of the Jakarta labour markets and their accessibility, the increase in educational facilities, and the growing attractions of modern urban life have led to the engagement of young Rikmokèri villagers in new and differently equipped spaces and places. I have discussed some of the implications this physical and social mobility has had on how family life functions and how it is perceived in Rikmokèri. Teenagers and those in their early twenties know that they will marry and start a family, and they are looking forward to it, like the earlier generations did. This much is unchanged, but their views on when to marry, with whom to marry, how to celebrate it, when and how to regulate childbirth, and how and where to live their married life all differ substantially from the ideas their parents and grandparents hold over these issues. More importantly, the realization of such aspirations is increasingly within the reach of the young because of their changed status, their growing autonomy, and their access to cash and formal education. What are the concrete implications of this for family life and the interactions between the generations in this village?

Above I referred to the feminization of family life. Women find themselves more on their own in facing daily life, in bringing up their children, in maintaining social relations and in fulfilling social obligations. Women always held a prominent position in family life but today women are on their own more because their husbands and children are simply not there most of the time. Ambiguously for the women, this implies an increase as well as a decline in their autonomy and freedom. Being on their own and having to decide on many things for themselves on the one hand enhances their decision-making power in certain realms. One woman explained that it is she who decides about the number of children because with her husband away all the time she is the one who bears the day-to-day responsibilities. By not being there most of the time, the husband has lost his vote, as it were. On the other hand, there are also quite a number of women who come to depend on the remittances. Since the power to decide over the use of the cash often lies in the hands of the one who earns it, women relinquish some of the power that they had in this field. What they earn in the village far from balances the wages their husbands or children bring in. Although most migrating children and husbands feel some degree of responsibility towards their own families, many are attracted by the more readily available consumer goods that they see around them: returning home with a leather jacket or a colour television set is at times more status-enhancing than the age-old tradition of supporting the family. As a result, positions within the family have shifted and this requires a renegotiation by all those involved to avoid conflicts or a retreat into silence. In either case, the new situation brings new tensions and makes new claims on people's adaptability.

At a time when access to cash is assuming mounting importance, this growing dependence on the remittances of husbands and children counters the autonomy women and mothers enjoyed in other fields. Women with husbands and children in Jakarta most of the time, are not only becoming more dependent financially but they are left behind with a family life which they did not really aspire. The older-generation women become more isolated because their offspring prefer not to have them in their house. Among the younger generations, the more recently married women have found networks of female friendships (sharing often a common background of having worked in Jakarta) which strengthen them both in economic and in emotional and social terms. It is primarily the single sons and daughters who can keep pace with change as they have been able to participate in the new options outside the village in work, in education, in personal development, in seeking experiences, and in leading more independent lives, and they have benefited from it. Their experiences have taken them in new directions, and their ideals of what kind of person they want to be have moved away from the ideals with which they were brought up. Since they marry according to their own rules and since the partner they marry very often has similar experiences, they want other things in their married lives and for their futures. Having been on their own in difficult circumstances, they seem to have all it needs to pursue their goals further, even when they return to the village to continue their lives.

Turning to the meaning of family life as such, several shifts have been observed. Rikmokèri consists predominantly of nuclear families. The ideal of setting up a neo-local household or family has a long history in Rikmokèri, but the young generation is realizing this ideal earlier in their married lives than any generation before them. Not only do they have the financial means to build a new house (often in association with others), but they also lead independent lives before their marriage and do not want to return to the parental home and live according to their parents' rules. This exerts pressure on the custom that at least one child must stay at home in order to take care of the parents: consequently this jeopardizes old age security systems which have existed for many generations in the village.

It is in marriage and childbirth, the two central bases of family life in Rikmokèri, where the shifts have been most distinct. Next to the rise in age at first marriage, the idea of marrying someone of one's own choice has gained ground. Children are still very much desired as they always were, but the access to modern family planning methods affords the younger generation more control over childbearing. It offers them the opportunity to attain the ideal of the small, happy and healthy family propagated by the New Order state and seen as a marker of modernity.

What then can be said in a nutshell about family life and relationships between the generations? Under the rapidly changing living conditions in Rikmokèri, the family as a framework and network of (grand)parent–child and husband–wife relationships and interactions is interpreted variously by the different generations. Relations between family members and the mutual expectations and reciprocal behaviours are challenged. With growing physical and socio-economic mobility, and the subsequent shifts in the realm of marriage and children, the positions of family members towards one another have to be redefined, which is not an easy task. In addition, the physical separation between family members because of migration or because they move into a house of their own is paralleled by cultural and psychological separation as people acquire different frames of reference induced by different experiences in different spaces. This culminates, finally, in new aspirations and practices of what kind of persons they wish to be, and in different perceptions and practices of what kind of family lives they wish to live.

Author's Note

The research on which this chapter is based received funding from The Netherlands Foundation for the Advancement of Tropical Research (WOTRO) and was carried out from October 1993 until October 1994 under the auspices of LIPI (Indonesian Institute of Sciences). The research was carried out in Rikmokèri (pseudonym), a Central Javanese village of some 630 houses and a population of almost 3,000 people. The village lies approximately 20 km inland from the main highway along the north coast connecting Jakarta and Surabaya. With the wide variety in means of transportation, the villagers can reach Jakarta in some eight to ten hours' travel.

Notes

1 Guyer (1981), Hartmann (1981), Guyer and Peters (1987), Fapohunda (1988), Moore (1988, 1994), Sen (1990), Wolf (1990, 1992a), Kabeer (1991, 1994), and Niehof (1994) all contributed to the understanding that 'the household' is anything but a static social unit and that household relationships are dynamic and fluid.

2 'While the deconstruction of households and the analysis of intra-household asymmetries has emerged in African and Latin American studies, considerable work is yet to be done in Asia, particularly Southeast Asia' (Wolf 1990: 67).

3   It has to be remarked that with the ongoing financial, political and ecological crises that are hitting Indonesia since mid-1997 the picture at present is more grim than when I conducted the research.

4   I was able to go back to the village from September 1998 until December 1998 to study the impact of the crises on households and labour. One quite surprising result surfaced from the village census that I conducted in October 1998. Notwithstanding the collapse of the construction sector in Jakarta, the labour migration to the capital did not diminish but instead involved an even greater number of families. Where the 1993 village census showed that 43% of all households had one or more family members working as migrants in Jakarta, the preliminary results of the 1998 village census show that 50% of all households now have a family member working there.

5   Rural Java studies in the 1960s found similar compositions, e.g. Hildred Geertz (1961: 32) who found 75% nuclear households and Jay (1969: 52) who came to a figure of 74% nuclear households. Later studies such as Hüsken (1988: 116) found 73% nuclear households, Hetler (1986: 130) 78%, Wolf (1992a: 57) some 60%, and Saptari (1995: 150) for two villages 66% and 54% respectively. White (1976: 219-220) found not more than 50% simple nuclear households alongside 18% single-headed households.

6   I am not arguing that such relationships were static in the past and that the more outward-oriented focus of present-day young villagers jeopardizes 'self-evident' behaviour patterns between generations. However, within a short time-span the generations of Rikmokèri villagers have been confronted as active partakers and passive witnesses, with the result that patterns and objectives that existed previously are no longer pursued or aspired to the extent they were before.

7   It has to be remarked that any references to the New Order relate to the New Order under president Suharto who stepped down as president in May 1998.

8   Although often translated as 'prosperous', *sejahtera* more literally connotes the state of 'welfare' or 'well-being' (not necessarily economically 'prosperous').

9   *Mbak* is the term of address for a young Javanese woman.

10 As for the discussion on the Javanese village as a 'construct' and the way the Javanese village here under study fits into that discussion, the interested reader can find the details in my thesis (Koning 1997: 27–41).

11 Some men also give savings to a co-villager who returns home earlier than they do. If one of the men returns, all women hope that he will bring with him some cash from their husbands.

12 Remittances are in most cases an issue between husband (the migrant labourer) and wife, or between parents and children (the migrant son or daughter).

11

Negotiating Gender, Kinship and Livelihood Practices in an Indonesian Transmigration Area

Becky Elmhirst

INTRODUCTION

As is the case in many parts of Indonesia that are affected by rapid environmental and political economic transformation, non-farm work is an important feature in both Javanese transmigrant and Lampungese host communities of North Lampung's transmigration zone. Where the experience of the two communities appears to diverge is in the contrasting ways in which unmarried daughters from each group engage in non-farm work. While the daughters of Javanese transmigrants remain in the transmigration settlement as wage workers on a nearby commercial sugar plantation, in recent years their Lampungese peers have been heading in ever greater numbers to the factories of Tangerang, crossing the Sunda Strait and, until the onset of the monetary crisis in 1997, returning to their natal villages just once a year. The purpose of this chapter is to explore this contrast in the lives of Javanese daughters and their Lampungese peers, focusing on the household as a site where negotiations over the employment of unmarried daughters takes place. The chapter draws on the 'bargaining model' of household relations, in which individuals' bargaining power depends on their position within the wider economy, and where intra-household cooperation takes place when it is in an individual's best interests (Sen 1990; Kabeer 1991).

In order to account for the differences in the experiences of Javanese and Lampungese daughters it is necessary to go beyond an exposition of household economics and examine also the contrasts in the rights, responsibilities and expected behaviours which have come to be associated with the kinship practices of each group. Of interest is the different ways in which these representations have shaped family decision-making, from the assertion of parental authority to its resistance by daughters themselves. Attention is directed to the ways in which household dynamics are shaped by forces not reducible to livelihood or economic goals, but which involve concerns such as prestige, power and morality

(Hefner 1990). To encapsulate these forces, I adopt the concept of a household 'moral economy', as a set of ideas about what is right and just in the household.

The idea of a moral economy was originally used to describe community-wide peasant reaction to capitalist penetration (Wolf 1971). Through Scott's work (Scott 1976), the concept has been linked to a Chayanovian concept of a risk-avoiding, utility-maximizing peasant, for whom a moral economy represents an ahistorical, pre-capitalist and preferred mode of behaviour (Brass 1991). While the existence of moral economies has been the subject of much theoretical dispute,[1] more recent approaches have suggested that the problem is not whether there is such a thing as a moral economy, but the fact that people often act in ways antithetical to prevailing ideas of social justice and morality, 'causing others to appeal to the idea of community/moral economy as they struggle to improve their lot' (Harriss 1994: 182; Scott 1985). While such analyses have been conducted at community level, there is also a case to be made for looking at the moral economy of the household, not as something that exists, but as a representation, an image, which is contested between different genders and generations who express alternative constructs of what a household moral economy should look like (Hart 1991; Agarwal 1994). This chapter explores variations in the construction of these 'household moral economies' between Javanese and Lampungese people, as they emerge from contrasting kinship ideologies. The point is that a 'household moral economy' is appealed to and contested in the decision-making process by daughters and parents alike, and that this, in turn, has given shape to the kinds of practices in which Lampungese and Javanese daughters engage.

BACKGROUND AND SETTING

The Sumatran province of Lampung, which straddles the traditional division between 'inner' (Java and Bali) and 'outer' Indonesia, provides the setting for this study. It owes most of its recent history and socio-economic conditions to the Indonesian government's transmigration programme, one of the largest resettlement schemes in the world. Transmigratie began in Lampung, as *Kolonisatie* under the Dutch in 1905, and since then, has brought major changes to the province, prompting spontaneous migration from Java, a twenty-fold increase in population, and profound changes to the ethnic structure of the province, where more than two-thirds of residents cite Javanese as the language they use at home (Hugo *et al.* 1987; Pain 1989).[2] Although Lampung was officially closed to inter-provincial transmigration in the late 1970s, local transmigration (*transmigrasi lokal* or *translok*) continues apace, resettling so-called 'forest squatters' from critical watersheds and government forest reserves in the south and centre of the province to less populated areas in the north.[3] *Translok* has had a major impact on regional development in North Lampung, 'bureaucratizing' formerly remote areas and the village structures of the original Lampungese population, bringing extensively or sporadically cultivated areas into permanent and intensive cultivation, and diversifying and 'developing' the regional economy in line with national economic objectives.

Local transmigration has brought changes in population density (as population has increased sevenfold in just ten years), changes in land tenure structures and a shift to private ownership, and the creation and dissolution of a range of income-generating possibilities associated with commercial plantation development in North Lampung. Furthermore, these changes have been accompanied by environmental problems associated with deforestation, including erosion and weed invasion. Together, environmental and politico-economic changes have placed considerable pressure on available cultivable land and on livelihoods in the area. Local transmigration has also had an indirect impact on livelihoods, as road development associated with the programme has meant greater overland access to other parts of Indonesia. Whereas prior to local transmigration most long-distance travel was by river boat, it is now possible to reach the provincial capital Bandar Lampung in five hours by bus, and Jakarta in about 18 hours by bus and ferry. The proximity of Lampung to Java, coupled with the infrastructural developments of local transmigration, means that even the far north of the province is now beginning to feel the impact of export-oriented industrialization to the west of Jakarta, particularly in Tangerang regency. More recently, as Indonesia's economic crisis has brought widespread job losses in the industrial sector, this in turn has affected the employment profile of North Lampung, particularly areas where a high proportion of people had been working in Tangerang.

Research was carried out in two neighbouring villages, the original Lampungese village of Negri Indah and the mainly Javanese transmigration settlement of Negara Sakti.[4] There are significant contrasts in the landscape and organization of these villages. Negri Indah is composed of 255 closely packed houses which are raised on stilts to avoid the seasonal flooding of the nearby Way Kanan river. Permanent cultivation is confined to a narrow strip of river flood plain where rice, maize and vegetables are grown in response to the rise and fall of flood waters. Fruit and rubber trees are grown at a distance from the village on plots of land that until recently were under shifting cultivation and extended fallow systems. A number of families have smaller, temporary houses in these more distant fields where people stay during the harvest or planting season. Land is increasingly in private hands, although some more distant areas still fall under *marga* [lineage] control, from which individual farmers are able to gain usufruct rights to cultivate. Uncertainties over land title, none of which has been formalized by the local authorities, means that there is considerable speculation, often resulting in conflict, among Lampungese families, and between other land users (government and private plantation companies, and transmigrants) in the area. Beyond the village and the household, the people of Negri Indah identify closely with their *marga* which distinguishes them from other Lampungese groups and, more recently, from incoming transmigrants. In the past, the *marga* chiefs (*penyimbang*) played an important part in strategic decisions, deciding the form and regularity of agricultural activities, and arbitrating patrilineal marriage and bride-price contracts (Hilman Hadikusuma 1989). As with other parts of Sumatra, much of this role has been superseded by local government which is now responsible for land title, the regulation of farming systems and even arbitration in marriage arrangements (Kato 1989). However, the tension between the *marga* system of power and authority, and government-imposed village government means that most village structures have the appearance of being rather ad hoc, and bureaucratic control is considerably looser than is common in Javanese villages. Patrilineal inheritance and marriage practices associated with the *marga* continue to be of significance in structuring everyday life, and the lineage frequently provides a basis for the development of economic and social networks extending from the village to the provincial capital where most *marga* chiefs now reside.

The second village, Negara Sakti, while only 7 kilometres away, is quite different. The village, a transmigration settlement, was founded in 1982 when around 800 families were resettled from other parts of the province. The resettlement policy tended to favour the movement of husband, wife and children, leading to a certain uniformity in household arrangements, which tend to be nuclear in form. Each family was given a house, a home garden plot and 1.75 hectares of land on which to plant upland rice, other food crops and perennials, and once again, this has led to relative uniformity in economic terms. A school, clinic, marketplace and mosque were provided, and new roads constructed, linking the settlement with the regional capital of Kotabumi. Both the landscape and village life are highly ordered, with evenly spaced house plots and a village administration which forms part of a hierarchy of state control over agriculture, village activities and life-choices, including movement into and out of the village.[5] Unlike the Lampungese case, where hierarchy is related to genealogy-based, patron–client ties, hierarchy in the transmigration village relates to local, government-based, patron–client ties. The ownership of land by transmigrants has been formally recognized through the government certification programme, although newly arriving families and second-generation transmigrants do not generally have official title to the land they own. The influence of a Javanese cultural ecology is noticeable in the landscape around the transmigration settlement, where wet rice-fields have been carved out in low-lying marshy areas, and upland crops such as cassava are commonplace. More recently, the landscape has been even more radically transformed by a nearby sugar-cane plantation, which has incorporated more than 70% of households into an outgrower scheme.[6] Beyond the village and household, transmigrants have relatively few ties. Many have lost touch with kin in Java (most were born in Lampung to couples who moved from Java in the 1950s) and most of the settlements in southern Lampung from which they were moved no longer exist.[7] Those networks that do exist are close-kin based, as some transmigrants are able to send a child to live with grandparents in the south or central regions of the province where they themselves grew up.

These contrasts, in the landscape ecology, social structures and village-level power relations, mark a line of difference which has been created historically and reproduced in particular ways by the transmigration experience (Guinness 1994). This provides the politico-economic and social context from which the livelihood practices of each group have emerged, in other words, contrasting 'life spaces' within which the activities of young, unmarried Javanese and Lampungese women must be situated.

Off-farm Work and Circular Migration in North Lampung

Work in rural Java has shown that the economic base of most households (and indeed the activity profile of many individuals) is marked by considerable diversity, with few household members engaged in own-farm agriculture alone (Alexander *et al.* 1991; Effendi and Manning 1994). According to this Java-based thesis, off-farm work includes small-scale trade (Alexander 1987; Evers 1991), construction work and transport (Firman 1994), petty commodity production (Grijns *et al.* 1994), work in rural factories (Wolf 1992), and activities that involve circular migration (Hugo 1982; Hetler 1990). Work elsewhere in Indonesia suggests that this picture is not confined to contemporary Java, but is apparent in many outer island rural areas also, with farm work combined particularly with plantation and large-scale agro-processing activities (Hill 1992).

The situation in North Lampung shares elements of both these patterns. While off-farm work is most frequently connected with plantation and agro-processing (including logging) in line with a rapid expansion of commercial plantations in the area, there is also some evidence of diversification into small-scale trade, transport and petty commodity production, and increasingly, following North Lampung's own *revolusi colt* [minibus revolution] (Dick and Forbes 1992), circular or temporary migration in search of work. Livelihood practices in the transmigration settlement of Negara Sakti share similar characteristics to that noted in transmigration settlements elsewhere in Indonesia, where migrant welfare is closely linked to the availability of alternatives to farm work (World Bank 1988; Leinbach *et al.* 1992; Watkins *et al.* 1993). In Negara Sakti, off-farm activities revolve around work at a nearby government sugar plantation (PTP), as seasonal and day labourers, and in a nearby forestry plantation (*hutan tanaman inti*). Men, women, sons and daughters are involved in each of these, earning wages of around Rp. 1,000 to Rp. 3,000 per day.[8] Men also frequently take part in (illegal) logging activities in the few remaining stands of forest. Petty trade, as might be expected according to studies done elsewhere, is the domain of married women (Alexander 1987). While plantation work is closely linked sequentially with the rice farming season, in many instances it is given priority, simply because it represents a stable, albeit small, income which is set against the uncertainties of farming where drought and pests are commonplace. People say: 'We are poor people (*kami orang ngak punya*). If we don't go to work at the plantation, we don't eat.' It is notable that there are few instances of circular migration among transmigrants, perhaps because of the availability of waged work nearby, and also because the cost of travelling to the city is out of reach for those living on such an economic knife-edge.

The importance of off-farm work is also apparent in the host communities around transmigration settlements, although this issue has received much less attention in the literature (Guinness 1994). In the Lampungese community of Negri Indah, while most households are nominally defined as farm households by their members, few engage in own-account agriculture alone. Typically, Lampungese men are involved in a number of loosely defined business activities aside from their farm work, including trade in animal skins, logging, marketing of locally caught fish and transport activities (by boat and overland). Many of these activities take them away from the village for lengthy periods, and sons who are no longer in school may accompany their fathers. Unmarried daughters also migrate for lengthy periods – in their case, to seek work in *peri*-urban[9] factories in West Java (Tangerang). While the economic crisis has meant that such work is harder to come by in recent times, young women continue to move to Tangerang, relying on a dense network of kinship ties to help them secure factory employment. Off-farm work is much less common among married Lampungese women, many of whom are left to take care of the fields. Among wealthier families who are able to pay others to work the land, married women may take up petty trade, but this is very much house-based work rather than market-based. It is fair to say that off-farm work is less an indication of crisis than an indication of a remunerative and less physically taxing alternative. Said one Lampungese farmer: 'We don't like to work hard on the land, Javanese farmers are the ones that are always working hard.'

While off-farm work is important in both villages, some activities are more common among one group than another. For example, most Javanese transmigrants work as plantation labourers, yet Lampungese will rarely pursue this option. Many Lampungese work for long periods of the year in another part of Indonesia. For transmigrants, this happens rarely. Significantly, this difference manifests itself most explicitly in terms of the contrasting activities of unmarried daughters in each group. If they work away from home, most unmarried Javanese women work either as off-farm labourers on the land of other transmigrants, or at the plantation as day labourers. Only in a handful of cases did unmarried transmigrant daughters migrate to urban factories, and those that did were the daughters of middle-income transmigrants: school teachers or members of the LKMD (village council).

Transmigrant daughters work at the plantation both in the sugar harvest during the dry season (at which time there is no work in their family's fields) and at other times of year when they take part in day work (*harian*) involving weeding or fertilizer application. Recruitment is via a *mandor* [labour broker] who is usually a neighbour. Each morning, at about 7.30 am, trucks arrive from the plantation to collect labourers, returning them to the village at 4 pm. The work is hard, hot and dusty, and those taking part find their skin is burned by the searing midday sun. Although there is an hour's break for lunch, day workers must provide their own food, and as noted above, wages are well below the regional minimum for meeting physical needs.

In the case of unmarried Lampungese women, it is rare that they will labour in and around the village. There were no cases of unmarried daughters working on the plantation, even though it was just a few kilometres away from the village. Invariably, these young women go further afield: to the factories of Tangerang in Java. When fieldwork began in 1994, this relatively new situation in the lives of young women had taken everyone in the village by surprise and was frequently commented on by old and young alike. Women agreed that it began when one young woman followed her cousin (who lives in the south of Lampung) to Tangerang to work. Since then, an informal peer-group/kinship network has emerged, drawing women from this relatively remote rural community, across the

Sunda Strait to work in *peri*-urban factories, principally in the Tangerang regency of West Java. Young women seek out employment themselves, on the advice of their friends, and their engagement depends on them passing a written test and interview. More recently, economic crisis and high levels of unemployment have meant that it is increasingly difficult to find work. Yet many women have remained in Tangerang, working on a casual basis in factories which hire and fire workers depending on the state of their order books. While there are a number of factories which employ young women from this particular village, it is clear that they tend to favour workers from more distant origins, in other words, an immigrant workforce.[10] In this sense, the situation of these women is very different from that documented by Wolf in her study of factory daughters in Central Java, many of whom lived relatively close to their families, and some of whom were able to commute. In this case, the link between rural home and urban factory is less strong: a fact which has implications for household negotiations over remittance practices. Visits home take place once a year, at the Muslim *Lebaran* festival, when young women return home with savings and gifts for their families.

To understand the different work practices of Javanese and Lampungese daughters means unravelling some of the gender processes which might be at work: on the one hand, how these may affect women's livelihood options, and on the other, how these themselves may be renegotiated in order to take on board new income-generating constraints and possibilities as they arise.

Locating the Working Lives of Daughters: Household and Beyond

Understanding the labour force participation of young women, in local off-farm work and employment involving temporary migration, has been approached from a number of different angles in the literature in Indonesia and beyond. Structural perspectives have tended to interpret rural female work and migration practices as responses to wider politico-economic forces. These might work to push young women out of farm-based activities, for example, declining farm-based income-generating activities or lack of available land to sharecrop (Hart 1989; Hardjono 1993; Singarimbun 1993), or to pull young women into alternative activities as the structure of the economy shifts towards export-based industrialization (Fernandez-Kelly 1983; Mather 1985). In North Lampung it is clear that wider structural changes associated with transmigration have altered the profile of income-generating possibilities in the area, as outlined in previous sections. Share-cropping possibilities are curtailed by the limited availability of cultivable land and the marketization of land transfer in the area (the buying and selling of land for cash rather than 'loaned' to relatives or inherited), while plantation development and better overland links to the industrial heartland of Java have brought new off-farm employment within reach of transmigrants and Lampungese people. Yet while structural change has been an important force in shaping the availability of different types of work in the area, it does not adequately explain why young Javanese or Lampungese women appear to be engaged in particular types of work.

Another type of explanation has looked to the household realm in order to account for the various work activities of different groups of people. Within household-based interpretations of female work practices, two main themes have emerged. The first of these has focused on economic aspects of the household, linking, for example, daughters' participation in relatively new income-generating activities to their role within an existing household division of labour in spatial and temporal terms. It is argued that where daughters play an important role in childcare, domestic work or work on the family fields, their participation in off-farm work must accord with these, taking place near enough to the family farm for activities to be combined, to a greater or lesser extent. By contrast, where young women have no productive role in the farm household, and therefore are of no value to the household (as is argued to be the case in parts of Latin America), they may be 'expelled' to work in urban areas where they can play a productive role as domestic servants or factory workers (Young 1982; Radcliffe 1993). Within this research theme, attention centres on the concept of labour allocation, offering a rather passive representation of daughters themselves.

The second theme to have emerged in household-based explanations of women's work practices marks a return to an earlier idea of the importance of kinship and family in underscoring the lives of household members (Moore 1988). In part, this renewed interest in kinship and all that it embraces, including gender and generational relations, inheritance and familial obligations, has been driven by a need to account for profound differences in the nature of female work practices in various parts of the world. It is also related to efforts to understand the internal dynamics of households, the ways in which various work practices emerge from contested interests within the household, and how internal processes are tempered by kinship ideologies and practices (Beneria and Roldan 1987; Wolf 1992). This conceptualization of female work practices marks a departure from the rather mechanistic depiction of household relations in labour allocation models and seeks to draw together cultural (kinship) and economic (the household economy) factors in order to arrive at a framework that can account for differences in the work practices of young women in different places (Kabeer 1991). In both Javanese transmigration settlements and Lampungese villages in North Lampung, the household is a central cultural configuration which, following Guyer and Peters (1987), embodies moral values of authority, property, kinship, marriage, residence and inheritance. The following section examines how contrasts in the working lives of Javanese transmigrant daughters and their Lampungese peers relate to distinctive kinship processes and household economies, in so far as these have emerged in this particular setting.

KINSHIP AND HOUSEHOLD ECONOMY: IDEOLOGY AND PRACTICE AMONG JAVANESE TRANSMIGRANTS

Around 90% of the transmigrant families in Negara Sakti described themselves as Javanese, that is, they spoke Javanese at home. In very general terms, the Javanese kinship system is usually characterized as bilateral, shaped by 'the need to maintain social relationships through rules of complementarity and similarity rather than hierarchy and opposition, and the need to reduce imbalances of power through mutual responsibility and cooperation rather than oppression and force' (Karim 1995: 16). The nuclear household has been regarded as an important unit through which economic and social support is channelled, although its boundaries are often stretched to include grandparents and recently married children where need arises (Geertz 1961; Jay 1969). Javanese marriage practices involve matrilocal residence, monogamy and relatively easy divorce. While marriage in Java is almost universal, marriages are frequently dissolved (Geertz 1961; Brenner 1995). Many women marry early by Western standards, at around the age of 19. The choice of spouse, while traditionally a decision made by parents, is increasingly made by couples alone (Wolf 1992). Girls and boys are equally able to inherit (although the influence of Islamic law means that a daughter is eligible for a third share of the property, while a son is entitled to two-thirds). Moreover, women are able to hold property and on divorce, take with them what they brought to the marriage (Brenner 1995).

A snapshot view of Javanese kinship and household practices in Negara Sakti reflects this broad pattern, but also indicates how kinship and household practices may be socially constructed in line with wider socio-economic influences. Migration (and in particular, the strictures of the transmigration programme), has meant that a particularly nucleated form of household is prevalent, comprising husband, wife and children. Only nuclear families were allowed to join the programme, and while there was no *de jure* prohibition on elderly relatives or large numbers of children accompanying couples, the amount of government food assistance given to transmigrants in the first year acted to limit household size. Title to and control of land (and other property) were handed exclusively to a male household head, and while inheritance practices continue to follow a bilateral pattern, in practice, the village government has, on occasion, intervened to prevent the subdivision and parcelling up of transmigrant land allocations between children.[11] Where land is held by women, it is because they are widowed or divorced, but usually the certification remains in their husbands' names. Spouse choice, as in contemporary Java, is frequently the prerogative of the couple themselves, but it should be noted that in Negara Sakti, the possibility of intermarriage between Javanese and Lampungese people (which is very rare) inspires a certain amount of fear for parents in both groups, and a desire to control their daughters' sexuality.

In terms of intra-household relations within Javanese families, lines of authority are both generational and gendered, with deference (respect or *hormat*) directed principally to elders, and particularly to the father who is regarded as having the final word on issues such as education, work and marriage partners, although mothers are also important decision-makers in day-to-day issues. *Hormat* implies both obedience to parents and responsibility for them in their old age. For daughters, a further power dynamic exists between them and their brothers, who are regarded (alongside parents, and particularly the father) as being the guardians of their sisters' personal morality and conduct.

At an economic level, it is difficult to characterize the features of a generalized 'Javanese household economy' beyond making some rather loose statements about the division of labour, gendered mobility constraints, and expectations about the economic contribution of different household members. While there are certain tasks that are defined as women's work and others that are regarded as male, none of these categories is exclusive. Generally, however, women are responsible for domestic and childcare tasks, they are closely involved with nearly all aspects of farming, and have a particularly strong role in small-scale trading (Stoler 1977; Alexander 1987). In Negara Sakti, economic marginality means that nearly every able-bodied adult has to work just to buy enough rice to feed the family. Men, women and children work at the plantation, although frequently men are recruited for the better-paid seasonal contracts, while women work on a daily basis, and frequently these tasks are combined with work on their own farm. For daughters this often means an early start to begin washing clothes and cooking before heading off to work at the plantation, then more cooking and childcare on their return. Mothers are particularly dependent on their daughters for lessening their own workload.

For women in Java, there are relatively few mobility constraints imposed on married women, and many must travel considerable distances in the course of their trading activities. One difference is that public transport is much less developed in North Lampung than on Java, and many women depend on men with motorbikes to ferry them across vast tracts of sugar-cane plantation to the next village. Mobility is more constrained for unmarried women, although seclusion does not feature in Negara Sakti. Groups of young women often wander around together, even after dark, which is unheard of in the Lampungese village.

With respect to the dynamics of the household economy in Negara Sakti, a number of points should be made. First, as has been outlined above, poverty means that there is strong pressure on all able household members to work, although whether this constitutes their participation in a household strategy is debatable. Generally speaking, cash is handed over to the mother (wife) who is responsible for buying food and for cooking. The fact that the mother (wife) is aware how much the going work rate is at the plantation (the principal source of off-farm income) means she is able to exert some pressure on people to comply. In this sense, transmigrant households represent fairly tight economic bundles. Second, the nature of the transmigration programme has meant that many wider kinship networks have been truncated and even severed. As a result, many households in Negara Sakti must operate as autonomous economic units, as they are only occasionally able to seek assistance via extra-local kinship networks, for example, by borrowing money from relatives, or by certain household members living with a relative while they work in another area of Lampung.[12] Where inter-household links have developed, these have tended to be on a neighbourhood basis within the settlement. Small sums of cash are borrowed and lent between neighbours, and the right to take part in the harvest or planting of rice is earned through neighbourhood ties, rather than extended family ties. Third, these points together (economic marginality and limited possibilities of using networks beyond the village) have curtailed the possibilities of circular migration for any household member. Raising the fare to get to Java, for example, is beyond the reach of most transmigrants where life is lived on a hand-to-mouth basis, and there is little possibility of being able to call upon relatives in migrant destinations to offer support.

The implications of kinship and household economy for daughters in Negara Sakti relate to an expectation that daughters will assist their mothers in childcare and household tasks, will raise sufficient income to support themselves within the household, will care for their parents in old age, and will act in ways that will maintain the respectability and standing of their family in the eyes of others. Poverty means that strong pressure is exerted on young women to contribute towards lessening the load on their parents, either by working at the plantation or by looking after siblings, cooking or other domestic responsibilities. This stands in contrast to what Geertz has termed the 'ego-centred' nature of Javanese family life, in which young people are indulged (Geertz 1961). As has been documented by others for rural Java, children (including adolescent girls) are expected to work (White and Hastuti 1980), although the boundary between work and play is often blurred. Where household incomes routinely fall short of household expenditures, the expectation that daughters will 'pay their own way' is understandable.[13] Furthermore, there is an expectation that daughters will be responsible for looking after parents as they reach old age and are unable to work. *Ibu* Jomangin was quite explicit about this point:

> If he can, I want my son to graduate from high school, then become a college student. For my daughter, just school here, so she can help me in the house. It's better for girls to stay near their parents, if they can.

Plantation work provides a local income opportunity through which all of these expectations can be met, without imposing an economic burden on other household members.

KINSHIP AND HOUSEHOLD ECONOMY: IDEOLOGY AND PRACTICE AMONG THE LAMPUNGESE OF WAY KANAN

Compared to the Javanese kinship system, far less has been written about Lampungese kinship. The people of Negri Indah belong to the Way Kanan group, whose kinship system is patrilineal and genealogy-based, located within a wider *marga* or clan system to which smaller family groupings defer in many family decisions, particularly those concerning property, inheritance and marriage (Hilman Hadikusuma 1989).[14] In terms of co-residence, family units stand in marked contrast to the nuclear family organization of the Javanese transmigrants. Households may comprise several married couples (blood relations through the male line), their children and elderly parents, all of whom may or may not share land, and may or may not eat from the same pot. In addition, several self-defined household members may live, on a temporary basis, in smaller, simpler houses close to the fields, in a system which resembles the *umbulan* of the past.[15] Furthermore, as *marga* links extend over a wide geographical area, a number of contributing household members may take up these networks to migrate on a temporary basis, either to clear new land for cultivation in the mountains, or to seek work in the city. In this sense, households as clusters of 'kinship-mediated economic flows' (Kabeer 1991: 8), are more diffuse than those of the Javanese. However, there is some evidence, based on the descriptions of older Negri Indah residents, that politico-economic change in North Lampung has had some influence on co-residential kin groupings, in that maintaining *umbulan* is less common as much of the distant land has been sold for plantation development: as the *marga* declines in influence, people look inwards to a more nuclear, immediate family for support. In addition, as the land market has increasingly been privatized (as opposed to people having the right to cultivate *marga* land), it makes less sense for large groups of people to co-reside.

Within the patrilineal Lampungese kinship system, property, family status and responsibility all pass down the male line through the eldest son, who is regarded as being responsible for his parents in their old age, although in practice this responsibility inevitably falls upon his wife. Newly-weds reside at the home of the husband's parents, if he is the oldest son. This house, and its contents, will become his in due course. If he dies young, the property is held by his wife until his oldest son comes of age to take it on. Privatization of *marga* land has translated into a patrilineal inheritance system also, although how far this has any meaning in the absence of land certification for Lampungese is open to question. The few cases of women holding land in Negri Indah involved widows with no sons. Second sons must buy or rent land and houses, although in practice many work together with their older brothers, or, more recently, move away altogether.

Lampungese marriage practices are characterized by patrilocal residence and a general absence of divorce.[16] There are occasionally polygynous marriages but these are more prevalent in wealthier communities. As with Javanese practice, in the past, many women married young (on average, aged 13) but this has risen and there are many single women aged up to 22. Choice of marriage partner rests with the couple, although they must have the tacit approval of both sets of parents, and, often, the consent of the wider sub-clan, particularly in instances where they belong to a 'good line'.[17] On marriage, a woman is considered to belong to her husband's family, and as such, is responsible for the care of his parents, over and above her own. Most women co-resided with their husband's parents, relieving the burden of his mother, but taking up much of the domestic work themselves.

In terms of intra-household relations within Lampungese families, lines of authority are both gendered and generational, as was the case in Javanese families, but if anything, gender is a stronger reference mark. Mothers may be observed deferring to their sons, and, more frequently, sisters to their brothers. In other words, all female household members are under the guardianship of male household members, whatever their age. Women are expected to obey their husbands, and daughters to obey their fathers, particularly when it comes to life-choices, such as education, marriage and work. However, authority does not end with the father (male head of household) for he is expected to defer to the wider lineage group (*marga*), particularly over marriage and property transfer decisions. The decision-making process regarding the marriage of *Mbak* Niah, a school teacher, involved her parents, her future husband's parents and the sub-clan, with whom a deal was worked out regarding the timing of the event, where the couple would live and work, and the payments to be exchanged between families. Although the idea to marry was the couple's, the decision had to be made by her father, but this itself was embedded in a wider sub-clan negotiation.

As economic units, households are extremely complex, made up as they are of a number of different conjugal units: grandparents (who may farm and cook together), their oldest son, his wife and children (who cook and eat together), and perhaps a younger son or daughter, who may contribute to either of these units. Land may be owned individually, but may be worked as a household group, with different household members having different authority over how it may be used. The division of labour between men and women is relatively clear-cut. While men and adult women work together in the fields, there are clearly identified male and female tasks, and women are solely responsible for all domestic work including processing the harvest (unless this is done by machine). Although the ideal for women is that they do not engage in agricultural work (they should stay home, keep their skins white and avoid building muscles), in practice this is rarely achieved, particularly among poor people. Unlike Javanese women, Lampungese women play little role in petty trade, unless it is via a small shop in the front of their house.

Partly, the restriction on women's participation in the labour force relates to normative constraints on their mobility. Even married women are not allowed to go out of the village unaccompanied, or to go to distant fields on their own. Widows would be seen accompanied by their sons as they made their way to tend their crops. Where these restrictions are particularly strong is in the case of unmarried girls, who, on reaching puberty, are not allowed to go out of the house except with parents or older brothers. Thus, they have little or no role in the farming system as they are precluded from taking part in any activity that takes them away from the confines of the house until they have married and borne their husband a child.[18] In view of this, the temporary migration of unmarried women to Tangerang, a practice which has only emerged in the last few years, is particularly noteworthy as it appears to flout these mobility restrictions.

In seeking to characterize the dynamics of the household economy in Negri Indah, the following points may be made. First, while poverty is no stranger to Negri Indah, for the most part, people are wealthier than their Javanese transmigrant neighbours. Many young people are educated to senior high school level and beyond, and there is less sense of a 'hand-to-mouth' existence, except among the poorest of families (generally female-headed households). Second, the relatively loose structure of the Lampungese household means that it is difficult to equate income flows with income-pooling. In other words, there is no one person who is solely responsible for control of income (there are a number of income control points, for example, the different wives within a dwelling), and although there is an expectation that at least some income will be pooled, this expectation does not apply to everyone in every circumstance. Third, it is clear that networks beyond the household (and even the village), many of which are kinship-based, are an important line of economic and social assistance for domestic groups. Several parents had a child living with relatives in the city to receive education (some as far afield as Yogyakarta, in Central Java), and young men and women often made use of wider networks to seek access to distant land for cultivation (in the case of men) or employment.

The implications of kinship and household economy for daughters in Negri Indah stand in marked contrast to the situation of daughters in Negara Sakti. In the Lampungese village there is little expectation that daughters will assist their mothers beyond elementary household duties, because of the constraints imposed on their working in the fields. In this sense, there is little expectation of daughters being able to support themselves through their own efforts, were they to remain in the village. In short, they have no local economic value. Furthermore, there is little expectation that daughters will be responsible for looking after their own parents as the latter reach old age and are unable to work (that responsibility falls upon the woman who marries their older brother). Daughters' responsibilities will lean towards the care of their future husband's family, but that is not something her natal family has to worry about. On the other hand, the position of daughters is entirely dependent on their making a suitable marriage, as they will have to look to their future husband for their future welfare. In view of this, daughters (and their families) need to negotiate a line of expected behaviours which will maintain their respectability and standing in the eyes of others. For these reasons, work in a Tangerang factory can be accommodated. It is not necessary for daughters to find local work to combine with on-farm duties, and as daughters are not expected to make any sort of economic contribution, nothing is lost by their going to Tangerang to work. One might even interpret their migration as an expulsion from the household (Young 1982; Radcliffe 1993). Furthermore, working in a factory does not incur the loss of prestige (*gengsi*) that working in the fields (or the plantation) would bring.

DAUGHTERS' AGENCY: PUSHING THE BOUNDARIES OF *ADAT* AND ECONOMICS

While this type of explanation correctly places young women's activities within the context of household relations, the emphasis on labour allocation obscures the intra-household negotiations which underlie work decisions and masks the intentionality of young women's (and parents') actions. In this conceptualization, daughters appear as passive, buffeted around by the requirements of the household economy and the desires of parents and authority figures, and there is little to suggest the role they themselves play in deciding how they want to spend their time, and the extent to which they are able to contest the boundaries that circumscribe their existence. Recent household studies have pointed to the importance of bringing the agency of women into the picture in order to reach a better understanding of the dynamics of household decision-making over work practices, arguing that it is necessary to look for points of resistance to household authority (Carney and Watts 1991; Hart 1991; Agarwal 1994). Others have looked beyond the power dynamic between husband and wife, to consider how household relations are also textured by the priorities, aspirations and negotiations of daughters, in other words, their agency (Wolf 1992).

The agency of both Lampungese and Javanese daughters with respect to their work practices can be couched very generally in terms of their wishing to develop or assert some kind of financial independence from their parents. This is set against the economic goals and aspirations of parents: on the one hand, of Javanese parents whose desire it is for their daughters to help their parents economically and care for them in old age, and on the other, of Lampungese parents who desire that their daughters make a successful marriage and not become a drain on family livelihood. Household dynamics, one would expect, involve give and take between the respective goals and aspirations of parents and daughters where these diverge.

However, there are two ways in which this conceptualization of household dynamics is inadequate. First, there is much in the situation of both Javanese and Lampungese family practices to suggest that social practice almost invariably exceeds any notion of economic space, as people's priorities include concerns such as prestige, power and morality (Verschoor 1992). In other words, the agency of daughters or parents is not necessarily reducible to economic or livelihood goals, but rather, embraces a set of non-economic priorities and preferences. These may be conceptualized in a number of ways. Bourdieu (1977), for example, writes of 'cultural capital' to include desired items which have no intrinsic economic value in and of themselves,[19] while Hefner suggests that maintaining identity and social morality may be a goal to be weighed against economic preferences (Hefner 1990). Such priorities may be significant where people are dependent on the esteem of their neighbours. Fear of ridicule or malicious gossip is particularly important where extra-household relations are important for maintaining the flow of everyday activities. In this sense, this fear is perhaps more important in the Lampungese village where ties between households, based on genealogy, are stronger. In the Javanese transmigrant village, migrants are less bound by a sense of community; if things fall apart, people can always leave. Stepping out of a genealogical tie is more problematic. Nonetheless, when questioned about their greatest worries, mothers and daughters in both villages regularly expressed fear of the wagging tongues of their neighbours and peers. If ideological or cultural factors are taken into account when analysing female labour, then it is necessary to consider the ways in which social values are enforced at the neighbourhood level (Vera-Sanso 1995). These values may not necessarily be rigid dictates but guiding principles around which household respectability is negotiated.

Within this, and with particular reference to work practices, it is necessary also to identify how value is attached to different types of work in ways that have little to do with economic factors (Verschoor 1992). This is particularly the case with plantation work in North Lampung, which, for the Lampungese, has particular connotations. Historically, this type of work was associated with Javanese contract labourers, regarded in Sumatra as occupying the lowest rung on the social ladder, earning the derisory name *Jakon*. Stories circulating in the Lampungese village about the social and sexual mores of female Javanese plantation labourers, not to mention the pity directed towards them, have been sufficient to ensure that no Lampungese person would be willing to take part in plantation work.

By contrast, plantation work does not have such negative cultural connotations for Javanese transmigrants, except that working there signifies poverty (*ekonomi ngak cukup*). Work in Tangerang is also accorded particular meanings. It is common for Lampungese daughters to describe themselves as *penjahit* [tailors] rather than *buruh pabrik* [factory workers], and this phraseology had been picked up by those parents who had consented to their daughters engaging in factory work. In the Lampungese village, the imagined space of the factory is one of 'white-collar' skilled work, an educated, urban workforce, with pale skin and soft hands, closely supervised by surrogate moral guardians in their hostels at the end of the working day. Significantly, these images are contested by those daughters (mainly Javanese) who have been unable or not permitted to go. Said one 18 year-old transmigrant daughter: 'They have to work long hours, they can't talk to each other and they have to sleep on the floor in rows in their hostels. I think they are pleased when they can come home to Negri Indah.' The point to make is that these representations and meanings accorded to different types of work colour what is deemed valuable and what is sought by different groups of people in ways that do not always overlap with economic criteria.

The second point to make is that the meanings and practices that are contested in the household are rarely negotiated in economic terms, but rather within an idiom of morality, through appeals to a family moral economy in which emphasis is placed on the moral rather than the economy by both daughters and parents. Household decision-making around the work practices of daughters involves negotiating the meaning and assessments of social morality, many of which are given what Li calls a 'vocabulary of legitimation' (Li 1996: 509) through the roles, obligations and responsibilities articulated in the kinship system. That there is a moral dimension to rural power struggles is not a new idea – it has been central to the work of Scott (1985; 1990). While this work has been subjected to much criticism (Hart 1991), where it can be defended and developed is in its portrayal of a moral economy as a set of ideas about what is right and just in rural communities and, by extension, in the household. Expectations of a moral economy are not always (maybe even rarely) met, and people can and do frequently transgress moral boundaries, particularly where earning cash is a goal (Harriss 1994). The point is not that a moral economy necessarily exists in the household, but that it is appealed to and contested by all parties within the decision-making process (Ilcan 1996). Thus, Javanese transmigrant parents will couch their arguments in terms involving the obligations of daughters to work hard and to care for them in their old age, while their daughters point to their obligations as parents to provide for them. Lampungese parents set great store by their daughters' obligation not to bring shame on their families, while daughters assert the ideal of parents' duties towards their children.

In the following section, a more closely textured reading of the decision-making process *vis-à-vis* work practices is offered, focusing on the diverging priorities and aspirations of daughters and parents, the ways in which gendered and generational power is asserted and subverted, and the ways in which appeals to a culturally embedded 'moral economy of the family and household' are articulated, comparing the experiences of Lampungese daughters and their Javanese peers.

LAMPUNGESE DECISION-MAKING AND WORK PRACTICES

The temporary migration of young, unmarried women from Negri Indah to work in textile factories in Tangerang is a phenomenon that has emerged in recent years, and which continues to be commented on by old and young alike. That it takes place in a context where normative codes point towards the seclusion of these young women is paradoxical, and that it has been prompted by the desires of young women themselves, suggests that daughters have been able to subvert parental power and aspirations, at least to some degree. As has been suggested, migration to Tangerang began when one young woman from Negri Indah followed her cousin (from the same lineage but living with her parents in the provincial capital Tanjung Karang) to work in a Tangerang factory. Effectively, this prompted a steady stream of young women, mostly her friends from Negri Indah, to follow suit, to the point that this peer group network to the factory became semi-formalized. Young women moved to Tangerang, stayed in the same hostels as those already working there, and approached the factories themselves. Labour brokerage has, until now at least, been administered at factory level, although there are signs that semi-formal brokerage takes place in the village too, particularly at the Muslim festival of *Lebaran* when women come home en masse, and new factory women return to Tangerang with them at the end of the holiday. As other studies have shown (e.g. Wolf 1992), young women are drawn towards work in the factories for a variety of reasons, few of which are purely economic, and none of which indicates their desire to help their families. *Ibu* Amatyani, now married, worked in a knitting factory for six months, sewing the sleeves on to sweaters for export. She went to Tangerang because she was bored hanging around at home with nothing to do. All her friends had already gone to work there, and she did not want to be left out. 'It was good in Tangerang, very busy (*ramai*). Here, people are very quiet, it is boring. In Tangerang there are lots of young women (*gadis*) who are working together, and it is more fun.' Much of the money she earned, she says, was used up in coming home for *Lebaran* and in buying presents for her family. She saved nothing, and gained little from it from a long-term financial perspective.

Parents have been reluctant to agree to their daughters' departure. There are fears about daughters' morality being compromised, about parents losing control of their daughters, and about their marrying someone who is not from the right Lampungese clan (let alone someone of a different ethnic group altogether). However, it is rare for parents to voice concerns about their daughters making an economic contribution, apart from the gifts they brought back with them at *Lebaran*. *Ibu* Mastura explained that both she and her husband had not wanted their daughter Yani to go to Tangerang originally. Now she was glad she had gone as her daughter now had some money and had sent gifts home. 'If she didn't work there, I would never have been to Java, ' she said. 'But I am afraid she will marry someone there. I want her to come home and not go back there again. But I expect she won't want to come back.'

Others were more interested in the economic contribution working daughters could make, for example, *Ibu* Kalsum, a widow, who had herself arranged for her daughters to work in Tangerang as soon as they had finished junior high school. Her male cousin had taken them there especially to find work, the idea being that they would be able to help her. She had lost everything when her husband died, having sold most of her belongings to pay for medicines to treat him. These days, she has come to rely quite heavily on the cash her daughters send home every month, even though it amounts to no more than Rp. 40,000 (about US$ 80 according to the exchange rate in 1995): 'If my children did not help, life would be very difficult'. Her case was unusual, however, and for the most part, the move to Tangerang was one that was prompted and negotiated by daughters themselves, often in the face of parental disapproval and concern over their moral welfare.

There are a number of issues which point to daughters being able to push back the boundaries of their existence. First, it is true to say that compared to Javanese daughters, most Lampungese daughters have greater access to money, either via the sale of personal possessions, or by borrowing from their friends, in order to raise the fare to get themselves to Tangerang in the first place. *Mbak* Yani had been forbidden to go with her friends to Tangerang by her parents. But she took matters into her own hands, selling all her gold jewellery to raise the Rp. 50,000 (US$ 100) to pay for the fare and lodgings, and confronted her parents with this fact. Although they were angry, they reasoned that the only way for her to get the money back would be to work. In other words, the agency of Lampungese daughters is less bounded in economic terms.

Second, daughters have been able to make use of peer group and kinship networks to a much greater degree than would have been the case for Javanese daughters. Indeed, it was a peer group–kinship network which had started the migration chain in the first place. Lampungese daughters were able to borrow money from friends already working in Tangerang, enabling them to accompany them on their return to the factory after the holidays, and it was certainly the case that parents regarded the main influence on daughters as being their friends. This peer group network has been of particular importance in the context of widespread unemployment, with young women sharing information about possible jobs as factories hire and fire workers practically on a daily basis (Elmhirst 1998).

Third, and related to both the above points, the temporary migration to factories of friends and kin has brought a new-found confidence among Lampungese daughters to challenge their parents' authority, and indeed, the gender structures of the community, in a very direct way. In asking permission to go to work in Tangerang (which all daughters do, although whether they will obey their parents is another matter), the leverage used by daughters to persuade their parents to go along with their plans is not so much an economic argument, but one which appealed to the parents' duty to appear to be providing well for their daughters, to be 'modern'. *Mbak* Rokiah described how she had persuaded her parents to let her go:

> They didn't have enough money to send me to senior high school even though I really wanted to continue. They knew that. I said, if I can't go to school, then I want to go to Tangerang instead. Because of that, they had to say I could go.

This course of events was later confirmed by her mother, who originally had not wanted Rokiah to go:

> She asked me first. I agreed to her wishes because before, she wanted to continue at school but I did not have the money to pay. She said, if I can't go to school, I want to go with my aunt [who lives in Tangerang]. I said OK. If she didn't have an aunt to keep an eye on her, she wouldn't be allowed. Her aunt already works at the factory. If she wasn't there, I wouldn't trust my daughter.

The comments by Rokiah's mother point to a fourth reason why it has been possible for daughters to push at the boundaries of village moral codes regarding the work practices of young women. The very existence of a network, and the fact that it is one based on kinship and common identity (belonging to the same clan) means that factory work can be accommodated within prevailing ideologies concerning young women's work and their obligations towards their natal household. In the eyes of parents (and their neighbours) factory work is not agricultural work ('they just pack soap or sew, it is not the same as work in the *ladang*, which is taboo'), and parents believe their daughters to be 'supervised' by older women for the time that they are at the factory. Furthermore, there is a sense among parents of young women who have gone to work in Tangerang that their daughters would never make a financial contribution to the household (because of their exclusion from farm work and constraints on their movement around the village). Compared with Javanese daughters, their role in helping their mothers (and later caring for elderly parents) is not so central, and in a number of households with daughters working in Tangerang, domestic responsibilities had already been handed over to a daughter-in-law, as is common Lampungese kinship practice. Thus, limited expectations about daughters' contribution means parents can afford to be more *laissez-faire* about daughters heading to the factories of Tangerang.

The point at which parental power over factory-employed daughters is asserted heavily, is when there is a likelihood of any sort of threat that they might marry someone who is not Lampungese. This was the most frequently expressed fear of mothers and fathers alike, as *Ibu* Mastura's remarks about her daughter Yani suggest (see above). While there have been cases of fathers or brothers going to Tangerang to bring errant daughters home, generally parental authority is asserted at the Muslim festival of *Lebaran*, which is when children come home to pay their respects to their parents. It is at this time that daughters are most likely to capitulate to their parents' wishes, as *Lebaran* itself encourages them to re-evaluate their behaviour towards their parents and whether this accords with their being good Muslims. During the week that they are at home, arrangements are made for daughters to marry young men from the village, which means that they must give up factory work.

Ibu Jariah had been working in Tangerang for two years when her parents learned that she had a Sundanese boyfriend. When she came home for *Lebaran*, arrangements were made for her to marry *Pak* Ibrahim, a man seven years her senior, of 'good lineage', and whom it had always been assumed she would marry. Her parents, his parents and *Pak* Ibrahim himself had told her that as soon as she had married, she would be allowed to return to Tangerang, and *Pak* Ibrahim would accompany her to work also (he is a second son, and therefore will not inherit land). That was more than a year ago and they still have not left. *Ibu* Jariah now feels it was a tactic to persuade her to marry. 'I am bored here. There, I had money of my own, I could buy what I wanted. Here, I have to ask my husband. Once you have a husband, you can't go anywhere', she said.

JAVANESE DECISION-MAKING AND WORK PRACTICES

Javanese transmigrant households have the appearance of following a corporate strategy that is directed by the income-securing goals set by the household head, and to which all household members, including daughters, seem to comply. But is the participation of daughters in plantation work a sign of compliance with their parents' wishes, or an assertion of their own desire to earn an income independent of that of their parents? Plantation work is rather different from factory work in Tangerang, and the household decision-making processes around it are not the same either. In most households in Negara Sakti, daughters began working at the plantation after they had left school, generally at the age of 13. Their leaving school very much reflected the difficult choice parents had to make between their long-term desire to educate their children, who might then become government employees and keep them in their old age, and their short-term need to meet subsistence requirements. It is fair to say that most parents wanted to keep both male and female children in school as long as possible, even to the point of selling land in order to meet the fees. Plantation work fills that period between finishing school and getting married, a period for which there is some ambivalence about what sort of contribution (if any) daughters should be making towards their keep, but negotiation is very much on a day-to-day basis, rather than in the form of a single life-choice.

Parental authority is directed towards ensuring that daughters who have nothing better to do (such as school or marriage) help their parents, either by lessening the load on their mothers or by bringing in cash of their own. To this end, parents call upon a set of economic and moral resources in order to persuade daughters to comply with this. In terms of economic leverage, parents are well aware that daughters may need to call upon their good-will when it comes to setting up their own homes. There is little chance for young people to buy land in the area, and there are few non-familial networks they can utilize as an alternative. For this reason, many newly married couples live with the wives' parents before building a small house in the latter's home garden. *Pak* Susanto and his wife, Ani, both 22 years old, had just built a small wooden house in Ani's parents' home garden. Ani had been a good daughter, according to her mother, always helpful and polite, and although her parents had not wanted her to work at the plantation, she had done so and helped pay her way in the family. Now married, *Ibu* Ani continued to help her mother, doing laundry and looking after children while her mother worked in the fields, as an acknowledgement of the economic assistance her parents had, in effect, given her.

Moral resources, appeals to a household moral economy, are also made as parents attempt to assert their authority over daughters. *Ibu* Alfiah's family provides a case in point. Her daughter, Rupi, was taken out of school when she was 14 as *Ibu* Alfiah and her husband were unable to find the fees. *Ibu* Alfiah explained:

> Now all she wants to do is play. She hates to go to the plantation. I tell her how hard we have had to work to give her a good life. She doesn't realize how hard it has been for us. If she doesn't help, then there will be even less for us all. Life is very difficult here, to live you need a system of family mutual assistance (*sistem gotong royong keluarga*).

Rupi reluctantly began going to the plantation just three days a week, but on some days she refused, saying she was afraid of riding in the truck which took her to work (*takut naik truk*). On the days that she did not go to the plantation, her mother went instead, leaving Rupi to cook, clean and look after the younger children. Rupi's story is an indication that daughters do not necessarily share the goals and aspirations of their parents, nor do they always capitulate to their authority.

However, the ways in which daughters in Negara Sakti are able to contest their obligations and the expectations of their parents are very limited by a number of factors. First, as earlier sections of this chapter have outlined, the process of transmigration has left Javanese transmigrant daughters with a limited number of networks that they are able to call upon as alternatives to the support of immediate family. Few have any other kin living in the village (such as grandparents or an aunt) with whom they might stay if relations with their own parents were to break down. In addition, their 'forced' removal from their natal village (not to mention the fact that most of these villages no longer exist) and the little knowledge that they have of surrounding areas (where local transportation is scarce) means there are few places for young women to run to. Second, a semi-formalized network has yet to develop linking the transmigrant village with the factories of Tangerang. This means that daughters are less able to arrange work in Tangerang without the consent and assistance of their parents. As most parents are unwilling to part with the fairly substantial amount of cash to pay for their daughters to go to Tangerang when there is no guarantee that the money they earn will be relayed back to the household, this opportunity is beyond the reach of transmigrant daughters. Following on from this, the absence of alternative ways of earning cash within the immediate area (beyond the plantation) and the limited possibilities of saving enough money to pay for the fare to go further afield, leave daughters with little option other than to stay with their immediate family. This lack of resources, either economic or social, has meant that few daughters have the confidence to offer a serious challenge to parental authority; indeed they are particularly dependent on the good-will of their parents and in maintaining good relations with them. *Mbak* Itah, the eldest of four children, has worked regularly at the plantation since she left school (at age 14) and since her younger sister began to be involved more in domestic work. She is resigned about it:

> It is true that if you don't work at the plantation, there is not enough food, particularly before the rains come, when it is difficult to live. You can earn a bit of money. Although my mother takes the money, sometimes I can buy something myself. There's nowhere else to get money here.

Like many daughters of her age in Negara Sakti, *Mbak* Itah would have liked the chance to work in Tangerang, but regarded it as an unrealistic proposition, and one which her parents would not agree to on principle: 'My mother wants me to stay home and work here, she says we are the children of farmers and that kind of work is not possible for farmers'. This is not to say that parental opposition to daughters working in Tangerang has not been strenuously contested. Wati and Mirah, daughters of one of the school teachers in Negara Sakti, had been sent to senior high school in the provincial capital Tanjung Karang by their parents, and were to stay in a lodging house run by some relatives of their father. After a few months at school, both daughters dropped out and began working in factories, not in Tangerang, but in North Jakarta. According to their mother, neither has sent money home, and although they continue to stay with her husbands' relatives, their mother still does not know where they work or what kind of factory it is:

> Certainly I am worried about them and what they are doing. It would be better if they stayed on at school. I am afraid what will become of them. It is not like when I was young and had to obey my parents. Young people today just do what they like.

While many parents spoke of young people just 'doing what they liked', in fact this was not really the case. The agency of daughters was very much bounded by economic and social circumstance: poverty and their status as migrants meant that their actions had little latitude. Instead, the opposition of daughters to parental authority regarding work practices tended to be manifest more in day-to-day circumstances, rather than in life-choice decisions. Rather than their challenging parental authority and heading off to the factories of Tangerang, daughters contested the boundaries of obligation regarding work at the plantation nearby.

Few daughters enjoyed working at the plantation. It was back-breaking work, hot and dusty, and at the end of the day, wages were often paid directly to their mothers (if they had come to the plantation with them). There was little direct personal benefit in going, other than the knowledge that there might be more to eat, perhaps vegetables to accompany the rice, cassava and chilli that made up most people's evening meal. Sometimes when parents (usually fathers) told daughters that they had to work on the plantation that day, daughters would refuse to go: not in a direct and confrontational way, but indirectly, Javanese-style. Either they would go and hide when the truck came round to pick them up, or they would say that they were sick, appealing to the obligation of their mothers to take care of them. Others, like Nita, challenged their parents more directly. Nita said she sometimes asked her parents why they were not a successful family like 'x', who did not make their daughters work at the plantation. The implication in this was that parents had somehow failed to uphold their role in the household moral economy. Although parents would certainly scold daughters and complain bitterly when they did not comply with their wishes, by far the greatest sanction on young women was the fact that if they did not work, they did not earn, and if they did not earn, they did not eat. Compared to their Lampungese peers, the latitude of Javanese daughters in

Negara Sakti to challenge parental authority was very much constrained by economic circumstance and social situation: as migrants with few resources to call upon beyond the immediate confines of the household, transmigrant daughters have little choice but to comply with parental wishes. Their resistance was one of innuendo and suggestion regarding the abilities of their parents to earn an income, of inaction rather than action (Scott 1990), which enabled them to appeal to a moral economy in which parents indulged them, but in ways that did not threaten their already precarious economic position.

Conclusion

Contrasts in the work practices of Javanese transmigrant daughters and their Lampungese peers can be linked to a complex relationship between the needs of the household to subsidize farm income with off-farm sources and, by contrast, the agency of daughters themselves, who are attracted by the autonomy that wage work appears to imply. When the two communities are compared, this relationship seems to be being played out rather differently. Among Javanese households, daughters' desires to strike out on their own appear to have been suppressed in the face of poverty, and in a situation where young women have few resources beyond the immediate family upon which they can call in order to challenge parental authority and push against the strictures that kinship norms and obligations demand. Furthermore, the nature of the work in which they engage is such that it is difficult for them to avoid contributing to the household, particularly when their mothers are employed alongside them. For these reasons, it is possible to note the appearance of a 'pulling together' of transmigrant families, where individual survival strategies appear to have converged, in line with a Javanese household moral economy in which there is an expectation that daughters will contribute their labour as carers in the parents' old age.

Among Lampungese daughters, the situation is rather different. Here, daughters are 'assumed out' of household economic equations. Their migration to Tangerang to work in factories is indicative of the ways in which daughters have been able to challenge parental authority by calling upon extra-household networks and resources. Although a tradition of seclusion for unmarried daughters remains, paradoxically, the position of daughters within a Lampungese household moral economy has been such that they have been able to negotiate their situation with parents, by presenting factory work in ways that offer no threat to household respectability. The bounds of female agency are felt more strongly once women are expected to marry, and at that point, the drawbridge on their autonomy is pulled up.

I have attempted to show that while the activities of daughters in the two communities are linked to cultural (moral) factors and economic realities, they are not reducible to either one. Cultural factors are important in shaping the meanings that are ascribed to different types of work, in mediating the ways in which daughters are attached to the household and family, and in providing a lexicon through which daughters' attachment is negotiated and renegotiated in moral terms. By contrast, economic factors are important for shaping the terms upon which different types of work are taken up by daughters, in mediating the terms through which daughters are obliged to contribute (or not) to the household and family, and in setting the boundaries within which daughters are able to operate. Thus, while an analysis of daughters' work practices involves an understanding of the household as a cluster of kinship mediated economic flows (Kabeer 1991), it also requires that the household be characterized as a central cultural configuration, a cluster of moral values embracing the rights, responsibilities, obligations and expectations of daughters and parents alike.

Author's Note

This chapter is based on doctoral fieldwork conducted in Indonesia between August 1994 and May 1995 under the auspices of LIPI (Indonesian Institute of Sciences) and funded by the British Economic and Social Research Council. More recent data is drawn from fieldwork conducted between March and May 1998 with financial support from the Economic and Social Research Council research award number R000222089. I am grateful to my sponsors in Indonesia, the Department of Forestry and the International Centre for Research in Agroforestry (ICRAF-Southeast Asia) for their support.

Notes

1. See Brass (1991) for an overview of critiques of the moral economy thesis as represented by the work of James Scott and Eric Wolf. See also Harriss (1994).

2. For reviews of the Indonesian transmigration programme in general, and its impact, see Hardjono (1977), World Bank (1988), Fasbender and Erbe (1990) and Tjondronegoro (1991).

3. *Translok* has received little attention in the literature. For a brief description see Pain (1989). The programme began with research in 1978 into possible sites for *translok* resettlement. Originally, around 50,000 families were to be moved with the aim of opening up isolated areas, rather than opening new forest, but in fact more than 100,000 households had been moved by 1993, with plans to resettle many more. The process is very similar to that of transmigration in terms of provision of housing, rural infrastructure and a 2-hectare land allocation to migrants designated for the cultivation of upland crops.

4. The names of villages and people have been changed to protect privacy.

5. The *Lembaga Ketahanan Masyarakat Desa* (LKMD) [village 'cabinet'] and *kepala desa* [village head] are the most important elements of village-level administration and have the power to compel people to take part in unpaid

communal activities (e.g. road-building). The village head is also able to exert influence over marriage, the sale of land and movement away from the settlement.

6   The term used in Indonesia for this arrangement is *tebu rakyat*; ostensibly it is a nucleus estate/smallholder plasma system in which farmers are contracted to grow a particular crop and sell it to the factory. The price obtained is used to pay off credit obtained for clearing the land, paying non-family labour and buying planting materials.

7   For example, the *kecamatan* [district] of Gunung Balak, from whence many were resettled, no longer exists. The villages were simply wiped off the map when the resettlement took place.

8   Figures are for the 1994/95 season and should be set against an average price for a kilogram of rice of Rp. 1,000 in the transmigration settlement.

9   *Peri*-urban refers to the semi-urban hinterland of cities where there is a mixture of urban and rural land uses and economic activities.

10 This marks a distinct category of factory work according to a survey of industrial labour in West Java (Hutagalung *et al.* 1994). This survey suggested that workers in such factories were from distant parts of Java, rather than outer-island regions. How far the participation of young women from outer Indonesia in factory work represents a new situation has yet to be researched.

11 There were several instances where the village head refused to allow the sale of land, and where he would not permit the *de jure* subdivision of land between siblings, although in practice, the land has been parcelled up. Were the legality of this to be questioned (for example, in one of the area's frequent land claim disputes) the position of the *de facto* landowners would be very uncertain.

12 It is also the case that many transmigrants (or their parents) had come to Lampung as 'runaways' and had thus lost all links with their natal villages in Java. Extended family networks have a limited role to play in the lives of transmigrants.

13 For at least six months of the year, many people's incomes could be described as *harian*, or daily. By working on the plantation, people would earn just enough to cover their food needs for one day. Were one adult household member to fall sick or not to work, it would be almost impossible for others to earn enough to subsidize their needs. Difficult decisions had to be made: one man had decided that his family could not afford to pay for his mother-in-law to visit hospital to have her broken arm set, as the money was needed for food for his six children. As his mother-in-law sat chewing betel to ease the pain, he explained that there was no point in paying for the treatment when she was too old to work in any case.

14 The ethnology of Lampung is very complex and not all sources agree. According to van Royen (1930) and Sevin (1989), the main original groups are Pubian, Abung, Pesisir and Menggala. Those originating in South Sumatra

in the eighteenth and nineteenth centuries include the Ogan, Sumendo and Mesuji. The Way Kanan are thought to belong to this latter, non-indigenous group, although their origins are Pesisir and this is reflected in their language, which has similarities to the language spoken in coastal areas in the south of the province (Lebar 1972). For a slightly different interpretation, see Hilman Hadikusuma (1989).

15 *Umbulan* were smaller, often temporary hamlets built close to fields and were inhabited for the course of cultivation during extended fallow cycles (shifting cultivation). Principal residence remained at the natal village (which was where older people and young daughters would stay).

16 There are instances of abandonment by either sex. In the one case where a wife abandoned her husband, she left the village to work land in South Lampung with her eldest son, but has not remarried.

17 The sub-clan system is hierarchical to the point where, if no partner of suitable rank is available, the person must remain single. This was the case of one sub-clan chief, who was still single at the age of 40.

18 Villagers link this practice to the possibility of 'abduction' marriage (*caripaksa*).

19 Educational qualifications might be an example of this.

12

Staying Behind
Conflict and Compromise in Toba Batak Migration

Janet Rodenburg

> [Migration] brings economic, social and geographic mobility, yet in other ways heightens social and economic dependence; it binds families together, whilst also pulling them apart; it is a central source of advancement, and a symbol of power, yet also resisted through stress upon local sources of power ... (Gardner 1995: 3–4).

INTRODUCTION

When *Nai*[1] Datir's husband left the village to work as a hawker in West Sumatra she, like dozens of other wives, dreamt of receiving regular remittances and educating her children. Today, she knows better. Rather than leading a life of relative leisure, she finds herself trapped by her husband's migration. During the five years that *Ama* Datir was physically absent most of the time, *Nai* Datir had to work his fields on her own with little or no financial support. To make matters worse, her husband started a relationship with someone else in West Sumatra and *Nai* Datir has not heard of him since.

Luckily, not all fare as badly as *Nai* Datir. Indeed, many Toba Batak are living outside their home area, mainly because of the success of those who have been able to improve their standard of living or to educate their children. Inspired by these and other stories of a good life, many families have one or more migrant members.

This chapter will consider the implications of male-dominated outmigration for gender relations and household organization in North Tapanuli, a relatively remote, mountainous area in North Sumatra.[2] Earlier anthropological studies on the effects of migration tended to accept the gender division of labour as given, so that women often disappeared from the discussion, tucked into the 'household' or 'domestic community', their concrete lives obscured behind abstract concepts such as reproduction and, even, gender (Wright 1995: 780). In this chapter I am particularly interested in the space of manoeuvre of the women staying behind in relation to the practice of patriliny, in which the nature of property and residence are central in defining women's rights and women's space. Given this context, male migration has contradictory consequences for women's bargaining power and control in particular and intra-household relations in general.

However, apart from focusing on consequences, it is important also to understand the converse: the ways in which kinship and household arrangements and the imperatives that emerge from such arrangements themselves shape the course of migration. It is easy to portray village women as passive victims, an image that relates to the undeniable reality of patriarchy[3] in North Tapanuli. In terms of residence patterns, access to resources, rights over children, and physical mobility, Toba Batak women come off worst. They are barred from domains of political and religious power and defer to their male elders over important decisions. In terms of legitimate power, men dominate.

The image of women as victims has by now been extensively criticized and for good reasons (Mohanty 1988). My findings confirm the view of most feminist anthropologists that women have not been merely passive victims of externally imposed codes of behaviour, swept along by the inexorable forces of history. The concept of agency – both in defence of and in rebellion against one's position – has cast new light on the life-worlds, strategies, and rationalities of actors in different social arenas (Long and Long 1992: 6). However, 'agency' can become a problematic concept if treated ahistorically. What needs to be avoided is an uncritical fusing of the notion of women's agency with that of women's resistance to oppression, and to gender oppression in particular (see Abu-Lughod 1990, Saptari this volume). Moreover, the analysis of women's agency should acknowledge the pervasiveness of women's conservatism, their resistance to change. Women have also acted as agents of gender socialization on behalf of the prevailing norms of their society, as mothers and teachers. Various reasons for women's acceptance of their position are suggested here: their own upbringing and the power of ideology; the limited alternatives available to them; as well as the risks of rebellion and the rewards of conformity. The penalties and the rewards should not be lightly dismissed. Women who rebel against their lack of land rights, for instance, face isolation and can no longer count on their brothers' good-will. At the same time, women's compliance to their ascribed roles as providers and mothers within the domestic sphere gives them an identity and social prestige.

In the following analysis I shall point out domains of non-formal power of women in the context of different forms of male migration. The aim is to investigate to what extent migration of male household members enables or hinders Toba Batak women's individual and collective efforts to improve their social and economic position within the community. I shall explore the extent to which male migration works to reproduce and reinforce patriarchal structures and power relations; or, to what extent migration of direct relatives may give rise to new forms of power and authority for women and may represent a resource in women's negotiations with men over access to property and social recognition.

As feminist anthropologists (e.g. Moore 1988; Di Leonardo 1991; Strathern 1995) have pointed out, there are other forms of power operating behind the scenes and women often use these to real effect. We must therefore look beyond the formal rules to the ways in which women strategize and informally negotiate their positions, as Gardner (1995) has so eloquently done in her study on migration in Bangladesh.

From this point of view migration no longer appears as some kind of structural force, inasmuch as it is a medium to achieve one's aims. It is recognized that 'structure is not as such external to human action, and is not identified solely with constraint' (Giddens 1987: 61). This model leaves analytical space for the role that women play in facilitating male migration, without overlooking the fact that migration in turn conditions and mediates their agency. Agents, whether migrants or stayers, use structures for their own individual ends.

Similarly, Toba Batak family and household networks can be seen as a medium, providing the background support that the migrant needs in order to undertake the risky business of migration. While much research on migration strategies (e.g. Arizpe 1982; Findley 1987) has treated the household as an undifferentiated, harmonious unit which is the lowest level of decision-making, this chapter takes note of more recent work on the complexity of intra-household relations. It questions the general assumption that individual members subordinate their private interests to the general good of the household and underlines the importance of relationships of power and subordination along age and gender lines.

North Tapanuli: Background of Migration

Batak history over the past century can be read as a case study of rapid modernization. Having been relatively isolated from external impacts until the coming of the Rhenish Mission and Dutch colonial control in the last decades of the nineteenth century, the Toba Batak embraced Christianity, education, the money economy and urbanization more wholeheartedly than most Indonesian people (Reid 1998).

Migration has been an integral part of this process of development. Even in pre-colonial and colonial times, Toba Batak men were known for their 'wanderlust', travelling to and from the coast to barter precious forest products for salt. Their womenfolk were left behind in the villages to take care of house and hearth (Burton and Ward 1827). Political independence offered opportunities to occupy former plantation land in the eastern lowlands, and Batak responded by beginning a mass outmigration from their impoverished homeland (Cunningham 1958; Rodenburg 1997). At the same time expanding urban, and particularly public, sectors opened up a 'window' of mobility which better-educated men in particular were able to exploit. There was a general belief in migration as the way to 'progress' (*hamajuon*), to new norms and values, to broaden one's horizon (Cunningham 1958; Bruner 1961; Rodenburg 1997).

The Toba Batak homeland of Tapanuli Utara is poor, ranking fifteenth of North Sumatra's 17 *kabupaten* [districts] in per capita GDP, above only remote Nias and Dairi (SUDA 1993: 731-734). Its historic core, the island of Samosir with Lake Toba, is dirt-poor even in this context, with a declining population, exhausted soils, and no industry except tourism (Reid 1998). Peasant smallholdings dominate the local economy. A clear agricultural policy is lacking and even in the irrigated areas there is only limited mechanization. In one of the research villages the average farm size per household was 9.5 *rante*, [0.38 ha], with 68% cultivating even less than that. Land ownership was fairly evenly distributed, with 77% of the households operating less than 1 ha and only 6% operating more than 2 ha. Most smallholders are able to obtain sufficient rice and root crops for their own needs if the harvest is good, but rarely have a surplus large enough to tide them over a bad year. One of the principal strategies to make ends meet under these economically harsh conditions has been circular migration in search for additional earnings.

While much of the early migration was temporary, male-dominated, and limited to short-term economic opportunities, during the last decades movements to Medan, Jakarta and other urban centres have been more permanent, involving both men and adolescent women, or whole households. Everybody has migrants among his/her family or friends. Thus, in 61% of the households at least one member had moved out, either a male 'head of household' and/or an adolescent son or daughter. In one of the villages a total of 39 married men (12%) were absent, most of them engaged in hawking activities in West and South Sumatra. Consequently, the male to female ratio among the adult population (those aged 25 to 59 years) was 56:100.

At the time of research two main types of migration were distinguished with differing implications for intra-household relations. Migrants were (a) male or female adolescents, or (b) married men. The latter paid periodic visits to the village, ranging from once a month to once a year. Related to these forms of migration are a number of factors: the motivation to leave (to gain employment or education); the flow of remittances (to or from the village); and the distance between the place of migration and the home village. Before delving into the implications of the migrants' prolonged absences from the village, it is necessary to take a closer look at Toba Batak kinship and household arrangements.

The *Ripe*, the *Marga*, and the *Huta*

Ripe

Although households are an integral part of Toba Batak lineages, in 'earning a living' domestic groups operate as relatively autonomous enterprises. In North Tapanuli over the past 70–80 years there has been a transition from multi-household to single-household dwellings. Elderly people still remember that as many as six related family groups might share one large *adat* house. The interior was divided into separate 'rooms', demarcated by walls of unrolled mats at night. Rice stores were kept in separate bins; shawls and other valuables in separate caches. Every domestic group [*ripe*] had its own fire-place in the centre of the house (Sherman 1990).

Whereas in the past male agnatic kin and their wives tended to live in extended and sometimes polygamous households, institutions and practices such as the nuclear family and monogamy were adopted under the influence of Christianity and colonial ideology. Most newly-wed couples tried to set up their own household (*manjae*) as soon as possible, usually before the birth of the first child. The young wife received a bag of hulled rice and some kitchen utensils from her mother-in-law, with which she could start her duties as a housewife on her own. The husband received a *hauma panjaean* [rice-field] from his father (Vergouwen 1964: 218). The *panjaen* was a proclamation that the newly-weds had become a fully responsible couple before the *adat*. In recent times, however, increasing land scarcity has complicated the traditional practice of endowing *panjaen* land (Simbolon 1998).

The villagers use the term *ripe* interchangeably with the Indonesian term *rumah tangga* to refer to what we call a couple or nuclear (or conjugal) family. Husband and wife, with their dependent children, comprise a *ripe*. Its members have mutual responsibilities for the production and provisioning of food, and this isolates this unit from wider groupings. These are also important components of official state ideology (*Pancasila*) which promotes the idea of the *keluarga sejahtera* [secure and peaceful family] in which men are responsible for women's economic and physical well-being.

The usual definition of the household in Southeast Asia is a group of people who live and eat together. However, in North Tapanuli the *ripe* is not simply a group of common consumers, for in addition it often involves joint property and economic cooperation with non-members. When examined more closely, the 'household' as a bounded unit becomes increasingly problematic, especially where migration is involved. In Tapanuli, for instance, some household members spend many years elsewhere. Likewise, economic cooperation may take place across spatial boundaries, where a wife cares for village property whilst her husband lives and works in other parts of the archipelago. In these cases, understanding the household simplistically as a 'common hearth' can be misleading (see also Gardner 1995: 100–01).

As the colonial courts, the Christian missionaries, the educational system and the New Order government actively promoted the ideology of the nuclear family, the current norm for Toba Batak households comprises a conjugal couple and their children who eat, work and sleep together. This is, however, just a norm, an imagined household. Although I witnessed a strong affective identification with the nuclear family, and children played an important role as the focus for family solidarity, only half of all households could be called nuclear. I found many other living arrangements and, as elsewhere, this has largely to do with the family's stage in the development cycle; instead of being a single type, households are constantly changing and evolving over time. Moreover, whereas the ideal household includes a conjugal couple, whose complementary labour contributes to the economic and social reproduction of the group, there is a considerable number of households without an adult male. Male migration means that men can belong to a household in name while being physically absent. Some of them hold such central positions or contribute so much to the upkeep of the village household that their presence is felt even though they live and work elsewhere. One of them, a man who worked as a teacher in another sub-district, acted as a deacon in the local church whenever he spent a weekend home. Another migrant had a (hereditary) position as hamlet head, even though he resided in the far south of Sumatra, some 1,200 km from his natal village.

In the following I shall therefore distinguish between village households (being bounded, localized units with members actually present at the time of enumeration) and translocal or migrant households (with members residing in different places). In the villagers' definition, the village household[4] is the unit of co-residence and consumption, although this unit is not necessarily self-sufficient since it may partly depend on the earnings of absent migrants. The translocal household is more loosely defined as a set of shared relationships among people that impose obligations and revolve around the pooling of common resources (Friedman 1984; Wolf 1986). However, as demonstrated below, in order to maximize security many women chose the strategy of laying claim to the obligations and solidarity of wider kin, thereby transgressing the boundaries of their own household.

Marga

To understand life in Tapanuli, the concept of *marga* [kin group] is crucial, for kinship is one of the principal factors of social, political and economic organization, structuring daily life.[5] To a large part it has influenced patterns of migration, for it is mainly through the *marga* network that people gain the initial capital and contacts which enable them to migrate. Just like the situation in North Lampung, described by Elmhirst (this volume), many Toba Batak villagers had a child living with an uncle or aunt in the city while attaining a higher education or looking for a job.

Kinship is essentially a set of organizational principles for the division of labour and the allocation of resources in the household; it is the main mechanism for the transmission of property, and the provision of care. It becomes effective through *adat* [customary law], the state and the economy, but it also exists as ideology in that it attributes values to these principles. Like all ideologies, however, actual practices may deviate from its normative prescriptions. Thus a kinship system that appears to stress functional complementarity between men and women may co-exist with actual relations that are full of tension and conflict (Scott 1994: 78).

Most commentators have characterized Toba Batak society as patrilineal. Descent is through men, and under customary law, daughters do not share in the inheritance of their fathers. For Toba Batak women it is crucial to bear sons because they continue the patrilineage. As a consequence, the custody of children is ultimately with the patrilineage. But it is also sons who endow a woman with prestige and economic power because they secure her access to her husband's land in case she becomes a widow.

However, women also maintain links with their matrilineal kin. Brothers, in particular, are expected to play important roles on various ritual occasions in women's lives. They may serve as authority figures for the sister's children, and marriage between a sister's son and a brother's daughter is actively encouraged. Emotional and ritual ties apart, a brother is expected to provide economic and social support when necessary. Although a woman cannot inherit land because she leaves her natal home upon marriage, she can be given a plot of rice-field (*pauseang*) by her father or her brothers if she asks for it (Vergouwen 1964: 258–59). This gift symbolizes 'honour' on her father's part because he is able to share his wealth with another *marga* to which his daughter now belongs. Simultaneously, the *pauseang* land (Simbolon 1998) strengthens the relationship between the two clans. However, a woman is not allowed to transfer the ownership[6] of the land to somebody outside her father's family. While it seems that the transfer of land gifts was relatively common in the past, in both research villages only a minority of the women (about 14%) had received land from their matrikin. The argument went that because of severe land shortage, few families today have sufficient land to support both a household head and his married sons' families, as well as afford the 'luxury' of letting a married daughter share in the property.

Notwithstanding the importance of matrikin, the basic issue remains that sons are permanent members of the family while daughters join the family into which they marry. This knowledge informs both the attitudes and the behaviour of the parents. Whilst we must not jump to conclusions about the powerlessness of women, it is certainly the case that this is a world where most of the cards, at least formally, are held by men. Likewise, the crucial importance rural women place on their relationships with brothers and on access to their natal homes can only be understood in the context of their overall life situations. These include: early arranged marriages; patrilocal residence; economic and social vulnerability in case of marital discord, marriage break-up or widowhood; and ritual connections and strong emotional ties with brothers. In one of the villages I witnessed how a young woman whose marriage had dissolved was welcomed in her brother's home and stayed for several months. However, instances of neglect and duplicity by brothers also abound, as recounted later in this chapter.

Huta

Even though people live in individual *ripe*, they often depend on members of other households for certain goods or services. Most cooperation takes place between people residing close to each other, often clustered in one hamlet (*huta*). Such *huta* originally consisted of two opposite rows of houses, the whole being enclosed by an earthen wall with tall bamboos, for protection against outside invaders (Vergouwen 1964: 105). Although today the walls and bamboo hedges are no longer maintained, the common courtyard (*alaman*) is still a perfect meeting and working place. Harvested rice is dried in the sun, while women chase off chickens and chat with their neighbours. Others cut wood for daily cooking or weave *pandanus* [reed-like grass] mats, and children play around. On festive occasions big meals are prepared for the kinsmen and kinswomen who attend *adat* ceremonies in front of the house of married or deceased residents. Male household heads in a *huta* are usually brothers or paternal cousins, while occasionally other kin may occupy one of the houses. Beyond the immediate *ripe*, there is no economic obligation towards other *huta* families, although the notion of duty (*kewajiban*), a key component of Toba Batak kinship ideology, means that where possible, support and economic help are rendered to other *huta* members if they are in need. Women in neighbouring or kin-related households may cooperate in agriculture (*marsiadapari*), they may look after each other's children, borrow utensils or give a loan. Male networks have mainly to do with house construction and repair, loaning of tools or a buffalo, or drinking together. Interestingly, few women of migrant households participated in cooperative farm activities because they said that they lacked the time and the people to reciprocate the labour.

Women play a prominent role in the hamlet community. Their conversation is neither dull nor subdued. Subjects of local interest – for example, feasts, marriages and disputes – are all discussed in a lively and opinionated manner. Women joke about certain men behind their backs and they also make fun of men in general ways. For example, a young man was ridiculed because he was about to marry a squint-eyed woman who was about five years his senior. To the village women it was obvious that he only married her because she was a successful trader in Padang, West Sumatra. The young man had never travelled before but went to Padang straight after the marriage.

The above example, however, is the exception that proves the rule that it is mainly women who stay behind in the villages while their menfolk migrate. In the following I shall therefore focus on inter-household dynamics fostering or constraining male migration.

Cooperative Conflicts and Perceived Interests

> Many boys and men who are out of the village ... have mothers, sisters or wives who remain at home, raising children and tilling the soil. In most cases, the women provide a good portion of the wherewithal for males who are attending school or engaged in other enterprises. Sisters thus occupied are by no means unconscious dupes. Many view themselves as helping their brothers and their parents. Some seemed to refuse offers of marriage to continue doing so (Sherman 1990: 199–200).

As stressed throughout this chapter, migration is not only about the people who move, but also about social and economic arrangements that permit certain household members to leave the village. These arrangements have been viewed in contradictory ways in assessing migration. Historical-structural studies (e.g. Wood 1981), for example, have recognized that the sustenance and reproduction provided by rural relatives to the urban migrants are essential to the latter's success. Nevertheless, the people who give this economic and emotional support are typically not regarded as actors in the migration process and are often classified as 'residual' population, 'left behind' in the countryside. Marxist-oriented studies (e.g. Meillassoux 1981) have specifically focused on this latter group, arguing that the so-called productive migrant actitivies of husbands, brothers and children may be parasitic on the work carried out in the rural household, such as farm labour, domestic work and the care of children: 'Women are tied hand and foot to the place where they live – men may escape their responsibilities in the towns. The migrant system therefore deepens the age-old exploitation of women and the weak' (Bush *et al.* 1986: 293).[7]

When combining the two approaches, we might argue that although there is some degree of cooperation, relations between household members may also be strained by conflicting interests inherent to the gender division of labour. Because of these opposing tendencies, Sen (1990: 129) suggests that household relations can best be understood in terms of 'cooperative conflicts'. The members of a household work together insofar as cooperative arrangements make each of them better off than non-cooperation. Individuals within the household are motivated not only by their individual well-being but also by their perceptions of obligations and legitimate behaviour to which they should ideally conform. Applying these ideas to Toba Batak migration, we see that cooperation is based on strong patrilineal kinship bonds, while at the same time conflicts may arise about who within the household is entitled to migrate,[8] the amount of remittances sent home, or the extent of support given to newly arrived kin in the city. Such conflicts are rarely resolved through coercion but rather through bargaining and negotiations. The gender division of labour makes it fruitful for the parties to cooperate, but the particular way in which the fruits are divided reflects the 'bargaining power' of the respective parties. In the context of this study, the obvious sources of bargaining power are: ownership of and control over land; access to employment and other income sources; and access to external support networks. Inequality between family members in respect of these power sources – often based on gender and age – gives some members a weaker bargaining position than others.

Perception plays a vital role in shaping these bargaining powers. How women see themselves, how they represent their situations, and how they value what they do may in part determine the positions they attain. Yet, given the nature of gender divisions inside and outside the household, perceptions of individual interests are not always clear-cut and unambiguous. While men's strategies are usually geared towards both collective and individual needs, women's strategies are mainly focused on the present and future situation of their children, and generally have a collective character. For instance, when I asked women what migration meant for them, they answered in terms of the well-being of the family more often than men did. This is not surprising, given that in a patrilineal society a woman's social status is mainly derived from her husband's status. Moreover, having children, and particularly sons, is in the self-interest of all mothers in a society that measures a woman's position by her reproductive performance. Potentially contestable issues are dismissed to the realm of what Bourdieu (1977) called 'doxa' – that which is part of 'undisputed tradition'.

To sum up, both cooperation and conflict characterize gender relations within the household. Their hierarchical character in any given context is maintained or changed through a process of (implicit or explicit) contestation or bargaining between actors with differential access to economic, political and social power. My concern in the following is to explore how intra-household inequalities among the Toba Batak - exemplified within marital, sibling and parental relationships - are structured and perpetuated, and how they are subject to change. In particular, what role does male migration play in structuring, maintaining and changing these relations?

Precious Partners

> Of course women participate in work in the fields. They all work in agriculture. To see a woman hoeing the field is a very natural thing. If they didn't, how could the men leave? (Female villager)

The majority of the migrated spouses on Samosir Island were pedlars in other parts of Sumatra, selling kitchen utensils or cloth. Some of them, particularly those who lived far away, visited their wives and children just every now and then, for instance once a year, but others came home more often. They returned for religious holidays (especially during Christmas), or when an emergency arose. At the end of their working lives, when travelling around started to undermine their health, they rejoined their *ripe* – or what was left of it. While many were part of a Toba Batak migrant network in the *pangarantoan* [migration area], it was clear that for the majority the emotional ties and to some extent their economic security (in the sense of land and/or kinship bonds) remained in the village.

The husband usually started to migrate during the early stages of the household's developmental cycle, when the couple had to provide for a growing number of children. Likewise, the majority of the married migrants were between 25 and 35 years of age. In the meantime, as providers for the rural household, the wives made a living from farming, selling shallots, cloves and cassava, sometimes supplemented with local petty trading. Like most villagers the women had been socialized to engage in farming from early childhood; they were used to making many kinds of decisions; they were knowledgeable about farming practices and could perform almost all the necessary stages in the agricultural cycle. As such, they fulfilled crucial productive and reproductive roles in relation to the land, their homes and their children. These were not merely supportive roles but central to the life of the migrants, the maintenance of the farms and the continuity of their families. The presence of women as a source of information back in the village was essential for migrant men.

Thus, one could argue that the circular migrant and his wife were mutually dependent. The migrant needed a stable place to which he could return and children who could support him in his old age; the wife relied on her husband for access to land and to finance their children's schooling. The following case is an example of cooperation between husband and wife, crossing spatial boundaries, and one that has borne fruit:

Case Study 12.1: *Ama* Bonggas

> In 1969 *Ama* Bonggas (then 29) went off to Kisaran (East Sumatra) to hawk cloth. His wife stayed behind in the village with five small children, the eldest being 8 at the time. *Nai* Bonggas helped her husband to start his business with her earnings from the shallot yields. In her husband's absence she worked the land, arranged for storage and sale of the agricultural produce, arranged for loans and returned loans, and ensured that the household's obligations to kin and affines were fulfilled. After three years *Ama* Bonggas was able to buy himself a house in Kisaran and some time later he purchased a second-hand motorbike to facilitate his hawking activities. He also bought some rice land in Kisaran which he share-cropped to others. According to his wife he earns some Rp. 200,000 a month, 'but I've never seen a coin of it'. At least half of the amount is used to support two sons who are in university. Four other children have joined their father because of better schooling facilities. By cultivating five *rante* (0.2 ha) of dry land, *Nai* Bonggas is able to maintain herself and her two youngest daughters.

Most women staying behind took on full responsibility in the village without hesitation, because this was their share in the migration project within the reorganization of the household. They saw migration as a joint strategy aiming at the long-term enhancement of the status of their family, and this also implied their own personal status.

Few of them had ever visited their husbands because it was often too far and, they said, they did not want to be considered as untrusting. Consequently, they lacked a clear idea of their husbands' whereabouts. In the words of *Ama* Bonggas:

> I do not expect my wife to share my experiences or to listen to my stories. This is men's business that does not interest her. As long as she is satisfied in the village and looks after the children, what else

can I desire? If I want to discuss things [upon my visits home], I go to the *lapo* [coffee shop] where I can meet my mates.

His wife commented, however:

> We women stay at home and do back-breaking work even if we are feeling ill or if we are pregnant. We never have a rest period. When the men come home it only means more work. We have to cook more and tastier food and feed the guests (who come to greet the husband) as well.

In everyday life Toba Batak women are hard-working and stoical. Scarcely educated, they are sharp of perception and tongue. Their talking, laughing and quarrelling are a vivid demonstration of their active participation in village life. Indeed, when living in North Tapanuli, I was struck more by the general competence of women in providing for the needs of their families than by the difficulties they experienced. Many wives back their husbands financially, for example by pawning some jewellery, by breaking into their secret savings, or by simply skimping on their daily food. If there are no savings, then land or a water buffalo may be sold in order to raise sufficient starting capital – to the detriment of the household's economic resources. After the actual departure, the wife's involvement increases, and can extend to several years of shouldering responsibilities and making sacrifices.

Daily life in the village must continue whether men are present or not. Children are born, go to school, get sick and recover, or in some cases die while their fathers are away. Only a few activities, like baptisms, funerals and marriages, are postponed or deliberately planned so that the husband may attend. In their spouses' absence it is the women who solely maintain social and kin obligations. Their responsibilities are not necessarily limited to the domestic sphere; the wives of absent hamlet heads, for instance, represent their husbands on several occasions within the *huta*, such as marriages, transfer of land (selling), or at the farewell ceremony of a migrant. Even when a married son lives in the same village, it is usually the migrant's wife who assumes these tasks.

Whether migration of husbands is viewed positively or negatively depends to a large extent on a woman's age and her position in the life-cycle. It was mainly elderly women who talked casually about their husbands' absence, being used to the pattern of female responsibility for the bulk of day-to-day household provisioning. Some of them rather pointedly commented that they were relieved to be without the tiresome bother of a man: 'You know, men usually expect you to be at their beck and call: "Is dinner ready? Have you polished my shoes?" I have more freedom when my husband is not around.'

Neither did the younger women perceive the absence of their husbands negatively, since the household needed the money, especially for children's education. When questioned further, however, they often added (with some irritation): 'Of course I don't like him being away all the time! A wife should be with her husband.' These younger women were also more inclined to mention loneliness. This is related to patrilocal residence rules entailing that young wives are newcomers in their husbands' *huta*. This feeling might be reinforced by the fact that nowadays more marriages are based on free choice and therefore these women really missed their life partners. But I also got the impression that the younger generation of wives – with a solid *Pancasila* education – want to live up to the state ideology of a happy and harmonious family. They cited a pattern in which the man provides the cash income for the household as the ideal distribution of financial responsibilities and power.

However, the overwhelming majority of the migrants returned to the village with only modest remittances in their pockets. Or, as one of the wives, commenting on her husband's absence, bluntly put it: 'The only difference is that now he can buy his own cigarettes.' Where the migrant visited the village only annually or biennially, he sometimes sent money. Whereas in other studies consumer durables, new furniture or house improvements usually rank high in migrant households, such expenditures were virtually absent in the Toba Batak villages. Only a handful of better-off households had a television set, for example, but this had not necessarily been bought with migrant remittances. Upon visiting the research villages in 1996 I detected no more than one dish antenna (*parabola*), whereas these devices mushroom in other parts of Sumatra.

Sibling Solidarity

In a patrilineal society like the Toba Batak, sons and daughters have different positions. Sons are the embodiment of the family's future and they are therefore entitled to more strategic resources – landed property, education, a good occupation – than daughters. As discussed before, this has to do with the fact that sons are long-term members of the family who have the obligation to care for their elderly parents, whereas daughters are temporary members who move away upon marriage. Therefore, virtually all parents aspire to have their sons achieve higher education and employment in the cities, even if, in the short run, it means loss of labour or income to the family. Admittedly, there are a growing number of daughters who go their own ways, looking beyond the boundaries of the rural household and identifying themselves with their peers in the city (Rodenburg 1997). But many seem still resigned to their roles as supporters, as the following case study demonstrates.

Case Study 12.2: Donna

> After the deaths of her parents Donna (26) saved every *rupiah* to finance her youngest brother's schooling. Although she does not know his field of study, Donna has paid the annual tuition fee of Rp. 160,000 (US$ 80) and Rp. 300,000 (US$ 150) for his board and lodging for four years. She speaks bitterly of her eldest brother who left the village many years ago. He has not contributed a single *rupiah* to the education of Dalmok, their youngest brother, and, what is worse, does not even fulfil his *adat* obligations. When Dalmok married recently it was Donna who took a bus to

Jambi with five *kaleng* (100 litres) of rice and 25 kg of pork as a contribution to the ceremony. Her youngest sister is still in secondary school and has until now been supported by her, but Donna worries how to finance her education in the future. She therefore asked Dalmok and his wife to take on this responsibility on the pretext that she would like to marry.

A sister who helps her brothers to migrate and become 'successful' may also be rewarded for her efforts, either directly or through her children. There were many examples of village youth living with their *tulang* [mother's brother] in town while attending their studies or looking for a job. But there might also be benefits within the village: Donna's migrated brothers allowed her to cultivate the family land so that she could support herself and her younger sister. Interestingly, even with a brother or other male kin residing in the village, a migrant might prefer a sister to till the land, a welcome gesture where farming land is scarce. The argument was that when the land is operated by a male relative there is a risk that this person may claim the land as his own (since it originally belonged to their common father or grandfather). Since female relatives could never be legal heirs, it is a safe strategy to let them cultivate the migrant's land.[9] In Muara I found at least 20 women (about 10% of the adult female population) who cultivated one or more plots for migrated male kin. Most of them share-cropped the land, while some enjoyed it for free. This resulted in a seemingly paradoxical situation in which the patrilineal system denies women ownership of land, but because of this very lack of ownership rights they had increased access to land.[10]

Altruistic Mothers

While a considerable number of village women had to manage without their husbands for extended periods, many more were confronted with the out-migration of at least one of their children. For an increasing number of parents, it has become normal and right that their sons should leave the village to make money elsewhere, either as traders or, ideally, in a professional career. A 50-year-old woman said: 'It is enough for me to suffer in the village. I don't want to see my son suffer as a farmer.' Another woman expressed a similar reaction to her son's migration: 'Even seeing him around the village frustrates me. There is no reason to stay here where there is no future.' She had great hopes for her children and was supportive of their desire to continue their studies in the city. She wanted them 'to become something big'.

Prestige evidently is a central value in competitive rural societies, as de Jong (this volume) has demonstrated for Flores. As discussed elsewhere (Rodenburg 1997), Toba Batak parents may go to great lengths to enable their children to move out successfully (read: receive higher education), selling productive assets like land or a water buffalo. It is believed that educated children will send remittances home, are dressed well, and can make a good marriage match. I knew several women who scraped together money from selling mangoes, cultivating shallots, or weaving *pandanus* mats. Some women had to accept prolonged separation from their husbands, who contributed to the children's schooling with the proceeds from hawking. Toba Batak motherhood is closely aligned with subjugation of self-interest and a predominant focus on 'children and their future'. The ideology of maternal altruism encourages women to devote their earnings to meeting collective rather than individual needs. However, a mother's aspiration to have successful children is not based only on the wish for her children to have a more prosperous life than she herself has had. Legendary for their hard work and self-sacrificing thrift, Toba Batak mothers nevertheless hope to receive financial support from their children one day. Whether they are physically present or not, sons in particular are expected to support their parents in their old age; not to do so is aberrant behaviour subject to disapproval. This was stressed by one woman who in rather direct terms explained: 'We have children to be assisted, at home and in the fields, and when they have become adults they can pay back what we have invested in them.'

ACCOMMODATION AND STRATEGIC COMPLIANCE

If migration is a strategy of men, so it is for women. This is the case even when they themselves do not leave the village, for in an indirect way women make migration a strategy to improve their lives. Frequently they are the primary agents of accumulation to make migration possible. It is not rare for a wife to push her husband to try his luck elsewhere, sometimes mobilizing her urban relatives to pave the way for him.

CASE STUDY 12.3: *NAI* TIURMA

> Although her husband had never migrated before, one year ago *Nai* Tiurma (30) encouraged him to look for additional income elsewhere. While his family had no trading experience, several of her relatives were pedlars in West Sumatra, willing to initiate *Ama* Tiurma in the art of trading. He thus went to live with his wife's brother who was hawking cloth in the vicinity of Padang. His wife ironically recounts how he dreaded to leave his family: 'He wept for two weeks prior to his departure.' He is the youngest son and occupies the parental house in Simarmata. *Nai* Tiurma cultivates 4 *rante* (0.16 ha) of land and takes care of the three children and her mother-in-law who lives with them. Her own (widowed) mother and a younger sister reside in the same village and occasionally share in childcare and farm activities.

Living in town with kin or co-villagers gives migrant men the opportunity to send home messages, and sometimes money, when one of them returns to the village. For a wife, this network also has social importance, since it means some kind of control over her husband's activities. Although the kin network is no guarantee, a wife would probably soon find out if her husband were to have an extra-marital affair. Especially in the case of matrikin, she would find solidarity on her side. One woman told me that when her husband proposed to move to Peninsular Malaysia where earnings were much higher, she rejected the plan since they did not know anyone there.

Some women reminded their husbands of the lengths to which they go to enable them to migrate. The effect of these remarks was to keep the men aware of their dependence on their wives, of how they must in their turn and in their own way sustain the family by reciprocating what the women do for them. If they fail to do so, their wives might summon them home, as the next case study demonstrates.

CASE STUDY 12.4: *NAI* AMSON

> After her husband had hawked cloth in Sibolga for 10 years, *Nai* Amson (55) called him home. He returned 'without a *rupiah* in his pocket', nor had he been able to send his children to senior high school, 'so what's the use of *mangaranto* [migrating]?' According to *Nai* Amson, many Batak men use the pretext of peddling 'just to be independent and *mardalani aja* [to roam about]' while their wives and children in the village live 'on the verge of starvation'. Now that *Ama* Amson is back again, he lends a hand in farming, which enables his wife to spend more time on local petty trade.

To many wives, the decision not to accompany their spouses but stay in the village was a conscious one. They did not see any productive role for themselves in the migration area and did not want to rely on their husbands' money. Some said they pitied migrant women in urban areas who had to live among strangers, squeezed together in crowded neighbourhoods. Instead, they preferred the countryside where they were 'free to breathe', and could speak the Toba Batak language.

In other instances, husband migration can be the first step towards 'familial migration'. This was the strategy that *Nai* Meida pursued. Her husband sold kitchen utensils in West Sumatra while she took care of the two small children. Because her husband was the youngest son, they were living in the household of her parents-in-law.

> Our problem is that we have so little money because my husband has not inherited any land yet. I try everything [I can] to get hold of some money. I make *pandanus* mats and sell them in the market. I try to economize, because I have a plan: I discussed the possibility of *mangaranto* with my husband, and I persuaded him that he must give it a try. I sold my bridal gold to help him to cover travel expenses and to start his business in Padang. I talked about that with my parents-in-law, and they agreed to his departure. I did not tell them that if he succeeds we will all move to Padang. Then we can separate from my parents-in-law and educate our children, so that they don't need to become farmers like me.

Nai Meida carefully worked out a long-term strategy to reach her aim. For her, living in a nuclear family, together with her husband and children, is definitely preferable to a life in the extended household of her parents-in-law. Especially a young wife may urge her husband to let his family join him if his enterprise turns out to be relatively successful. In fact, nowadays a family's reunion in the *pangarantoan* is an important sign of a migrant's success. Often the wife too starts trading in the market when she arrives in the city.

Even whilst formally it is the men who call the shots, it is important not to underestimate the extent to which women control resources from behind the scenes. One woman explained, with a knowing wink: 'If a woman wants to get her way with her husband in some matter, then she can always refuse what he wants of her at night.' Persistent complaining, pleading ill-health, playing off male affines and consanguines against each other and threatening to return to the natal home are all means by which women try to get their own way within the family. Women's opportunities for informal strategies may change over time: newly married wives without sons have far less influence than their mothers-in-law.

Women's opportunities also depend on their position within the family. The following example describes the case of an adult daughter who achieved her aim while conforming to male authority and playing 'the game'. This implied recognizing certain power rules and not transgressing any social norms.

Case Study 12.5: *Nai* Tony

> As all her brothers had migrated and held well-paid positions in town, *Nai* Tony was the only one of the family remaining in Tapanuli. Her parents had joined one of their sons, a lawyer, in Jakarta, but when her father felt the end approaching, he came back to his natal village to die and to be buried in the family grave. During the last weeks of his life he was carefully nursed by his daughter, while all her siblings gathered to bid him farewell. *Nai* Tony had cultivated most of her father's land, but upon the division of the estate she would run the risk of being evicted by her brothers. In order to safeguard her access to the land, she requested her dying father to give her part of the property as *pauseang*. Before asking her father, however, she consulted with her brothers since her request would affect her brothers' personal interest in the land. She was obviously downplaying the potential of herself and her husband, stressing her image as uneducated, poor and left behind (*ditinggalkan*), but with success: before her father breathed his last, *Nai* Tony got her plot of land.
>
> *Nai* Tony knew that to reach her aims she would have to subordinate herself, begging her father and brothers and give them their due quota of power. She made her relatives see that she had no intention of running counter to the interests of men (by going to court, for example, to request her rightful part of the inheritance) or of challenging traditional female roles. Instead, she spoke the language of subordination in order

to extract benefits from it, while at the same time to some degree subverting this ideology. (See also Villareal 1992)

I have described the above cases to illustrate how women, while not themselves moving out, can utilize migration for their own ends. These women do not openly call into question, or revolt against, their position within the household, but they remain integrated in the village society's normative system and conform to it. They have realized the chances that the migration of their husbands or brothers might offer, and use it as an informal strategy to enhance their own position. Rather than lamenting about suppressive structures and their inability to overcome them, they find out the potentials inherent in these structures and use them for their own interests, similar to what Gardner (1995) has called their 'strategic compliance'. The appearance of compliance need not mean that women lack a correct perception of their best interests; rather it can reflect a survival strategy stemming from the constraints on their ability to act overtly in pursuit of those interests.

SHATTERED EXPECTATIONS: SOME 'NEGATIVE CASES'

There is often a gap between the model of the household as an economic unit, based on income-pooling and complementary gender roles, and the behaviour of individuals within households. Indeed, the extent to which households are units and what strategies of members conform to common goals are issues that lie just below the surface of discourse in Tapanuli. Women complain about husbands who do not support them and their children, while parents complain about indifferent children. In this respect, other household members can use the ideal of an economically unified household as a claim on men's, and children's, resources.[11]

Deserted Wives

Only a handful of the women with migrant husbands received regular remittances, and few of them knew how much money their spouses made. To my surprise, this seldom appeared to be a source of conflict. The wives interpreted this withholding of information as a sign of their husband's independence which they seemed to accept. Another potential source of conflict was the prolonged absence from wife and children, which in some cases posed a serious threat to marital relations. Living away from their families gave men the opportunity to engage in gambling (*marjuji*) or to start liaisons with other women (*marboru-boru*), a fact which some of them tended to boast about rather than try to hide. While it was no secret that migrant men might have adulterous affairs, the threat of gossip seemed enough to keep their village wives from having extra-marital liaisons.

The attention which economists have begun to pay to 'bargaining' processes is an important step in the analysis of gender conflicts of interest and their resolution. However, most analyses adopt an open, face-to-face model of bargaining, which presumes that people are certain of and can act on their own interests, and do so overtly. My findings in Tapanuli suggest a rather different picture. Women with clear complaints of male inadequacy seldom quarrelled openly. Why? I would suggest that the private activities, kin relationships and networks of reciprocity which women so keenly pursue provide them with security. This enables a woman who benefits little from migration in the short term nevertheless to ensure her own or her children's welfare perhaps in the long term.

Consequently, most wives tried to avoid quarrels and open conflict as much as possible. They either accepted their husbands' freedom or they turned a blind eye to their behaviour. Women tended to anticipate possible negative reactions by their husbands and to resign themselves to the current situation in order to prevent disruption or outright conflict. However, as Sen (1990: 126) argues: 'It can be a serious error to take the absence of protests and questioning of inequality as evidence of the absence of that inequality.'

This leads me to suggest that the main reason for a Toba Batak woman to reconcile herself to her husband's whims is not to keep harmony in the household, but is related to her weak bargaining position to enforce a more favourable situation. Any open resistance would probably only work against her. If her recurrent criticisms led to the husband abandoning her, the wife would certainly be considered the instigator, thereby losing her the sympathy of her in-laws. However, in cases where migrant husbands had deserted their wives, the man was criticized while sympathy was extended to the wife – unless she was childless or sonless. 'The idea is that a woman [...] has given him all that he could desire of her, she has contributed to the building up of his 'house' and therefore she should not be at the mercy of any inclination of his to get rid of her' (Vergouwen 1964: 254). Abandoned women might even be supported by their family-in-law, as shown in the following case.

Case Study 12.6: *Nai* **Rintu**

Nai Rintu (41) lives with her two school-age daughters in one of the upland *huta* on Samosir island, her husband's native hamlet. Right after their marriage the couple went to live in Tebing Tinggi (East Sumatra), where *Ama* Rintu started to trade in cloth. To meet their subsistence needs they rented ten *rante* (about 0.5 ha) of rice-fields, cultivated by *Nai* Rintu. During this period five children were born, two of whom survived. When his trade dwindled, *Ama* Rintu decided to try his luck in a neighbouring area. He moved on his own because there was little paddy available to feed the family. For two years he returned regularly and supported the family. However, when *Nai* Rintu was pregnant with her youngest child she learned that her husband was having a relationship with a Javanese woman. Soon after that she had to give up the land in Tebing as the owner needed it himself. Being derived of her sole source of income, she felt compelled to return to her husband's natal village. Her mother-in-law (whose late husband used to have a second wife in the *pangarantoan* as well) provided her with a house and some land to cultivate for free. The eldest son, Rintu, was offered accommodation with his father's brother in Medan, where he attends university. From the sale of shallots and cloves, his mother somehow manages to scrape together the money for his tuition. Although the couple has not been in touch for years, *Nai* Rintu prefers not to dissolve the marriage. As a divorcée she would no longer be entitled to work her husband's land, and, being beyond reproductive age, her chances for remarriage – in order to secure her livelihood – are virtually zero.

In one of the villages I found nine women (a quarter of all women staying behind) who had been deserted by their spouses. When the remittances and visits became few and far between and eventually ceased, the assumption was that 'he has found himself another woman over there'. This assumption was soon to be confirmed by fellow-migrants from the same village. The wives claimed that the separations were the result of the husband falling in love with someone else rather than of specific marital conflicts. Most said that their spouses had simply withdrawn from the scene. One woman, living in an old shack with her three children, cursed the day she had helped her husband to set up his business in West Sumatra:

> I had ordered (*diperintah*) him to search for a living, but instead he searched for a wife. Looking back, I wonder how much I benefited from his trading. Until he went away, that is for the first three years of our marriage, we used to stint on everything and save so that he was able to accumulate the necessary starting capital. Now I find that all the sacrifices I have made have gone totally unrewarded through no fault of mine. Life would have been better if he had not migrated at all. Do no forget that it was largely with money from my savings and jewellery that he could even think of leaving the village.

I am not trying to suggest that such cases of desertion could only occur when the husband was earning away from home; simply that such circumstances made it easier for the husband to drift into a situation where he was in practice no longer supporting his wife and children. Most men are in their early thirties when they abandon their wives. When they get older the wives feel more confident because they no longer consider their husbands to be attractive to other women or, as one of them said of her 54-year-old spouse: *Ndang langku be'* [he is no longer wanted].

In general, where male kin controls access to land, women rarely initiate conflicts about their husbands' absence, because such action could deprive them of essential access to productive resources. A woman who initiates divorce loses her claim on any of the couple's joint possessions, other than what she herself has brought to the marriage.[12] In addition, the fact that in case of divorce a Toba Batak wife has no rights over the children has far-reaching effects in maintaining marriages, in spite of long periods of separation. In other words, in conflict situations the bargaining power of women is weakest when they live in patrilineal societies and when they work primarily for the farm or business of the household head, because their lack of access to productive resources creates 'systematic biases in the perception of who is 'producing' what and 'earning' what within the household' (Sen 1990). This paternal-privileging principle appears to curtail women's strategies.

In contrast, in bilateral societies, women seem to be in a much stronger bargaining position. As described by Jayawardena (1977), in some parts of Aceh, North Sumatra, a wife could renounce and divorce her migrant spouse if he failed to support his family. A wife was in a position to do so because she owned and managed individual property and, due to matrilocal settlement, further sustenance could be expected from her natal family. Another study (Siegel 1969: 117) in the same area found that 39% of all marriages ended in divorce, more than half of them being related to financial conflicts, and in each of these cases it was the woman who took the initiative to split up.

In contrast to her Acehnese sisters, I have not heard of any Toba Batak woman seeking legal forms of redress when the husband no longer contributed to the family income. Instead, if a wife loses her husband's affection while he is in the *pangarantoan*, this is frequently blamed on other women. Blaming another woman for marital breakdown may also be easier than accusing one's husband (and thus, by association, the patriarchy which gives men so much power).

Duped Sisters

How does the affective brother–sister relationship, as outlined in Toba Batak kinship ideology, match reality? In particular, to what extent do brothers meet women's expectations of practical help in times of need? The evidence is mixed. Brothers generally appear to fulfil their ceremonial roles, such as giving marriage gifts at the weddings of sisters' children. Stories about their reliability in an economic crisis are less consistent.

In the foregoing I have outlined that a number of women enjoyed increased access to land as a result of their brothers' migration. While this gives the women the opportunity to earn extra income, the economic position of these 'privileged' women ultimately depends on the good-will of the migrants, who can reclaim the land at any time. Thus, there is more to the story of Donna (related earlier) who worked the land of her two migrated brothers. During my stay in the village, Donna's eldest brother suddenly turned up and, without consulting his sister, pawned their single rice-field to solve his financial problems. From then on, in order to feed both herself and her sister, Donna had to sharecrop someone else's field. This example shows that women's access to migrants' land, just like *pauseang*, is merely another kind of male largesse upon which the women can never rely.

Few village women were aware of the national Land Law, which stipulates that sons and daughters have equal inheritance rights and that they are equally entitled to parental land. They did not wish to sour or break their relationships with their brothers and, consequently, I did not come across any cases in which women had claimed a rightful share of their fathers' inheritance.[13] Most villagers agreed that a woman should never exercise her formal rights, by taking the matter to court for example. She would then be severely criticized by relatives and associates because this act is regarded as threatening to the traditional kinship system and as destroying the intimate relationship between a brother and sister.

Although according to Toba Batak *adat* women have a right to ask, brothers can refuse, which gives the sisters little room for bargaining. A brother might return to his natal village after years of residence elsewhere and it would still be recognized (although sometimes reluctantly) by his family that he had the right, 'if he had the need', to claim his land, as illustrated in the following account.

Case Study 12.7: *Ama* Nurita

> Directly after marriage, *Ama* Nurita (now 42) left his home village and went with his wife to Rantau Prapat, where they bought about 25 *rante* (1 ha) of *sawah*. When, 10 years later, they had four daughters and no son, they were summoned by a *datu* [traditional healer] to return to the *bona ni pasogit* [ancestral homeland]. *Ama* Nurita is the youngest son of a family of five. Since his only brother is a teacher in Pematang Siantar, *Ama* Nurita is entitled to the parental land: 4.5 *rante* of *sawah* and 1.5 ha of *ladang*. In his absence he had allowed his three sisters (two of them widowed) to operate most of the fields. Upon his return, however, *Ama* Nurita reclaimed the land and mortgaged two plots to his sisters. In other words, they were allowed to continue the cultivation of his land but now had to pay for it. When I returned in 1996 the much desired son had not been born.

While some village women may still perceive themselves as 'helpers' of their male relatives, I found evidence of an increasing number of young women challenging their traditional position and migrating, to obtain a higher education or an independent income (Rodenburg 1997: 64–73). Although daughters are still less entitled to education than sons, to some extent education and access to the urban labour market have removed women from patriarchal control and given them an independent means of support (van Bemmelen 1992). While young women have the possibility of 'voting with their feet', for elderly women one way to increase status is through their children.

Disappointed Mothers

> A woman, especially an old one, who must hoe her own land is a sad sight, but no disgrace stems from her having to do this work. If economic necessity has forced all children to leave in search of their own fortunes, disgrace may well be felt though, because of the fact that she has no family to help her (Cunningham 1958: 41).

As discussed earlier, motherhood is the main avenue to whatever control and authority a Toba Batak woman may gain. A woman's status is linked especially to that of her son and, particularly in later life, to the care and respect he shows to her. In the past, the reproductive success of a Toba Batak woman was defined in terms of having mature sons resident with or near her. A mother had access to her son's labour and, in addition, she could delegate part of her work to her daughter-in-law. Landed property was dispensed in such a way as to guarantee the care of the older generation. If a son did not fulfil his obligations, he ran the risk of being disinherited by his parents.

Today, when a son wants to migrate, the parents can no longer credibly use disinheritance as a threat. With the continuing decline of smallholder agriculture and increased education, employment opportunities elsewhere have become more attractive even for landed sons. There was often bitterness and suspicion on both sides: the old felt they were mistreated, while the younger generation resented their parents' attempts to retain control.[14] With women living longer than men, and often being younger than their husbands, the older generation was often represented by widows. The following example shows that the out-migration of a son may cause tensions between the migrant's individual aspirations and old age security systems. It also shows the crucial position of daughters-in-law in providing for parents' old age.

Case Study 12.8: *Ama* Lamsar

> Despite his parents' wish to keep their only son in the village, *Ama* Lamsar (now 32) left Simarmata at the age of 20. He went to Padang, where he engaged in hawking. Two years later he was called home to marry at his parents' instigation; directly after the wedding ceremony he returned to Padang. His parents had summoned his wife to keep them company and to cultivate the 6 *rante* of *ladang* [dry field]. Because of domestic tensions, however, *Nai* Lamsar followed her husband to Padang within a year, against the old couple's wishes. For seven years they lived in Padang, where they raised four children and built a house. But a year ago *Ama* Lamsar was called back to the village because his father was dying. After the funeral he resumed his trading activities, but his mother insisted that her daughter-in-law and the children should stay and take care of her. When I asked *Ompu* [grandmother] Lamsar (a shrivelled but sharp old woman) about the possibility of joining her son in Padang, she definitely rejected the idea: she had always lived in Tapanuli and felt afraid of moving to an urban area. Her daughter-in-law added with a sigh: 'After her death she wants to be buried in the family grave, that's why she'd better remain in the village; the transportation of a corpse from Padang to Samosir Island would be too expensive.'

A woman who feels neglected can bring pressure to bear on her immediate dependants by hinting at the disasters that might befall them were she to die with anger in her heart (and thus perhaps to take revenge as a ghost). Indeed, I witnessed several ceremonies in which it was said that an ancestral spirit had taken possession of one of its descendants in order to express its dissatisfaction with the conduct of its offspring. In one case the spirit reproached her survivors of having left the *bona ni pasogit* [ancestral homeland]; in another case blame was attached to a family that had built a new, modern house in favour of the traditional Batak house.

While the outmigration of *Ama* Lamsar involved extensive negotiation – with his wife as an important bargaining asset – for an increasing number of parents, having a successful migrant son lends prestige to the whole family. To many Toba Batak parents the best strategy to optimize life options is to ensure that their children have secure employment; this will enable them to support their parents in their old age. Some children are successful as migrants and manage to support their rural families. But in many cases their economic activities are increasingly centred on the urban economy, and their remittances tend to be low and intermittent. Thus, a mother complained that after giving life, education and a job to her son, now that the latter was earning he seemed to have forgotten his parents. Many of the ties between Toba Batak urban professionals and their rural relatives now appear to be largely symbolic, with grandchildren being baptized in the natal village and monuments being erected by migrants on ancestral land to show off the success of their clan. Their wives live with them in urban areas and their own children have never spent more than a few days at a time with their grandparents in the village. A telling example is the recently built hotel in Muara, which a number of well-to-do urban Batak prefer to spending the night in their rural 'home' where they have to make do without electricity or sanitary facilities.[15] It is hard to imagine them keeping their rural ties active.

Conclusion

If there is one overall conclusion to be drawn from this chapter, it is that the situation of Toba Batak women is ambiguous. On the one hand, the ability of rural women to run the farm and give active support to the migration of their kin demonstrates how difficult it is to view them as passive victims. As the status of the household reflects on that of the women in it, the adoption of migration strategies by the women enhances their individual status. If the migrating husbands, brothers or sons are successful in the *pangarantoan*, then the women staying behind or their children will also ultimately profit. It is with this hope in mind that they juggle their tasks and obligations, for this is their contribution to make migration a success. As protectors of ancestral land and maintainers of social networks, the women provide a safety-net to retired migrants or to those whose migrant enterprise fails. Stability is associated with women, as it is they who live on and use the land, attend to rituals, safeguard knowledge, and nurture the next generation. They act as temporary trustees, ensuring the continued association of the land with the migrant/patrilineal group. As such, they are powerful images for the migrant's roots.

But one should also beware of romanticizing the way in which these women cope, as the meagre resources available to them limit their efforts dramatically. Since the household economy is founded on a very weak base, women simply have no other alternatives. And to the extent that they receive remittances, these are seldom invested in agriculture. Moreover, although some wives and mothers may take on the position of farm manager, we should remember that one of the main reasons that men have moved away is because local agriculture is marginal:

> To till the soil today is a despised activity which is not very lucrative. One can argue that this was historically always the case. Perhaps the difference is to be found in the fact that such dichotomies (rural/urban, traditional/modern, etc.) increasingly meet gender divisions (Abaza in Weyland 1993: 204).

Simply because women play a prominent role in agriculture does not mean that they control the resources, which are often in male hands. Women with migrant husbands thus do not necessarily enjoy an increase in domestic power. I would, therefore, agree with Gardner (1995: 212) who states that 'it is misleading to assert that women who head their own households, with no adult men, are better off than their neighbours, for female power is always dependent upon access to resources and male support.' The limitation on women's life choices in the rural community is one of the main reasons why an increasing number of young, educated women migrate, breaking out of their traditional gender roles.

But also women staying behind have their own interests and try to realize them, and in this endeavour may actively use structures for their own aims. They are not confronted with the results of 'impacts' and 'effects' inasmuch as they try to put structures to profitable account or turn them into a resource. That this is the case has been demonstrated in this chapter by showing that migration can also be a strategy of non-migrating women. As Villarreal (1992: 261–62) puts it:

> Though we should not blind ourselves to the ways in which women are constrained and moulded by circumstances and conditions – some of which they themselves recreate and forge – we must acknowledge on the other hand that they have the capacity to manipulate these limitations ... in order not only, as it were, to survive in deep water, but to use the current whenever possible to bring the boat in their direction.

Acknowledgements

I want to thank the Centre for Development Research in Copenhagen for hosting me while revising this chapter. In particular, I am grateful to the members of the gender section for their stimulating comments.

NOTES

1. *Nai* [mother of] and *Ama* [father of] are used before the name of one's first child, in this case Datir (a pseudonym).

2. Fieldwork was undertaken during 1988–89 in two villages: one in subdistrict Muara, the other on the island of Samosir (see Rodenburg 1997). The villages were briefly revisited in 1996.

3. In this chapter 'patriarchy' is used in a fairly loose descriptive sense to refer to institutionalized patterns of gender relations which involve inequalities of power, sexuality and resource allocation favouring men over women. Despite the debates within feminism over the usefulness of the concept, the term captures the gender-specific nature of women's oppression and indicates that this is rooted in, although not necessarily confined to, the family (Scott 1994: 78).

4. Village households in North Tapanuli varied considerably in size: while the smallest units were those consisting of single persons, the largest units included 11 members. The average number of members per household was 4.4, which was below the average figure (5.6) for North Tapanuli as a whole – no doubt a result of extensive outmigration.

5. This chapter does not allow for a more elaborate discussion of Toba Batak kinship principles. For more information, see Vergouwen (1964), Niessen (1985), Simbolon (1998).

6. The idea of ownership among Toba Batak, as in other kin-based societies, is highly complex. The simplest way of understanding some of the major problems is to separate property rights into two: use rights and rights to alienate (rights to sell). While in non-kin-based societies ownership is regarded as consisting of both classes of rights, in North Tapanuli ownership tends to mean use rights for the individual, as the community is the legal land-owning entity (see also Simbolon 1998).

7. Although most of these Marxist-oriented studies were developed in Southern Africa, where race relations cut across gender and class relations, I think that the basic ideas are also relevant in Asian situations.

8. Papanek (1990: 170) defines entitlements as the 'socially and culturally recognized rights of specific categories of persons to particular resource shares'. She argues that the greater entitlement of one person often becomes the increased responsibility for care by another. Focusing on a migration-oriented society, we might expect that a man's entitlement to migrate will translate into increased responsibility for his 'caretaker', who is usually his wife, mother or sister.

9. Another option for migrants is to leave the land uncultivated, a general practice with plots far removed from the village, especially when they are not particularly fertile. In this case, however, the migrant runs the risk of the land being confiscated by the government to be used for economic development (Rodenburg 1997; Simbolon 1998).

10 However, because these caretakers have no permanent rights to the land, they will not opt to invest in the land or to plant perennials.
11 See also Francis (1995: 208), who observed a similar pattern in relation to changing divisions of labour due to migration in Western Kenya.
12 For a similar situation in North Bali, see Jennaway, this volume.
13 However, already in the 1930s there existed resentment among educated Tapanuli Batak women over being excluded by *adat* from inheritance rights, as depicted in the journal *Soeara Ibu* [Voice of Women] (Blackburn and Hatley, this volume). These urban women probably dared to raise their voices because they were economically less dependent on kinship relations.
14 For a comparable situation in Central Java, see Koning (this volume).
15 From the way it is constructed – on the edge of Lake Toba, but not overlooking the lake – it is clear that the hotel is not meant for tourists (who do not frequent Muara anyway).

SECTION V: BEYOND THE DICHOTOMIES

The distinction between home and workplace, between productive and reproductive activities, has often been too sharply drawn in feminist literature. The chapters in this section focus on the ways in which women cross such boundaries with relative ease, showing their dynamism in redefining their roles.

Willemijn de Jong's chapter on 'Women's Networks in Cloth Production and Exchange in Flores', looks at the influence of the productive and distributive activities of female weavers on intra- and inter-household relations in a village society. Since independence women participate decisively in creating and maintaining networks of social security by their increased exchange activities. As cloth producers, as owners of cloth wealth, and as household managers of food and money, the women define, and at the same time are defined by, asymmetric and symmetric economic relations. As traders of cloth, whereby men partly function as regional intermediaries, they also contribute to inter-village relations. By their productive and distributive activities Lio cloth producers thus clearly cross the cultural boundaries of the domestic unit and create and maintain social networks of households of neighbours and kin within the village and beyond.

In 'Networks of Reproduction among Cigarette Factory Women in East Java', Ratna Saptari attempts to break the sharp distinction between ideology and practice and reveals how ideology is redefined through practice. Through her examination of cigarette factory households, she shows how the workings of ideology at the practical level are complex and multifaceted. The gender ideologies can be distinguished between notions of what men and women should do in the home, and notions about mothers or wives as wage-earners. In the first case there has not been much change; in the second case, there have been clear shifts in the last 30 to 40 years. Saptari points out that individual interests may be served as well as household interests in the choices or activities which household members adopt. Again intra-household relations influence the content of this inter-household reciprocity, namely whether husbands allow their wives to go to work when there are very small children. It is this mingling of ideology and practice, of household units and inter-household networks, which makes the analytical dichotomies, which we ourselves create, quite often more a hindrance than a help.

G.G. Weix's chapter 'Hidden Managers at Home: Elite Javanese Women Running New Order Family Firms' looks at a similar theme, namely how elite women integrate home and workplace to their own benefit. She first looks at the social organization of family firms and women's position in managing home-based production on Java. She characterizes this pattern as the hidden management of family firms by elite women from within their homes, particularly labour relations through distribution of gifts and largesse. Because throughout the twentieth century these elite women have combined socialization and other domestic processes with supervision of wage work and relations of production associated with the workplace, their actions and strategies have empowered the household to be a hybrid social domain. The women not only secure their own livelihood by managing a family firm or enterprise, they also employ other women in their factories and they hire servants to care for and accompany their children throughout their lives. And finally they negotiate relations of authority with a wide entourage of employees, all within the familiar settings of their own home.

13

Women's Networks in Cloth Production and Exchange in Flores

Willemijn de Jong

INTRODUCTION

Production of prestigious cloth for wear and for gift exchange is today still an important task for women in many rural households in Indonesia as a way of supplementing their income. In Java (Antlöv and Svensson 1991) and in some parts of Bali (Ramseyer 1988) the manufacture of hand-made cloth is more industrialized and the producers have often lost control over their products. In the outer Indonesian islands such as Flores, however, production is still principally domestic, with the weavers themselves being petty entrepreneurs.[1] In contrast to symbolic studies about textiles, research on the economic, sociopolitical and cultural dimensions of cloth producers and of cloth-producing households in Indonesia and elsewhere is still scant.

Flores belongs to one of the poorest, most isolated and least developed provinces of Indonesia, East Nusa Tenggara (NTT) (Corner 1989; Kameo 1996; Zeuner 1996). Agriculture is still mainly subsistence-oriented and there are villages who subsist in large part on the domestic production of cloth. Not surprisingly, this female-dominated economic sphere is scarcely statistically recorded yet, so there are no reliable figures on the production of hand-woven cloth and on cloth-producing households.

Most of the regions in Flores are traditionally divided into weaving and non-weaving areas, to stimulate trade between coastal communities with regular food shortages due to drought, and inland communities in the mountains with more abundant food supplies (Barnes and Barnes 1989; Hamilton 1994a). Institutionalized by customary law, which the Lio people today designate with the Indonesian term *adat*, this regional division of labour often included a weaving taboo for non-weaving communities. Probably the regional trade of textiles already existed before the beginning of Dutch colonial rule in 1906 and before the concomitant missionary influence of the Catholic Church on Flores (van Suchtelen 1921).

I shall focus on one of the most important villages of the weaving area of the Lio in Central Flores where I conducted altogether two years of field research. The Lio, or the Ata Lio as they call themselves, number about 150,000. They are one of the eight ethno-linguistically and culturally differentiated groups[2] in Flores and have so far been insufficiently described.[3] Almost 20 villages in the area of the dry south coast mainly subsist on weaving (see Orinbao 1992; Hamilton 1994b). In these villages of the Southern Lio, as I call them, almost all households produce cloth, apart from food. The research village of Nggela consisted of 257 households in 1990 with an average of four persons per household, and the number of its inhabitants amounted to 1,283 (551 men and 712 women; sex ratio 0.774).[4] The gender relations in this village hold largely true for the Southern Lio in general.

Hand-woven cloths are considered by Lio females and males as important prestige goods and items of wealth. As sarongs and shoulder cloths, they are worn by women and men in everyday life, at feasts and as burial shrouds, as gifts they are bestowed in ritual exchange; and as trade items they are converted into cash.

My aim is to show what kind of influence the productive and distributive practices of the women as weavers have on intra- and inter-household relations in the village society. Therefore I shall first elaborate on the notions of the household and other units of the social structure. Then I shall outline the organization of cloth production and exchange of cloth in rituals and trade. Subsequently intra- and inter-household relations are analysed. My suggestion is that women's cloth production and distribution strengthen their influence and power in other spheres of their households and beyond. This makes a strict dichotomization of domestic and public spheres obsolete. Moreover, by their increased exchange practices of textiles since Indonesian independence in 1945 and especially since the 1970s, women participate decisively in creating and maintaining networks of social security.

Notions of the Household and of Other Social Units

The most important categories and groups in the social structure of the village society are the household, the house segment and the house. The notion 'household' among the Lio is equated with 'hearth' (*bu'u waja*). The idiom 'people with a hearth' (*ata eo no'o bu'u waja*) designates married people (cf. also Arndt 1933). This indicates that on marriage an old household breaks up and a new one develops. Indeed, newly-wed couples are classified as having economic, social and ritual responsibilities independent of their parents. Consequently they have to establish a domestic unit of production and distribution of their own. This is a reason why young women and men frequently express opposition to marriage for some time: often women do not marry before they are 25 years of age, men not before 30.

It also turns out that the Lio household, besides being a unit of social reproduction, is primarily a unit of production and distribution, if we follow the analytical device that Yanagisako (1979: 186) proposes, 'to begin with an investigation of the *activities* [or 'practices' according to actual anthropological idiom] that are central to the domestic relationships', especially 'by identifying the important productive, ritual, political and exchange transactions in a society'.

The villagers usually relate their rights and duties in household and family affairs to *adat*. The influence of Roman Catholicism[5] and of the Indonesian nation-state in this respect is rather formal. This is confirmed by other studies about the Lio. John Prior (1988: 195) for instance elucidates, that

> meaning is found in life not through what is taught at the school bench nor from church pulpit nor from the radio nor from the national government. The priest's role has been largely reduced to that of dispenser of the sacraments and administor of the Parish. The national government has succeeded in providing a wider sense of belonging whereby the Lionese know themselves to be Indonesian [*sic*] citizens ... The radio is used largely for popular music and news from afar. But for all this outside influence, daily life gains a meaning precisely from the Lionese culture itself, where the contradictions and paradoxes of life are viewed in a dyadic symbolic network of complementary opposites. Life gains meaning through the harmony of paired contradictions.

According to men's and women's representations of *adat* in Nggela, wives hold power inside the household, husbands outside the household. The Ata Nggela have thus constructed a pair of 'complementary opposites', or a 'paired contradiction' in Prior's terms, between a domestic unit which is conceptualized as female dominated and an extra-domestic unit that is male dominated. Indeed, women manage, and control for a large part, household resources such as food and money and are responsible for the education of the children, whereas men are the heads who represent the household in wider kin and village matters. This corresponds with their position in the local descent groups as heirs of land and successors to political office (*ana dari nia*). Only in exceptional cases of strong husband dominance and weak support of a wife's brother or natal family, does the husband rather than the wife control household resources. At first sight this would imply that men are usually subordinate to women in inter-household affairs, and women subordinate to men in extra-household affairs. There are, for instance, a great many widows, but few widowers, who run a household. In 1990, 15% of the households were female-headed. But if a husband is absent, the wife represents him.

Households often include non-nuclear family members who are integrated in production and distribution, for example foster children of near kin, and formerly, slaves, who performed domestic labour and for whom bridewealth was exchanged. The individual composition of households changes strongly over time, not only due to their 'developmental cycle' (Fortes 1958), but also because of migration and of child fostering.

The ideology of post-marital residence is uxorilocal in Nggela and virilocal in other Lio villages. In practice, residential units in Nggela may temporarily consist of extended families of two generations, namely of parents, a daughter with her (future) husband and further unmarried children. If the younger couple is already married, this residential unit consists of two households. The same applies to patrilocal Lio villages, but with a married son. So we cannot speak here of a household as a co-residential group, as scholars often do (see Yanagisako 1979: 164), also with regard to Indonesia (see Wolf 1990: 45); nor can we speak of a consumption or a pooling unit in the strict sense of the word (see Sahlins 1972: 94).

To my knowledge there is no term for 'family' in the Lio language, but in Nggela there exists the notion 'pot' (*podo*), comprising a group of brothers with their nuclear families which is a sub-unit of the lineages or houses. In former times such house segments used to pay common tributes of field produce to the head of the house, probably lived in the same house, and also constituted a consumption unit in the sense that they cooked and ate together. They might have constituted household units in pre-colonial days. Today groups based on house segments factually act as so-called wife-givers and wife-takers at occasions of marriage and other life-cycle rituals.

Descent categories called *suku* can be considered as lineages. They are connected with food taboos related to known ancestors (*embu*). Physically and symbolically they are represented in ceremonial houses (*sa'o nggua* or *rumah adat*) where the ancestors are worshipped (see also Howell 1995). Membership of the houses as corporate local descent groups is patrilineally transmitted. Part of the house is headed by a titled noble male (*mosa laki*) and a titled noble female (*laki ata fai*). Again, these female heads fulfil important tasks of a ritual kind inside the house, and the male heads outside the house. Moreover, before independence the titled male heads constituted the village council as lords of the land. The houses functioned as social groups, particularly on the occasion of agricultural rituals (*nggua*) until 1980[6] and during land conflicts until today. And because of lineage exogamy the houses are formally partners in marriage alliances.

Other important social categories that are identified by the Ata Nggela are ranks or estates, which cross-cut the houses. Three ranks are distinguished, based on descent categories called *kunu*. The latter can be considered as clans, as they are connected with food and behavioural taboos related to animals and plants (*tebu*). The ranks comprise descendants of nobles or high-ranking people (*ata ria*) from senior clans; descendants of commoners or middle-ranking people (*ana fai walu*) from junior clans; and descendants of slaves or low-ranking people (*ata ko'o*). Membership of the clans and subsequently of the ranks is transmitted matrilineally. With independence this ranking system, based on the ascribed criteria of descent and seniority, was formally abolished, but informally it still influences economic, social and political life decisively. Thus, the ranking system is only slowly penetrated by a class system, based on achieved criteria of education, occupation and income.[7] And until now that class system has had a stronger impact on generational relations than on gender relations (see de Jong 1998a).

According to notions of descent theory in the tradition of British anthropology, the kinship system of the Southern Lio can thus be classified as a double descent system with on the one hand matriclans, transferring rights on ritual and politico-jural offices as well as skills in craft and healing, and on the other hand patrilineages, mainly transferring rights on land (see also Sugishima 1994). Male property consists of land, houses, bride-wealth jewellery and animals. It is transmitted in the male line, in fact from father to mother and then to son. Female property consists of gold jewellery for adornment and cloths, which are transmitted from mother to daughter.

Further, according to concepts of alliance theory in the tradition of Dutch and French anthropology, the marriage system can be classified as an asymmetric alliance system, as in most parts of Eastern Indonesia (see de Josselin de Jong 1935), with unequal bride-wealth according to rank and wealth. Formal alliances between houses as wife-givers and wife-takers are initiated or maintained through marriage, which are strengthened by reciprocal gift-giving of the individual households of the houses at later life-cycle feasts. Thereby wife-givers are ideologically superior to wife-takers. This type of marriage system does, however, by no means automatically imply that women are mere objects in male marriage transactions (see also Postel-Coster 1988; de Jong 1998a, 1998c).

Associated with the cultural notion of 'hearth', households are thus important social units in the village society, especially in economic and ritual life. Most of the households in Nggela are closely connected by kinship and neighbourhood ties which are reproduced by regular, and often elaborate exchanges of gifts and services. As such, a range of decisions that are made within the household are also influential in the village society at large. However, as I shall show in more detail below, these households differ considerably according to rank and wealth. This is not self-evident. The village of Nggela resembles in this respect some other centres of Lio culture, but it distinguishes itself from many other, more egalitarian Lio villages (cf. Prior 1988).

THE ORGANIZATION OF PRODUCTION, RITUAL EXCHANGE AND TRADE OF CLOTH

Cloth production is organized according to a labour division of gender, age, rank and wealth. Today the men are barely subsistence producers of food. They cultivate mainly maize and cassava in swidden agriculture, and besides, they breed horses, pigs and goats on a small scale for ritual purposes. The women, on the other hand, are both subsistence and market producers of cloth. They manufacture tubular female and male sarongs, male shoulder cloths, and scarves. Thereby women provide for clothing for public occasions of the household members, for cloth gifts in ritual exchange, and for additional food, school fees and possibly for consumer goods by selling their cloth wealth.

According to general views in the region, the highest quality of Lio *ikat* cloths are produced in Nggela. Its repertoire of cloth comprises more than 30 different types (de Jong 1994). All cloths are now produced with machine-spun thread and most of them with chemical dyes. The production of a shoulder cloth takes about two weeks, while a sarong takes about one month.[8] Cloths with natural dyes (indigo and morinda), which are hardly produced in other Lio villages any more, take at least two years to finish, because the red dyeing process has to be repeated again and again.

The manufacturing process, which the weavers organize autonomously, consists of three phases: tying of the motifs (called *ikat* after the Indonesian term), dyeing and weaving. *Ikat* work is artistically most demanding and is valued as most prestigious. Formerly, high-ranking weavers created the highest valued designs and monopolized it by means of an *ikat* taboo. After independence the national government officially abolished the feudal ranking system of nobles, commoners and slaves and its prerogatives. Thus also the monopoly of prestigious weaving motifs by high-ranking weavers in the village could not be legitimated and maintained any longer. It shifted to a monopoly of these motifs by women who had passed the menopause, albeit of all strata. This indicates a certain division of labour according to age with older women mostly engaged in the *ikat* work and younger women who mainly weave.

There also exists a division of labour according to rank and wealth. By taking a somewhat simplified categorization, we can discern three groups of weavers: middle-ranking weavers who as a rule only produce for their own household; wealthy, high-ranking weavers who additionally place orders; and poor, low-ranking weavers who additionally accept orders on a regular base. There is no group of non-producers (virtually all the 'order-placing' women, as I designate them, are engaged in cloth production themselves. So it would be misleading to call them employers in an industrial capitalist sense. This form of labour organization already existed before independence, but seems to have been on the increase since that time. Remuneration is still in kind (thread, maize, cassava, rice or indigo) and otherwise in money.

Ritual exchange of cloth is practised at all life-cycle feasts (*pulu*), such as birth, first communion, marriage, house-building and death. Cloth gifts (*luka lawo*) together with rice and other luxury foods, fall within the female gift category. They are bestowed by the wife-givers as counter-prestation for the male gifts of the wife-takers, namely animals (*éko*) and money (*kerta*]) (as well as gold jewellery (*wéa*) in case of bride-wealth delivery). According to the concepts of the Ata Nggela, this concerns an exchange of goods between a married brother and sister. They say: 'The brother gives cloth, and the sister gives animals' (*Nara pati luka lawo, weta pati éko*). Women as well as men thus officially participate in gift exchange. The brother is expected to render gifts of cloth and ritual services at life-cycle events of his sister's children, whereas the sister makes her husband give animals to her brother at similar events of his children. In the most ideal case, this gift exchange of animals and cloth takes place at the preferred marriage of the brother's daughter with the sister's son. Today this is only occasionally practised among high-ranking families.

Translated into intra-household categories and in transfer of property between households, this means that a wife gives from her cloth wealth to her husband's sisters and parents, and a husband gives from his wealth of animals to his wife's brothers and parents. Gift exchange thus mainly takes place between households related by affinal ties.

Furthermore, an exchange of gifts and services occurs between households related by consanguinal ties of the same gender, thus sisters help one another with cloth gifts and brothers with animals. These transactions are more informal than those between households related through affines.

Trade of cloth occurs, if cash is needed, especially during the yearly 'hunger period' before the harvest. Since the 1970s the weavers also sell when they have to pay school fees. Trade cloths include new pieces of lower quality, used pieces for wear and, if good prices are offered, new high-quality pieces.

The weavers autonomously sell their cloths to local and regional petty traders in the village or on the regional markets and to tourists, who increasingly visit Nggela since it was officially designated by the regional government as a 'tourist village' (*desa pariwisata*) at the end of the 1980s. By selling to tourists, the weavers can earn a daily wage, which is up to three times higher (about Rp. 1,500) than if they were to sell to traders or work for other weavers (about Rp. 500).[9] However, selling to tourists is not easy. It is very time-consuming, and the market price can drop since less expensive cloths are also available at some newly developed tourist sites in the Lio area, for example near the famous Kelimutu volcano. Prices for sarongs in Nggela varied in 1990 from Rp. 15,000 up to Rp. 250,000 and for shoulder cloths from Rp. 10,000 up to Rp. 75,000.

With the spread of the monetary economy and with the increasing importance of formal education since the 1970s, as well as with the development of a regional tourist market in the 1980s, the production and distribution of cloth wealth have grown considerably in the villages of the Southern Lio. This was also facilitated through the import and increased use of machine-spun thread and chemical dyes as well as through changes in the *ikat* technique. At the same time, due to soil deterioration and migration, food production and distribution have declined, but small-scale animal breeding for ritual purposes has remained more or less constant. Whereas in the past the weavers were oriented in their production strategies mainly towards subsistence needs, the display of cloth in agricultural and life-cycle rituals and the demands of the regional market have meant that at present the weavers are chiefly oriented towards both the prestige system of gift exchange and the profit system of the tourist market.

Because the trade of cloth has increased, the decision-making power of weavers as breadwinners in the household and beyond seems to have grown with it. However, the more the weavers produce, the more they also bestow gifts (cf. de Jong 1995, 1998c). At least the system of ritual exchange absorbs one-third of the cloth that is produced each year. From a Western point of view, such management of resources is paradoxical and makes the aims of rural development uncertain. What motivates the women to participate increasingly in gift exchange?

Organizing life-cycle feasts with gift exchange is seen as crucial to gain prestige (*gai naja*). Prestige evidently is still a central value in this competitive village society, both for men and for women. Another important function of the exchange of goods and services on such occasions is to guarantee social security, as the weavers also compare these reciprocal arrangements of kin networks with savings associations (*arisan*). Although women sometimes speak of cloth-giving as a burden, the bestowing of textiles evidently endows them with prestige and social security, or more generally, with some influence in public opinion and on social relations. But what kind of influence do the weavers have on social relations in their households and beyond? In the next sections I shall analyse this issue more in detail.

INTRA-HOUSEHOLD RELATIONS AND PRACTICES RELATED TO PRODUCTION AND REPRODUCTION

A household's productivity in cloth manufacture and its subsequent distribution of cloth are affected by the additional tasks of an average weaver in agricultural production and in social reproduction. The most important responsibilities are: housework, childcare and care of sick kin, organizing life-cycle feasts of the children, services at feasts of kin and neighbours, mourning duties after the death of kin and neighbours, as well as communal services. Women thus perform a whole range of domestic tasks, defined in older publications on gender as activities around a mother(child group, as well as public tasks, defined as activities that link mother–child groups (cf. Rosaldo 1974). Through these economic and social practices the women create manifold intra- and inter-household relations. Here I shall focus first of all on the intra-household relations.

The most important productive relations within the household are (a) the gender relation between husband and wife and (b) the generational relation between mother and daughter. In a cloth-producing household the wife autonomously organizes cloth production, housework and the rearing of small children, while the husband takes care of food production and tasks such as construction. In addition, both cooperate in the domains of the other. A husband helps the wife with cloth production, for example with winding up thread, with caring for the children and sometimes with cooking, and a wife helps the husband with food production, for example by assisting in planting and harvesting, and with construction. The same applies to adolescent female and male children. Both perform unremunerated work for their parents' household until they are married, except if they enrol in formal education outside the village and migrate. Only at harvest time, especially in April, does agricultural work take priority over textile work for the female members of a household. We can thus speak of a balance of autonomy and cooperation of the husband–wife pair in the productive and reproductive spheres of the household, and thus of a gender symmetry (cf. also de Jong 1996).

This is strengthened by representations about working tasks. The domesticated role of women as wives and mothers is not undervalued. Yet both females and males value the role of the woman as cloth producer more highly than the role of mother, and also more highly than the role of food producer. The technology of cloth production is considered as more developed, and as the workplace is at home, their skin stays whiter which is highly appreciated. Moreover, cloth producers can gain more prestige with their products. Still more highly valued is the role of employees, particularly civil servants, because of their regular monthly wages.

The gender concepts of this rural community thus clearly contrast with the middle-class-oriented emphasis on reproduction and on the role of the mother as advanced by the Indonesian state. These views are particularly expressed in the governmental women's groups (PKK) which officially operate at all administrative levels from the national centre to the local villages (see TP PKK 1989). In Nggela, however, the PKK hardly existed during the 1990s.

A mother is hampered in her role as a cloth producer until her children are able to walk. Her productivity at this time decreases about 50% or more, and her production costs may rise, because she often starts to place some weaving work outside. Nevertheless, she will regularly make textiles, though in smaller quantities. As her husband also helps her, a weaver does not need to rely totally on female kin of other households to conduct her own productive activities. Small children tend to play near the *ikat* frame or the loom while the mother is doing *ikat* work or weaving.

Mothers educate their daughters in small tasks in cloth production from an early age. Daughters of marriageable age are very productive and creative, which increases the productivity of the household considerably. Besides weaving, the daughters perform more agricultural work as well as services at life-cycle feasts of neighbours and kin than do their mothers. The latter then concentrate on *ikat* work and housework. Under the regime of her mother, the daughter feels more free than under the authority of the mother-in-law during the marriage process or when she has the responsibility of her own household after marriage.

Because more males than females migrate, there are quite a number of spinsters who stay in the households of their mothers. Neither the imbalance of males and females nor the high number of unmarried women causes much debate within the village. It is more an issue of concern of descendants from the village living in town. Although not being married is less valued than being married, spinsters are nevertheless appreciated as *ikat* weavers.[10] And, what is perceived as more relevant, they contribute more to the survival and in certain cases to the wealth of the households. So a family has some advantage in not marrying out all the daughters.

The increased productivity in cloth manufacture as a household matures in the developmental cycle is important, because a mother normally increasingly engages in life-cycle feasts with gift exchange as she gets older, and her children and those of her nearest consanguinal and affinal kin marry and also have children. The organization of life-cycle feasts for the children is a cooperative effort of productive male and female household members in the first place, which is hardly possible without the engagement of at least one elder woman, usually the wife.

If a married daughter (or daughter-in-law) lives together with her mother (or mother-in-law), which is often the case for some years, they cooperate in cloth production, housework and the nursing of children, but, as already mentioned, they produce and distribute their cloth wealth separately.

The mother–daughter relation is generally asymmetric, as it is based on the principle of seniority. However, through recent changes this generational hierarchical difference decreases, which is especially manifest in that daughters can choose their marriage partners more autonomously (see also de Jong 1998b).

Now I would like to examine the control or the decision-making power over household resources and property in the household as well as the relations of dependence. One of the elder weavers once persuasively stated:

> The men do not possess money, not even 100 *rupiah*. And they also don't know how to manage money. Until they die, they don't dispose of money. To contribute to school fees for the children, they can at best breed horses or pigs and sell them. Since former times the women have made money. We have the money in our hands. The women are stronger than the men are. The women can decide more than the men can.

And the husband of a weaver said:

> The wife has the power at home. She has to control everything, such as money and food. The husband is not allowed to do that. If a men disposes of money, which is sometimes the case, then he is too free.

The income of a household depends mainly on the sale of cloth, but occasionally also on the sale of animals or food. Further contributions derive from scarce wage labour in agriculture, from the more frequent wage labour in textile manufacture, and in rare cases from wages through employment of the household members. Indeed, it is mainly the women who as weavers earn regular money; the men as peasants only sporadically contribute financially to the household income. This makes husbands dependent on wives, for example for their spending money, and makes the children dependent on mothers, for example for school fees.[11] Even male civil servants normally hand all of their wages over to their wives. This practice is reinforced by the idea advanced by women and men that men cannot reasonably manage money.

Average monthly expenditures in 1990 amounted to about Rp. 8,000 mainly for additional food and about Rp. 10,000 for weaving materials. In particular, expenditure on formal education varies greatly. Additionally, all but the poorest women deposit cash or rice in one or more of the rotating savings associations, usually run in the neighbourhood. The savings are mainly used for school fees and for life-cycle feasts.

Wives are very much in control of all the household resources: the food products which the husband, unmarried sons and possibly future son-in-law cultivate; the textiles which the unmarried daughters manufacture; and the money which mostly they themselves contribute to the household income by selling their cloths. The women themselves can decide what happens with their cloth wealth, as marriage with bride-wealth does not imply that the husband has rights over the production or products of the weavers. Moreover, a legally married woman obtains rights over the distribution of food, and over the property of the husband after his death. Based on these rights of control over important resources, the women exercise authority in the sense of juridical legitimized power, and some decision-making power over their husbands' and their children's products and activities. Control over their own labour products and over those of other household members is thus crucial to the strong position of the weaver in the domestic domain.

Simultaneously, and somewhat contradictorily, the idea exists that husband and wife should consult each other about domestic and extra-domestic affairs. In reality, women often seem to take the lead, especially if cloth gifts are at issue. This is expressly indicated by the distanced view of an elder spinster:

> Most of the time the husband loses, although he has more power [in extra-domestic affairs]. That is to say, he has the right to organize the gifts for the kin persons. But often the wife wins. So it is in this village. Actually the husband has the right, but mostly he loses. If the wife does not agree with something, then it does not happen, for example the giving of gifts to the family of the husband.

Because the wife has the right to inherit her husband's property after his death, as already mentioned, it seems that she already exerts influence over it during his lifetime. Thus she also influences the giving of animal wealth and gold jewellery.

To summarize, the women as household managers have considerable decision-making power, which is to some degree juridically legitimized or formal, via the customary law of the village society. To some degree though, it is informal, ascribed to competitive social relations and circumscribed with 'winning' (*utu*). This especially applies if they can dispose of the labour of other household members, particularly their husbands and one or more daughters. This decision-making power, mainly due to their production and distribution of cloth wealth, evidently has an impact on other spheres of production and reproduction as well, which is particularly obvious in their role in marriage (cf. also de Jong 1998a).

INTER-HOUSEHOLD RELATIONS AND PRACTICES RELATED TO RANK AND WEALTH

The most important relations between households, besides tenancy relations,[12] are productive relations in the context of cloth production on the one hand and exchange relations of goods and services in the context of life-cycle rituals on the other hand. Whereas the households in the first context are not related by close kinship ties, because exchange of labour between near kin is usually not remunerated with goods or money but based on reciprocity of services, the households in the latter context are kin-based, at least in a classificatory sense. What practices do the women pursue in these contexts?

In the context of productive relations, weavers of wealthy, mostly high-ranking households control the labour and labour products of weavers of poor, often low-ranking households. Order-placing and order-taking relations often exist between such households in a neighbourhood, so that a certain supervision is guaranteed. To grasp these relations, it makes sense to outline first the differences in property and income of these households, as these factors determine production and distribution strategies.

There are large differences in property *vis-à-vis* land, housing, money and valuables of gold jewellery and cloth between households. Differences in landed property originate from allocation of land among the houses according to seniority and marriage alliances. This is to a large degree related to rank, as only high-ranking men could become titled landlords with allocative authority. Wealthy households may possess at least four plots of fertile land, partly cultivated by sharecroppers, valuables of several pieces of gold jewellery, larger savings of money and about 20 pieces of cloth.[13] Poor households normally possess no land or only one plot, a house with hardly any furniture, one or two pigs, no gold jewellery, and money to the value of about Rp. 5,000 in 1990. Their most important possessions tend to be the wealth the weavers have produced themselves or have received as gifts at life-cycle rituals. This female wealth consists sometimes of up to ten pieces of cloth with an equivalent value of at least Rp. 350,000.[14] The poorest households, however, only possess one or two pieces of cloth.

Whereas in the case of one of the wealthiest households (where both spouses are civil servants) the monthly income can amount to Rp. 300,000 with another Rp. 300,000 yearly coming from the cloth trade, for the poorest households the income from cloth trade may be less than Rp. 30,000 per annum. In wealthier households further proceeds may come from former household members who have migrated, mostly remittances from older unmarried or married children, possibly also from foster children, who work as employees in provincial towns. Only these households are able to provide for higher education and to enter into a desirable white-collar job by means of available kinship connections and assets.

Poor weavers often have to interrupt cloth production for their own household, and to take outside orders to be able to buy the necessary weaving materials. This severely limits their cloth output. Order-placing weavers on the other hand can increase their output considerably. To illustrate this I would like to outline the relations of production between two weavers[15] with very different social and economic positions in 1990, whose households are related by order-placing and order-taking.

Case Study 13.1: *Ibu* Maria and Mama Nika

> *Ibu* Maria (56) was of high rank and worked both as a teacher with a monthly wage and as a weaver. Her husband was a retired teacher with a monthly pension and he held an important political office in the village.

Two young foster children lived in her household, her own marriageable and married children had all migrated. Because *Ibu* Maria needed many cloths for her family and kin and because she was wealthy, she regularly gave orders to other weavers. Her output of cloth amounted to 13 pieces in 1990. Because she had left the village for five months to seek medical care for her husband in Bali and Java, this was below her average. It also was below the average amount of cloths produced in a household at that time, which was about 15 pieces.

Because Mama Nika (37) had only one son she worked alone, and because her household was extremely poor she regularly had to take orders from other weavers. Most often she worked for her neighbour *Ibu* Maria. In 1990 she produced only five pieces of her own. Her productivity during that year may also have been limited by family problems. Her husband, with whom she had one child, had left her some time before. Afterwards she lived with her second partner in a consensual union and bore two children, both of whom died after some years. This man owned plenty of land, but he did not cultivate it, as he preferred to do irregular wage-labour in construction in the village. And exceptionally, he was in control of the household resources. In 1990 he took a lover and had a child with her. Some time later he returned to Mama Nika, got seriously ill and died. After his death Mama Nika did not benefit from the rights to his property, which a legal widow normally can.

Ibu Maria remunerated Mama Nika irregularly. The two women had no clear arrangement about payment. For some time after the death of her consensual partner, Mama Nika even resided with *Ibu* Maria, who provided her with food and gave her several kinds of gifts.

Asymmetric economic relations between households, maintained by women, are thus fundamental to the basic livelihood of at least part of the households, and also for the additional wealth of another part of them. Only the relations of the women's saving associations, which also connect households in a neighbourhood, are symmetric.

In ritual exchange both husband and wife initiate and maintain relations with other households. As cloth gifts have increased considerably since independence, wives have exerted a stronger impact on inter-household relations between kin within the village and with migrated kin beyond the village. In other words, social networks have a strong female component. Households related by gift-giving at life-cycle feasts concern particularly those of poor weavers who concentrate on cloth production for gift-giving, and of wealthier weavers who produce cloth for both giving and selling. The poorest weavers are not able to give or sell, they only produce for their own wear. Moreover, there are wealthier weavers who mainly focus on selling, especially to tourists. Weavers who practise these latter distribution strategies are socially rather isolated and forfeit prestige and security.

It is particularly noticeable that poor women emphasize the gift-giving of cloth more than the selling of it. Why do they pursue such a social practice? For poor weavers (in contrast to the poorest weavers), gift exchange is important, because by this kind of extra-domestic cooperation they can achieve some prestige and enhance long-term security for their households. Wealthy weavers can additionally obtain power by gift-giving, if they bestow poor kin with gifts that these cannot reciprocate except through labour or services.

If we look at the case of *Ibu* Maria again, it is striking that as a wealthy weaver she maintains a large network with households of kin in Nggela, with households of kin in the neighbouring village from where she originates, especially with her brother's household, and with households of kin in the neighbouring town. In 1990 she invested more than half of her cloth produce (nine pieces) in gift-giving, and she also received several cloths (four pieces). Its extent depends on the number of life-cycle feasts that are occurring in households to which a women is related by consanguinal and affinal ties.

In contrast, Mama Nika as a very poor weaver did not bestow one piece of cloth during that year. She hardly possesses any pieces of cloth of her own. Moreover, relations with her consanguinal and affinal kin are strained, because neither her husband nor her consensual partner have given adequate bridewealth gifts for Mama Nika, who actually was of high rank. Subsequently she did not obtain support from her natal family, and she became socially isolated.

At the death of Mama Nika's consensual partner, *Ibu* Maria was one of the few persons who gave her a piece of cloth, as a classificatory relative. To reciprocate this kind of gifts, Mama Nika could only perform *ikat* and weaving work for *Ibu* Maria and also would give her and her husband political support, if necessary. By gift-giving *Ibu* Maria not only influenced social relations to obtain prestige and security, as most women do, but also to achieve power, which was possible because she was an older and wealthy, high-ranking woman.

The different sizes and intensities of the kin networks that women decisively create and maintain thus strongly depend on the mostly symmetrical, but sometimes asymmetrical exchange relations with available consanguinal and affinal kin as well as with classificatory kin. Gift exchange normally starts with the marriage of a women. The beginning of exchange relationships is a delicate and conflictive matter, which does not succeed in all cases (as evidenced by Mama Nika). This subsequently influences the economic and social practices of a weaver as well as her support network. Unsuccessful exchange relations between the families of husband and wife may in certain cases even lead to the separation of the spouses. Usually a woman increasingly engages in gift exchange as she gets older, because through the growing-up of her children and the children of her nearest consanguinal and affinal kin, she becomes more and more involved in life-cycle rituals (as happened for *Ibu* Maria). This gives her the potential to exert more influence and, where she also enjoys high rank, wealth and advanced age, it also gives her more power.

CONCLUSIONS

The cultural notion related to *adat*, of a marked dichotomy between the female domestic and the male extra-domestic sphere among the Ata Nggela and the Southern Lio people, generally contradicts their social practices. Such an *emic* concept, like the strict *etic* segregation of the domestic and the public domain, conceals the important role men play in the domestic domain and the role of women in the extra-domestic domain in these weaving villages. Actually, both domains strongly overlap, as in other non-industrial societies (see Comaroff 1987). Southern Lio households are, for instance, the most important social locus of 'public' work and of decision-making for both women and men. Moreover the widespread practice of child fostering obfuscates a clear boundary.

The organization of activities between husband and wife is fairly symmetric, but the wife has control over labour products and the income of household members, so that from this perspective the domestic domain can indeed be deemed female-dominated. At least Lio cloth producers have considerable 'bargaining power', as elsewhere in Indonesia (see Papenek and Schwede 1988). Based on their control over own cloth wealth and over the agricultural and textile products of other household members, women also exercise a strong influence in economic and ritual affairs in the extra-domestic or public sphere, usually in both trade and life-cycle ceremonies.

This particularly applies to wealthy, high-ranking weavers who additionally control textile products of weavers of poor households and thus may accumulate and distribute more cloth wealth. The restricted part played by a weaver in ritual exchange may be attributed to the following economic conditions: first there may be no male household member to perform agricultural subsistence production (and/or some kind of scarce wage labour), so that a weaver has to provide for all the food; second, a women may have to provide to a large extent for the formal education of her children. Moreover, a basic social condition for restricted involvement in gift exchange is a conflictive relationship with kin to whom a woman otherwise would have gift-giving obligations. From these results we can infer that for the women of the poorest households, the economic interests of mere survival take precedence in the distribution practices of cloth. In other words, for the women of poor households, economic and social interests are paramount, whereas for the wealthy women, economic and political interests are at stake.

According to an early study by Sanday (1974), women in pre-industrial societies who possess power in the public domain, dispose of wealth beyond the domestic unit and their products are valued market goods. These conditions apply too to most of the Lio weavers. As producers and distributors of cloth wealth, the case of the Lio weavers supports the thesis of Weiner (1986) – but more at the level of social practices than at the symbolic level. Weiner states that women who produce cloths and exchange them in rituals exercise power in the domestic domain and that certain women therefore occupy powerful positions in the extra-domestic domain.

As far as gifts in ritual exchange in general are concerned, Godelier (1995) has recently pointed to the duality of the gift: on the one hand it creates solidarity and closeness in social relations by sharing; on the other hand it creates dependence and distance in social relations by inducing debts. That is why gift-giving as an individual act is a means *par excellence* of serving all kinds of interests. He states particularly that, unlike trade, any kind of gift exchange creates debts that cannot really be paid off; otherwise the exchange of similar gifts, which occurs in certain pre-industrial societies, could not be explained. I assume that in a similar vein, Lio weavers have recently used their prestige products increasingly as gifts to exert influence by building relations of solidarity, especially if they are poor, and by creating relations of dependence, if they are wealthy and of high rank.

Considered from a bird's eye view, the households in the village community constitute networks and are related in different ways, in which the women play a crucial role. As cloth producers (by participating in order-placing and order-taking), as owners of cloth wealth, and as household managers of food and money (by participating in rotating savings associations), the women constitute asymmetric and symmetric economic relations respectively between households in their neighbourhood. As givers of cloth wealth they are active in maintaining mostly symmetric relations, and as elite cloth-givers they sometimes also create asymmetric relations between households of kin within the village, and (because of migration) sometimes within the region. This serves them and other household members with respect to economic support, social security, prestige and possibly power. And finally, as traders of cloth, whereby men partly function as intermediaries, women also contribute to inter-village and to village–town relationships, i.e. to regional networking.

By their productive and distributive strategies Lio cloth producers thus clearly cross the cultural boundaries of the domestic unit and create and maintain social networks of households of neighbours and kin within the village and beyond. Proceeding from their historically specific socio-political, economic and cultural contexts, this places them in a strong position in their household and in their local society at large.

As far as the near future is concerned, household relations probably will not change dramatically. With the economic recession in Indonesia since 1997, it can be supposed, however, that also in the weaving region of the Lio practices to satisfy subsistence needs will be intensified and with that intra-household relations. At the same time inter-household networks based on gift-giving at a village and regional level may become even more important in terms of mutual economic support and social security.

Author's Note

With a grant provided by the canton of Zurich, postdoctoral fieldwork in Flores was conducted in 1987/88 and 1990/91 under the auspices of the Indonesian Academy of Sciences (LIPI) and supported by Universitas Indonesia in Jakarta and Universitas Nusa Cendana in Kupang.

Notes

1 See Niessen (1985) for Western Indonesia as well as Barnes and Barnes (1989) and Geirnaert-Martin (1992) for Eastern Indonesia. We cannot speak here of 'homeworking' in the sense of 'work under employment conditions for an

2   agent or entrepreneur who puts out work to the individual homes of the workers' (Holzner 1995: 1), as weavers on Flores are as a rule petty entrepreneurs themselves.

2. Koentjaraningrat (1971) distinguishes the people of Manggarai, Riung, Ngada, Nage-Keo, Ende, Lio, Sikka and Larantuka.

3. There exist only a number of articles and a few books mainly on socio-symbolic aspects, which have appeared particularly since the late 1980s.

4. If not indicated otherwise, the statistical figures in this article are all based on two sources: *Daftar Isian Potensi Desa dan Kelurahan Tahun* 1989/90, *Desa Nggela* and *Kecematan Wolowaru Dalam Angka* 1990. *Kantor Statistik Kabupaten Ende.*

5. In broad conformity to the population of Flores in general, 93% of the villagers adhere to Roman Catholicism and 7% to Islam.

6. Agricultural rituals ended in 1980, because the village elders quarrelled about the proper performance of the rituals, which means that they disagreed about the right order of their ranking positions. The deeper reasons for the breakdown of the cycle of agricultural rituals are to be worked out in a forthcoming comprehensive publication.

7. According to my own investigations, in 1990 only 2% of the productive village population belonged as civil servants to the socio-economic group of employees.

8. In other Lio weaving villages, such as Jopu, the manufacture of one piece of sarong takes only about two weeks because of different production methods and the different quality of the textiles.

9. This equalled the costs for 1 kilo of rice in 1990. At that time the value of 1,000 Indonesian Rp. was about US$ 0.55.

10. To become a Catholic nun, a nurse or a teacher is not really an option for unmarried women. Spinsterhood is only apparent later in the life-cycle of a woman, because the age of marriage is rather high. Moreover, the number of nuns and nurses in Flores used to be rather small (cf. Stegmaier 1977). And as far as female teachers are concerned, they are desired marriage partners because of their monthly wages.

11. From figures of enrolment in formal education in Nggela, I could infer that both boys and girls are equally encouraged to get through primary and secondary education. A Catholic secondary school (SMPK) was built in the village at the end of the 1960s, while a Catholic primary school (SDK) was founded at the beginning of the 1920s.

12. In 1990 about 20% of the households were landless.

13. Whereas the villagers openly talk about their income, they try to conceal their valuables, which makes it very hard to get exact information.

14. I calculated here average prices paid by villagers; prices paid by tourists are up to three times as high.

15. The names of the women are changed. On Flores *Ibu* is used to designate female teachers and other employees, whereas married peasant women are referred to with *Mama*.

14

Networks of Reproduction among Cigarette Factory Women in East Java

Ratna Saptari

INTRODUCTION

The critical examination of the household concept in the last two decades has opened up new lines of enquiry for scholars who view it as central to an understanding of the position of women and men in the process of social change. As households are considered to mediate between individuals and society, the way in which scholars view and define households, shapes the way in which this process of articulation occurs. The critique against the universality of the nuclear family-based household has been set up on the realization of variations in domestic and kin-based units that function to care for the daily maintenance of its members and their social reproduction. The (non-nuclear) co-residential extended family (F. and K. von-Benda Beckmann this volume), the non-co-residential extended family and the women-based kin networks (Lamphere 1974; Stack 1974; Yanagisako 1977) are such examples. Within this framework, scholars attempting to identify trends and changes in household composition are confounded by the difficulties in measuring and placing boundaries. This has led to an emphasis on activities rather than boundaries; on function rather than form (Yanagisako 1979; White 1980).

The first aim of this chapter is to contribute critically to this discussion. By emphasizing the diversity of domestic units, scholars have tended to ignore the ways in which units and sub-units are linked and may perform the same functions at different points in time or different functions at the same time. Thus boundaries between domestic units are still crucial, because they highlight the nature of exchange. Inter- and intra-household relations of reciprocity differ according to the membership status that one has to a specific household. The daily maintenance of social units may consist of a wide range of activities and these may not necessarily be shared with members of the unit for which such activities are undertaken, but with members of other units.

What I would like to show in my study in a village in Malang, East Java, is that the nuclear family-based household still emerges as the dominant form of domestic unit. However, in order to support the daily maintenance of this household, the services of individuals outside these households are needed. The village of Kayuwangi in Malang is representative of many other villages in the area in that it has undergone a long history of proletarianization through forced colonial sugar-cane cultivation and later on through an intensive commercialization process in the form of agricultural intensification and industrialization. My earlier research examined the development of the cigarette industry in the area and how it influenced the lives of the women workers who constitute the bulk of its labour force. In this chapter I shall look at the way in which women factory workers, who are mainly married and have children, have established networks of reproduction in order to ensure the daily maintenance of households and at the same time allow their entry into factory work. By establishing such networks, the nuclear household as a co-residential and consumption unit remains more or less intact with its traditional gender division of labour where women still bear the prime responsibility for domestic work. This situation evokes another crucial question: why has the gender division of labour remained the same while women's freedom of (physical) movement has in the last decades increased? In this case we see the retention of ideological views concerning women's work and men's work at home. At the same time the acknowledgement of women's role as income earner has been greatly enhanced. Indeed, the workings of ideology at the practical level are complex and multifaceted. Therefore, in looking at ideology and its relation to practice, we need to examine closely the different aspects of ideological notions and how they are constituted through social relations.

The second line of enquiry arising from the critique of household studies has been the attempt to open up the 'black box' (Niehof 1994) and investigate the internal dynamics of the household by looking not only at how household members negotiate differences and work in the interests of the household but also how internal conflicts may affect the continuity of the household as a unit. In this analysis, individual interests may result in the depletion of household resources for the purpose of individualistic goals (Sen 1980; Folbre 1988; Wolf 1990; Niehof 1994). This line of argument contributes to the critique on the term 'household strategy' as we have learned to distinguish between different levels of analyses (household and individual). What is still under-exposed in these arguments is the analysis of the overlap and contradiction of individual vs. household strategies. This is based on the undeniable fact that individuals at times work not only for their own interests but also in the interests of the household and sometimes work for both simultaneously. This problem is compounded by the methodological complications involved. Intentions can be deduced either by verbal statements, or by the actions themselves (which are subject to the researcher's interpretation), or by the results of such actions (i.e. who benefits most from such actions). In this study it will be shown that the distinction between individual and household interests cannot be sharply drawn, since both can operate simultaneously when an individual undertakes certain actions. The setting up of women's kin-based networks facilitates women's entry into the workforce and therefore enhances their decision-making powers in the household and their ability to take charge of their own lives. At the same time the income earned by these women strengthens the existence of their households, at least for the short term, as reproduction needs of its members are temporarily met.

In other words, the ways in which households mediate women's entry into the 'public sphere' are much more complicated than is often assumed since, at least in the case of the cigarette workers' households in Malang, it is not only the internal dynamics, but also the networks which women make with other women in different households that shape women's position in the workplace. The presence of the latter allows the household gender division of labour to remain intact as women enter the factories.

This chapter is organized as follows: the section below provides the context in which individual household members are integrated into the labour market in general and women into the cigarette industry in particular. The next section looks at the types of households, here defined as co-residential units, existing in the village. This is followed by an examination of the social reproduction of women workers and the households, focusing on the types of domestic activities undertaken and who are involved in these activities. Finally, some brief conclusions are drawn.

THE GENDERING OF WORK IN MALANG

It is a commonplace to say that women have a different position in the labour market than men. In households where the members are mainly wage dependent, the kind of work from which women can obtain an income differs from men's. In Kayuwangi, a rice-cultivating village where the majority of the households do not own land,[1] within the landless/near-landless category, men are more evenly distributed across the job spectrum. Women, on the other hand, are almost or entirely absent in construction work, salaried employment, transportation and renting/sharecropping arrangements (most of the arrangements being made by their husbands). The wives usually become 'family labour': they are concentrated primarily in factory work and agricultural work; many of them classify themselves as 'unemployed' [*nganggur*].[2] The availability of jobs outside the village is also more limited for women. In the mobility patterns of the household members of Kayuwangi, men are twice as likely to commute daily to their jobs than are women;[3] and in the period of research, except for one woman, all the individuals who migrate temporarily (and therefore are living outside the boundaries of the village) are men.

Although most of the Kayuwangi factory workers are from landless households, factory work is also important for women of the small landowning households. Those in factory work are employed mainly in cigarette factories. There are around 20 factories in the vicinity and the workforce is predominantly made up of women, both married and unmarried, old and young. Although production is often unstable and wages are not very high, entry into the cigarette labour force does to a certain extent ensure some kind of stability in income since the closing down of one factory would not necessarily mean the loss of a factory job. Those who go to the factories are not limited to cigarette production, since other factories, mostly owned by domestic capital, exist within a radius of 5 kilometres of the village. Other factories in the area can also see segregation by gender in the recruitment of labour. For instance, the sugar, paper-processing, and car repair services recruit men, whereas women are mainly absorbed in the food-processing, weaving or cigarette industries. If we further examine the factories separately, a more differentiated picture emerges. First of all, hierarchies between factories, objectively and subjectively, do exist. Certain factories, like the sugar factory and some cigarette factories, are more stable sources of employment and provide workers with some form of security, if not high wages. Other factories are less stable or are located further away, which means high transportation costs.

The patterns indicated above show that the labour market in Malang has always been segregated along gender lines. Such a distinction is often explained by the patriarchal ideology deriving from gender division in the home (Beneria 1979; Hartmann 1979; Elson and Pearson 1981). Patriarchal relations at home are reproduced in the workplace and this in turn implies that women's employment in the labour market will not change their position in the home, as women's income does not have the same meaning as men's (Whitehead 1981). This point of view is helpful in pointing us to the social relations at home as a significant factor in shaping relations at the workplace. However, since other forces (such as the market, differing employer strategies, and changing boundaries of the reproductive units) mediate the link between home and workplace such a point of view needs to be qualified. In the Malang area, where the village of Kayuwangi is located, the content of gender segregation has shifted through the decades as certain industries were open to women at one period in time and closed to them at another.

This can be clearly seen if we look at the development of the cigarette industry and what it meant for women's employment through the decades. The emergence of the cigarette industry in Malang dates back to the early 1920s, when a large number of medium-size firms managed to establish themselves and rapidly grew in number. By 1977, Malang had more than 50 *kretek* enterprises. The size of these enterprises also grew, as evidenced by the fact that in 1987 the workforce had grown to almost 30,000 (from 18,932 ten years before) yet the number had shrunk to about 20 enterprises (Saptari 1995). Thus enterprises became bigger and factory buildings had to accommodate this growing workforce. Originally, the balance between men and women workers employed in this industry was quite even, with men filling both the upper and lower ranks of the industry. However, since the early 1960s this industry has rapidly transformed itself into a 'female' industry, where the men comprise a significant minority but fill the better-paid sections, working either as supervisors, security guards or in secure, permanent jobs.

Women's entry into the factory work, which occurred in the 1920s, was not without social tensions. Moralistic views of a woman's place being with the children and family- dominated local discourse, and factory work was often linked to sexual 'looseness'. At that time women seldom travelled far in search of work. With bad transportation facilities and the availability of some work in the vicinity (in sugar fields, family farms or agricultural wage labour), not many women went to the factories that were located in the town of Malang. In Kayuwangi, there were not more than ten women who ventured beyond their village boundaries to reach the cigarette factories. Most of them walked to the factories in twos or threes, although one or two were accompanied by their husbands.[4] For some women the husbands condoned factory work; for others it was an escape from them (or from fathers). The trickle of workers from the village to the factories in Malang, particularly in the early 1940s, cannot be separated from the economic changes during those years. The Depression of the 1930s and the period prior to the Japanese invasion were periods of extreme hardship. After the Japanese occupation with the experience of forced labour of the male household heads, food rationing, inflation and a general situation of extreme poverty, wage levels in the larger cigarette companies were considered somewhat higher than for agricultural or other types of work.

In Kayuwangi, where a large percentage of households did not not have access to the means of production, and most of the men – particularly from the landless and small landowning households – were employed on a seasonal basis, the economic imperatives of survival outweighed the need to retain women at home, if that need ever existed. Indeed, even when there has been an attempt to constrain the movement of women to the factories or the labour market, the alternatives and networks that women have at their disposal quite often provides a foil to any such attempt. In addition to this the *kretek* cigarette industry with its long history in Java, plus the fact that different generations of men and women have at one or another point in their lives been employed in the industry, casts it in a different light from the new factories emerging in the industrial estates in the large cities of Java, where young women migrants are employed.

Many parents feel guilty when they cannot give money to their children and prefer to let them earn it themselves. As one woman said, 'What can we do? We cannot give them any pocket money so why not let them find their own money?'

The divergent positions of household members strongly influence their decision to seek factory work and the constraints or responses they may face from the other members, either parents or husbands. For men, the problem is different, since it is not a question of whether to work or not but whether to accept a job with a specific wage level.

For most women of the villages, the motivation to go to the cigarette factories is primarily, but not solely, economic. Besides the economic benefit of having one's own supply of money, there is also the satisfaction of being able to get away from domestic problems or even boredom. One woman whose children had left the home said: 'Why should I stare at the wall if I can go out and meet friends?' She was referring not to the small amount of domestic work she had to do but more to the social isolation she felt if she stayed at home.

The gender ideologies at work and at home are then not totally inflexible structures that shape women's position in all the social and economic arenas. Boundaries between these ideologies and practice are difficult to demarcate sharply as the different notions of womanhood and manhood influence and are influenced by the social, economic and political expediencies.

It will be shown below that the relative ease with which women entered the factories was a result of changing views of women's position in the household and the nature of their work; however, this was particularly accommodated by the networks which women established with their female kin from other households. The entry of women into factory work did not markedly change the gender division of labour within the household. The context within which such changes did or did not take place can only be understood if we look at the household structures in the village of Kayuwangi, as shown below.

HOUSEHOLD TYPES AND INTRA-HOUSEHOLD RELATIONS IN KAYUWANGI

In order to look at the link between the gender ideologies and intra- and inter-household relations related particularly to domestic work, we must first look at the prevailing household forms in this community. Table 14.1 gives a general picture of this based on a survey of the 141 sample households undertaken in 1988. Since it is often assumed that rural class position influences household composition, I have linked access to land with household forms.

Table 14.1: Household type by land ownership, Kayuwangi, 1988

Land Ownership (Hectares)	Sub-nuclear %	Sub-nuclear N	Nuclear %	Nuclear N	Extended %	Extended N	Total %	Total N
0.000–0.049	7	7	66	70	27	29	100	106
0.050–0.490	9	2	73	16	18	4	100	22
0.500–0.990	-	-	63	5	37	3	100	8
>1.00	-	-	60	3	40	2	100	5
Total	6	9	66	94	27	38	100	141

Source: household survey 1988.

In all the different landowning categories, it seems that the most predominant household form is that of the nuclear family, consisting of a conjugal couple and their unmarried children.[5] However, at the same time, the non-nuclear category (which can be subdivided into the extended and the sub-nuclear type) is also quite significant since more than one-third of the households take this form. The extended household (which consists of a nuclear or sub-nuclear family plus other relatives often consisting of more than two generations) is the most frequently found, whereas only a small number of the non-nuclear category are of the sub-nuclear type (households consisting of a widow/er or divorcee living alone or with other unmarried children, siblings or relatives). Proportionately speaking, the extended form is slightly more frequent for the landowning groups compared to the nuclear form, although this may not be as significant as it looks considering the small size of this group. This trend is also not consistent since the percentage does not become higher the larger the size of landholding.[6]

These sample households include those that do not consist of cigarette factory workers. If we concentrate on those households with cigarette factory workers in order to see the link between women's factory work and household compositions, we will find more or less the same proportions in household forms. Of the 141 sample households, one quarter (35 households) have one or more members who are cigarette factory workers. However it should be added that many of these sample households have members who once were cigarette factory workers, which would give a general notion of the involvement of the households in the cigarette factory work. Of the cigarette households, 60% are of the nuclear type, 28% are extended and only 10% are sub-nuclear. As can be seen from Table 14.2 below, more than 53% of the female cigarette factory workers in our sample are wives of household heads.[7] Most of these women (57%) are in the 25–39 year age category.

Table 14.2: Household position of cigarette workers (women and men) by household type, Kayuwangi, 1988

Rel. with Hh head	Sub-Nuclear	Nuclear	Extended	Total	%*
WOMEN					
Household head	2	-	-	2	7
Wife	-	13	4	17	61
Daughter	1	3	2	6	21
Daughter-in-law	-	1	1	2	7
Sister	-	-	1	1	4
Total	3	17	8	28	100

Table 14.2: Household position of cigarette workers (women and men) by household type, Kayuwangi, 1988

MEN					
Household head	-	4	1	5	72
Son	1	-	-		14
Son-in-law	-	-	-	-	-
Brother	-	-	-	-	-
Grandson	-	-	1	1	14
TOTAL	1	4	2		100

Source: household survey 1988; * in rounded figures.

Of the 35 households of cigarette workers, 48% (17) have small children that still need taking care of. How do these women deal with the task of child-rearing? How do they deal with the other functions that need to be undertaken (food preparation, cleaning and washing) for the daily maintenance of the household? How does their employment affect the division of labour at home? Many scholars have shown that the household may expand or contract according to (a) the demographic cycle of the household and (b) economic exigencies that take its members out of the household to obtain waged work. Other members may be drawn in to facilitate the continuation of the daily maintenance of the household. In the sections below it will be shown that this is only part of the story; the other part is that we have to look beyond the household units and at the networks between households to see how reproductive tasks are solved.

DOMESTIC WORK IN THE HOUSEHOLDS

Although ideological notions of women staying in the domestic sphere have changed and there are few social impediments to women working full-time in paid employment, the division of labour within households is often retained. Many comparative studies have found that despite women's employment outside the home, the number of hours that men spend on housework is little affected (Blumberg 1991; Coleman 1991; Standing 1991; Safa 1995). In Kayuwangi, women usually do childcare and cooking and men's involvement is considered to be the exception. The task of fetching water or firewood would usually involve more men, but this also depends on the occupation of other members (whether this would enable them to get firewood easily) and the kind of technology to which they have access. In certain situations those who had agricultural work would be in charge of gathering firewood. The availability of kerosene cooking stoves also makes a difference.[8] Access to tap-water or well-water reduces the workload, but women are often still the ones to fetch the water from these sources. Cleaning the house is something that men occasionally engage in, but only in their spare time. Washing clothes is usually done by each person individually (men and women), while the ironing is done mainly by the women.

Young married women tend to face different problems in the intra-household division of labour than do older married women. For households with small children, it is primarily childcare that is the major area of contention between husband and wife. Although husbands often have to capitulate to the wife's demand to return to work, they place more stress on child-rearing, since women with young babies are considered not ready to leave for work. How then, do women factory workers deal with this relative inflexibility of intra-household notions of domestic work? To a certain extent this is resolved by adding hours of work at home on top of their factory work. This is vividly portrayed in the classical term of women's 'dual burden'. In Kayuwangi, prior to going to work, most cigarette factory women have to cook rice, warm up yesterday's meal and get their children something to eat before they go to school or are dropped off at their grandmothers' or other female kin. On the way home from work, cigarette factory women would buy food ingredients from the foodstall near the factory or close to their homes to cook when they get home. Only once did I come across a case where the husband cooked the rice in the morning and warmed up the food. A woman from a wealthier household conveyed this to me in terms of incredulity, which revealed prevailing notions of women's and men's link to domestic work in the community.

In addition to the added burden that women bear with waged employment, they also count on the services of other women in the household or outside the household.[9] It will be shown below how exchanges of services can occur between female members of households who are kin. This can be seen in the cooking and purchasing of food, but it is particularly crucial in the case of childcare. In the Table 14.2 it was shown that extended families (where other members such as parents or siblings constitute the co-residential unit), constitute almost one third of the cigarette households (11 households). In seven of these, the cigarette workers are married women with small children. In four of the seven households, the child(ren) is (are) taken care of by their mothers who are also in the same households. In three of these, the mother-in-law takes care of the child-minding duties. The section below will focus further on these exchanges and the networks that women forge among family members.

WOMEN'S NETWORKS OF REPRODUCTION

In Kayuwangi, there is an abundance of examples of the exchanges of services and goods between households. Such exchanges may involve relations between sisters or between sisters and their mother; between women and their mothers-in-law. They may involve different types of exchange or reciprocities, and also different services that are exchanged. One illustration below shows the multiple types of services that are exchanged between three households. The network exists between a 60-year-old widow, from a sub-nuclear household, with her two daughters who are both employed in the cigarette factory and have children, and are part of their own nuclear households.

Case Study 14.1: Parti

> Parti from Kayuwangi, a former cigarette factory worker and one of the first few who ever worked in a (foreign) cigarette company, has five married children (one son and four daughters). Two of the daughters set up their own households elsewhere during the period of my stay. Two of her daughters who were living in the same hamlet worked in the cigarette factory, 15 minutes' walk away from where they lived. Daughter number three, Rukmini, a cigarette factory worker who lives four houses away from her mother, has three children, the youngest of whom was 6 months old and the oldest 6 years old when I started my fieldwork. The two youngest always stayed at Parti's place during the day (while the mother went to work in the factory).
>
> Parti herself has a foodstall and normally a heavy schedule. She was usually already awake at 3.00 am to do her own shopping at the big market in Malang. At 6.00 she would be preparing her various dishes and before 7.00 she was ready with food for her customers who had to start work either in the fields or the factory. At about 6.30 am Rukmini would arrive with the children, bringing with her also a pot of steaming cooked rice. She would either have breakfast first or leave without breakfast. Because the preparation of the food for the stall was usually rushed and intensive, especially with the extra burden of the children to watch over and feed, Parti had arranged for her granddaughter from daughter number one, Sumi (who was also living in the same hamlet but farther away to the south) to come and live with her. This granddaughter was in her teens and was constantly in conflict with her grandmother because she preferred to earn her own money rather than help her grandmother. But she stayed anyway, since she couldn't yet find a job and she had finished primary school long ago. Parti's daughter number one, Sumiati, who was also working in the factory did not need her daughter to help out in the house because she only had one other child (a son) who was also quite big and thus didn't need to be taken care of. Occasionally, when Sumiati did not have time to cook herself, she would take some of the food that was left over from her mother's foodstall, on the way home from the factory.

In the case above, childcaring services are exchanged with white rice and occasionally some money. However, Parti is helped out in her foodstall by the teenage daughter of her eldest daughter. Parti herself was once a factory worker and so, although she has her hands full in trying to earn an income, she supports her daughter. Such provision of services is certainly not about material benefits alone: it is also linked to feelings of obligation, the 'duties of a mother'.

Another example concerns a mother who does not herself engage in productive activities but is totally devoted to the care of her daughters' needs.

Case Study 14.2: Tarmi

> Paini (household D) has just had a baby one month ago and Tarmi (household A), Paini's mother, has moved to her house to help take care of it. The father stays with household B and household C. Besides taking care of Paini's baby, Tarmi goes regularly to the house of household C because her other daughter is doing the cooking for Paini. So Tarmi walks between three households every day (sometimes up to 10 times, so that she complains that her legs feel very tired). Between Sumi (household C) and Imah (household B) there is also some cooperation: Imah buys the rice; Sumi buys the food and gives her money to shop. Sumi is not working because she has a child to take care of; she also used to work in the factory but stopped four years ago.

Sometimes the networks of reproduction involve exchanges between siblings and their mother. A case in point is the network revolving around Sariyah's household.

Case Study 14.3: Sariyah's Household

> Sariyah is an elderly cigarette worker with four married daughters, each of whom lives in her own household in quarters that adjoin each other. Daughters number two and three also work in the cigarette factory. All households keep their own budgets (*menyimpan uangnya sendiri-sendiri*). Daughter number one, who used to work in the factory, has now stopped because she has a child to take care of, and at the same time, she also takes care of her second daughter's daughter. The one who does the cook-ing is daughter number two. This is why she is not seeking more work (*moncok*) in company D which is now opening up to workers from other factories (to do extra work), because the children will be angry if they don't have any food when they get home.
>
> The decision to stop work may have to do with the specific situation in the household of daughter number 2, which may not have been influenced by the network itself but works to the benefit of the other members.

From the above examples it can be seen that even the types of occupation that members have and the availability of female members who can take over part of the chores in exchange for others, are crucial to the working out of shared domestic duties.

THE NATURE AND LIMITS OF RECIPROCITY

As the cases have indicated, the negotiations and agreements made are not always based on the full approval of the women who have to shoulder the domestic duties, particularly childcare. On the one hand, a wage income is much welcomed by any parent, but on the other hand, older women are overburdened and hardly compensated monetarily for their efforts. In addition to this, since most of these women are not too old to engage in some self-employment activity, many of them consider it a missed opportunity to earn their own income (which is considered better than asking for money from their children). The quotes and case study below portray some of the feelings and tensions that mothers face in taking over the task of childcare:

> It is actually not very nice to stay at home all the time, not having one's own money. But because I have to take care of my niece, who is the daughter of my sister, I have to stay at home. Actually I am doing this because when Sumi was still unmarried (*gadis*) she took care of my child when I went out to work. (A middle-aged former cigarette factory worker)

A woman in her fifties, when her daughter was not around one Sunday, complained that her daughter only gave her Rp. 1,000 a week to take care of her child. She had once said to her daughter that she should hire a servant (*buruhkan orang*) to take care of her child as this would allow her to earn her own money. But her daughter only answered : 'There's no money for that.'

Case Study 14.4: Parti Again

> Parti, who had to take care of her three grandchildren for her number three daughter, was busy in her foodstall serving a customer, so she told the 6-year-old granddaughter, Lia, to hold the 2-year-old grandson. But a few minutes later Lia was already interested in something else and dumped her brother on the floor. Parti got angry at Lia saying she didn't know how to *momong* [care for a small child] properly. Parti, who was already about 60 years old, had to bend down to lift her grandson who was not getting lighter, then tried to chase after Lia yelling at her: Lia, here, this is your *momongan*! Lia came back to get her brother, but not long after that went out again to play with her friends and left her brother on the bench in the foodstall. Parti was muttering to herself as she took the little boy in her arms and used a long cloth slung across her shoulders to try to get the boy to sleep. She then said to me: 'Taking care of these children makes me quite tired (*kesel*, which can mean, physical as well as mental tiredness). They eat my food, they get snacks from my stall, and their mother gives me only Rp. 2,000 a week.'

So why are these women willing to sacrifice their energy and time to serve the interests of their daughters, when they themselves get little in exchange? As mentioned above, such exchanges are not only about material rewards. In the case of mother–daughter networks, the notion of 'balanced reciprocity' as coined by Sahlins (1965) cannot be applied. More appropriate would be that of 'general reciprocity', where the expectation for a return service is not for the immediate future but for old age security.

In the case of exchange between female siblings, the sharing of childcare is usually done alternately, where one sister who is (temporarily) out of the labour market, either because she herself has her own child to take care of (and no one to help her) or because she has just been laid off, or because she is still too young to find a factory job, will take care of her working sister's child on the proviso that some time in the future when she also has a job, her sister will return the service.

Thus the flow of female workers to the factories has been made possible not only by the domestic labour of those no longer (or not yet) able to enter the labour market. Quite often the backbone of the domestic labour force is the women who are still potentially active and still wanting to earn money either to cover household needs or to obtain some degree of independence. For this group the income, if not for themselves, at least can enhance their status by enabling them to provide pocket money or clothes for their grandchildren or children.

ALLOCATION OF INCOME: SERVING INDIVIDUAL, HOUSEHOLD OR EXTRA-HOUSEHOLD INTERESTS?

With all the efforts expended by women's networks to facilitate the entry of some of its members into the cigarette labour force, we wonder what happens to the income earned by these women? To what extent does it come back to the women who helped the factory women in the first place? It seems that although extra-household support was obtained to allow women to work in factories, the material benefits of such employment go back to the nuclear-family-based household. And within the household, the income does give the woman some leverage in the husband–wife relationship. However, the main share of the income usually goes on the daily maintenance of the household.

If we concentrate first on the income management patterns in Kayuwangi, two main types emerge. In the first pattern, the individual members of the household each retain a small amount of their own income and then submit a share to the household pot. In the case of husbands or wives, depending on the income levels, usually there is some agreement as to the division of financial expenditure. For instance, the husband's income may be allocated to pay for electricity, schooling and taxes, whereas the wife's income is generally spent on daily food consumption. Or if the wife's income is more stable (e.g. factory work) even if it is lower than the man's, it will be used for putting into *arisan* (this will be discussed below) whereas the husband's income will be for daily expenditures. In the second pattern the husband gives all his earnings to his wife and she will 'manage' its allocation with or without consulting her husband. The difference between the two patterns is usually rather blurred, since having reached some kind of decision as to how the incomes are to be allocated, the husband may then give all his earnings to his wife and let her handle the actual expenditure.

For some feminists and most policy-makers, the concentration and emphasis on income-creation programmes have been based on an assumption that the more income women can bring into the household, the more say they will have in decisions concerning their own and their family's well-being. It has been argued strongly, however, that there is no straightforward relation between income earned and increased power and authority within the household. As

Whitehead (1981: 89) has argued, male and female money wages are valued differently when they enter the household; therefore whatever the level of income, a woman's earnings may not always be recognized in the same way as men's. This is further augmented by the fact that in the labour market, women's labour is often valued less *because* it is considered as supplementary to the husband's wage.

A woman's access to an independent wage, and her capacity to take part in major decision-making on how it should be used, are often mediated by several factors: the ideological notions of women's and men's wages and the pre-existing power imbalance between female and male members of the household (Roldan 1988: 230); the way household income is managed; the income level of the household; and the stage in the life-cycle of the earner (Standing 1991: 88). These factors may be closely interrelated with one another; thus, for instance, ideological notions on wages may depend on the income level of the household. In wealthier households, assuming that most of the wealth is not a result of the woman's income but from inheritance and/or the income of the (male) household head, any income brought in by the wife may not be valued as crucial to the status and well-being of the family and so may be trivialized. The reverse usually holds for the poorer households. The life-cycle stage of the earner may also be linked with either household income or the way that household income is managed. The significance of an individual's income may be different if the earner is an unmarried daughter, a married daughter, or wife of the household head; it may be different in households of different class status, and also depend on whether and to what extent it is 'diluted' by being pooled with other members' earnings.[10]

Whatever a woman's wage level, how it is translated in terms of power can be measured by the degree to which she is able to control the allocation of income. In many societies women are given the responsibility of pooling the incomes earned by other members of the household and this is usually linked to the responsibility to allocate income. However, the act of allocating income cannot automatically be translated into greater power for women, since the right to decide how money is to be spent may not be theirs alone.[11] This distinction is significant since women usually have management roles but have little power to make the major decisions. In the example below, a woman's power to further her own interests (which ultimately benefits the household also) in keeping her job in the factory is facilitated by the mother's support:

Case Study 14.5: Paini

> Paini (mentioned in case study 14.2) had just given birth to a daughter and was planning to go back to work after one month. Her husband prohibited her from going back to work in the cigarette factory, saying that he would 'take care' of the housekeeping money (*uang belanja*). When Paini objected, he threatened to cut her household money by half (which meant she had to cope with only that money for the household). But Paini did not want to capitulate and got very angry at him.[12] She was also supported by her mother who offered to take care of the baby while she worked, since the factory was only 15 minutes walk away, and she could

come home at lunchtime to breast-feed the baby. The following Monday, Paini went back to work. Paini felt especially sure of her position because her husband was the stranger in the village and she was the one who could rely on her family network to provide the necessary support. Added to this, she felt she was in a strong position because the house they lived in had been built with her own money. The cost of building the house was Rp. 300,000, a sum which she had obtained through the sale of the gold necklace which she had bought with money saved in her *arisan* [rotating saving] group.

Many observers of Javanese household economies have commented on the significance of *arisan* as a way in which individuals can store up their income (or that of other members of the household, as will be shown below) at a certain point in the *arisan* cycle (Willner 1961; Papanek and Schwede 1988). These *arisan* groups are informally constituted yet have quite stringent rules which all the members must obey. All members pool an agreed amount of money at a stipulated time regularly, either weekly, monthly or fortnightly. At regular periods (usually when the money is being pooled) one or more members draw lots to see who gets the total amount pooled (or half the amount depending on how many people are allowed to draw the lottery).

Considering that *arisan* activities compel the members to contribute a fixed amount of money regularly, one would expect that members of the *arisan* would be mainly those who have fixed incomes, i.e. factory workers or civil servants. Indeed, those who chose not to join *arisan* groups did so out of fear that they would not be able to meet their obligation when the time came. For example Riyanto, a construction worker, didn't want to join any *arisan* group, even the one in the village (which was considered to have lower dues) because he was afraid he would not be able to pay his weekly dues at times when his income was irregular.[13]

However on further examination it was found that the majority of the *arisan* members, in Kayuwangi at least, were 'unemployed' women.[14] The second largest occupational group was the factory workers[15] and the rest were divided between those working in agriculture (both wage workers and owners), trade, outworking, civil service and others.

How can this anomaly be explained and what is its significance? It provides at least one significant insight into the internal workings of the household economy, in that although one cannot speak of 'household strategies', we can see how individual strategies may work for the common good of the household. Thus the household is still considered as the site for reproduction and accumulation/savings despite some tendencies of 'each person for him/herself'. What usually happens is that the women without their own earnings obtain money for the *arisan* contributions through other members of the household who do have regular earnings. This means that although income pooling is not necessarily a feature of the internal economics of households, members with steadier incomes usually do pool part of their income to let a member join one of the groups.

In poorer households the members seem to pool incomes to a greater extent, since income levels are so low that even for food some kind of contribution is needed from other members of the family, particularly when no one has a stable income. A case in point (not from the sample) is a female head of a three-member household with only two income earners, whose incomes were low and unstable. The woman, who was a cutter in a cigarette factory (the lowest paid of all) earned only Rp. 600 a day. Her mother, a widow, was a masseuse and because she was old she was already losing out to competition from two younger masseuses in the village. For daily subsistence, the daughter would provide the rice and the cooking oil, while the mother would be responsible for providing for the *sayur* [vegetables].

Conclusion

The discussion above has shown that the functioning of households as domestic units and the division of labour within households are inextricably linked to the nature of their embeddedness in the larger society. Through these links they are also able to forge kin-based networks which incorporate other households. This embeddedness is reflected in the types of wage employment held by the members of these households and the characteristics of such members. In this sense the nuclear, family-based household (which has been dismissed by many other chapters in this volume) is still important as a unit of analysis in the context of Java, and of Malang in particular. However, why this unit is relatively inflexible in terms of the gender division of labour and in terms of composition, can only be explained by the networks formed by the women members to take over some of the domestic tasks for other members engaged in wage employment.

The gender ideologies can be distinguished between notions of what men and women should do in the home, and notions about mothers or wives as wage-earners. In the first interpretation there has not been much change; in the second interpretation, there have been clear shifts in the last 30 to 40 years. Although this can only be based on assumptions, it is possible that the importance of the woman's wage in the household economy itself has become the reason for the retention of the traditional division of labour at home. As men's employment becomes more unstable and seasonal, the need to retain their self-respect as male bread-winner becomes more imperative. Therefore even if women are becoming more visible as providers of small but secure incomes, they still attend to domestic chores at home. This view is shared by women, too, and therefore the networks are created to maintain the reproductive tasks that they view as their own.

While the male wage-earner's income may cover the daily expenses, the money obtained from the *arisan*, which is often in the name of the woman or wife, may allow visible improvements in the household economic position, such as the renovation of the house or the ability to pay for the children's education. The availability of women's networks also takes off the edge of the extra burden of domestic work when women go to the factories.

The account above has also shown the interweaving of individual vs. household interests. The distinction between the two may be clear in cases when household interests actually clash with individual ones. The employment of women in the factories has enabled the enhancement of household interests (the support of the household economy through women's income) at the same time as the individual interest (the freeing of one's total dependence on another person's income) is also served. However defining 'household interest' is not as easy as it seems. In the case of a clash of individual interests, as shown by the case of the husband who preferred his wife to stay at home to take care of the new-born baby, the husband may use 'household interest' as a blanket term for his own self-interest to maintain his position as the main family bread-winner.

The utilization of networks of women between households also reflects certain ideological notions. The notion of the 'sacrificing mother' and her obligations to the happiness of her daughter seems partly to explain why mothers or mothers-in-law are willing to expend so much energy and time at the cost of their own independence. This is clear because wages earned by the daughters whose interests are served here, do not directly go back to their mothers, although complaints have often been voiced by the mothers about this. On the other hand, their willingness to provide child-caring duties (or other domestic tasks) cannot be explained solely by ideological notions concerning a mother's obligations. It also has its material side, although maybe indirectly, in the form of old age security. In the case of sisters, reciprocity also has its material and immaterial sides, but here the material becomes more obvious. The question is the speed with which one service can be repaid by another. Again intra-household relations influence the content of this inter-household reciprocity, namely whether husbands allow their wives to go to work when there are very small children. It is this mingling of ideology and practice, of household units and inter-household networks, which often makes the analytical dichotomies, which we ourselves create, into more of a hindrance than a help.

Author's Note

This study is based on research conducted in 1988–90 funded by The Netherlands Science Foundation (NWO/WOTRO). Annual visits have been made since then and two one-month studies were also conducted in January and August 1997.

Notes

1   74.5% of the sample households own only 0.3% of all land; while 99.7% of the land is owned by slightly above a quarter of the households (Saptari 1995).

2   This point needs to be critically questioned since not many women from landless households can afford to be unemployed.

3   A total of 62 men compared to 24 women commute to various places.

4   For instance, one woman had a husband who owned a horse and cart: thus she was brought by him daily, quite often with two fellow workers who would pay their fare at the end of the month. Another woman walked together with her husband who was a trader in the large market in Malang.

5   The existence of nuclear family households is not new in Java. See Koning (1997) and her chapter in this volume.

6   It is interesting to note however, that only two of the nine sub-nuclear households in Kayuwangi have access to land (however, in both cases the female household head is not involved in the actual cultivation of the land) and that all these sub-nuclear households are female-headed. Since there are 19 female single parents in Kayuwangi, the rest are incorporated within extended households.

7   As registered in the village registry.

8   But most households who already have such a stove usually combine it with the old cooking furnace involving firewood, because these are considered to give a better flavour in the cooking than the modern stoves.

9   Standing (1991) also states that rather than work being shared between men and women, the division of labour within the household is one between female members (or between female members and domestic servants for the middle-class household). See also Mackintosh (1989: 164).

10 It is in looking at the income contribution of young unmarried daughters in East Asian households where income is pooled that Kung (1983) and Salaf (1981) come to the conclusion that employment does not improve the position of female workers in their households.

11 Using Pahli's distinction, a separation should be made between 'control' (being the ability to make major intra-household decisions of a 'policy-making' kind) and 'management' (being the capacity to put policy decisions into action) (Standing 1991: 89).

12 When describing this event Paini used the term *ta' amuki* which means 'I let out my rage at him'.

13 Cigarette factory incomes are also irregular but the difference is that workers know that some time they will be able to get work again and even if the factory closes down, they will have not so much difficulty in getting another job in another cigarette factory.

14 A total of 32 women were classified as 'unemployed' compared to 29 women factory workers.

15 Fifteen of the 20 factory workers were cigarette workers.

15

Hidden Managers at Home
Elite Javanese Women Running New Order Family Firms

G.G. Weix

INTRODUCTION

How do we account for the 'productive' side of Javanese households and its implications for theories of social reproduction and labour relations when configuring the boundaries of household as an analytical unit (cf. Netting *et al.* 1984; Medick and Sabean 1986)? We must first consider the social organization of family firms and women's position in managing home-based production in Java, two topics which have, by and large, eluded ethnographers of Javanese society. The migration of young women to work in large factories in the export zones of major cities has been the subject of much sociological research in the last two decades. This has tended to focus on 'factory daughters', who increasingly come into conflict with parents, and divergent interests centred in the households of workers themselves, rather than those of the firm owners (Wolf 1992; Elmhirst this volume). In this essay though, I shall analyse several aspects of the homes of factory owners themselves, particularly the social context of households within which one sees negotiation of labour and corporate relations as a curiously domestic management of enterprise by elite women.

Such domestic management occurs in relative seclusion, which may account for the theoretical and empirical elision of elite women in the comparative studies of households. In contemporary Indonesia, families who secure their wealth through private enterprise typically build residences as small compounds separating home and street. Quite expansive and private residences, garages, workshops, offices and even warehouse or storage buildings are connected by courtyards and paths and surrounded by high walls, often 10–20 feet in height. These residential enclaves give the spatial impression of a secluded home life; yet because they encompass home-based production, these 'households' challenge our model for domestic domain as distinct from modern capitalist enterprises. This elaborate architectural effort to combine home and workplace has several different historical origins; one pattern lies in the domestic arrangements of urban trader communities in entrepreneurial enclaves of north coast Javanese towns. I characterize this pattern as the hidden management of family firms by elite women from within their homes, particularly labour relations through the distribution of gifts and largesse.

Previous Studies of Javanese Households

> Household: a group of people who live in a house ... [There is] considerable variation in the composition of Javanese households (Geertz 1961: 33, 44).

When Hildred Geertz described the Javanese family in the 1950s she implicitly theorized household as a bounded unit coincident with nuclear family and hearthhold in urban and rural communities (1961: 30–36). Her colleague Robert Jay strengthened this association with his etymological analysis of *somahan*, noting that the root word for 'house' (*omah*) was modified with the prefix *se-* for 'a social unit' and the suffix *-an* for the product of a union, such as children (Jay 1969: 55). He also defined the social and economic context for *somahan* as 'a unit subject to taxes and neighbourhood labor duties, representation at *slametan*, recruitment of food gifts, of labor, and of invitations to family celebrations and to sharecropping agreements' (ibid.: 53). Both ethnographers agreed that Javanese households were a domain of linguistic socialization, economic independence and social reproduction. Because Jay noted the central role of food gifts and labour exchange distinguishing each unit in inter-house-hold relations, one might assume that family and household are coincident, and therefore not notice that such strands of exchange occur within households as well.

However, these ethnographies remain insightful 40 years later because both authors recorded anomalies to the dominant pattern. For instance, Jay (1969: 51) notes: 'In addition, more well-to-do households may have other dependants living singly with them, kinsmen or non-kinsmen.' And Geertz (1961: 33) writes extensively of urban neighbourhoods where,

> sometimes – particularly in town where living conditions are crowded – there are two households, sometimes related, sharing the same living space but with separate budgets and a sense of separateness. Two sisters and their husbands and children may live together but cook separately, side by side, in the kitchen. Or a young bachelor earning wages in a cigarette factory may lodge with his kin but eat in one of the nearby food stands. In some of the more crowded parts of town inhabited by a sort of urban proletariat – laborers in the small factories making such things as cigarettes or carbonated drinks or a kind of Javanese potato chip – several unrelated families may live in the same house but maintain completely separate households.

We can now read these allusions to the 'well-to-do' or 'a sort of urban proletariat' as domestic arrangements of residence structured by the unstated factor of class. Clearly, emerging economic transformations of the Indonesian economy in the late 1950s were influencing local household structure, composition, and the social processes by which kin and non-kin lived together in East Javanese urban residences. Strikingly, these allusions to class did not alter the standard anthropological/sociological portrait of household, even though the examples cited suggest that Javanese domestic life was extraordinarily heterogeneous and flexible in the negotiation of boundaries between social groups, interdependencies of individuals of all ages, and architectural spaces.

A second, related social fact about household was its matrifocal nature: Javanese women enjoyed an unusual economic autonomy emanating from their control over money and household budgets (Geertz 1961: 122–27; Jay 1969: 92). In a more recent study of batik market traders in Surakarta, Central Java, Suzanne Brenner elaborates on this economic and social asymmetry in money matters as it reinforces gender ideologies about desire and personal control (Brenner 1995: 28–31). Not only do Javanese women control household budgets, supervise servants and boarders, and predominate in the more public trade and market venues, they also operate successful home-based businesses. They are, I would argue, hidden managers at home, both of petty commodity production and of much larger enterprises. Throughout rural and urban Java, women run enterprises out of their homes, they employ wage workers and supervise small workshops located in, or adjacent to their households, and they reinvest capital in home and retail enterprises. Thus the linguistic, social and economic distinctions between family and stranger do not only define domains of home and society; they can also characterize a social context in which home and workplace overlap in the spaces of the household enterprises, as Geertz herself noted 40 years ago:

> Even these townsmen who are self-employed as, for instance, a man with a small cigarette factory, do not organize their enterprise in the form of a family business, but employ outsiders just as frequently as family members (Geertz 1961: 3).

It is striking that Geertz mentions 'a small cigarette factory' as a quintessential example of a family business, since the cigarette industry is one of the few enduring legacies of early Indonesian capitalism and home-based commodity production in an otherwise agrarian society on Java (Robison 1986: 26). The industry originated in the provincial town of Kudus, 60 kilometres west of Semarang, and its outlying villages. Kudus remains one of three national centres for the industrial production of clove cigarettes (cf. Saptari 1994). The industry was dominated by both Muslim Javanese and Chinese family firms throughout the twentieth century; the local commercial organization had a fluctuating membership from 20 to several hundred enterprises. Some even flourished over several generations, although inheritance conflicts lessened the degree to which these family firms could transmit their capital successfully to succeeding generations (Castles 1967: 58–66).

The home-based production of the clove cigarette industry thrived alongside factory production; until the 1940s a broad, pervasive system of piecework known as *abon* was contracted to peasants and urban day workers. Before the Second World War, entrepreneurs in Kudus stored raw materials (both tobacco and cloves) in warehouses near their homes; they then contracted hand-rolled cigarette production as piecework to rural women who travelled to town daily to pick up materials and to deliver completed bundles. However this contracted *abon* system grew cumbersome and caused traffic problems in the narrow alleys of the mosque compounds in West Kudus. As early as 1913 firms also located workshop production of hand-rolled cigarettes in warehouses built within the mosque compounds of West Kudus, or in factories on the outskirts of town. The newly designed workshop and warehouse complex typically was located next to the owner's home, with offices and additional buildings nearby. Thus storage, production, management and home life coexisted within the same spatial and social arena.

In addition to managing this expanded version of home-based production, many of the early entrepreneurs attempted to keep their children close to home as well. Some firm owners also built adjoining residences for their married daughters and their children next to their own homes. Both Haji Moeslich and Nitisemito, two of the famed first generation entrepreneurs, constructed contemporary mansions for their daughters; Nitisemito even built two identical residences for his twin daughters, one on either side of the river, Kali Gelis, both within sight of his own residence. Contemporary entrepreneurs whom I met in the 1980s also encouraged their children to settle next door to them; Nitisemito's grandson converted the warehouse and workshop next to his garage into a two-store modern home for his son and his new wife when they married.

Elite women – the wives, sisters, and daughters of cigarette firm entrepreneurs – have been quite active in the management of these firms, past and present. The crucial difference in men's and women's management styles has been their social location: women have supervised factory labour relations from within their households while their husbands, brothers and sons have traversed more public arenas, 'going to the office', even if this is located just across the street. These women's management practices, past and present, alter our theoretical perception of the household as a private social arena; even in the supervision of servants, a domestic idiom of patronage and gift-giving has supplanted contractual labour relations (Weix, in press). Because throughout the twentieth century these elite women have combined socialization and other domestic processes with supervision of wage work and relations of production associated with the workplace, their actions and strategies constitute the household as a hybrid social domain. The purpose of this chapter is to describe and analyse this hybrid domain ethnographically as it appeared in the 1980s and early 1990s, in order to reach a better understanding of Javanese domestic social relations and the agency of women who seek to secure their own personal and family rank predicated upon entrepreneurial success.

ELITE WOMEN'S AGENCY: CONSOLIDATING PRESTIGE

The privileges of wealthy women in Javanese communities as they translate into unusual forms of autonomy and agency have been noted by feminist anthropologists, but are only beginning to be analysed for their cultural and historical implications for patterns of social organization. For example, we know that peasant landowner women in rural Java augment their family status through specific practices of material and symbolic consolidation of prestige (Stoler 1977; cf. Hart 1986). In the village economy of the 1970s, wealthy peasant women negotiated other women's contract labour for planting and harvesting at a favourable rate; however they also distributed *slametan* baskets at neighbourhood ritual exchange in patterns to differentiate the status of recipients. Wealthier peasant women, Ann Stoler has argued, emphasize differential rank through these symbolic as well as material means: their strategic distribution of *slametan* baskets at life-cycle rituals strengthens both the hierarchy and ties between households, just as manipulating labour relations with landless peasants secures and enhances their family's material interests. Stoler combines class and gender effectively in her analysis because she posits wealthy women as primary agents of social reproduction of material and symbolic capital in the rural agrarian economy. In a similar vein, Valerie Hull has examined the social position and interests of middle-class urban women who have emerged as significant social groups for studies of enhanced social status based on education and the new ideology of domesticity (Hull 1986).

Despite these two pioneering works, gender is rarely part of the analysis of elite Indonesians, particularly of urban community leaders and the new elites (Emmerson 1976: 111) Since Indonesian women are often marginal to formal analyses of the political order, Jamie Mackie has even referred to them as 'a classless class' (quoted in Abeyaskere 1990). Recent efforts to integrate gender into analyses of the 'new rich of Asia' rely more on personal consumption patterns than relations of production as the arena in which high rank and differential status are consolidated and secured (Robison 1996).

Elite women strive for prestige, certainly; my question is how their strategies involve the domestic arena of their own households and the interests of other women (and men). While women of all socio-economic levels integrate economic livelihood with domestic tasks, cope with pregnancy and child-rearing and negotiate access to resources with other family members, elite women are a noteworthy sociological exception. Not only do they secure their own livelihood by managing a family firm or enterprise, but they also employ other women in their factories; they engage (sometimes scores) of servants to care for and to accompany their children throughout their lives; and they negotiate relations of authority with a wide entourage of employees – all within the familiar settings of their own homes. Their status as employer is conflated with their domestic roles as mothers, wives and household managers. Privileges of wealth can even seclude and shield them from analytic enquiry altogether; it is often difficult to observe the lives of elites in familiar settings for extended periods.

In addition to this paucity of empirical evidence, there is little theoretical or conceptual framework for studying elites anthropologically; the term itself is criticized as vague, obscuring more global or structural analysis of class and rank (Marcus 1983). One advantage of speaking of elites is to ground social analysis in specific and ethnographic contexts and to focus on the processes by which elite groups form and change over time (Marcus 1983: 6–8). For Indonesian studies, Emmerson's study of political elites scarcely mentions women because, as he puts it, so few are visible in public life (Emmerson 1976: 117). We have only begun to ask in what ways women in Java secure high rank, power and prestige and become the subject of study, in part because we have not turned to the social arenas in which they are constantly visible, namely their own households.

A second question is that of the logical consequence of their actions. Do elite women gain high rank as a consequence of cultural distinctions of gender itself, or do they gain prestige through kin roles and ties to powerful men? The ethnographic and historical study of Indonesian women suggests the former (Locher-Scholten 1987; Ong and Peletz 1995; Sears 1996). Since money, economic activity and agricultural fertility are associated with the female in Indonesian and Malay societies, their social autonomy is secured because as women, they are authorized to run both their own households and, collectively, the local market economy. Despite this relative advantage for women in Malay societies, gender as a basis for social distinction is muted compared with hierarchy in societies across the archipelago (Errington 1990; Keeler 1990). Moreover, in the New Order era (1966 to the present) Indonesian women are losing ground in terms of personal autonomy and the efficacy of their actions in economic matters (Sears 1996). Indonesian gender and kin roles have become ideologically fixed within the homes and domesticated as part of state-sponsored agenda (Baried 1986). For example, the term for mother, *Ibu*, implies heightened status and social obligations for women in general but particularly for social dependants, a process which Djajiningrat-Nieuwenhuis has coined 'Ibuization' (Djajadiningrat-Nieuwenhuis 1987). Yet neo-traditional Javanese values have further heightened this hyperbolic referral to the past; and the domestication of women has increasingly relegated them to the home as an appropriate domain or sphere.

Is it a New Order phenomenon to domesticate Indonesian women in their kin-based role as *Ibu* and confine their social agency to the household? If so, paradoxically, elite women in particular may become more influential by remaining within the domestic sphere and cultivating their authority from their positions in the household (cf. Pemberton 1994 on the concept of domestication in New Order Indonesia). Within their homes they can develop a broad range of networks with social dependants and still remain aligned with publicly broadcast, neo-traditional values. Their privilege and access to resources are mobilized, yet domestic; their activities transform their households into a site for generating symbolic capital, in particular relations of social indebtedness.

They do so differently than Javanese men, who emphasize either civil servant status or 'the office' as the site for brokering power (Suryakusuma 1996: 99–102). Thus, an asymmetry between husbands and wives makes elite homes a locus for symbolic and social capital primarily for women. This leads to diverging strategies for men and women who manage businesses, since women can create social debts and build enduring social connections and relations of dependency among staff, employees and workers.

In this chapter I shall focus on a certain class of Javanese elite women and the domestic strategies of labour management within their homes, in part to understand broader processes of social differentiation, rank and relations of dependence in contemporary Javanese households. Since the families which I shall describe here own and manage corporate firms of some significance, they reproduce class relations and differential social rank among not only their domestic staff of less than a hundred individuals, but also potentially thousands of employees in their enterprises. Second, elite women's agency, autonomy and central position to supervise home production are all predicated upon an unusual and expanded definition of household, in which the workplace is, in part, structured as a spatial and social aspect of an elite family's home. We can attend to elite women's strategies of labour management as 'a domestic project' by observing not only interactions linking on the factory floor, but also the everyday practices of communication and exchange negotiating the social spaces of activity within the factory owners' homes and private compounds. Operating simultaneously in multiple roles as firm manager, employer and supervisor of a large household, these wealthy women manage labour relations of a wide entourage of servants, staff and other social dependants, as well as the employment of day workers in factory workshops adjacent to their homes. They articulate the differences between 'staff' and 'workers' in a single enterprise; the processes of recruitment or dismissal are initiated often in their living room. Thus social differences of rank and class among household staff and factory workers themselves are constituted not simply in the home or workplace, but in the distinction between these two aspects of this expanded domestic setting.

BACKGROUND AND CASE STUDY SETTING

This chapter draws on field research on indigenous capitalist firms in Kudus, Central Java since 1986 (Weix 1990). I shall describe several families within a larger network of clans who own and operate an international cigarette firm, P.T. Dukun (a pseudonym), located outside Kudus in a village where the original founder, *Pak* Warno, lived in the 1950s. Today his children live in the village, in Kudus, Semarang and Jakarta and operate several subsidiary branches of the original firm, which has expanded into retail sales, batik production, paper mills and textile production as well. Specific social practices initiated and maintained by three generations of women contribute directly to the management and decision-making of their family business; these women contribute indirectly to the firm's success through specific acts of patronage towards staff and social dependants. Based on this case study, I shall argue that elite women monopolize aspects of gift economy in contemporary labour relations, and through strategic distribution of ritual exchange, display and patronage, they attempt to position themselves (and their family firms) as a source of generosity and largesse towards staff and workers. Their actions to maintain patronage with a wide circle social dependants ensure the success of their firms; and they also demonstrate how elite patronage practices are inflected by gender in ways hitherto unacknowledged in the literature on patron–client relations in Java. Finally, the fact that these practices are socialized from one generation to another illustrates how Javanese women incorporate a wide range of 'strangers' within the familial order of Javanese households, even on the grand scale of elite homes, and continually innovate domestic relations and their own heightened autonomy, as well as that of their daughters and daughters-in-law.

The following case study is of three generations of women associated with a prosperous and influential firm in Kudus. *Ibu* Warno, the wife of the founder, is deceased, although her reputation remains strong among the village where she lived as the firm grew in the 1950s and 1960s. *Pak* and *Ibu* Warno had five children, three sons and two daughters, all of whom manage the family firm, P.T. Dukun, or its subsidiary firms which receive raw materials from the parent firm. The second daughter, whom I shall call *Bu* Haji, married the son of another famous entrepreneur, whose enterprise went bankrupt in the 1960s. *Bu* Haji and her husband have four children, three boys and a girl. Their daughter, Wiwit, was a teenager attending high school during the years of my research. *Bu* Haji and her household in Kudus generate these examples although I shall also refer to her siblings and their residences.

The P.T. Dukun firm's founder, *Pak* Warno, and his wife are both deceased and buried in a family tomb near the homes of their children. They remain an important model for moral behaviour, and they are evoked at family gatherings. On the date of the founders' deaths every 35 days – when the national seven-day week and the market five-day week coincided (e.g. Juma'at Legi) – Bu Haji and her brothers and sisters visited the graves of their deceased parents, holding a prayer meeting and reading verses from the Qur'an. Their portraits hang in the offices, and in the home of their eldest son. Stories circulate about *Pak* Warno's thrift and *Bu* Warno's generosity, as we shall see. On the site of their original house, their eldest son has built a magnificent mansion; his siblings have built similar homes nearby. Both *Bu* Haji and her sister have moved away from the village, and reside in Kudus and Semarang, respectively.

Case Study 15.1: Bu Haji

> *Bu* Haji was in their thirties when I met her (in 1986) and had operated her own branch firm under a different logo since she was married. Her older sister supervised a branch firm in Semarang. Both women managed several factories in cigarette production, textiles and retail business. Their enter-

prises received materials from P.T. Dukun, including cloth for mass-produced batik production, tobacco for hand-rolled cigarettes, and paper for retail sales. *Bu* Haji told me that she and her husband managed labour relations together, and I witnessed them paying staff and employees from their home. Her husband oversaw marketing and the recipes for the sauce – a blend of cloves, sugar and other ingredients – used in cigarette production; he and his son tested samples and received market distributors and brokers in their living room almost daily. However, *Bu* Haji managed labour relations of workshop production and ordered supplies for the commercial ventures including a store, a batik factory and numerous contractual arrangements associated with the upkeep of their large household. She supervised 10 staff and 30 servants of all ages who lived in her house compound, or who worked there daily and returned to other residences in the evenings.

Wiwit helped her mother with running the household; at age 15 she could already instruct staff and servants in tasks, pay wages and expenses, and organize food preparation or hosting of guests, albeit with some assistance or guidance from her mother. She deferred to her parents and to her older brother, who married in 1992 and settled next to this parents' home. *Bu* Haji's children will inherit from the grandparents' firm as well as her own enterprises, including extensive interests in textiles, paper and manufacturing. In preparation, both Wiwit and her brother attended college in Jakarta to study business, engineering, and textile production and design. At home, however, Wiwit was already adept at managing servants and labour, including cultivating the extensive knowledge her mother shared about the major events in the lives of those who worked for them. All life-cycle rituals, births, deaths and marriages, were acknowledged in some way with gifts.

Bu Haji's children are not unusual in this respect; all *Pak* and *Ibu* Warno's adult children teach their own children to cultivate local exchanges between households in the neighbourhood. Even *Bu* Haji and her sister, having moved to the town and city, still remain deeply involved in household exchanges in the village. *Bu* Haji's primary relationships with her siblings, especially her eldest brother who supervises the family firm, are reinforced through daily contacts and visits to each other's homes. Kudus is just a short distance from the village where P.T. Dukun operates, and both the firm's buildings and their households are landmarks along the rural route. All neighbours know the homes of the firm owners, though few visit them casually.

This attention to gift-giving is the central concern of elite women in their homes. Second, the relationship between men and women, as spouses and as siblings, makes the political positions of their husbands, brothers and fathers visible as patrons, insofar as their wives, sisters and mothers are able to secure wide networks of patronage. A crucial question is how workers and employees themselves perceive such networks, as generosity or as payment.

P.T. Dukun was typical of one of the largest firms in Kudus; it employed some 8,000 workers, the majority of whom were women in the tobacco sectors, with equal numbers of men and women employed in manufactured cigarette production, textiles and linkage industries (paper, transportation and marketing). During the 1980s the four largest firms in Kudus employed 90% of all workers in the cigarette industry, and while the competition between these four corporations was constantly alluded to, the families who owned the firms often socialized in formal settings, e.g. *arisan*, public ceremonies, and civil service-sponsored-events. It is important to note the public nature of these events and socializing; it did not occur in elite homes, and elite women rarely attended. *Bu* Haji would claim to be too tired to attend a ceremony and would ask me to go instead and tell her who attended.

Visits to elite homes were central to forming new relationships of patronage. When I approached the P.T. Dukun firm to tour and to observe the workshops for my research, *Bu* Haji gave me a letter of introduction to her elder brother, who managed the firm. She had instructed me to take the note and visit her brother at his home in the afternoon. Not fully sensitive to these instructions, I delivered the note to the office receptionist, and met her brother at his office, which perplexed him. An assistant escorted me to the entry hall of his home across the street, where I waited until I could meet with his wife to introduce myself and my purpose. Such introductions indicate where the locus of social connections lies: reception of guests in one's home. I met with *Pak* Warno's eldest son because he had inherited the role of running the family business, and he was empowered to give me permission to observe factory workshops. Despite six months of field research in different sections of the firm, I found that the visits to *Bu* Haji's brothers' and sisters' homes, and numerous visits to her household in Kudus, proved unexpectedly fortuitous in understanding wage labour relations I witnessed in the workplace.

Only in elite households can one see not only the process of negotiating the conditions of wage labour, but also the cultural forms of compensation offered for work. This comprises not only wages, but also prepared food, baskets of rice distributed on *Idul Adha* and *Idul Fitri*, company calendars, and numerous other in-kind gifts distributed to workers in the shops next door, or across the street, while the distribution and preparation of life-cycle gifts occur in the elite women's home. While these practices may be idiosyncratic to this particular clan or industry, they nevertheless illustrate an important theme in contemporary Indonesian life: that wage work is always embedded in social contexts, in this case, the inter-household exchanges which a woman supervises from within her home.

Clove cigarette firms were initiated in Kudus at the turn of the century (including *Pak* Warno) by men who are made legendary as exemplary patrons of their communities, religious schools and local associations. In the Kudus museum displays and other locally produced histories, their wives and sisters are never mentioned, though they are crucial to maintain the prosperity of firms (Weix 1997). However *Bu* Haji and other elite women consolidate gift distribution as a sphere of influence of a particular firm. They keep a precise record of individual life-cycle rituals, and they plan more mass distributions to mark major Islamic holidays. The practice of patronage mediated by these women in the home makes the politics of their relations with their brothers, husbands and fathers visible, even as it shelters the women themselves from view.

These elite women facilitate the broader networks of patronage attributed to their fathers, husbands and brothers. The term 'patronage' brings to mind a traditional relationship between a powerful man and his clients, or followers symbolically cast as a father and children. In the Javanese context, the ability of a leader to gather followers can be based on moral authority as well as on the obligations of higher rank. However, most relationships of personal dependency rely on access to largesse as well as on personal authority. Scott comments that 'a patron must be a government official or a merchant with the ability to contribute more, and fulfil the obligations of high rank' (Scott 1977: 22). In Javanese society patronage with merchants or traders traditionally flows from a source different from the largesse of government officials. Traders in Central Java were brokers of materials, not of labour. Those in Kudus accumulated capital from dealing in tobacco and cloves stored for local production and distribution. If they did manufacture their own cigarette brands, they negotiated daily wages, or credit, with contracted day labourers and pieceworkers from urban compounds and nearby villages. In-kind support rarely entered into contractual labour for the thousands of workers and peasants from villages in and around Kudus.

However, in-kind benefits do play a crucial role in Javanese patronage managed by elite women. In the Javanese context, patronage is literally the offer to feed and provide for someone in return for his or her loyalty and deference. Since patronage is a relationship of dependency based not on access to land, or use-rights, but rather on benefits contingent upon personal and flexible ties: whoever accepts this relationship has some degree of social mobility. There is some sense then, in which social rank and prestige are at issue and may be negotiated. As firm owners expand the firm, they broaden their circles of social dependants through gifts of food, cloth, credit; they thus elaborate patronage between themselves and a set of permanent employees. These gifts of patronage are all in lieu of payment, or monetary compensation.

In order for this patronage to remain possible, money must be made to fit a social context. For Javanese, the point is not simply to make money, but to bring money into this relationship with hierarchy, either in familial or religious terms. This is accomplished by distinguishing family and non-family as different communities of debt, in which credit displaces deference in social relationships.

Family marks the circulation of talk and credit, instead of the circulation of money, to keep separate the effects of wealth on social rank and prestige from those spheres. Patronage thereby extends diffuse ties of family beyond the household to include additional members within the security of a familial order. Patronage, and the social distinctions it implies, presumes a disjunction between the circulation of money and social hierarchy – a gap which patronage serves not so much to bridge as to accentuate. In the next section I shall describe how elite women are able to accomplish these goals: to cater workers and staff; to provide a certain circulation of credit to make money appear unnecessary; and to strengthen their own position by staying at home.

In the village where P.T. Dukun is located, neighbours frequently spoke of *Ibu* Warno as 'a generous woman' who would always feed people well, and also give small gifts to people she met in the market. I asked the neighbours who worked in the factory if they had known *Bu* Haji's mother. One young woman responded, 'She was so generous. If you met her in the market [the booths set up along the factory walls] she would always give you something.' Similar words of praise described other elite women past and present as 'good and kind' because they gave small presents; James Scott has described this as dissimilated discourse on the symbolic capital of generosity shown by elites in Malay villages (Scott 1985). Both analytical and local explanations for this gift-giving therefore focused on this redistribution of goods as a means of garnering reputation and prestige. Yet it struck me as an odd story about everyday exchanges. Markets are not places to demonstrate generosity, nor are they sites of surplus to be given away; market stalls are temporary nodes of calculation, the tug of trade, the appraisal of means and opportunity in which women in particular are thought to excel. Why then, would village factory workers conflate the rhetoric of elite generosity with entrepreneurial women?

If *Bu* Haji's mother or any elite woman went to market, her meandering over produce would hardly be a place for her to assert her elite status *vis-à-vis* other villagers. More likely she would stress common origins as resident of the village, her mansion as 'just another household' along the road. The significance of her wealth and elite status only stand out at moments when she distributes gifts. *Bu* Haji inherited her mother's reputation for generosity, however *Bu* Haji was known more for receiving guests in her home, which became the locus of elite patronage to villagers and employees. It is rare for women like *Bu* Haji to initiate moments of exchange; it is far more common for villagers to attempt to position themselves as recipients of the fabled generosity. To approach a factory owner for assistance, one must visit the couple in their home, and more often than not, be received by the woman of the house. When *Bu* Haji holds audiences with her staff, and her husband entertains and meets both clients and distributors, she clearly dominates management of both exchange and labour relations for her and her husband's firm. As the daughter of a successful trader, and a wealthy business woman herself, she garners respect among urban civil servants. Nevertheless she is careful to nurture her ties to her natal village by participating in both urban and rural household exchanges.

Once elite women such as *Bu* Haji gain a reputation for generosity, they cultivate this through the reception of numerous visitors in their homes. I witnessed many occasions of visitors requesting *Bu* Haji's assistance at the end of their visit. Even though *Bu* Haji and her family often left Kudus for trips to Jakarta, Singapore or even Europe, their local reputation as elites whose homes were open to many strengthened the perception of them as generous people who distributed largesse. When *Bu* Haji was 'at home' receiving guests, she rarely left her household, but preferred to host gatherings such as savings association meetings or prayer readings. When she does venture out to visit other households, she will visit several in one day.

These avenues to patronage are centered on the home, not the office, and thus accent the position of elite women in distributing largesse to social dependants. The largesse is distributed in elaborate ways to supplement monetary compensation for labour. Gifts from elite women on behalf of their family firms to individual employees include not only personal assistance, but also meals during work, *slametan* baskets, cloth or clothing, calendars from the firm, and even annual bonuses. All these are in lieu of monetary compensation, and become emblematic of the patron's generosity and wealth itself.

HOMES AS ICONS OF LARGESSE

A second way in which elite families in Kudus have consolidated their domestic lives as the site for building symbolic capital has been to renovate their private residences adjacent to the factory complex. All of *Pak* Warno's sons have built their new homes since 1967 as landmarks of display in the village where P.T. Dukun is located. Most villagers calculate the location of neighbourhood residences by the distance between their houses and '*Pak* Warno's house'. By the 1980s each of the brothers had married and settled in a large household adjacent to the office building and factory complex. *Bu* Haji and her elder sister had built spacious homes in Kudus and Semarang with workshops adjacent to their residences; and by 1993 *Bu* Haji had replaced the workshops with a modern two-storey home for her eldest son who had just married. Each household is sumptuous, spacious, and an extravagant display of rank with marble floors, chandeliers, art and numerous rooms in which to host guests. In this *Bu* Haji follows the tradition of her grandparents and her husband's grandparents, who also built large mansions in their compounds near the factories in Old Kudus with tiled floors imported from Holland, and teak furniture commissioned from Jepara. The form and function of such large residences are designed not only for the comfort of the family and staff who occupy it daily, but also for the preparation and hosting of numerous rituals, prayer meetings and events. The most striking example of this use of household space occurred early in my field research when I assisted with a *wewehan* ceremony which *Bu* Haji hosted for 2,500 people.

As Jay describes in the 1950s, life-cycle rituals such as *wewehan* are interpreted as moments of redistribution and exchange in Javanese village life. *Bu* Haji and her sisters attempt to gain autonomy and to distance themselves from neighbours by secluding their homes as a private realm. However, they cannot remove themselves from the networks of community and neighbourhood engagements and life-cycle events without sacrificing the symbolic resources which they value most: reciprocal visits and exchanges with neighbours, employees and customers. On the contrary, *Bu* Haji often hosts larger and more elaborate *slametan* than anyone could possibly reciprocate. Planning began two weeks before an enormous event to celebrate the birth of her fourth child.

Bu Haji closed her factory early in the afternoon and enlisted the workers from her own branch firm next door to meet in the hallways of her home to assemble the first 800 *slametan* baskets which were later that evening distributed to the workers' homes. This first level of distribution was quite modest: a rice strainer filled with cooked rice, and some stewed goat in a small bowl. The strainer was tied up in a batik cloth printed for the occasion, and a flyer announcing the event tucked in the folds.

The second level of distribution prepared the following day was planned for some 600 neighbours, relatives and acquaintances, many of whom came on different days to help (*rewang*) prepare the vegetables and special dishes for the different levels of extravagance. The entire preparations lasted a week, with seven levels in all. The final distribution level for family members comprised *slametan* baskets that were tiny towers of bowls, baskets and boxes of sweets, requiring several young men to lift them for transportation. So the complete *wewehan* encompassed the entire social spectrum associated with P.T. Dukun and its branch firm.

Bu Haji, her mother before her, her sisters and sisters-in-law, and her daughter all demonstrate an active engagement and overlap of home and workplace, because their agency links the two social spheres during ritual exchanges and visits. As influential and powerful women, they draw upon their authority as employers to bring workers into their home for preparation and distribution of *slametan* baskets and gifts. Factory workshops are physically separated from the home and the wage work appears unrelated, except when a *slametan* arises and preparations draw the workers into the home to arrange the hundreds of baskets. Then suddenly the two spheres are joined with an *Ibu* at the helm. Similarly for prayer circles or life-cycle rituals, factory workers produce specially printed batik for the guests, or they join in life-cycle preparations just as neighbours and relatives would in a village context.

Bu Haji places herself at the apex of household exchange and draws her employees into the process. In managing labour relations and wage work more directly, *Bu* Haji and her sister each supervise a branch firm and direct daily management from their homes. It is not uncommon for the entire morning to be taken up with visits from factory managers and staff consulting with *Bu* Haji and her husband over decisions in the workplace. The one task elite women take on personally is the payment of wages and presentation of bonuses to staff and household workers at *Lebaran*. Husbands and wives run firms with interdependent styles of accommodating both modern financial practices and sex segregation of Muslim conventions. For example, if there were a meeting of firm representatives, *Bu* Haji would never attend. She preferred to send her husband, or even me as a representative for ceremonies such as the opening of the museum, to report back to her on who attended and what happened. However secluded they appear from public life, women like *Bu* Haji manage the crucial conversion of debt to patrimonial relations necessary to ensure the expansion of firms into significant institutions of employment, support and local patronage.

Finally, elite women distinguish workers from staff and employees connected to their households through their actions of gift-giving and attentive gestures of generosity. As the wives and sisters of firm owners, they manage the distribution of in-kind support with the exaggerated rhetorical role as *Ibu*, a mother who cares for social dependants. The security and protection of a patron is supplemented by the offer of women to feed their employees. To feed someone, one of the most mundane yet significant acts to establish relative status in a Javanese context, not only provides for others by offering them food and drink; it becomes the way to distinguish home from work. We can see this distinction replayed in factory production where pieceworkers typically do not eat or drink during their hours in workshops, whereas staff are generally given meal tokens, or breaks during which they can leave the factory complex.

In contrast, a worker who refuses to obey or complete the tasks at hand is said to be on a hunger strike (*mogok makan*). This remains one of the recurring issues in debates over industrial labour policy: provision of non-monetary compensation, usually a meal or tea served in the workplace. Grijns cites cases of opposition – not to conditions, but to supervisors. Women workers in shoe manufacturing have gone on strike and 'thrown away food given to them.' (Grijns *et al.* 1994: 162). Patronage in these settings is familial, a constantly shifting set of expectations. The process of circumscribing patronage in a Javanese context generates not simply a large family, but involves the distinctions among family members and strangers on a larger scale. It is in this sense that *Bu* Haji is engaged, albeit on a very large scale, with the same social processes that Geertz and Jay noted for household relations in the 1950s.

Conclusion

In reviewing these strategies of reputation, patronage and asymmetrical exchange in consolidating the prestige of the firm as practiced by *Bu* Haji, her mother, sister and potentially, her daughter, three themes stand out:

- The boundaries between household and workplace do more to identify the domestic unit as a crucial nexus from which to negotiate labour relations as a context for wage payment.

- The dichotomy between production and reproduction in any analysis of family firms is difficult to sustain, given the empirical evidence of Javanese home-based workshops located next to the owner's residence, and workers participating in life-cycle rituals on a regular basis.
- Female agency should discuss not only the dynamics of the nuclear family, but the role of elite women in shaping other women's lives, as their servants, staff, employees and entourage of social dependants and acquaintances.

Despite this augmented role for elite women, we should recognize that they are in turn circumscribed by the same ethos of moral economy as elite men. The difference worth noting is that women's generosity is predicated upon gifts as well as security of protection, and without this gendered aspect of patronage, much of what passes for a discussion of elite prestige may be obscuring the experience of those gift exchanges crossing class and shaping New Order household relations in contemporary Indonesia.

Bibliography

Abeyaskere, Susan (1990) 'Women and Class in Indonesia'. In Richard Taylor and Kenneth Young (eds), *The Politics of Middle Class Indonesia*. Monash University CSEAS Papers no. 19, pp. 1–16.

Abu-Lughod, L. (1990) 'The Romance of Resistance: Tracing Transformations of Power through Bedouin Women'. *American Ethnologist* 17, pp. 41–55.

Agarwal, Bina (1994) 'Gender, Resistance and Land: Interlinked Struggles over Resources and Meanings in South Asia'. *Journal of Peasant Studies* 22 (1), pp. 81–125.

Alderson-Smith, G. (1984) 'Confederations of Households: Extended Domestic Enterprises in Cities and Country'. In N. Long and B. Roberts (eds), *Miners, Peasants and Entrepreneurs; Regional Development in the Central Highlands of Peru*. Cambridge Latin American Studies 48. London, New York: Cambridge University Press, pp. 217–34.

Alexander, Jennifer (1987) *Trade, Traders and Trading in Rural Java*. Singapore: Oxford University Press.

Alexander, Paul, Peter Boomgaard and Ben White (1991) 'Introduction.' In Paul Alexander, Peter Boomgaard and Ben White (eds), *In the Shadow of Agriculture: Non-Farm Activities in the Javanese Economy, Past and Present*. Amsterdam: Royal Tropical Institute, pp. 1–13.

Alexander, Sally (1984) 'Women, Class and Sexual Differences in the 1830s and 1840s: Some Reflections on the Writing of a Feminist History'. *History Workshop Journal* 17, pp. 125–49.

Alisyahbana, Sutan Takdir (1961) *Indonesia in the Modern World*. Bombay: Congress for Cultural Freedom.

—— (1983) 'Sistem Matrilineal Minangkabau dan Revolusi Kedudukan Perempuan di Zaman kita' [The Minangkabau matrilineal system and the revolution of women's status in our time]. In A.A. Navis (ed.), *Dialektika Minangkabau Dalam Kemelut Sosial dan Politik* [Minangkabau dialectics in the social and political crisis]. Padang: Genta Singgalang Press, pp. 13–26.

Almagor, U. (1971) 'Gerontocracy, Polygyny and Scarce Resources'. In J.S. La Fontaines (ed.), *Sex and Age as Principles of Social Differentiation*. London: Academic Press.

Anderson, Benedict R.O'G. (1972) 'The Idea of Power in Javanese Culture'. In Claire Holt (ed.), *Culture and Politics in Indonesia*. Ithaca: Cornell University Press.

—— (1990) *Language and Power. Exploring Political Cultures in Indonesia*. Ithaca and London: Cornell University Press.

—— (1991) *Imagined Communities: Reflections on the Origin and Spread of Nationalism*. London: Verso.

Anderson, P. (1980) *Approaches to the Study of the Western Family, 1500–1914*. Cambridge: Cambridge University Press.

Antlöv, Hans and Thommy Svensson (1991) 'From Rural Home Weavers to Factory Labour. The Industrialization of Textile Manufacturing in Majalaya'. In Paul Alexander *et al.* (eds), *In the Shadow of Agriculture: Non-Farm Activities in the Javanese Economy, Past and Present.* Amsterdam: RTI, pp. 113–26.

Appadurai, A. (1986) 'Introduction: Commodities and the Politics of Value'. In A. Appadurai (ed.), *The Social Life of Things.* Cambridge: Cambridge University Press, pp. 3–63.

Arizpe, L. (1982) 'Relay Migration and the Survival of the Peasant Household'. In H. Safa (ed.), *Towards a Political Economy of Urbanization in Third World Countries.* Delhi: Oxford University Press, pp. 19–45.

Arndt, Pater Paul S.V.D. (1933) *Lionesisc–Deutsches Wörterbuch* [Lio–German dictionary]. Ende: Arnoldus.

Atkinson, Jane and Shelly Errington (1990) *Power and Difference: Gender in Island Southeast Asia.* Stanford: Stanford University Press.

Bank, Jan (1983) *Katholieken en de Indonesische Revolutie* [Roman Catholics and the Indonesian revolution], Baarn: Ambo.

Baried, Baroroh (1986) 'Islam and the Modernization of Indonesian Women'. In Taufik Abdullah and Sharon Siddique (eds), *Islam and Society in Southeast Asia.* Singapore: Institute of Southeast Asian Studies, pp. 139–54.

Barnes, Ruth (1989) *The Ikat Textiles of Lamalera. A Study of an Eastern Indonesian Weaving Tradition.* Leiden: Brill.

—— and R.H. Barnes (1989) 'Barter and Money in an Indonesian Village Economy'. *Man* [N.S.] 24, pp. 399–418.

Barrett, Michelle (1990) *Women's Oppression Today.* London: Verso.

Beauvoir, Simone de (1952) *The Second Sex.* New York: Vintage Books.

Bell, D. (1993) 'Introduction 1: The Context'. In D. Bell, P. Caplan and W. Jahan (eds), *Gendered Fields; Women, Men and Ethnography.* New York: Routledge.

Bemmelen, Sita van (1982) 'Enkele aspecten van het onderwijs aan Indonesische meisjes 1900–1942' [Some aspects of the education of Indonesian girls 1900–1942], Unpublished MA thesis, Department of History, Utrecht University.

—— (1983) 'Wege zur Veränderung der Position der Indonesische Frau durch die protestantische Mission im 19. und 20. Jahrhundert'. In: J. Gerwin *et al.* (eds), *Alltäglichkeit und Kolonisierung. Zur Geschichte der Ausbreitung Europas auf die übrige Welt.* Oldenburg: Bibliotheks- und Informationssystem der Universität Oldenburg, pp. 97-117.

—— (1992) 'Educated Toba Batak Daughters as Mediators in the Process of Elite Formation (1920–1942)'. In S. van Bemmelen *et al.* (eds), *Women and Mediation in Indonesia.* Leiden: KITLV Press, pp. 135–165.

Benda-Beckmann, F. von (1979) *Property in Social Continuity: Continuity and Change in the Maintenance of Property Relationships through Time in Minangkabau, West Sumatra.* The Hague: M. Nijhoff.

—— (1987) 'De Ijsjes van de Rechter: een Verkenning van Complexe Sociale Zekerheidssystemen' [The ice-sticks of the judge: exploring complex social security systems]. *Recht der Werkelijkheid* vol. I, pp. 69–82.

—— (1990a) 'Sago, Law and Food Security on Ambon'. In J.I. Bakker (ed.), *The World Food Crisis: Food Security in Comparative Perspective*. Toronto: Canadian Scholars' Press, pp. 157–199.

—— (1990b) 'Ambonese *Adat* as Jurisprudence of Insurgence and Oppression'. *Law and Anthropology* 5, pp. 25–42.

Benda-Beckmann, F. and K. von Benda-Beckmann (1978) 'Residence in a Minangkabau *Nagari*'. *Indonesia Circle* 15, pp. 6–17.

—— (1987) *Verwantschap tussen Dorp en Staat* [Kinship between village and state]. Paper presented at the 6th Conference on Tropical Asia (KOTA). June 1987, Amsterdam.

—— (1991) 'Law in Society: From Blindman's-bluff to Multilocal Law'. In *Living Law in the Low Countries*. Special Issue of *Recht der Werkelijkheid*. Amsterdam: Vuga, pp. 119–139.

—— (1994) 'Property, Politics and Conflict: Ambon and Minangkabau Compared'. *Law and Society Review* 28, pp. 589–607.

—— (1995) 'Rural Populations, Social Security, and Legal Pluralism in the Central Moluccas of Eastern Indonesia'. In J. Dixon and B. Scheurell (eds), *Social Security Programs: A Cross-Cultural Perspective*. Westport: Greenwood, pp. 75–107.

—— (1998) 'Where Structures Merge: State and Off-State Involvement in Rural Social Security on Ambon, Indonesia'. In S. Pannell and F. von Benda-Beckmann (eds), *Old World Places, New World Problems: Exploring Resource Management Issues in Eastern Indonesia*. Canberra: The Australian National University, Centre for Resource and Environmental Studies, pp. 143–180.

Benda-Beckmann, F. von and T. Taale (1992) 'The Changing Laws of Hospitality: Guest Labourers in the Political Economy of Rural Legal Pluralism'. In F. von Benda-Beckmann and M. van der Velde (eds) *Law as a Resource in Agrarian Struggles*. Wageningse Sociologische Studies 33, pp. 61–87. Agricultural University Wageningen.

—— (1996) 'Land, Trees and Houses: Changing (Un)certainties in Property relationships on Ambon'. In D. Mearns and C. Healy (eds), *Remaking Maluku: Social Transformation in Eastern Indonesia*. Darwin: Centre for Southeast Asian Studies, NT University. Special Monograph No. 1, pp. 39–63.

Benda-Beckmann, K. von (1988) 'Social Security and Small-Scale Enterprises in Islamic Ambon'. In F. von Benda-Beckmann, K. von Benda-Beckmann, E. Casiño, F. Hirtz, G.R. Woodman and H. Zacher (eds), *Between Kinship and the State: Law and Social Security in Developing Countries*. Dordrecht-Holland/Cinnaminson-USA: Foris Publications, pp. 451–471.

—— (1991) 'Development, Law and Gender Skewing: An Examination of the Impact of Development on the Socio-Legal Position of Women with Special Reference to Minangkabau'. *Journal of Legal Pluralism* 30/31, pp. 87–120.

—— (1991) 'Developing Families: Moluccan Women and Changing Patterns of Social Security in The Netherlands'. In H. Claessen, M. van den Engel and D. Plantenga (eds), *Liber Amicorum Els Postel*. Leiden: Faculty of Cultural Anthropology and Research Centre for Women and Autonomy of the University of Leiden, pp. 35–60.

—— (1992) 'Joint Brokerage of Spouses on Islamic Ambon'. In S. van Bemmelen, M. Djajadiningrat-Nieuwenhuis, E. Locher-Scholten and E. Touwen-Bouwsma (eds), *Women as Mediators in Indonesia*. Leiden: KITLV Press, pp. 13–32.

—— (1996) 'The Practice of Care: Social Security in Moslem Ambonese Society'. In D. Mearns and C. Healy (eds), *Remaking Maluku: Social Transformation in Eastern Indonesia*. Darwin: Centre for Southeast Asian Studies, NT University. Special Monograph No. 1 pp. 121–139.

Bender, D.R. (1967) 'A Refinement of the Concept of Household, Families, Co-residence and de jure Households in Onde'. *American Anthropologist* 73, pp. 223–241.

Beneria, Lourdes (1979) 'Reproduction, Production and the Sexual Division of Labor'. *Cambridge Journal of Economics* 3 (3), pp. 203–225.

—— and Martha Roldan (1987) *The Crossroads of Class and Gender*. Chicago: University of Chicago Press.

Berg, A. van den (1997) *Land Right – Marriage Left: Women's Management of Insecurity in North Cameroon*. Leiden: CNWS Publications.

Bhavnani, Kum-Kum (1988) 'Empowerment and Social Research: Some Comments'. *Text* 1 (2), pp. 41–50.

Blackwood, Evelyn (1993) 'The Politics of Daily Life: Gender, Kinship and Identity in a Minangkabau Village, West Sumatra, Indonesia'. PhD thesis, Stanford University.

—— (1995) 'Senior Women, Model Mothers and Dutiful Wives: Managing Gender Contradictions in a Minangkabau Village'. In Aihwa Ong and Michael Peletz (eds), *Bewitching Women, Pious Men: Gender and Body Politics in Southeast Asia*. Berkeley: University of California Press.

Bledsdoe, C. (1993) 'The Politics of Polygyny in Mende Education and Child Fosterage Transactions'. In B. Miller (ed.), *Sex and Gender Hierarchies*. Cambridge: Cambridge University Press.

Blumberg, Rae Lesser (1984) 'A General Theory of Gender Stratification'. In Randall Collins (ed.), *Sociological Theory*. San Francisco: Jossey-Bass, pp. 83–101.

—— (ed.) (1991) *Gender, Family and Economy: The Triple Overlap*. London: Sage Publications.

—— (1991) 'Introduction, the 'Triple Overlap' of Gender Stratification, Economy, and the Family'. In R.L. Blumberg (ed.), *Gender, Family, and Economy. The Triple Overlap*. London/New Delhi: Sage, pp. 7–32.

Boeke, J.H. (1926) 'Inlandsche budgetten' [Budgets of the Natives], *Koloniale Studiën* no volume number, pp. 229–334.

Boomgaard, Peter (1981) 'Female Labour and Population Growth in Nineteenth-Century Java'. *Review of Indonesian and Malaysian Affairs* 15 (2), pp. 1–31.

Boserup, E. (1970) *Women's Role in Economic Development*. London: Earthscan.

Bourdieu, Pierre (1977) *Outline of a Theory of Practice*. Trans. Richard Nice. Cambridge: Cambridge University Press.

BIBLIOGRAPHY

Bowen, E. (1954) *Return to Laughter.* New York: Harper & Bros.

Bradley, Harriet (1989) *Men's Work, Women's Work.* London: Polity Press.

Branson, Jan and Don Miller (1988) 'The Changing Fortunes of Balinese Market Women'. In G. Chandler, N. Sullivan and J. Branson (eds), *Development and Displacement: Women in Southeast Asia.* Monash: Monash University Press.

Brass, Tom (1991) 'Moral Economists, Subalterns, New Social Movements, and the (Re)emergence of a (Post-)modernized (Middle) Peasant'. *Journal of Peasant Studies* 18, pp. 173–205.

Brenner, Suzanne (1995) 'Why Women Rule the Roost: Rethinking Javanese Ideologies of Gender and Self-control'. In Aihwa Ong and Michael Peletz (eds), *Bewitching Women, Pious Men: Gender and Body Politics in Southeast Asia.* Berkeley: University of California Press, pp. 19–50.

Brouwer, A. (1990) 'Science, Social Security and Sago'. Unpublished research thesis, Agricultural University Wageningen.

—— (1996) 'Sustainability and Social Security in Central Moluccan Resource Management'. In D. Mearns and C. Healy (eds), *Remaking Maluku: Social Transformation in Eastern Indonesia.* Darwin: Centre for Southeast Asian Studies, NT University. Special Monograph No. 1, pp. 64–79.

—— (1998) 'From Abundance to Scarcity: Sago, Crippled Modernization and Curtailed Coping'. In S. Pannell and F. von Benda-Beckmann (eds), *Old World Places, New World Problems: Exploring Resource Management Issues in Eastern Indonesia.* Canberra: The Australian National University, Centre for Resource and Environmental Studies, pp. 336–387.

Bruce, J. and D. Dwyer (1988) 'Introduction'. In D. Dwyer and J. Bruce (eds), *A Home Divided: Women and Income in the Third World.* Stanford: Stanford University Press, pp. 1–19.

Brugmans, I.J. (1938) *Geschiedenis van het onderwijs in Nederlandsch-Indië* [Educational history in the Netherlands Indies]. Groningen/Batavia: Wolters.

Bruner, Edward M. (1961) 'Urbanization and Ethnic Identity in North Sumatra'. *American Anthropologist* 63, pp. 508–521.

Burger, D.H. (1975) *Sociologisch-Economische Geschiedenis van Indonesie* [Socio-economic history of Indonesia]. Amsterdam: Koninklijk Instituut voor de Tropen.

Burton, R. and N.M. Ward (1827) 'Report of a Journey into the Batak Country, in the Interior of Sumatra, in the Year 1824'. *Transactions of the Royal Asiatic Society of Great Britain and Ireland* 1, pp. 485–513.

Bush, R., L. Cliffe and V. Jansen (1986) 'The Crisis in the Reproduction of Migrant Labour in Southern Africa'. In P. Lawrence (ed.), *World Recession and the Food Crisis in Africa.* London: James Currey, pp. 283–299.

Butler, Judith (1994) 'Bodies that Matter'. In Carolyn Burke, Naomi Schor, Margaret Whitford (eds), *Engaging with Irigaray.* New York: Columbia University Press.

Carney, Judith and Michael Watts (1991) 'Disciplining Women? Rice, Modernization, and the Evolution of Mandinka Gender Relations in Senegambia'. *Signs* 16 (4), pp. 651–681.

Castles, Lance (1967) *Religion, Politics, and Economic Behaviour: The Kudus Cigarette Industry.* New Haven: Yale University Press.

Chatterjee, Partha (1993) *The Nation and Its Fragments: Colonial and Post-colonial Histories.* Princeton: Princeton University Press.

Cheater, Angela (1991) *Social Anthropology.* London: Routledge

Chow, Rey (1991) *Women and Chinese Modernity: The Politics of Reading between East and West.* Minneapolis: University of Minnesota Press.

'Christen Inlanders' (1917), *Encyclopaedie van Nederlandsch-Indië* [Christian natives, Encyclopaedia of the Dutch East Indies], The Hague/Leiden: Nijhoff/Brill, vol. I.

Clifford, J. and G. Marcus (eds) (1986) *Writing Culture: The Poetics and Politics of Ethnography.* Los Angeles: UCLA Press.

Clignet, R. (1970) *Many Wives, Many Powers.* Evanston, USA: North Western University Press.

—— (1971) 'Determinants of African Polygyny'. In J. Goody (ed.), *Kinship; Selected Readings.* Harmondsworth, UK: Penguin.

Cohen, M.L. (1976) *House United, House Divided: The Chinese Family in Taiwan.* New York: Columbia University Press.

Coleman, R. (1991) 'The Division of Household Labour: Suggestion for Future Empirical Consideration and Theoretical Development'. In R.L. Blumberg (ed.), *Gender, Family and Economy: The Triple Overlap.* London: Sage Publications, pp. 251–264.

Collier, Jane F. and Sylvia J. Yanagisako (eds), (1981) *Gender and Kinship: Essays toward a Unified Analysis.* Stanford: Stanford University Press.

Comaroff, John (1987) '*Sui Genderis*: Feminism, Kinship Theory, and Structural Domains'. In Jane F. Collier and Sylvia J. Yanagisako (eds), *Gender and Kinship: Essays toward a Unified Analysis.* Stanford: Stanford University Press, pp. 53–85.

Connor, L. (1995) 'Dying by Fire and Kris: Speaking to Women in the Realm of Death'. Paper presented at the Third International Bali Studies Workshop, University of Sydney, 3–7 July.

Cooley, F.L. (1962) *Ambonese Adat: A General Description.* New Haven: New York University.

Cooley, Laura (1992) 'Maintaining Rukun for Javanese Households and for the State'. In S. van Bemmelen *et al.* (eds), *Women and Mediation in Indonesia.* Leiden: KITLV Press.

Corner, Lorraine (1989) 'East and West Nusa Tenggara. Isolation and Poverty'. In Hall Hill (ed.), *Unity in Diversity. Regional Economic Development in Indonesia since 1970.* Singapore/Oxford/New York: Oxford University Press, pp. 179–206.

Covarrubias, M. [1973] (1989) *The Island of Bali.* Singapore: Oxford University Press.

Creese, H. (1995) 'Images of Women in Kakawin Literature'. Unpublished paper, Canberra: Australian National University.

Cunningham, C.E. (1958) *The Postwar Migration of the Toba-Bataks to East Sumatra*. Southeast Asia Studies 5. New Haven: Yale University.

Daftar Isian Potensi Desa dan Kelurahan Tahun 1989/90, *Desa Nggela*

Danu Rudiono (1992) 'Kebijaksanaan Perburuhan Pasca Boom Minyak' [Labour policy in the post-oil-boom period]. *Prisma* 1, pp. 61–80.

Davis, Carol (1995) 'Female Cooperative Networks in Minangkabau Life-cycle Rituals'. Paper presented to conference on Indonesian Women in the Household and Beyond. Leiden.

Dawson, Gaynor (1995) 'Women, Men and Merantau: Shifting Gender Relations in Transmigrant Households'. Paper presented at conference on Indonesian Women in the Household and Beyond. Leiden.

Deere, Carmen Diana (1995) 'What Difference Does Gender Make? Rethinking Peasant Studies'. *Feminist Economics* 1 (1), pp. 53–72.

De Kat Angelino, A.D.A. (1930) *Staatkundig Beleid en Bestuurzorg in Nederlandsch Indie* [State policy and administration in the Netherlands Indies]. 's-Gravenhage: Martinus Nijhoff.

De Oliveira, M. (1992) 'Family Change and Family Process: Implications for Research in Developing Countries'. In E. Barch and P. Xenon (eds), *Family Systems and Cultural Change*. Oxford: Oxford University Press, pp. 201–214.

Dick, Howard and Dean Forbes (1992) 'Transport and Communications: a Quiet Revolution'. In Anne Booth (ed.), *The Oil Boom and After: Indonesian Economic Policy and Performance in the Soeharto Era*. Singapore: Oxford University Press, pp. 258–282.

Di Leonardo, M. (ed.) (1991) *Gender at the Crossroads of Knowledge. Feminist Anthropology in the Postmodern Era*. Berkeley and Los Angeles: University of California Press.

Djajadiningrat-Nieuwenhuis, Madelon (1992) 'Ibuism and *Priyayi*zation: Path to Power?'. In: E. Locher-Scholten and A. Niehof (eds), *Indonesian Women in Focus. Past and Present Notions*. Leiden: KITLV Press, pp 43–51.

Donzelot, Jacques (1977) *The Policing of Families: Welfare versus the State*. London: Hutchinson & Co.

Dorjahn, V. (1959) 'The Factor of Polygamy in African Demography'. In M. Herskovits and W. Bascom (eds), *Continuity and Change in African Cultures*. Chicago: University of Chicago Press.

Dt. Rajo Penghulu, Idrus Hakimy [1978] (1986a) *Rangkaian Mustika Adat Basandi Syarak di Minangkabau* [A collection of precious *adat* based on Islamic law in Minangkabau]. Bandung: Remadja Karya.

—— [1978] (1986b) *Pegangan Penghulu, Bundo Kanduang, dan Pidato Alua Pasambahan Adat di Minangkabau* [Guidelines for the lineage head, senior woman, and ritual speech in Minangkabau]. Bandung: Remadja Karya.

Duff-Cooper, A. (1985) 'Notes on Some Balinese Ideas and Practices Connected with Sex from Western Lombok'. *Anthropos* 80 (4–6), pp. 403–419.

Dwyer, Daisy and Judith Bruce (1988) *A Home Divided: Women and Income in the Third World*. Stanford: Stanford University Press.

Effendi, T. and Chris Manning (1994) 'Rural Development and Nonfarm Employment in Java'. In Bruce Koppel, John Hawkins and William James (eds), *Development or Deterioration? Work in Rural Asia*. Boulder and London: Lynne Rienner, pp. 211–247.

Ellis, F. (1988) *Peasant Economics: Farm Households and Agrarian Development*. Cambridge: Cambridge University Press.

Elmhirst, Rebecca (1996) 'Transmigration and Local Communities in North Lampung: Exploring Identity Politics and Resource Control in Indonesia'. Paper presented to the Association of Southeast Asian Studies UK annual conference on 'Power and Identity in Southeast Asia: Local, National and Regional Dimensions', School of Oriental and African Studies, London, 23–27 April 1996.

—— (1998) 'Daughters and Displacement: Migration Dynamics in an Indonesian Transmigration Area'. Paper presented at a workshop on 'Migration and Sustainable Livelihoods', at the University of Sussex Poverty Research Unit, 5–6 June 1998.

Elson, D. and R. Pearson (1981) 'The Subordination of Women and the Internationalisation of Factory Production'. In K. Young *et al.* (eds), *Of Marriage and the Market*. London: CSE Books, pp.144–166.

Elwert, G. (1980) 'Überleben in Krisen, kapitalistische Entwicklung und traditionelle Solidarität' [Surviving under Crisis Conditions, Capitalist Development and Traditional Solidarity]. *Zeitschrift für Soziologie* 9, pp. 343–365.

Emmerson, Donald (1976) *Indonesia's Elite: Political Culture and Cultural Politics*. Ithaca: Cornell University Press.

End, Th. van den (1991) *De Nederlandse Zendingsvereniging in West-Java 1858–1963. Een bronnenpublicatie* [The Dutch Missionary Society in West Java 1858–1963], Alphen aan de Rijn: Aska.

Errington, Shelly (1990) 'Introduction'. In J. Atkinson and S. Errington (eds.), *Power and Difference: Gender in Southeast Asian Societies*. Stanford: Stanford University Press. pp. 1–36.

—— (1990) 'Recasting Sex, Gender, and Power: A Theoretical and Regional Overview'. In J. Atkinson and S. Errington (eds), *Power and Difference*. Stanford: Stanford University Press.

Evans, A. (1991) 'Gender Issues in Rural Household Economics'. In S. Joekes and N. Kabeer (eds), *Researching the Household: Methodological and Empirical Issues*. IDS Bulletin 22, no. 1, pp. 51–59.

Evers, Hans-Dieter (1991) 'Trade as Off-Farm Employment in Central Java'. *Sojourn* 6, pp. 1–21.

Evers, H.D., W. Clauss and D. Wong (1984) 'Subsistence Reproduction: A Framework for Analysis'. In J. Smith, I. Wallerstein and H.D. Evers (eds), *Households and the World-Economy*. London: Sage, pp. 23–36.

Fapohunda, Eleanor (1988) 'The Nonpooling Household: A Challenge to Theory'. In D. Dwyer and J. Bruce (eds), *A Home Divided: Women and Income in the Third World*. Stanford: Stanford University Press, pp. 143–154.

Fasbender, Karl and Suzanne Erbe (1990) *Towards a New Home: Indonesia's Managed Mass Migration. Transmigration between Poverty, Economics and Ecology.* Hamburg: Verlag Weltarchiv GMBH.

Fernandez-Kelly, Maria-Patricia (1983) 'Mexican Border Industrialization, Female Labour Force Participation, and Migration'. In June Nash and Maria-Patricia Fernandez-Kelly (eds), *Women, Men and the New International Division of Labour.* Albany: SUNY Press, pp. 205–223.

Finch, J. (1989) *Family Obligations and Social Change.* Cambridge: Polity Press.

Findley, S. (1987) *Rural Development and Migration. A Study of Family Choices in the Philippines.* Brown University Studies in Population and Development 5. Boulder: Westview.

Firman, Tommy (1994) 'Labour Allocation, Mobility, and Remittances in Rural Households: a Case from Central Java, Indonesia'. *Sojourn* 9, pp. 81–101.

Florida, Nancy (1996) 'Sex Wars: Writing Gender Relations in Nineteenth-Century Java'. In Laurie J. Sears (ed.), *Fantasizing the Feminine in Indonesia,* Durham and London: Duke University Press, pp. 207–224.

Folbre, Nancy (1986) 'Cleaning House: New Perspectives on Households and Economic Development'. *Journal of Development Economics* 22, pp. 5–40.

—— (1988) 'The Black Four of Hearts: Toward a New Paradigm of Household Economics'. In D. Dwyer and J. Bruce (eds), *A Home Divided: Women and Income in the Third World.* Stanford: Stanford University Press, pp. 248–262.

Fortes, M. (1966) 'Introduction'. In J. Goody (ed.), *The Development Cycle in Domestic Groups.* London: Athlone Press, pp. 1–14.

Foulcher, Keith (1998) 'Culture and Colonialism in the Essays of Armijn Pane, 1933–1953'. In A. Liem and H. Poeze (eds), *Lasting Fascinations: Essays on Indonesia and the Southwest Pacific to Honour Bob Hering.* Edisi Sastra Kabar Seberang Sulating Maphilindo 28/29, Stein, pp. 131–152.

Fraassen, Chr. F. van (1972) *Ambon-Rapport* [Ambon Report]. Leiden: Stichting WSO.

Francis, E. (1995) 'Migration and Changing Divisions of Labour: Gender Relations and Economic Change in Koguta, Western Kenya'. *Africa* 65 (2), pp. 197–215.

Freiberg-Strauss, J. and D. Jung (1988) 'Social Security in a Peasant Society: The Case of Boyocá, Columbia'. In F. von Benda-Beckmann, K. von Benda-Beckmann, E. Casiño, F. Hirtz, G.R. Woodman and H. Zacher (eds), *Between Kinship and the State: Law and Social Security in Developing Countries.* Dordrecht-Holland/Cinnaminson-USA: Foris Publications, pp. 229–267.

Friederich, R. (1959) *The Culture and Civilization of Bali.* Calcutta: Susil Gupta (India).

Friedman, K. (1984) 'Households as Income-pooling Units'. In J. Smith *et al.* (eds), *Households and the World Economy.* Beverly Hills: Sage, pp. 37–55.

Gardner, K. (1995) *Global Migrants, Local Lives: Travel and Transformation in Rural Bangladesh.* Oxford: Clarendon Press.

Geertz, Clifford (1960) *The Religion of Java.* New York: The Free Press of Glencoe (also London and Chicago: University of Chicago Press).

Geertz, Hildred (1961) *The Javanese Family. A Study of Kinship and Socialization*, New York: Free Press of Glencoe.

—— and C. Geertz (1975) *Kinship in Bali.* Chicago: University of Chicago Press.

Geirnaert-Martin, Danielle (1992) *The Woven Land of Laboya. Socio-Cosmic Ideas and Values in West Sumba, Eastern Indonesia.* Leiden: Centre of Non-Western Studies, Leiden University.

Giddens, Anthony (1984) *The Constitution of Society: Outline of the Theory of Structuration.* London: Polity Press.

—— (1987) *Social Theory and Modern Sociology.* Cambridge: Polity Press.

Godelier, Maurice (1995) 'L'énigme du don, I. Le legs de Mauss'. *Social Anthropology* 3, pp. 15–47.

Goode, W. (1963) *World Revolution and Family Patterns.* New York: Free Press.

Goody, Jack (1972) *Production and Reproduction: A Comparative Study of the Domestic Domain.* Cambridge: Cambridge University Press.

—— (1973) 'Polygyny, Economy and the Role of Women'. In J. Goody (ed.), *The Character of Kinship.* Cambridge: Cambridge University Press.

Gordon, Linda (1990) 'The New Feminist Scholarship on the Welfare State'. In Linda Gordon (ed.), *Women, the State and Welfare.* Madison: The University of Wisconsin Press, pp. 9–35.

Gouda, Frances (1995) 'Teaching Indonesian Girls in Java and Bali, 1900–1942: Dutch Progressives, the Infatuation with "Oriental" Refinement and "Western" Ideas about Proper Womanhood', *Women's History Review*, vol. 4, pp. 25–62.

—— (1995) *Dutch Culture Overseas. Colonial Practice in the Netherlands Indies 1900–1942*, Amsterdam: Amsterdam University Press.

—— (1998) 'Good Mothers, Medeas, or Jezebels: Feminine Imagery in Colonial and Anticolonial Rhetoric in the Dutch East Indies, 1900–1942'. In Julia Clancy-Smith and Frances Gouda (eds), *Domesticating the Empire: Race, Gender and Family Life in French and Dutch Colonialism.* Charlottesville: University Press of Virginia, pp. 236–254.

Grijns, Mies (1987). 'Tea-Pickers in West Java as Mothers and Workers'. In E. Locher-Scholten and A. Niehof (eds), *Indonesian Women in Focus.* Dordrecht: Foris Publication, pp. 104–119.

——, Ines Smyth, Anita Van Velzen, S. Machfud and Pujiwati Sajogyo (eds) (1994) *Different Women, Different Work: Gender and Industrialization in Indonesia.* Aldershot: Avebury.

Guest, Philip (1989) *Labor Allocation and Rural Development: Migration in Four Javanese Villages.* Boulder, Col.: Westview Press.

Guinness, Patrick (1994) 'Local Society and Culture'. In Hal Hill (ed.), *Indonesia's New Order: the Dynamics of Socio-Economic Transformation.* Sydney: Allen & Unwin, pp. 267–304.

Guyer, J. (1981) 'Household and Community in African Studies'. *African Studies Review* 24 (2/3), pp. 87–138.

—— (1988) 'Dynamic Approaches to Domestic Budgeting: Cases and Methods from Africa'. In D. Dwyer and J. Bruce (eds), *A Home Divided: Women and Income in the Third World*. Stanford: Stanford University Press, pp. 155–172.

—— and P. Peters (eds) (1987) 'Conceptualizing the Household: Issues of Theory and Policy in Africa'. *Development and Change* 18 (2), pp. 197–213.

Hall, Catherine (1979) 'The Early Formation of Victorian Domestic Ideology'. In Sandra Burman (ed.), *Fit Work for Women*. London: Croom Helm.

Hamidah (1935) *Kehilangan Mestika* [Lost jewels]. Jakarta: Balai Pustaka.

Hamilton, Roy W. (1994a) 'Behind the Cloth. The History and Culture of Flores'. In Roy W. Hamilton (ed.), *Gift of the Cotton Maiden. Textiles of Flores and the Solor Islands*. Los Angeles: UCLA Fowler Museum of Cultural History, pp. 20–38.

—— (1994b) 'Ende Regency'. In Roy W. Hamilton (ed.), *Gift of the Cotton Maiden. Textiles of Flores and the Solor Islands*. Los Angeles: UCLA Fowler Museum of Cultural History, pp. 123–147.

Hardjono, Joan (1977) *Transmigration in Indonesia*. Kuala Lumpur: Oxford University Press.

—— (1993) 'From Farm to Factory: Transition in Rural Employment in Majalaya Sub-district, West Java'. In Chris Manning and Joan Hardjono (eds), *Indonesia Assessment 1993. Labour: Sharing the Benefits of Growth?* Research School of Pacific Studies monograph no. 20. Canberra: Australian National University, pp. 273–289.

Harris, Olivia (1981) 'Households as Natural Units'. In K. Young *et al.* (eds), *Of Marriage and the Market*. London: CSE Books, pp. 49–68.

Harriss, John (1994) 'Between Economism and Post-modernism: Reflections on Research in "Agrarian Change" in India'. In David Booth (ed.), *Rethinking Social Development: Theory, Research and Practice*. Harlow: Longman, pp. 172–196.

Hart H.M.J. (1936) 'De daling van de kosten van levensonderhoud van ambtenaarsgezinnen te Batavia' [The decline of the costs of living of families of civil servants in Batavia]. *Koloniale Studiën* 3: 43–80.

Hart, Gillian (1978) 'Labor Allocation Strategies in Rural Javanese Households'. Unpublished PhD thesis, Cornell University.

—— (1986) *Power, Labor and Livelihood: Processes of Change in Rural Java*. Berkeley: University of California Press.

—— (1989) 'Agrarian Change in the Context of State Patronage'. In G. Hart, A. Turton and B. White (eds), *Agrarian Transformations: Local Processes and the State in Southeast Asia*. Berkeley: University of California Press, pp. 31–49.

—— (1991) 'Engendering Everyday Resistance: Gender Patronage and Production Politics in Rural Malaysia'. *Journal of Peasant Studies* 19 (1), pp. 93–121.

—— (1992) 'Imagined Unities: Constructions of "The Household" in Economic Theory'. In S. Ortiz (ed.), *Understanding Economic Process*. Lanham, Md: University Press of America.

——, Andrew Turton and Benjamin White (eds) [1989] (1992) *Agrarian Transformations: Local Processes and the State in Southeast Asia*. Berkeley: University of California Press.

Hartmann, Heidi (1979) 'Capitalism, Patriarchy and Job Segregation by Sex'. *Signs* 1 (3), pp. 137–168.

—— (1981) 'The Family as the Locus of Gender, Class and Political Struggle: The Example of Housework'. *Signs* 6 (3), pp. 366–394. (Also in S. Harding (ed.), *Feminism and Methodology*. Bloomington: Indiana University Press and Milton Keynes, Open University Press.)

Haryono Suyono (1993) 'Keluarga Berencana sebagai Gerakan Pembangunan Keluarga Sejahtera' [Family planning as the movement to build a prosperous family]. Badan Koordinasi Keluarga Berencana Nasional, Jakarta.

—— (1994a) 'Membangun Keluarga Sejahtera Sebagai Wahana Pengamalan Pancasila'. [Building a prosperous family as the vehicle to implement the state ideology] Kantor Meneteri Negara Kependudukan, Badan Koordinasi Keluarga Berencana Nasional, Jakarta.

—— (1994b) 'Pembangunan Keluarga Sejahtera di Indonesia Bedasarkan UU NO 10 Tahun 1992 dan GBHN 1993' [Building a prosperous family in Indonesia according to Law No. 10 of 1992 and the broad outlines of the Nation's Direction of 1993]. Kantor Meneteri Negara Kependudukan, Badan Koordinasi Keluarga Berencana Nasional, Jakarta.

Heeren, H.H. (1967) *Transmigratie in Indonesië, Interne migratie en de verhouding van immigranten/autochtonen speciaal met betrekking tot Zuid- en Midden-Sumatra* [Transmigration in Indonesia. Internal migration and the relationship of immigrants/autochtonous population, especially with regard to South and Central Sumatra], Meppel: Boom.

Hefner, Robert (1990) *The Political Economy of Mountain Java: an Interpretive History*. Berkeley: University of California Press.

Heng, Geraldine and Janadas Devan (1992). 'State Fatherhood: The Politics of Nationalism, Sexuality and Race in Singapore'. In Andrew Parker *et al.* (eds), *Nationalisms and Sexualities*. London: Routledge.

Hetler, Carol (1984) 'Female-Headed Households in Indonesia'. Paper presented at the IUSSP Seminar on Micro-Approaches to Demographic Research, Australian National University, Canberra.

—— (1986) 'Female-headed Households in a Circular Migration Village in Central Java, Indonesia'. PhD thesis, Australian National University

—— (1990) 'Survival Strategies, Migration and Household Headship'. In Leela Dube and Rajni Palriwala (eds), *Structures and Strategies; Women, Work and Family*. New Delhi: Sage, pp. 175–199.

Hiatt, L. (1980) 'Polyandry in Sri Lanka; A Test Case for Parental Investment Theory'. *Man (N.S.)* 15, pp. 583–602.

Hill, Hal (1992) 'Regional Development in a Boom and Bust Petroleum Economy: Indonesia since 1970'. *Economic Development and Cultural Change* 40, pp. 351–379.

Hilman Hadikusuma (1989) *Masyarakat dan Adat-budaya Lampung* [Society and Lampungese custom]. Bandung: Mandar Maju.

Hoëvell, G.W.W.C. Baron van (1875) *Ambon en Meer Bepaaldelijk de Oeliassers* [Ambon and, more particularly, the people from the Lease Islands]. Dordrecht: Van Blussee en Van Braam.

Holleman, F.D. (1923) *Het Adat-grondenrecht van Ambon en de Oeliassers* [Adat land law of Ambon and the Lease Islands]. Delft: Molukken Instituut.

Holzner, Brigitte M. (1995) 'Homeworking and Intra-household Relations. A Case Study from East Java'. Paper presented at the Third WIVS Conference on Indonesian Women's Studies: 'Indonesian Women in the Household and Beyond. Reconstructing the Boundaries'. Leiden, 25–29 September.

Hong Le Koan (1928a) 'Persatuan jang diharap' [The hoped-for organization]. *Panorama*, 7 January.

—— (1928 b) 'Puteri Salome' [Princess Salome]. *Panorama*, May–July issues.

Hospes, O. (1996) *People that Count: Changing Savings and Credit Practices in Ambon, Indonesia*. Amsterdam: Thesis Publishers.

Howell, Signe (1995) 'The Lio House. Building, Category, Idea, Value'. In Janet Carsten and Stephen Hugh-Jones (eds), *About the House. Lévi-Strauss and Beyond*. Cambridge: Cambridge University Press, pp. 149–169.

Hsiung, Ping-Chun (1996) 'Between Bosses and Workers: The Dilemmas of a Keen Observer and a Vocal Feminist'. In D.L. Wolf (ed.), *Feminist Dilemmas in Fieldwork*. Boulder Col.: Westview Press.

Hugo, Graeme (1982) 'Circular Migration in Indonesia'. *Population and Development Review* 8, pp. 59–83.

——, Terence Hull and Valerie Hull (1987) *The Demographic Dimension in Indonesian Development*. Singapore: Oxford University Press.

Huizenga, L.H. (1958) *Het koeliebudgetonderzoek op Java in 1939–40* [The Coolie Budget Research on Java in 1939–40], Wageningen: Vada.

Hull, Terence (1975) 'Each Child Brings its Own Fortune'. Unpublished PhD dissertation, Australian National University.

Hull, Valerie (1975) 'Fertility, Socioeconomic Status and the Position of Women in a Javanese Village'. PhD dissertation, Australian National University.

—— (1986) 'Women in Java's Rural Middle Class: Progress or Regress?'. In V. Hull (ed.), *Women of Southeast Asia*. University of Illinois: Southeast Asian Studies Monograph Series no. 17.

Humphries, Jane (1977) 'Class Struggle and the Persistence of the Working Class Family'. *Cambridge Journal of Economics* 1 (3), pp. 241–258.

Hüsken, F. (1988) *Een Dorp op Java. Sociale Differentiatie in een Boerengemeenschap, 1850–1980* [A village in Java. Social differentiation in a rural community, 1850–1980]. Overveen: ACASEA.

Hutagalung, N., Mies Grijns and Ben White (1994) 'Women as Wage Workers'. In Mies Grijns, Ines Smyth, Annette Van Velzen, S. Machfud and Pujiwati Sajogyo (eds), *Different Women, Different Work: Gender and Industrialization in Indonesia*. Aldershot: Avebury, pp. 147–172.

Ilcan, Suzan (1996) 'Fragmentary Encounters in a Moral World: Household Power Relations and Gender Politics'. *Ethnology* 35, pp. 33–49.

Jaggar, Alice (1983) *Feminist Politics and Human Nature*. New Jersey: Rowman & Allanheld.

Janssens, A. (1991) 'Family and Social Change. The Household as Process in an Industrializing Context, Tilburg 1840–1920'. PhD thesis, Catholic University of Nijmegen.

Jassin, H.B. (1987) *Pujangga Baru: Prosa dan Puisi* [The Pujangga Baru in prose and poetry]. Jakarta: Haji Masagung.

Jay, Robert (1969) *Javanese Villagers. Social Relations in Rural Modjokuto*. Cambridge, Mass.: MIT Press.

Jayawardena, C. (1977) 'Women and Kinship in Acheh Besar, Northern Sumatra'. *Ethnology* 16 (1), pp. 21–38.

Jennaway, M. (1996) 'Sweet Breath and Bitter Honey; HIV/AIDS and the Embodiment of Desire among North Balinese Women'. PhD Thesis, University of Queensland, Brisbane.

Jensen, G. and Luh Ketut Suryani (1992) *The Balinese People: A Reinvestigation of Character*. Singapore: Oxford University Press.

Jong, Willemijn de (1994) 'Cloth Production and Change in a Lio Village'. In Roy W. Hamilton (ed.), *Gift of the Cotton Maiden: Textiles of Flores and the Solor Islands*. Los Angeles: UCLA Fowler Museum of Cultural History, pp. 210–227.

—— (1995) 'Cloth as Marriage Gifts. Change in Exchange among the Lio of Flores'. In *Contact, Crossover, Continuity: Proceedings of the Fourth Biennial Symposium of the Textile Society of America, Los Angeles, California, 1994*. Los Angeles: Textile Society of America, Inc., pp. 169–180.

—— (1996) 'Gleichgewichtige Formen des Zusammenlebens in fremden Kulturen'. *Szondiana* 1/96, pp. 21–40.

——(1998a), *Geschlechtersymmetrie in einer Brautpreisgesellschaft. Die Stoffproduzentinnen der Lio in Indonesien*. Berlin: Reimer.

—— (1998b) 'Rang, Reichtum und Geschlecht. Hierarchische und komplementäre soziale Differenzen auf Flores'. In Brigitta Hauser-Schäublin and Birgitt Röttger-Rössler (eds), *Differenz und Geschlecht*. Berlin: Reimer, pp. 260–276.

—— (1998c) 'Vom Brautpreis zur Mitgift? Heiratstransaktionen in Ostindonesien'. *Asiatische Studien* LII.2, pp. 445–471.

Josselin de Jong, J. P. B. de (1935) 'The Malay Archipelago as a Field of Ethnological Study'. In P. E. de Josselin de Jong (ed.), *Structural Anthropology in the Netherlands. A Reader*. The Hague: Nijhoff, pp. 166–182.

Kabeer, Naila (1991) 'Gender, Production and Well-being: Rethinking the Household Economy'. Discussion paper no. 288. Brighton: Institute of Development Studies, University of Sussex.

—— (1994) *Reversed Realities: Gender Hierarchies in Development Thought*. London: Verso Press.

BIBLIOGRAPHY

Kameo, Daniel D. (1996) 'Social Economic Problems in Agricultural Development in East Nusa Tenggara and East Timor'. *Ekonomi dan Keuangan Indonesia* XLIV, pp. 33–53.

Kano, Hiroyoshi (1977) *Land Tenure System and the Desa Community in Nineteenth Century Java*. Tokyo: Japan. Occasional Paper Series no. 5. Institute of Developing Economies.

Karim, Wazir Jahan (1995) 'Introduction: Genderizing Anthropology in Southeast Asia'. In Wazir Jahan Karim (ed.), *'Male' and 'Female' in Developing Southeast Asia*. Oxford: Berg Publishers, pp. 11–34.

Kato, Tsuyoshi (1982) *Matriliny and Migration: Evolving Minangkabau Traditions in Indonesia*. Ithaca and London: Cornell University Press.

―― (1989) 'Different Fields, Similar Locusts: *Adat* Communities and the Village Law of 1979 in Indonesia'. *Indonesia* 47, pp. 89–114.

Kecematan Wolowaru Dalam Angka 1990. Kantor Statistik Kabupaten Ende. [Sub-district Woluwaru in Numbers 1990. Statistics Office of the Ende District].

Keeler, Ward (1990) 'Speaking of Gender in Java'. In Shelly Errington and Jane Atkinson (eds), *Power and Difference: Essays on Gender in Southeast Asia*. Stanford: Stanford University Press, pp. 73–90.

Keesing, Roger M. (1976) *Cultural Anthropology, A Contemporary Perspective*. New York: Holt, Rinehart & Winston.

Kemp, J. (1988) *Seductive Mirage. The Search for the Village Community in Southeast Asia*. Comparative Asian Studies/3, Centre for Asian Studies Amsterdam. Dordrecht: Foris Publications.

Kipp, Rita (1998) 'Emancipating Each Other: Dutch Colonial Missionaries' Encounter with Karo Women in Sumatra, 1900–1942'. In Julia Clancy-Smith and Frances Gouda (eds), *Domesticating the Empire: Race, Gender and Family Life in French and Dutch Colonialism*. Charlottesville: University Press of Virginia, pp. 211–235.

Kloek E. (1981) *Gezinshistorici over Vrouwen; een Overzicht van het Werk van Gezinshistorici en de Betekenis daarvan voor de Vrouwengeschiedenis* [Family historians on women: an overview of the work of family historians and its significance for the history of women]. ASVA/SUA scriptie reeks no. 4. Amsterdam: Sua.

Knaap, G. (1987) *Kruidnagelen en Christenen: De Verenigde Oost-Indische Compagnie en de Bevolking van Ambon 1656-1696* [Cloves and Christians: the Dutch East Indies Company and the population of Ambon, 1656–1996]. Dordrecht: Foris.

Koentjaraningrat, R.M.1960) 'The Javanese of South Central Java'. In G. Murdock (ed.), *Social Structures in Southeast Asia*. Chicago: Quadrangle.

―― (1967) 'A Survey of Social Studies of Rural Indonesia'. In Koentjaraningrat (ed.), *Villages in Indonesia*. Ithaca: Cornell University Press, pp. 1–29.

―― (1971) 'Kebudayaan Flores' [The culture of Flores]. In R.M. Koentjaraningrat (ed.), *Manusia dan Kebudayaan di Indonesia* [The people and cultures of Indonesia]. Jakarta: Djambatan, pp. 183–197.

―― (1985) *Javanese Culture*. Singapore and Oxford: Oxford University Press.

Koning, J. (1996) 'Family Planning Acceptance in a Rural Central Javanese Village'. In P Boomgaard, R. Sciortino and I. Smyth (eds), *Health Care in Java. Past and Present*. Leiden: KITLV Press, pp. 147–169.

—— (1997) 'Generations of Change. A Javanese Village in the 1990s'. PhD thesis, University of Amsterdam.

Koppel, Bruce, and John Hawkins (1994) 'Rural Transformation and the Future of Work in Rural Asia'. In Bruce Koppel, John Hawkins and William James (eds.), *Development or Deterioration? Work in Rural Asia*. London and Boulder: Lynne Rienner, pp. 1–46.

Kopytoff, I. (1986) 'The Cultural Biography of Things: Commoditization as Process'. In A. Appadurai (ed.), *The Social Life of Things*. Cambridge: Cambridge University Press, pp. 64–91.

Korn, V. (1941) 'De Vrouwelijke Mama' in de Minangkabause Familie'. [The female uncle in the Minangkabau family] *BKI* 100, pp. 301–338.

Kraan, A. van der (1985) 'Human Sacrifice in Bali: Sources, Notes and Commentary'. *Indonesia* 40, pp. 89–121.

Krause-Katerla, H.J. (1986) 'Die Gewürznelkenproduktion auf den Molukken: soziale Auswirkungen langfristiger Weltmarktintegration'. Bielefeld, unpublished dissertation.

Krishnaraj, M. and K. Chanana (eds) (1989) *Gender and the Household Domain; Social and Cultural Dimensions*. New Delhi: Sage.

Krulfeld, R. (1986) 'Sasak Attitudes towards Polygyny and the Changing Position of Women in Sasak Peasant Villages'. In L. Dube, E. Leacock and S. Ardener (eds), *Visibility and Power*. Oxford: Oxford University Press.

Kung, L. (1983) *Factory Women in Taiwan*. Ann Arbor: University of Michigan Press.

Lamphere, Louise (1974) 'Strategies, Cooperation, and Conflict among Women in Domestic Groups'. In M.Z. Rosaldo and Louise Lamphere (eds), *Women, Culture and Society*. Stanford: Stanford University Press, pp. 97–112.

Laslett, P. (1972) 'Introduction: The History of the Family'. In P. Laslett and R. Wall (eds), *Household and Family in Past Time*. Cambridge: Cambridge University Press.

Leach, E. (1971) 'Polyandry, Inheritance and the Definition of Marriage'. In J. Goody (ed.), *Kinship; Selected Readings*. Harmondsworth, UK: Penguin.

—— (1991) 'The Social Anthropology of Marriage and Mating'. In V. Reynolds and J. Kellet (eds), *Mating and Marriage*. Oxford: Oxford University Press.

Lebar, Frank (ed.) (1972) *Ethnic Groups of Insular Southeast Asia. Volume One. Indonesia, Andaman Islands and Madagascar*. New Haven: Human Relations Area Files Press.

Leinbach, Thomas, John Watkins and John Bowen (1992) 'Employment Behaviour and the Family in Indonesian Transmigration'. *Annals of the Association of American Geographers* 82, pp. 23–47.

Lelyveld, J.E.A.M. (1992) '*Waarlijk geen overdaad, doch een dringende eisch*' [Surely no excess but a strong demand]. 'Koloniaal onderwijs en onderwijsbeleid in Nederlands-Indië 1883–1942' [Colonial education and educational policy in the Netherlands Indies 1883–1942]. Unpublished PhD Thesis, University of Utrecht.

Lévi-Strauss, C. (1969) *The Elementary Structures of Kinship*. Trans. J. Bell, J. von Sturmer and R. Needham. Boston: Beacon Press.

Li, Tania (1996) 'Images of Community: Discourse and Strategy in Property Relations'. *Development and Change* 27, pp. 501–527.

Liechty, M. (1995) 'Media, Market, and Modernization, Youth Cultures in Kathmandu'. In V. Amit-Talai and H. Wulff (eds), *Youth Cultures. A Cross-Cultural Perspective*. London: Routledge, pp. 166–201.

Locher-Scholten, Elsbeth (1987) 'Female Labour in Twentieth Century Java: European Notions – Indonesian Practice'. In E. Locher-Scholten and A. Niehof (eds), *Indonesian Women in Focus. Past and Present Notions*. Leiden: KITLV Press, pp. 77–103.

—— (1994) 'Orientalism and the Rhetoric of the Family: Javanese Servants in European Household Manuals and Children's Fiction', *Indonesia*. Cornell University Press, vol. 58, pp. 19–40.

—— (forthcoming in 2000) 'Marriage, Morality and Modernity. The Debate on Monogamy in a Colonial Context'. In E. Locher-Scholten (ed.), *Women and the Colonial State. Essays on Gender and Modernity in the Netherlands Indies 1900-1942*. Amsterdam: Amsterdam University Press.

Long, N. and A. Long (1992) *Battlefields of Knowledge. The Interlocking of Theory and Practice in Social Research and Development*. London and New York: Routledge.

Mackintosh, M. (1989 *Gender, Class and Rural Transition: Agribusiness and the Food Crisis in Senegal*. London: Zed Books.

Maijer, L.Th. (1894) *De Javaan als mensch en als lid van het Javaansche huisgezin* [The Javanese as a human being and as part of the Javanese household]. Batavia and Solo: Albrecht & Rusche.

Manderson, Lenore (ed.) (1983) 'Women's Work and Women's Roles: Everyday Life in Indonesia, Malaysia, and Singapore'. ANU: Development Studies Monograph 32, pp. 1–14.

Marcus, George (1983) 'Introduction: 'Elite' as a Concept, Theory and Research Tradition'. In George Marcus (ed.), *Elites: Ethnographic Issues*. Albuquerque: University of New Mexico Press, pp. 3–27.

Mather, Celia (1982) 'Industrialization in the Tangerang Regency of West Java: Women Workers and the Islamic Patriarchy'. Working Paper no. 17. Centre for Sociology and Anthropology, University of Amsterdam.

—— (1985) 'Rather than Make Trouble, It's Better Just to Leave. Behind the Lack of Industrial Strife in the Tangerang Regency of West Java'. In H. Afshar (ed.), *Women, Work, and Ideology in the Third World*. New York: Tavistock, pp. 153–177.

Mayr, E. (1963) *Animal Species and Evolution*. Massachusetts: Belknap.

McDonald, Peter (1992) 'Convergence or Compromise in Historical Family Change?' In E. Berquo and P. Xenos (eds), *Family Systems and Cultural Change*. Oxford: Clarendon Press, pp. 15–30.

—— (n.d.) 'Issues in the Analysis of Javanese Marriage Patterns'. Mimeo. Department of Demography, Australian National University.

Medick, Hans and David W. Sabean (eds) (1986) *Interest and Emotion: Essays on the Study of Family and Kinship*. Cambridge: Cambridge University Press.

Meillassoux, C. (1981) *Maidens, Meal and Money; Capitalism and the Domestic Community*. Cambridge: Cambridge University Press. [Original title: *Femmes, greniers et capitaux*, 1975.]

Mershon, K. [1937] (1971) *Seven Plus Seven; Mysterious Life-Rituals in Bali*. New York: Vantage Press.

Meyer, Paul (1981) 'The Value of Children in the Context of the Family in Java'. Unpublished PhD dissertation, Australian National University.

Mohanty, C. (1988) 'Under Western Eyes: Feminist Scholarship and Colonial Discourses'. *Feminist Review* 30, pp. 61–88.

Moore, Henrietta (1988) *Feminism and Anthropology*. Cambridge: Polity Press.

—— (1994) *A Passion for Difference. Essays in Anthropology and Gender*. Cambridge: Polity Press.

Morris, Lydia (1990) *The Workings of the Household*. Cambridge: Polity Press.

Mrázek, Rudolf (1994) *Sjahrir. Politics and Exile in Indonesia*, Ithaca, New York: Southeast Asia Program, Cornell University.

Mubyarto (1987) *Politik Pertanian dan Pembangunan Pedesaan* [Agricultural Politics and Rural Development]. Jakarta: Penerbit Sinar Harapan.

Musisi, N. (1991) 'Women, "Elite Polygyny", and Buganda State Formation'. *Signs* 16–4), pp. 757–786.

MWO: *Onderzoek naar de mindere welvaart der Inlandsche bevolking op Java en Madoera* [Research on the lesser welfare of the native population in Java and Madoera]. (1911) *IXd. Adatregelingen in de Inlandsche Kristengemeenten op Java* [Research into the lesser welfare of the native population in Java and Madoera. *Adat* regulations in the native Christian communities in Java], Batavia: Kolff.

—— (1914a) *IX b3. Verheffing van de Inlandsche vrouw* . [Elevation of the native woman]. Batavia: Papyrus.

—— (1914b) *X a. De Volkswelvaart op Java en Madoera. Eindverhandeling van 't onderzoek naar de mindere welvaart der Inlandsche bevolking* [The populiation welfare in Java and Madoera. Final treatise of the research into the lesser welfare of the native population]. Batavia: Ruygrok.

—— (1914c) *XII.* Batavia: Papyrus.

—— (1936) *VIII. Overzicht voor Nederlandsch-Indië* [Survey of the Dutch East Indies], Batavia: Landsdrukkerij.

Naim, Mochtar (1984) *Merantau: Pola Migrasi Suku Minangkabau* ['Merantau': migration patterns of the Minangkabau]. Yogyakarta: Gadjah Mada University Press.

—— (1985) 'Implications of Merantau for Social Organization in Minangkabau'. In L.L. Thomas and F. von Benda-Beckmann (eds), *Change and Continuity in*

BIBLIOGRAPHY

Minangkabau: Local, Regional and Historical Perspectives on West Sumatra. Ohio: Ohio University Monographs in International Studies, Southeast Asia Series, pp. 111–120.

Navis, A.A. (1985) 'Perempuan Dalam Masyarakat Matrilini Minangkabau' [Women in Minangkabau matrilineal society]. Paper Seminar Kebudayaan Minangkabau, Bukittinggi.

Netting, R., R. Wilk and E. Arnould (1984) *Households. Comparative and Historical Studies of the Domestic Group.* Berkeley: University of California Press.

Nicholson, Linda (1990) *Feminism/Postmodernism.* New York: Routledge.

Niehof, A. (1985) 'Women and Fertility in Madura'. PhD thesis, University of Leiden.

—— (1994) 'Het duveltje uit de zwarte doos: de ongemakkelijke relatie tussen gender en huishouden' [The devil from the black box: the uneasy relationship between gender and household]. Inaugural lecture. Agricultural University Wageningen.

—— (1995) 'Who Benefits from Income-Generation? Some Theoretical Considerations and Evidence from West Java'. Paper presented at conference on Indonesian Women in the Household and Beyond. Leiden.

Niessen, Sandy A. (1985) *Motifs of Life in Toba Batak Texts and Textiles.* Dordrecht: Foris Publications.

Ochse, J.J. and G.J.A. Terra (1934) 'Geld en producten huishouding, volksvoeding en gezondheid in Koetowinangoen' [Money and product household, people's nutrition and health in Koetowinangoen]. In *Het onderzoek naar de economischen en landbouwkundigen toestand en het voedselgebruik te Koetowinangoen* [Research in the economic and agricultural situation and food intake in Koetowinangoen]. Departement van Economische Zaken. Buitenzorg: Archipel.

Ong, Aihwa and Michael Peletz (1995) 'Introduction'. In Aihwa Ong and Michael Peletz (eds), *Bewitching Women, Pious Men: Gender and Body Politics in Southeast Asia.* Berkeley: University of California Press, pp. 1–18.

Oorzaken der mindere welvaart.[XII. Causes of the Lesser Welfare] (1914). Batavia: Kolff.

Orinbao, P. Sareng (1992) *Seni Tenun Suatu Segi Kebudayaan Orang Flores* [The art of weaving as a cultural issue among the people of Flores]. Ledalero, Nita, Flores: Seminari Tinggi St Paulus.

Ortner, Sherry (1974) 'Is Female to Male as Nature is to Culture?'. In M.Z. Rosaldo and Louise Lamphere (eds), *Women, Culture and Society.* Stanford: Stanford University Press.

Pain, Marc (ed.) (1989) *Transmigration and Spontaneous Migrations in Indonesia.* Bondy: ORSTOM.

Pak, Ok-Kyung (1986) 'Lowering the High, Raising the Low: The Gender, Alliance and Property Relations in a Minangkabau Peasant Community of West Sumatra, Indonesia'. PhD thesis, Toronto University.

Pane, Armijn (1964) *Belenggu* [Shackles]. Jakarta: Pustaka Rakyat.

Papanek, Hanna (1990) 'To Each Less than She Needs, From Each More than She Can Do; Allocations, Entitlements, and Value.' In Irene Tinker (ed.), *Persistent Inequalities. Women and World Development.* Oxford: Oxford University Press, pp. 162–185.

—— and Laurel Schwede (1988) 'Women Are Good with Money: Earnings and Managing in an Indonesian City'. In D. Dwyer and J. Bruce (eds), *A Home Divided: Women and Income in the Third World.* Stanford: Stanford University Press, pp. 71–98.

Parker, L. (1993) 'Witches, Bees and IUDs; Sexuality and Fertility Control in Bali'. Paper presented at the 'State, Sexuality and Reproduction in Asia and the Pacific' Conference, ANU, Canberra, July 16–18.

Parsons, T. and R. Bales (1955) *The Family: Socialization and Interaction Process.* New York: Free Press of Glencoe.

Pasternak, B. (1976) *Introduction to Kinship and Social Organisation.* New Jersey: Prentice-Hall.

Pateman, Carole (1988) *The Sexual Contract.* Stanford, California: Stanford University Press.

Peletz, Michael G. (1994) 'Neither Reasonable nor Responsible: Contrasting Representations of Masculinity in a Malay Society'. *Cultural Anthropology* 9, pp. 135–178.

Peluso, Nancy (1992) *Rich Forests, Poor People.* Berkeley: University of California Press.

Pemberton, John (1994) *On the Subject of 'Java'.* Ithaca: Cornell University Press.

Pittin, Renée (1987) 'Documentation of Women's Work in Nigeria, Problems and Solutions'. In: C. Oppong (ed.), *Sex Roles, Population and Development in West Africa.* Portsmouth: Heinemann, pp. 25–45.

Poerbani, Arti (1948) *Widijawati, het Javaanse meisje* [Widijawati, the Javanese girl], Amsterdam: Keizerskroon.

Postel-Coster, Els (1985) *Het Omheinde Kweekbed: Machtsverhoudingen in de Minangkabause Familieroman* [The seed-bed fenced in: power relations in the Minangkabau family saga]. Delft: Eburon.

—— (1988) 'Women as Gifts. An Observer's Model'. In D. Moyer and H. Claessen (eds), *Time Past, Time Present, Time Future. Essays in Honour of P.E. de Josselin de Jong.* Dordrecht: Foris Publications, pp. 245–258.

Prihatmi, S. Rahayu (1977) *Pengarang-pengarang Wanita Indonesia: Seulas Pembicaraan* [Indonesian Women Writers: A Discussion]. Jakarta: Pustaka Jaya.

Prindiville, Joanne (1985) 'Mother, Mother's Brother, and Modernization: The Problems and Prospects of Minangkabau Matriliny in a Changing World'. In L.L. Thomas and F. von Benda-Beckmann (eds), *Change and Continuity in Minangkabau: Local, Regional and Historical Perspectives on West Sumatra.* Ohio: Ohio University, Monographs in International Studies, Southeast Asia Series, pp. 29–45.

Prior, John M. (1988) *Church and Marriage in an Indonesian Village. A Study of Customary and Church Marriage among the Ata Lio of Central Flores, Indonesia, as a Para-*

digm of the Ecclesiastical Interrelationship between Village and Institutional Catholicism. Frankfurt am Main/Berne/New York/Paris: Lang.

Pyle, David (1985) 'East Java Family Planning, Nutrition, and Income Generation Project'. In C. Overholt *et al.* (eds), *Gender Roles in Development Projects.* West Hartford, CT: Kumarian Press.

Rabinow, P. (1986) 'Representations are Social Facts; Modernity and Postmodernity in Anthropology'. In J. Clifford and G. Marcus (eds), *Writing Culture: the Poetics and Politics of Ethnography.* Berkeley: University of California Press.

Radcliffe, Sarah (1993) 'The Role of Gender in Peasant Migration'. In Janet Momsen and Vivian Kinnaird (eds), *Different Places, Different Voices: Gender and Development in Africa, Asia and Latin America.* London: Routledge, pp. 278–316.

Raffles, Thomas Stanford (1817) *History of Java.* London: Black, Parbury etc., [2 vols] vol. I.

Ramseyer, Urs (1988) 'Die Weberinnen von Sidemen. Zeichen der Frühindustrialisierung in einem balinesischen Dorf'. In Brigitta Hauser-Schäublin (ed.), *Mensch, Kultur, Umwelt 3. Kleidung und Schmuck.* Basel pp. 65–72.

Rapp, Rayna (1982) 'Family and Class in Contemporary America: Notes toward an Understanding of Ideology'. In Barrie Thorne and Marilyn Yalom (eds), *Rethinking the Family.* New York: Longman, pp. 168–187.

Reenen, Joke Van (1996) *Central Pillars of the House: Sisters, Wives, and Mothers in a Rural Community in Minangkabau, West Sumatra.* Leiden: CNWS Publications.

Regt, Ali de (1993) *'Arbeiders, burgers en boeren: gezinsleven in de negentiende eeuw'* [Labourers, Burghers and Farmers: Family Life in the Nineteenth Century]. In: Ton Zwaan (ed.), *Familie, huwelijk en gezin in West-Europa. Van Middeleeuwen tot moderne tijd* [Family, Marriage and Household in Western Europe. From Middle Ages to Modern Times]. Amsterdam/Heerlen: Boom/Open Universiteit, pp. 193–218.

—— (1993) 'Het ontstaan van het "moderne" gezin, 1900–1950' [The origin of the "modern" family], in: Ibid., pp. 219–239.

Reid, Anthony (1988) 'Female Roles in Pre-Colonial Southeast Asia'. *Modern Asia Studies* 22 (3), pp. 629–645.

—— (1988) *Southeast Asia in the Age of Commerce 1450–1680. Vol. One: The Land below the Winds.* New Haven: Yale University Press.

—— (1993) *Southeast Asia in the Age of Commerce 1450–1680. Vol. Two: Expansion and Crisis.* New Haven: Yale University Press.

—— (1998) 'Why do Bataks Erect Tugu?' Canberra: The Australian National University. Unpublished paper.

Reiter, R. (1975) *Toward an Anthropology of Women.* New York: Monthly Review Press.

Resink-Wilkens, A.J. (1936) 'Huishoudonderwijs voor het dessameisje' [Education in home economics for the *desa* girl]. In: M.A.E. van Lith-van Schreven and J.H. Hooykaas-van Leeuwen Boomkamp (eds), *Indisch vrouwenjaarboek* [Indies women's yearbook]. Jogjakarta: Kolff-Buning, pp 61–67.

Ricklefs, M.C. (1991) *A History of Modern Indonesia since c.1300*, Houndsmill, Basingstoke and London: Macmillan Press.

Robison, Richard (1986) *Indonesia: the Rise of Indonesian Capital.* Singapore: Asian Studies Association of Australia, Southeast Asia Publication Series, no. 13.

Rodenburg, A.N. (1993) 'Staying Behind: Rural Women and Migration in North Tapanuli, Indonesia'. PhD thesis, University of Amsterdam.

Rodenburg, Janet (1997) *In the Shadow of Migration. Rural Women and Their Households in North Tapanuli, Indonesia.* Leiden: KITLV Press.

Roesli, Marah (1922) *Sitti Noerbaja.* Batavia: Balai Poestaka.

Roldan, M. (1988) 'Renegotiating the Marital Contract: Intrahousehold Patterns of Money Allocation and Women's Subordination among Domestic Outworkers in Mexico City'. In D. Dwyer and J. Bruce (eds), *A Home Divided: Women and Income in the Third World.* Stanford: Stanford University Press, pp. 229–247.

Rosaldo, Michelle Z. (1974) 'Woman, Culture, and Society. A Theoretical Overview'. In Michelle Z. Rosaldo and Louise Lamphere (eds), *Woman, Culture and Society.* Stanford: Stanford University Press, pp. 17–42.

—— and L. Lamphere (1974) *Woman, Culture and Society.* Stanford: Stanford University Press.

Royen, J.W. van (1930) 'Nota over de Lampoengsche Merga's'. Batavia: Departement van binnenlandsch bestuur, Weltevreden. [Note on the Lampungese clans] (Translated from the Dutch into Bahasa Indonesia by Ibu M Robbana Rusli. Jakarta: Department of the Interior).

Sacks, Karen (1979) *Sisters and Wives: The Past and Future of Sexual Equality.* Westport, Conn.: Greenwood Press.

Saefullah, Asep Djadja (1979) 'The Value of Children among Tea Estate Workers' Families: A Case Study in a Village of West Java, Indonesia'. Unpublished Master's Thesis. Department of Demography, Australian National University.

Safa, H. (1995) *The Myth of the Male Breadwinner: Women and Industrialization in the Caribbean.* Boulder: Westview Press.

Sahlins, M. (1965) 'On the Sociology of Primitive Exchange'. In M. Banton (ed.), *The Relevance of Models for Social Anthropology.* London: Tavistock Publications, pp. 139–189.

—— (1974) *Stone Age Economics.* London: Tavistock.

Said, Edward W. (1984) *Orientalism.* Harmonsworth: Penguin Books (first edn 1973).

Salaff, J. (1981) *Working Daughters in Hong Kong: Filial Piety or Power in the Family?* Cambridge: Cambridge University Press.

Salmon, Claudine (1977) 'Presse féminine ou féministe?'. *Archipel* 13, pp. 157–191.

—— (1984) 'Chinese Women Writers in Indonesia and their View on Emancipation', *Archipel* 28.

Sanday, Peggy R. (1974) 'Female Status in the Public Domain'. In Michelle Z. Rosaldo and Louise Lamphere (eds), *Woman, Culture and Society.* Stanford: Stanford University Press, pp. 189–206.

―― (1990) 'Androcentric and Matrifocal Gender Representations in Minangkabau'. In Peggy R. Sanday and Ruth G. Goodenough (eds), *Beyond the Second Sex: New Directions in the Anthropology of Gender.* Philadelphia: University of Pennsylvania Press, pp. 139–168.

Saptari, Ratna (1994) 'Gender at Work and the Dynamics of the Workplace: Indonesia's Kretek Cigarette Industry in the 1980s'. In David Bourchier (ed.), *Indonesia's Emerging Proletariat: Workers and Their Struggles.* Clayton: Monash University CSEAS monograph series, no. 17, pp. 27–43.

―― (1995) 'Rural Women to the Factories. Continuity and Change in East Java's *Kretek* Cigarette Industry'. Unpublished PhD thesis, University of Amsterdam.

Schlegel, Alice (1990) 'Gendered Meanings: General and Specific'. In Peggy R. Sanday and Ruth G. Goodenough (eds), *Beyond the Second Sex: New Directions in the Anthropology of Gender.* Philadelphia: Philadelphia University Press, pp. 21–42.

Schouten, M. (1995) 'From *Anak Piara* to PKK: Ideologies and History of Minahasan Women's Household Duties. Paper for the WIVS conference on Indonesian Women in the Household and Beyond: Reconstructing the Boundaries. Leiden.

Schrieke, B. (1960) *Indonesian Sociological Studies.* Bandung: Sumur Bandung.

Schwede, Lauren Kathleen (1991) 'Family Strategies of Labor Allocation and Decision-making in a Matrilineal, Islamic Society: The Minangkabau of West Sumatra, Indonesia'. PhD thesis, Cornell University.

Scott, A. MacEwen (1994) *Divisions and Solidarities. Gender, Class and Employment in Latin America.* London and New York: Routledge.

Scott, James (1976) *The Moral Economy of the Peasant: Rebellion and Subsistence in Southeast Asia.* New Haven: Yale University Press.

―― (1977) 'Patronage or Exploitation?'. In E. Gellner and J. Waterbury (eds), *Patrons and Clients in Mediterranean Societies.* London: Duckworth, pp. 21–38.

―― (1985) *Weapons of the Weak: Everyday Forms of Peasant Resistance.* New Haven: Yale University Press.

―― (1990), *Domination and the Arts of Resistance: Hidden Transcripts.* New Haven: Yale University Press.

Sears, Laurie (ed.) (1996) *Fantasizing the Feminine in Indonesia.* Durham and London: Duke University Press.

―― (1996) 'Introduction: Fragile Identities, Deconstructing Women and Indonesia'. In Laurie Sears (ed.), *Fantasizing the Feminine in Indonesia.* Durham and London: Duke University Press, pp. 1–46.

Selasih (1933) *Pengaroeh Keadaan* [The influence of circumstances]. Jakarta: Balai Pustaka.

―― (1969) *Kalau Tak Untung* [If fortune does not favour]. Djakarta: Balai Pustaka (8th reprint, original 1933).

Sen, Amartya (1990) 'Gender and Cooperative Conflicts'. In I. Tinker (ed.), *Persistent Inequalities. Women and World Development.* Oxford: Oxford University Press, pp. 123–149.

Sen, G. (1980) 'The Sexual Division of Labor and the Working Class Family: Towards a Conceptual Synthesis of Class Relations and the Subordination of Women'. *The Review of Radical Political Economics* 12 (2), pp. 76–86.

Sen, Krishna (1998) 'Indonesian Women at Work: Reframing the Subject'. In Krishna Sen and Maila Stivens (eds), *Gender and Power in Affluent Asia*. London: Routledge, pp. 35–62.

Sevin, Oliver (1989) 'Lampung: History and Population'. In Marc Pain (ed.), *Transmigrations and Spontaneous Migrations in Indonesia*. Bondy: ORSTOM, pp. 13–124.

Sharma, Ursula (1980) *Women, Work and Property in North-West India*. London: Travistock Publications.

Sherman, D.G. (1990) *Rice, Rupees, and Ritual. Economy and Society among the Samosir Batak of Sumatra*. Stanford: Stanford University Press.

Siegel, J. (1969) *The Rope of God*. Berkeley: University of California Press.

Silverblatt, Irene (1991) 'Interpreting Women in States: New Feminist Ethno-histories'. In Michaela di Leonardo (ed.), *Gender at the Crossroads of Knowledge: Feminist Anthropology in the Postmodern Era*. Berkeley: California University Press.

Simbolon, I.J. (1998) 'Peasant Women and Access to Land. Customary Law, State Law and Gender-Based Ideology. The Case of the Toba-Batak (North Sumatra)'. PhD thesis, Wageningen Agricultural University.

Singarimbun, Masri (1993) 'The Opening of a Village Labour Market: Changes in Employment and Welfare in Srihardjo'. In Chris Manning and Joan Hardjono (eds), *Indonesia Assessment 1993. Labour: Sharing the Benefits of Growth?* Research School of Pacific Studies monograph no. 20. Canberra: Australian National University, pp. 261–272.

—— and Shafri Sairin (eds) (1995) *Lika-Liku Kehidupan Buruh Perempuan* [Details of the lives of female labourers]. Yogyakarta: Pustaka Pelajar.

Smyth, Ines (1986) 'Ideology and Practice of Marriage in West Java'. Unpublished paper. Institute of Social Studies, The Hague.

—— (1993) 'A Critical Look at the Indonesian Government's Policies for Women'. In J.P. Dirkse *et al.* (eds), *Development and Social Welfare*. Leiden: KITLV Press.

Snouck Hurgronje, Ch. (1915) *Nederland en de Islâm*, Leiden: Brill, (2nd edn).

Soewarsih, Djojopoespito (1975) *Manusia Bebas* [Free human beings]. Jakarta: Djambatan.

Sollewijn Gelpke, H.F (1879–1880) *Naar aanleiding van Staatsblad 1878, no. 110*. No place: Ogilvie & Co., [3 vols.] vol. I.

Spivak, Gayatri (1988) 'Can the Subaltern Speak?'. In Cary Nelson and Lawrence Grossberg (eds), *Marxism and Interpretation of Culture*. Urbana: University of Illinois Press, pp. 271–313.

Stack, Carol (1974) *All Our Kin*. New York: Basic Books.

Standing, H. (1991) *Dependence and Autonomy*. London: Routledge.

BIBLIOGRAPHY

Steady, F. (1987) 'Polygamy and the Household Economy in a Fishing Village in Sierra Leone'. In D. Parkin and D. Nyamawaya (eds), *Transformations of African Marriage*. Manchester: Manchester University Press.

Stegmaier, Ortrud (1977) 'Missionsdienst am eigenen Volk'. *Verbum SVD* vol. XVIII, pp. 66–80.

Stephens, W. (1963) *The Family in Cross-Cultural Perspective*. New York: Holt, Rhinehart & Winston.

Stichter, S. and J. Parpart (1990) *Women, Employment and the Family in the International Division of Labour*. Basingstoke: Macmillan.

Stivens, Maila (1985) 'The Fate of Women's Land Rights: Gender, Matriliny and Capitalism in Rembau, Negri Sembilan, Malaysia'. In H. Afshar (ed.), *Women, Work and Ideology in the Third World*. London: Travistock, pp. 3–36.

—— (1991) 'The Evolution of Kinship Relations in Rembau, Negeri Sembilan, Malaysia'. In F. Hüsken and J. Kemp (eds), *Cognation and Social Organization in Southeast Asia*. Leiden: KITLV Press, pp. 71–89.

—— (1994) 'Gender at the Margins: Paradigms and Peasantries in Rural Malaysia'. *Women's Studies International Forum* 17 (4), pp. 373–390.

—— (1998) 'Theorising Gender, Power and Modernity in Affluent Asia'. In Krishna Sen and Maila Stivens (eds), *Gender and Power in Affluent Asia*. London: Routledge, pp. 1–34.

—— (ed.) (1991) *Why Gender Matters in Southeast Asian Politics*. Monash: Monash Papers on Southeast Asia, no. 23.

Stoler, Ann (1976) 'Garden Use and Household Consumption Patterns in a Javanese Village'. *Masyarakat Indonesia*, 3.

—— (1977) 'Class Structure and Female Autonomy in Rural Java'. *Signs* 3 (1), pp. 74–89 (also in Wellesley Editorial Committee (eds), *Women and National Development*. Chicago: University of Chicago Press).

—— (1986) 'The Company's Women: Labour Control in Sumatran Agribusiness'. In Kate Young (ed.), *Serving Two Masters: Third World Women in Development*. Ahmedabad: Allied Publ. Ltd.

Strathern, M. [1972] (1995) *Women In Between. Female Roles in a Male World: Mount Hagen, New Guinea*. Maryland: Rowman & Littlefield Publishers.

Streatfield, K. (1986) *Fertility Decline in a Traditional Society; the Case of Bali*. Canberra: Department of Demography, Australian National University.

Suchtelen, B.C.C.M.M. van (1921) *Ende (Flores)*. Weltevreden: Papyrus.

SUDA (1993) *Sumatera Utara Dalam Angka 1993* [North Sumatra in numbers 1993]. Medan: Kantor Statistik Propinsi Sumatera Utara.

Sugishima, Takashi (1994) 'Double Descent, Alliance, and Botanical Metaphors among the Lionese of Central Flores'. *Bijdragen tot de Taal-, Land- en Volkenkunde* 150, pp. 146–170.

Sukarno [1947] (1984) *Sarinah*. Jakarta: Inti Idayu Press, Yayasan Pendidikan Soekarno.

Sullivan, Norma (1989) 'The Hidden Economy and Kampung Women'. In Paul Alexander (ed.), *Creating Indonesian Cultures*. Sydney: Oceania Publications, pp. 75–90.

—— (1994) *Masters and Managers: A Study of Gender Relations in Urban Java*. St Leonards: Allen & Unwin.

Suryakusuma, Julia (1996) 'The State and Sexuality in New Order Indonesia'. In Laurie Sears (ed.), *Fantasizing the Feminine in Indonesia*. Durham: Duke University Press, pp. 92–119.

—— (1988) 'PKK: The Formalization of the Informal Power of Women'. Paper presented to 'Women as Mediators in Indonesia. International Workshop on Indonesian Studies No. 3'. Royal Institute of Linguistics and Anthropology. Leiden, The Netherlands.

Taale, T. (1991) 'Looking for a Livelihood in Hila: Continuity and Change in Land Use and Its Implications for Social Security in an Ambonese Village'. Unpublished Masters thesis, Agricultural University Wageningen.

Takdir Alisjahbana (1936) *Lajar Terkembang* [With sail unfurled]. Jakarta: Balai Pustaka.

Tanner, Nancy (1974) 'Matrifocality in Indonesia and Africa and among Black Americans'. In M.Z. Rosaldo and L. Lamphere (eds), *Woman, Culture and Society*. Stanford: Stanford Univeristy Press, pp. 129–157.

—— and Lynn L. Thomas (1985) 'Rethinking Matriliny: Decision-Making and Sex Roles in Minangkabau'. In L.L. Thomas and F. von Benda-Beckmann (eds), *Change and Continuity in Minangkabau: Local, Regional and Historical Perspectives on West Sumatra*. Ohio: Ohio University, Monographs in International Studies, Southeast Asia Series, pp. 45–73.

Teeuw, A. (1979) *Modern Indonesian Literature*, vols 1 and 2. The Hague: Martinus Nijhoff.

Termorshuizen, Gerard (1991) 'A Life Free from Trammels: Soewarsih Djojopoespito and her Novel Buiten Het Gareel', *Journal of Netherlandic Studies* 12 (2), Spring.

Tilly, L. and J. Scott (1978), *Women, Work and the Family*. New York: Holt, Rhinehart & Winston.

Tiwon, Sylvia (1996) 'Models and Maniacs: Articulating the Feminine in Indonesia'. In Laurie Sears (ed.), *Fantasizing the Feminine in Indonesia*. Durham: Duke University Press, pp. 47–70.

Tjondronegoro (1991) 'The Utilization and Management of Land Resources in Indonesia, 1970 to 1990'. In Joan Hardjono (ed.), *Indonesia: Resources, Ecology and Environment*. Singapore: Oxford University Press, pp. 17–35.

TP PKK (Tim Penggerak PKK) (1989) *Inang. Hidup dan Bhaktiku* [Motherhood, life and responsibilities]. Provinsi NTT.

Trivers, R. (1972) 'Parental Investment and Sexual Selection'. In B. Campbell (ed.), *Sexual Selection and the Descent of Man*. London: Heinemann.

Tsing, Anna Lowenhaupt (1993) *In the Realm of the Diamond Queen*. Princeton, New Jersey: Princeton University Press.

Vera-Sanso, Penny (1995) 'Community, Seclusion and Female Labour Force Participation in Madras, India'. *Third World Planning Review* 17, pp. 135–167.

Vergouwen, J.C. (1964) *The Social Organisation and Customary Law of the Toba-Batak of Northern Sumatra*. The Hague: Nijhoff. [Translated by J. Scott-Kemball from *Het rechtsleven der Toba-Bataks*, 1933; KITLV, Translation Series 7.]

Verschoor, Gerald (1992) 'Identity, Networks and Space: New Dimensions in the Study of Small-scale Enterprise and Commoditization'. In Norman Long and Anne Long (eds), *Battlefields of Knowledge. The Interlocking of Theory and Practice in Social Research and Development*. London: Routledge, pp. 171–188.

Verslag van de arbeidscommissie betreffende de wettelijke vaststelling van minimumloonen voor werknemers op Java en Madoera [Report of the labour commission on the fixation by law of minimum wages for employees on Java and Madoera] (1920). Batavia: Kolff.

Villarreal, M. (1992) 'The Poverty of Practice. Power, Gender and Intervention from an Actor-oriented Perspective'. In N. Long and A. Long (eds), *Battlefields of Knowledge. The Interlocking of Theory and Practice in Social Research and Development*. London and New York: Routledge.

Volkstelling van Nederlandsch-Indië 1930 (1934) *III. Oost-Java* [Census of the Dutch East-Indies 1930. III East-Java], Batavia: Landsdrukkerij.

Vollenhoven, C. van (1918) *Het adatrecht van Nederlandsch-Indië*. (93 vols), I. Leiden: Brill.

Vreede-De Stuers, Cora (1959) *L'Emancipation de la Femme Indonésienne* [The emancipation of the Indonesian woman]. Paris/The Hague: Mouton & Co.

—— (1960) *The Indonesian Woman: Struggles and Achievements* The Hague: Mouton.

Walby, Sylvia (1990) *Theorizing Patriarchy*. Oxford: Basil Blackwell.

Walle, E. van de and J. Kekovole (1984) 'The Recent Evolution of African Marriage and Polygyny'. Paper presented at the Annual Meeting of the Population Association of America, Minneapolis.

Wallerstein, Immanuel and Joan Smith (1991) 'Households as an Institution of the World-Economy'. In R.L. Blumberg (ed.), *Gender, Family, and Economy: The Triple Overlap*. London/New Delhi: Sage, pp. 225–243.

—— (1992) 'Introduction: Households as an Institution of the World Economy'. In J. Smith, I Wallerstein, M. Carmen Baerga, M. Beittel and K. Friedman Kasabaet (eds), *Creating and Transforming Households: The Constraints of the World Economy*. Cambridge: Cambridge University Press.

Warren, C. (1993) *Adat and Dinas: Balinese Communities in The Indonesian State*. New York: Oxford University Press.

Watkins, John, Thomas Leinbach and Karen Falconer (1993) 'Women, Family and Work in Indonesian Transmigration'. *Journal of Developing Areas* 2, pp. 377–398.

Watson, C.W. (1991) 'Cognatic or Matrilineal: Kerinci Social Organization in Escher Perspective'. In F. Hüsken and J. Kemp (eds), *Cognation and Social Organization in Southeast Asia*. Leiden: KITLV Press, pp. 55–71.

Weiner, Annette B. (1986) 'Forgotten Wealth. Cloth and Women's Production in the Pacific'. In Eleanor Leacock and Helen Safa (eds), *Women's Work. Development and the Division of Labor by Gender.* Massachusetts: Bergin and Garvey, pp. 96–110.

Weintraub, J. (1997) 'The Theory and Politics of the Public/Private Distinction'. In J. Weintraub and K. Kumar (eds), *Public and Private in Thought and Practice: Perspectives on a Grand Dichotomy.* Chicago: The University of Chicago Press, pp. 1–42.

Weix, G.G. (1990) 'Following the Family/Firm: Patronage and Piecework in a Kudus Cigarette Factory'. Doctoral Dissertation, Cornell University.

—— (1997) 'Displaying the Post-colonial Past: the Kudus Clove Cigarette Museum'. *Visual Anthropology Review* 13 (1), pp. 28–39.

—— (in press) 'Inside the Home and Outside the Family: Domestic Estrangement of Javanese Servants'. In Kathleen Adams and Sara Dickey (eds), *Home and Hegemony: Domestic Service in South and Southeast Asia.* Ann Arbor: University of Michigan Press, pp. 190–225.

Weyland, P. (1993) *Inside the Third World Village.* London and New York: Routledge.

Wertheim, W.F. (1964) *Indonesian Society in Transition: A Study of Social Change.* The Hague: W. van Hoeve.

White, Benjamin (1976) 'Production and Reproduction in a Javanese Village'. Unpublished PhD thesis, Columbia University.

—— (1980) 'Rural Household Studies in Anthropological Perspective'. In Hans Binswanger and R. Evenson (eds), *Rural Household Studies in Asia.* Singapore: Singapore University Press, pp. 3–25.

—— and E.L. Hastuti (1980) 'Different and Unequal: Male and Female Influence in Household and Community Affairs in Two West Javanese Villages'. Agro-economic Survey, Bogor Agricultural University, Indonesia (also The Hague: Institute of Social Studies).

Whitehead, Ann (1981) 'I'm Hungry, Mum: The Politics of Domestic Budgeting'. In K. Young, C. Wolkowitz and R. McCullagh (eds), *Of Marriage and the Market: Women's Subordination in International Pespective.* London: CSE Books, pp. 88–111.

—— (1990) 'Food Crisis and Gender Conflict in Africa'. In H. Bernstein (ed.), *The Food Question: Profits Versus People?* London: Earthscan, pp. 54–68.

Wieringa, Saskia (1988) 'GERWANI and the PKK: Brokers on Behalf of Whom?' Paper presented to 'Women as Mediators in Indonesia. International Workshop on Indonesian Studies No. 3', Royal Institute of Linguistics and Anthropology, Leiden, The Netherlands.

—— (1995) 'The Politicization of Gender Relations in Indonesia: The Indonesian Women's Movement and Gerwani until the New Order State'. Unpublished PhD Thesis, University of Amsterdam.

Wikan, U. (1990) *Managing Turbulent Hearts: a Balinese Formula for Living.* Chicago: University of Chicago Press.

Wilk, Richard and Robert McC. Netting (1984) 'Households: Changing Forms and Functions'. In Robert McC. Netting, Richard Wilk and Eric Arnould (eds), *House-*

holds: Comparative and Historical Studies of the Domestic Group. Berkeley: University of California Press.

Williams, Linda (1990) *Development, Demography, and Family Decision-Making.* Boulder Col.: Westview Press.

Williams, Raymond (1977) *Marxism and Literature.* Oxford: Oxford University Press.

Willner, Anne Ruth (1961) 'From Rice Field to Factory: The Industrialization of a Rural Labor Force in Java'. PhD thesis, University of Chicago.

—— (1980) 'Expanding Women's Horizons in Indonesia: Toward Maximum Equality with Minimum Conflict'. In S. Chipp and J. Green (eds), *Asian Women in Transition.* University Park, PA: Pennsylvania State University Press.

Wilson, E. (1975) *Sociobiology.* Cambridge, Mass.: Belknap.

Wolf, Diane L. (1986) Paper prepared for session on 'Gender, Race, and Labor in the World Economy', Annual Meeting of the American Sociological Association, New York.

—— (1990) 'Daughters, Decisions and Domination: An Empirical and Conceptual Critique of Household Strategies'. *Development and Change.*21 (1), pp. 43–74.

—— (1991) 'Female Autonomy, the Family and Industrialization in Java'. In R.L. Blumberg (ed.), *Gender, Family, and Economy: The Triple Overlap.* London, New Delhi: Sage, pp. 128–148.

—— (1992) *Factory Daughters. Gender, Household Dynamics, and Rural Industrialization in Java.* Berkeley: University of California Press.

—— (1992). 'Industrialization and the Family: Women Workers as Mediators of Family Change and Economic Change in Java'. In S. van Bemmelen, M. Djajadiningrat-Nieuwenhuis, E. Locher-Scholten and E. Touwen-Bouwsma (eds), *Women and Mediation in Indonesia.* Leiden: KITLV Press, pp. 89–108.

—— (1996) 'Situating Feminist Dilemmas in Fieldwork'. In D.L. Wolf (ed.), *Feminist Dilemmas in Fieldwork.* Boulder Col.: Westview Press.

Wolf, Eric (1971) *Peasant Wars of the Twentieth Century.* London: Faber.

Wong, D. (1984) 'The Limits of Using the Household as a Unit of Analysis'. In J. Smith, I. Wallerstein and H.D. Evers (eds), *Households and the World-Economy.* London: Sage, pp. 56–63.

—— (1987) *Peasants in the Making: Malaysia's Green Revolution.* Singapore: Institute of Southeast Asian Studies.

Wood, C.H. (1981) 'Structural Changes and Household Strategies; A Conceptual Framework for the Study of Rural Migration'. *Human Organization* 40, pp. 338–344.

World Bank (1996) *World Development Report.* Washington DC: World Bank.

—— (1988) *Indonesia: The Transmigration Program in Perspective.* Washington DC: World Bank.

Wright, C. (1995) 'Gender Awareness in Migration Theory: Synthesizing Actor and Structure in Southern Africa'. *Development and Change* 26, pp. 771–791.

Yanagisako, Sylvia J. (1977) 'Women-Centered Kin Networks in Urban Bilateral Kinship'. *American Ethnologist* 4 (2), pp. 207–226.

—— (1979) 'Family and Household: The Analysis of Domestic Groups'. In *Annual Review of Anthropology* 8, pp. 161–205.

—— and Jane F. Collier (1987) 'Toward a Unified Analysis of Gender and Kinship'. In Jane F. Collier and Sylvia J. Yanagisako (eds), *Gender and Kinship. Essays toward a Unified Analysis*. Stanford: Stanford University Press, pp. 14–51.

Young, Kate (1982) 'The Creation of a Relative Surplus Population: a Case Study from Mexico'. In Lourdes Beneria (ed.), *Women and Development: the Sexual Division of Labour in Rural Societies*. New York: Praeger, pp. 149–177.

Zendingsstatistiek (1937) *Zendingstijdschrift De Opwekker* [Missions' statistics, *Missions' Journal: the Awakener*], vol. 83.

Zeuner, Géraldine (1996) 'Nicht-Regierung-Organisationen und akteurzentrierte Entwicklung im ländlichen Raum. Eine empirische Untersuchung am Fallbeispiel Flores, Indonesien'. Unpublished thesis, Geographical Institute of the University of Zurich.

GLOSSARY

A = Ambonese
B = Batak
Bal = Balinese
D = Dutch
J = Javanese
L = Lio
Lamp = Lampung
M = Minangkabau

Words without notation are Indonesian

abon	technical term in the cigarette industry of the 1930s describing piece-rate contract work
adat	tradition/customary law
ama (B)	father (of)
ana (L)	child
ana dari nia (L)	male heir within a patrilineage or house
ana fai walu (L)	commoner
arisan	rotating savings and credit association
ata (L)	human being; people
ata ko'o (L)	slave
ata ria (L)	nobleman, noblewoman
balu (Bal)	divorcee
banjar (Bal)	hamlet or residential cluster of households linked by social, economic and ritual ties
berani	brave, assertive
bona ni pasogit (B)	ancestral homeland
buruhkan orang	to hire workers
bu'u waja (L)	hearth, household
caripaksa	abduction marriage
dati (A)	landholding clan segment
datuk; datuak (M)	title for the male heads of matrilineages or matriclans. In the local Rao-Rao dialect *datu(a)k* had a wider meaning; it was used for senior women as well as senior men, namely: a person's mother's mother (MM), mother's father (MF), father's mother (FM), father's father (FF), mother's mother's brother (MMB), father's mother's brother (FMB)
desa	village

desa adat	customary village
desa dinas	Indonesian administrative village
desa parawisata	tourist village
Dharma Wanita	association for the wives of civil servants
eko (L)	animal
galak	fierce, easily angry
gengsi	prestige
hak ulayat	traditional community rights
halus	refined
harato pusako (M)	ancestral property; common property of a lineage or lineage segment
harian	daily
hormat	respect
huisvrouw (D)	housewife
huta (B)	hamlet or part of a village
ibu	mother, honorific for adult women
ibu teladan	model mother
Idul Adha	Muslim holiday commemorating the Day of Sacrifice
Idul Fitri	Muslim holiday marking the end of the fasting period
isteri	wife, woman
jaba (Bal)	collective term for non-caste Balinese
jodoh	marriage partner, predestined mate
kamaduang (Bal)	to be made into a co-wife
kampung	hamlet
keluarga	family
keluarga kecil bahagia	small happy family
keluarga sejahtera	prosperous and tranquil family
kemadjoean (kemajuan)	progress
kepala keluarga	head of the family; household head
kerta (L)	money
kodrat	God's will; natural, pre-ordained character or role
kodrat wanita	women's essential nature
kolonisatie (D)	transmigration under colonial administration
kretek	clove cigarettes
kunu (L)	patrilineage
kuren (Bal)	symbolic hearth or kitchen, household
ladang	dry field
laki ata fai (L)	titled noblewoman

GLOSSARY

luka lawo (L)	cloth, male and female
luung (Bal)	good, desirable
luungan nganten (Bal)	better to marry
madu (Bal)	co-wife; honey
mamak (M)	real or classificatory maternal uncle
mandor	supervisor, work gang leader often functioning as labour broker
mangaranto (B)	to travel in search of work; to migrate
manjae (B)	to set up one's own household
marga	clan or lineage group
masohi (A)	mutual help; co-operation
matua (Bal)	parents-in-law
mbak (J)	young woman
mémé matua (Bal)	mother-in-law
menyimpan uang	to save money
mitra sejajar	equal partners
momong	child minding
mosa laki (L)	titled nobleman; lord of the land
nagari (M)	village or village community; lit: socio-political unit according to *adat*
nai (B)	mother (of)
(nga)maduang (Bal)	to bestow a co-wife upon one's wife
nganggur	not working; unemployed
nggua (L)	agricultural ritual
nilai-nilai luhur	high values
Orde Baru	New Order
paceklik	scarcity (of food), crisis
pekarangan	house-yard; house compound
pangarantoan (B)	migration area; destination area of migrants
panjaen (B)	a piece of land endowed to a newly-wed couple to start an independent household
paon (Bal)	kitchen
pauseang (B)	land given by parents to their daughter
peladang berpindah	shifting cultivators
pembangunan	development
pemukiman kembali	resettlement
penghulu(s)	village chief, lineage head
penyimbang (Lamp)	lineage chief or aristocrat
peradaban	civilization

perempoean (perempuan) woman	
periuak (M)	cooking pot; group of people sharing a cooking pot
perkawinan	marriage
perusa (A)	property acquired by a person's own efforts
PKK	*Pembinaan Kesejahteraan Keluarga*, Family Welfare Programme, a village-level programme to educate women on various aspects of family welfare
podo (L)	pot, house segment
priyayi	nobility, elite
pulu (L)	life-cycle ritual
pusaka	inherited property
rantau	migrate, destination of migration
rewang (J)	mutual help
ripe (B)	household; family
roemah (rumah) tangga	household
rukun	in harmony, concord
rumah adat	ceremonial house
rumah gadang	traditional Minangkabau house
rumah keluarga	household
rumah pusaka	large houses which are inherited property of clans
rumah tangga	household (for official purposes)
rumah tau (A)	patrilineage; clan
rupiah	Indonesian currency divided in 100 cents
samande (M)	the unit of mother and children, which is the smallest kinship unit in Minangkabau *adat*
sa'o nggua (L)	ceremonial house
sa'o (L)	house
sawah	wet-rice field
selir (J)	co-wife, often of lower descent, of the Javanese nobility
slametan	ritual communal meal
soa (A)	clan associations in Ambonese villages
somah(an)	household
suku (L)	matriclan
sumando (M)	inmarried males; husbands of female lineage members
sumber daya manusia	human resources
tani	peasant, farmer
tebu rakyat	smallholder sugarcane outgrower scheme
transmigrasi lokal	local transmigration
triwangsa (Bal)	collective term for the Balinese caste-bearing nobility

GLOSSARY

tuyul (J)	gremlin-like spirit; a mischievous spirit
tweedehands (D)	second-hand, hand-me-down
umbulan (Lamp)	temporary hamlet of shifting cultivators
utu (L)	to win; having decision-making power
wahana sosialisasi	socializing receptacle
wanita	woman, lady (a term which came into popular usage from the 1940s onwards)
warong/warung	shop, food-stall
wéa (L)	gold jewellery
wewehan (J)	ritual marking the 35 days after a child's birth

OVERVIEW OF PAPERS PRESENTED AT WIVS CONFERENCE

S. van Bemmelen, 'Women's Issues between the Family and the Household'

K. and F. von Benda-Beckmann, 'Houses, Housing and Households: the Fluidity of Ambonese Living Arrangements'

S. Blackburn, 'Women and the Household in Colonial Indonesia: Insights from the Women's Press'

C. Davis, 'Female Cooperative Networks in Minangkabau Life Cycle Rituals'

G. Dawson, 'Women, Men and Merantau: Shifting Gender Relations in Transmigrant Households'

F. Dharmaperwira and M. Nolten, 'Rosa and Nina. Two Sumatran Women and Their Support Networks'

M. Djajadiningrat, 'A Household or a State within the State? Women at the Central Javanese Courts'

B. Elmhirst, 'Javanese Households in Transmigration, Lampung'

M. Grijns, 'From Blueprint to Actual Households, Coconut Farmers in West Java'

B. Hatley, 'The Household Model of a Woman's Place: Reflections in Indonesian Women's Writing and Performance'

B. Holzner, 'Homeworking and Intra-Household Relations: a Case Study from East Java'

M. Jennaway, 'Bitter Honey: Female Polygynous Destinies in North Bali'

W. de Jong, 'To Give or to Sell? Female Distribution Strategies in Cloth Producing Households in Flores'

M. Jufri and B. Watson, 'Decision-making in Rural Households in Kerinci and Minang'

N. Kariani Purwanti, 'The Change of Household Structure and its Impact on Dayak Women'

J. Koning, 'The Nuclearization of the Nuclear Family: an Illustration from North Central Java'

E. Locher, 'Colonial Perceptions of Women in the Indonesian Household'

A. Nakatani, 'Private or Public? Female Roles in the Maintenance of Ceremonial Ties between Balinese Households'

A. Niehof, 'Who Benefits from Income-Generation? Some Theoretical Considerations and Evidence from West Java'

OVERVIEW OF PAPERS PRESENTED AT WIVS CONFERENCE

J. van Reenen, 'Woman/Centre and Male/Periphery: Gender and the House in Minangkabau'

J. Rodenburg, 'Gender, Households and Migration in a Toba Batak Village'

D. Rutherford, 'The Family and the Foreign in Biak, Irian Jaya: a Domestic Economy of Shock'

R. Saptari, 'Labouring Women, Households and Ideologies: the Case of Cigarette Factory Workers in East Java'

M. Schouten, 'From *Anak Piara* to *PKK*: Ideologies and History of Minahasan Women's Household Duties'

L. Sciortino and I. Smyth, 'The Triumph of Harmony, the Formal Denial of Domestic Violence on Java'

S. Thambiah, 'Women Carry the Household, the Bhuket of West Kalimantan'

G.G. Weix, 'Strange Gifts: Elite Homes in Java'

D. Wolf, 'Beyond "Women and the Household" in Indonesian Studies: Theory, Practices, and Challenges'

T. Yusmadiana and Yusnaini, 'Family Structure, Female Autonomy and Fertility in the Village of South Sumatra'

INDEX

agency 1, 6, 7, 10, 12, 19–22, 23, 72, 86, 93, 97, 98, 99, 143, 154, 159, 221–22, 226, 230–31, 236–37, 257, 259, 302, 303–05, 312, 314
agriculture 74, 17, 25, 210, 211, 212, 238, 242, 244–45, 264, 268, 273, 295
Association of Housewives in the Indies 29, 40, 41

balanced reciprocity 292
bargaining 16, 23, 243–44, 252–53, 256, 258
    model 87, 208, 252–53
    power 87, 208, 236, 243, 255
Boedi Oetomo 41

census (Java 1930) 31
children 4, 5, 18, 22, 31, 34, 35, 37, 40, 42, 52, 53, 54, 88, 95, 99n. 2, 156, 158, 187, 195–97, 201, 218, 236, 241, 245, 248–49, 254, 262, 263, 266, 267, 269, 271, 272–73, 274, 275, 276, 277, 278, 285, 287, 288, 289, 290–93, 296, 297, 300, 302, 306–07, 309
Christian missions 29, 36, 38, 43
cooking pot; cooking pot unit 3, 164–65, 173
cooperative conflict 243, 242
cultural capital 222

decision-making 20, 87, 90, 91, 92, 118, 135, 186, 208–09, 224, 220, 222, 223, 227–28, 270, 273, 274, 278, 283, 294, 305
    power 273, 274, 283
dichotomies 1, 6, 7, 8, 12, 13, 125, 262, 297
discourse 13, 18, 24, 28, 34, 45, 56, 68, 81, 88, 97, 98, 143, 146–47, 158–60, 285, 310
domestic work 95, 217–21, 227, 282, 286, 289, 296

education 18, 25, 28, 29, 30, 31, 33, 35, 36, 37, 38, 39, 40, 41, 42, 43, 46, 50, 70, 186, 201, 204, 216, 220, 237, 239–40, 246–48, 256–58, 266, 267, 270, 271, 273, 275, 278, 280, 296, 303
empirical 85, 144, 299, 304, 314
ethnographic 147–148, 304

family
    autonomy 185, 187, 204–05
    feminization 189, 204
    New Order 187–88, 262, 299
    separation 206, 277
female night labour 34–35
fiction 31, 44, 55, 57, 59, 64, 146, 158

genealogical 148, 222
generations (problem of) 34, 183, 186, 188, 200, 204, 209, 215–16, 219, 257–58, 267, 285, 287, 301, 305, 306
gifts 241, 255, 262, 264, 265, 268, 269, 270, 271, 272, 274, 276–79, 300, 306–12, 314
    duality of 278
    exchange of 264, 265, 268, 269, 270, 271, 272, 276–78, 300, 314

hawk(ing) 235, 238, 244–45, 249–50
house 4, 11, 17, 19, 22, 25, 107–10, 116, 119–21, 134, 137–38, 265, 267, 268, 288, 290, 291, 295, 296, 307
    segment 265, 267
household
    composition 185, 190, 281, 286, 287, 300, 301
    debates 184, 102, 104
    decision-making 91, 186, 209, 214, 216, 233n. 13, 221–24, 228, 237
    development cycle 189, 192, 239
    economic behaviour 252
    European 30, 41
    gender and 105, 186, 209, 215–16, 185, 219, 235, 237

INDEX

intra-household relations 22, 98, 206n. 2, 182, 185, 186, 208, 215–16, 219, 222, 236–38, 281, 297
moral economy 209, 224, 228, 231, 314
multiple 238, 191
nuclear 4, 5, 18, 21, 189, 190, 191, 199, 211, 216, 281, 282, 290, 293, 296, 297
studies 8, 181, 182, 186, 222, 282
housewife 15, 18, 19, 39, 42, 43, 51, 53, 73, 78, 88, 94

ideology 7, 8, 13, 14, 18, 28, 29, 35, 38, 41, 45,46, 55, 78, 88, 89, 90, 91, 93, 94, 98, 187, 222, 236, 239–40 247, 249, 252, 262, 267, 282, 297, 303
imagined community 78
income 7, 16, 20, 42, 86, 88, 91, 92, 93, 96, 98, 126, 132, 264, 267, 273–74, 275, 278, 280, 282, 283, 284, 290, 291, 292, 293–96, 297, 298n. 10
allocation 203, 205
management 202, 217, 221, 225, 227
inheritance 50, 126, 211, 215–16, 218–19, 240–41, 251, 255–57, 261n. 13, 294, 301

Java 5, 15, 17, 20, 25, 40, 76, 88, 89, 181–207, 208–233, 262, 264, 276, 281–98, 299–314

Kartini 25, 46, 70
Foundation 39
kin 3, 4, 11, 16, 20, 21, 22, 53, 95, 96, 97, 258, 262, 266, 271, 273, 274–79, 281, 286, 289, 300, 301, 304
-based networks 7, 22, 211, 213, 217, 219, 221, 233n. 12, 237, 240, 249, 286
selection theory 144
kinship 11, 21, 25, 116, 143–44, 185, 186, 208, 215–16, 218–19, 221, 223, 226, 229, 231–32, 236, 238, 240–41,243–44, 256, 206n. 5, 268, 274, 275
ideology 209, 215, 218, 242, 255, 261n. 13

labour 5, 7, 12, 14, 17, 19, 25, 68, 69, 75, 80, 83n. 14, 83n. 16, 87, 88, 90, 94, 95, 97, 99, 231, 240, 257, 262–80, 281–98, 299, 300, 302, 303, 305, 306, 307, 308, 313
allocation 95, 215, 221
market 19, 96, 283, 284, 285, 293, 294
relations 306–08, 310–11, 312
legislation 83n. 16
levels of meaning 14
livelihood practices 211–12, 208
local transmigration 209, 210

Majapahit 146
Mamak 167–68, 173, 176–77
marriage 6, 10, 14, 16, 18, 19, 25, 52, 55, 59, 62, 63, 83n. 12, n. 13, 112, 121, 148, 156, 189, 193–95, 198, 199, 206, 210–11, 215, 218–22, 233n. 5, 234n. 18, 241, 248, 254, 255, 265, 267, 268, 269, 270, 272, 273, 274, 275, 276, 280, 282, 307
materiality 69, 70
matriarchal household 80
matriclan 268
matriliny 163
matrilineal 11, 15, 165, 178
migration 8, 88, 94, 168, 177–78, 199, 204, 206, 209, 213–14, 216, 219–20, 226, 231, 235–61, 266, 270, 279, 299
circular 182, 200, 212, 218, 238
migrant 8, 200, 208, 214, 218, 222, 230–31, 232n. 3, 235–61, 285
minimum wages 34, 213
modernity 206
moral economy 86, 209, 232n. 1, 223–24, 231, 314

networks of reproduction 281–98
non-kin based networks 22, 185, 190, 201, 205, 213, 217, 224, 226, 228
nuclearization 21, 89, 184, 199

off-farm work 212–13, 214–15, 217

parental investment theory 144, 161n. 4, 249
patrilineage; patrilineal 11, 18, 20, 143, 156, 158, 210–11, 218–19, 235, 240–41, 243–44, 247–48, 255, 268
Periuak 164, 173
PKK 18, 28, 29, 43, 95, 272
polyandry 143–44, 157

polygamy 10, 53, 56, 62, 112, 148, 239
polygyny 73, 142–46, 148, 154–55, 157–60, 161n. 2, n. 14, 219
priyayi 13, 30, 32, 33, 36, 48, 50, 51, 66n. 5, 92
progress 49, 53, 60, 237
property 12, 13, 16, 77, 78, 80, 81, 130, 157–58, 215–16, 218–20, 236, 239–41, 260n. 6, 247, 251, 255, 257, 268, 270, 273, 274, 275
    ancestral 165–66, 168, 177
    relationships 117–19, 134–35, 137

remittances 187, 199–203, 205, 207n. 12, 214, 235, 243, 247–48, 252, 254, 258–59, 275
representation 1, 10, 12, 13, 14, 15, 16, 18, 19, 23, 25, 45, 72, 82, 215, 266, 272, 300
residence 8, 11, 16, 30, 31, 37, 73, 88, 110, 121–22, 215–16, 219, 234n. 15, 236, 241, 247, 267, 299, 301, 302, 306, 307, 311, 314
    co-residentiality 11, 103, 106–07, 125, 130, 137–39, 218–19, 240
    pattern 16, 37, 111–13, 138, 166, 194, 197, 236
rumah gadang 165–66, 171–72, 175

Sarekat Islam 41, 42
security 83n. 4, 5, 14, 126, 195, 205, 244, 253, 257, 262, 265, 271, 276, 277, 279, 284, 292, 297, 310, 313,314
segregation by gender 217, 224, 231, 284
senior woman 15, 164, 172–73
social security 4, 262, 265, 271, 279

sociobiological 144
South Sumatra 4, 7, 35
Steinmetz, H.E. 32, 37
strategies 231, 236, 237–38, 240, 243–45, 248–52, 255, 258–59, 263, 270, 275, 276, 279, 282, 284, 295, 302, 303, 305, 313
    of distribution 275, 276, 279
    of production 270, 275, 279
structural 19, 21, 237, 304
    change 86, 87, 99
structural-functionalist 144
subjective 3, 20, 143, 160
Sumando 167, 177

tani 30, 34, 35, 36
transmigration 34, 35, 74, 76, 83n. 17, 208–12, 229, 232n. 3

universality 281

Van Deventer Foundation 38
VOC (East India Company) 34

weavers
    order-placing 269, 275, 279
    order-taking 275, 279
women
    fiction (*see under* fiction)
    magazines 13, 47, 54, 64, 65
    networks 20, 21, 22, 23, 25, 226, 262, 264–79, 283, 285, 286, 289–91, 293, 296, 297
    organizations 18, 47, 48, 52, 73
workplace 8, 262, 263, 272, 283, 284, 299, 301, 302, 305, 308, 312, 313

The Nordic Institute of Asian Studies (NIAS) is funded by the governments of Denmark, Finland, Iceland, Norway and Sweden via the Nordic Council of Ministers, and works to encourage and support Asian studies in the Nordic countries. In so doing, NIAS has published well in excess of one hundred books in the last three decades, most of them in co-operation with Curzon Press.